Sexual Diversity and Catholicism

Sexual Diversity and Catholicism

Toward the Development of Moral Theology

Patricia Beattie Jung with Joseph Andrew Coray

Editors

A Michael Glazier Book
THE LITURGICAL PRESS
Collegeville, Minnesota

www.litpress.org

A Michael Glazier Book published by The Liturgical Press.

Cover design by Ann Blattner. Watercolor by Ethel Boyle.

Unless indicated otherwise, the Scripture quotations are from the New Revised Standard Version Bible, Catholic edition, © 1989 by the Division of Christian Education of the National Council of Churches of Christ in the U.S.A. Used by permission. All rights reserved.

2	3	4	5	6	7	8

Library of Congress Cataloging-in-Publication Data

Sexual diversity and Catholicism : toward the development of moral theology / Patricia Beattie Jung with Joseph A. Coray, editor[s].
    p. cm.
    "A Michael Glazier book."
    Includes bibliographical references and index.
    ISBN 0-8146-5939-X (alk. paper)
    1. Homosexuality—Religious aspects—Catholic Church. 2. Homosexuality—Biblical teaching. 3. Catholic Church—Doctrines. I. Jung, Patricia Beattie. II. Coray, Joseph A.

BX1795.H66 S49   2001
261.8'35766—dc21

                                      00-064974

For all who struggle faithfully with sexual diversity
and in celebration of the loving devotion of
Stephen and Ken

Contents

Acknowledgments

We are grateful to Dr. John McCarthy and Dr. Robert Di Vito, chairs of the Theology Department and Graduate Program in Theology at Loyola University Chicago, respectively, for their encouragement and provision of two graduate research assistants to help with this volume. We are deeply appreciative of the general editorial assistance of Douglas Bowden and Timothy Sever, both doctoral students in moral theology at Loyola University Chicago, who were diligent in their searches for missing citations and helped us enormously with their careful reading of the essays. We acknowledge with thanks the guidance of Dr. Joseph R. Sherwin from the Office of Research Services at Loyola University Chicago. Without the receipt of a John and Theresa Mulcahy Research Support Grant on Catholic Issues from that office, we would not have been able to gather together for a working symposium on this volume.

We are most grateful, of course, to the scholars who chose to participate in this conversation and to contribute essays to this volume. Thanks for your hard work drafting your thoughts and your willingness to submit them to review by others outside your field, to read and critique the essays of other contributors and to revise your essays. Such interdisciplinary work requires dedication to the truth, patience, and courage.

Patricia Beattie Jung
Joseph Andrew Coray

Introduction

Patricia Beattie Jung

*I*t is simply a matter of fact that in the United States we discriminate as a matter of public policy on the basis of sexual identity. We
give preferential treatment in a variety of ways to heterosexual
people and treat gay men, lesbians, bisexuals, and transgendered people
(hereafter GLBT) prejudicially in regard to jobs, housing, credit, and
public accommodations. Though this discrimination is often accompanied by, and is certainly reinforced by homophobia, fear and hatred are
not always the driving force behind these policies. Sometimes what
undergirds them is the heterocentric conviction that there is something
wrong with—that is, either imperfect, defective, diseased, or downright
evil about—homosexual desires and activities. Because people are divided in their basic moral evaluation of homosexuality in particular,
and about sexual diversity in general, they are divided about how to respond to the differential treatment based on sexual identity inherent in
many of our public policies.

Through its official teachings on homosexuality the Roman Catholic Church sends "mixed" signals in regard to such heterosexist policies.
On the one hand the Church has repeatedly and unambiguously condemned verbal abuse of and violent attacks against GLBT people.[1] In
1986 the Vatican Congregation for the Doctrine of the Faith (hereafter
CDF) noted in its "Letter to the Bishops of the Catholic Church on the
Pastoral Care of Homosexual Persons" (hereafter PCHP) that "it is
deplorable that homosexual persons have been and are the object of
violent malice in speech and in action. Such treatment deserves condemnation from the Church's pastors wherever it occurs."[2] Reiterating
the point for the United States Catholic Conference (hereafter USCC),

Bishops Joseph Charron and William Skylstad argued in 1996 that "gay people deserve respect, compassion, understanding and defense against bigotry, attacks and abuse."[3]

Furthermore, the Roman Catholic Church has clearly taught that at least some types of discrimination based on sexual orientation should be dismantled. In 1976 the bishops of the USCC taught that gay people "like everyone else should not suffer from prejudice against their basic human rights. They have a right to respect, friendship and justice. They should have an active role in the Christian community."[4] More recently this same regional teaching body called "on all Christians and citizens of good will to confront their own fears about homosexuality and to curb the humor and discrimination that offend homosexual persons. . . . First and foremost, we support modeling and teaching respect for every human person, regardless of sexual orientation."[5] "The intrinsic dignity of each person must always be respected in word, in action and in law," the Vatican has long proclaimed.[6] This was reiterated by the CDF in its 1992 letter to the bishops, "Some Considerations Concerning the Response to Legislative Proposals on the Non-Discrimination of Homosexual Persons" (hereafter SCC),[7] and then again two years later in the *Catechism of the Catholic Church,* which declares, "Every sign of *unjust* discrimination in their regard should be avoided."[8]

On the other hand, because the Roman Catholic Church clearly advocates a heterocentric sexual ideal, it endorses some forms of discrimination based on sexual orientation. This should come as no surprise. These mixed messages do not come from an "incoherent" or "confused" teaching but from carefully nuanced distinctions informing a quite consistent teaching. And while there is much room for debate, even among conservative Catholics, about how this heterocentric ideal might best be applied in our particular cultural context, it is important to recognize that this normative framework establishes at least the possibility that some heterosexist policies might be deemed not only just but morally required. Thus when the Vatican issued the PCHP in order to combat what it perceived as a growing confusion about its teachings about homosexuality and related issues, the Church reiterated its traditional position that "no one has any conceivable right"[9] to homosexual behavior. It further specified that efforts associated with what it labeled the "pro-homosexual" movement to dismantle some expressions of heterosexism "threaten the lives and well-being of a large number of people" and "put in jeopardy" the family.[10] Therefore the CDF concluded that all Church-related institutions should withdraw support from organizations "which seek to undermine the teaching of the Church, which are ambiguous about it or which neglect it entirely."[11]

Though generally considered less authoritative in status, the Vatican's SCC declares that discrimination based on sexual orientation is "not only just but morally required" in several arenas: specifically noted were policies regarding the placement of children for adoption and foster care, the employment of teachers and athletic coaches, military recruitment, and even housing (especially when the rights of GLBT people are compared to the needs of "genuine" families). Landlords are described as expressing a legitimate concern when they screen potential tenants on the basis of sexual orientation. Why? Because the Vatican presumes GLBT people (like those with contagious diseases, it is suggested) pose a real threat to the common good. Specifically, the Church teaches that they recruit youth and attack the institution of (heterosexual) marriage and family.[12]

Again, while some of these specific applications of official Church teaching on homosexuality were not well received by some Catholics in the United States, many believe that at least some forms of heterosexist discrimination are not only justified but morally required. Many U.S. Catholics believe, for example, that our present marriage laws are a paradigmatic example of a "legitimate" instance of "just" discrimination or differential treatment based on sexual orientation; by pooling their discretionary funds the bishops of several Roman Catholic dioceses in California became the largest single donor in support of the Knight Initiative (which would ban same-sex marriages in California.) The many benefits and protections associated with marriage make it clear that much is at stake in the contemporary debate about the civil licensing of same-sex marriage.[13]

These Catholics are not alone in their judgment. Christians across many denominations see the effort to dismantle our present marriage laws as misguided at best, and at worst as a dangerous moral outrage. Many denominations teach officially that this particular discriminatory practice is just, indeed necessary, to protect the public good. Bishops Charron and Skylstad spoke not only for the USCC but for many others when they concluded that "no same-sex union can realize the unique and full potential [for mutual love and support, for the reproduction and education of children, for the imaging of God's love for people] which the marital relationship expresses."[14]

Arguments for the proscription of same-sex marriage rest in part on the claim that heterosexuality is more than simply *part* of God's good creation. Rather, it is the *only* moral, or at least the morally ideal, form of human sexuality; in the terms of official Catholic teaching, arguments against same-sex marriage hinge on the conviction that a homosexual "inclination" or "tendency" is "objectively disordered." This is so, according to Roman Catholic Church teaching, because authentic love-making is *only* possible under two interrelated conditions. Sexual partners can only truly make love when they (1) are open to the possibility of procreation and (2) are expressing that sort of self-giving presumed possible only between persons whose genders are complementary. See also the Vatican statement presented by the Pontifical Council for the Family on July 26, 2000, which explicitly addresses such legislative initiatives entitled "Family, Marriage and 'De Facto' Unions" (especially Section 23).

DOES HETEROSEXISM HAVE A BIBLICAL FOUNDATION?

It can be easily established that these two tenets had been thought to rest upon a descriptive account of human sexuality as "naturally" structured around procreativity and male-female complementarity. Yet, as Stephen J. Pope notes, these teachings are no longer based on "a rationally developed philosophical analysis nor a scientifically informed account of human nature but a direct and straightforward appeal to biblical revelation."[15] Hence he argues that contemporary expressions of this traditional Church teaching are most aptly categorized as representative of a form of "revealed" natural law, resting decisively as they do on certain traditional interpretations of biblical texts judged by the official magisterium to be key to this question. The significant, if not decisive, role of biblical interpretation in its present teachings is noted by the Church itself. These moral convictions, the Church has argued, are based "on the solid foundation of a constant Biblical testimony."[16]

Whether the biblical texts frequently cited in official Church teachings[17] can be *reasonably* interpreted to support this heterocentric sexual ideal, and consequently at least some heterosexist practices, is one of the questions explored in this volume. Indeed, this was the question that led originally to this interdisciplinary study. Thus some of the essays collected here explore the relationship between contemporary biblical scholarship and Roman Catholic magisterial teachings about the morality of homosexuality. The biblical renewal of moral theology encouraged by the Second Vatican Council[18] invites all teachers of the Church to ask: can contemporary biblical scholarship confirm that the

Bible "reveals" what has officially been taught in this regard—specifically that human sexuality is so designed as to be structured exclusively around procreativity and male-female complementarity, and therefore that homosexual activity is immoral? Are magisterial interpretations of key biblical texts regarding human sexuality corroborated by reasonable biblical exegesis?

MORAL DISCERNMENT OF THE LIVING TRADITION

Obviously, however, the question of what constitutes the criteria for *reasonable* biblical interpretations is significant. It has always been the Roman Catholic position that the discernment of the living tradition is rooted in the consilience of insights[19] not only from traditional sources (such as Sacred Scriptures and Church teachings), but also from secular disciplines and human experience. Truth is such that it is logical to expect reasonable biblical interpretations to cohere not only with cogent Church teachings but also with the wisdom emerging from sound scientific studies,[20] well-constructed philosophical analyses, and properly interpreted human experiences. Each source of moral wisdom—traditional Church teachings and practices, the Bible, the data of secular disciplines, and human experience—requires interpretation.

Such interpretation is best done dialogically; through such interplay these sources are allowed to mutually correct as well as corroborate each other. Thus for biblical scholarship to contribute to the renewal of moral theology, exegetes must enter into conversation not only with theologians but with scientists, philosophers, and pastors. Thus it was that most of those who contributed essays to this volume met at Loyola at the Cenacle in Chicago in October 1999. During that working symposium the contributors struggled faithfully in small interdisciplinary groups to allow their own reflections on human sexual diversity to be informed by the insights and wisdom emerging in other fields. While working primarily out of their respective disciplines, the authors listened to each other and worked together toward moral discernment. Following that symposium they each revised their essays in an effort to contribute with more discernment to the development of Catholic teaching on sexual diversity.

That such moral discernment is a Protestant as well as Catholic agenda goes without saying. Yet how precisely the insights of experience, secular disciplines, and the Scriptures relate to traditional Church teachings, and to the teaching office of the Church, is part of what has historically divided Roman Catholics and Protestants. And it raises additional methodological questions. Complicating the scholarly pursuit of the question of whether insights from these various sources of wisdom cohere with and undergird traditional heterocentric Church teachings (or not) are debates among Catholics about the proper understanding of the relationship among these sources of wisdom. Consider, for example, the relationship in principle between the Bible and magisterial teachings on specific moral matters. Can the biblical renewal of moral theology result not only in the reinforcement, but at least on occasion in the further development, indeed even the reform of traditional Church teachings?

Magisterial Teachings and Insights from the Bible, Secular Disciplines, and Human Experience

Fidelity to authoritative teachings on highly complex moral matters generally requires that these teachings be engaged by theologians (constructive and moral), biblical scholars, scientists, philosophers, and pastors in a variety of ways. For example, it requires that arguments in their defense be both sympathetically constructed and critically evaluated. The potential applicability of these teachings to the contemporary situation needs to be both appreciated and tested. In regard to teachings about homosexuality and heterosexism, an exploration of the exegetical and hermeneutical arguments foundational to magisterial teachings is obviously part of their faithful appropriation.

While engaged in this work, moral theologians ought neither absolutize nor overlook magisterial interpretations of the Sacred Scriptures. It is reasonable to expect Church teachings, received with the presumption of truth, to be readily corroborated by the best of biblical scholarship and to cohere with cogent interpretations of relevant human experiences and with the best scientific data and philosophical arguments available. Thus the genuine *appreciation* of official Church interpretations of the Bible is not antithetical to their critical analysis. The theological reception of authoritative Church teachings is not properly conceived of as separable from the exposure of these same teachings to rigorous scholarly analysis and debate. Vigorous *suspicion* can be an expression of the faithful appreciation of tradition. The dichotomization of these two hermeneutical approaches is false.

Many in the academy, however, continue to assume that a commitment to wrestle faithfully with Church teachings will prove inescapably parochial. Such tenacity reflects, they most likely presume, a blind and immature submission of inquiry to an excessively authoritarian voice. Certainly, if one were to ascribe a preemptive form of authority to Church teachings on specific moral matters, that would be the case. Whenever one grants primacy *a priori* to a source of wisdom (whether that be official Church teachings or contemporary secular viewpoints) over all others, then one rules radical disagreements "out of order," and eclipses even the possibility of mutual correction and learning.

The Church recognizes of course that there is a debate, confusing for many of the faithful, about how best to interpret the witness of Scripture on the subjects of same-sex behavior, homosexuality, and heterosexism. Indeed, according to the official *magisterium* those exegetes who argue "that Scripture has nothing to say on the subject of homosexuality, or that it somehow tacitly approves of it, or that all its moral injunctions are so culture-bound that they are no longer applicable" are "gravely erroneous."[21] However, since the guidance of the Holy Spirit has never been understood to be restricted to the official magisterium, the discernment of the living Tradition by the teaching Church remains in principle open to developments triggered by insights stemming from other sources of moral wisdom. The Catholic tradition remains in principle open to developments in moral theology triggered by the skills, expertise, disciplines, and insights stemming from many— some not even explicitly Christian—sources of moral wisdom.

Teaching Authority

The promise of biblical renewal for moral theology is not easy to characterize, but it most certainly holds some rather surprising ecclesiological implications for Christian communities, Protestant and Catholic alike. Since as far back as the sixteenth century, exegetes have recognized the practice of "private" exegesis to be very dangerous. Taking biblical texts seriously as sources of moral wisdom requires that their interpretation be done in conversation with Christian traditions in communion with the Church. In 1993 Stanley Hauerwas, arguably the best-known Protestant ethicist in the country, shocked many of his Protestant readers when he argued that "most Christians assume that they have a right, if not a pious obligation, to read the Bible. I challenge that assumption. No task is more important than for the Church to take the Bible out of the hands of individual Christians in North America."[22] This was shocking because to conclude that biblical interpretation should take place only when "controlled" by the Church simply goes against the piety of much of American Protestantism.

As the title of his book *Unleashing the Scriptures* indicated, Hauerwas was driven to this conclusion by the conviction that the Bible is being held captive by North American political interests and prejudices. Few would deny the merits of his concern. Some scholars call the ideological corruption of Christian teaching and preaching by the biases of any given culture "eisegesis." It is always a real and present danger. It is surely the concern that lay behind the Vatican's desire to clarify its teaching on homosexuality in 1986. It has long been understood that the primary problem in the use of Scripture in moral arguments is that of control. Thus resolving questions about the control of the interpretative process will prove central to the biblical renewal of moral theology.

The Bible as Scripture

It has become commonplace to note that people are narratively constructed. We live out of many different scripts. The messages that bombard us from all quarters get organized more or less by the master story in accord with which we live. When the Bible is faithfully appropriated, it functions precisely as such an identity-conferring master story. When we are authored by it, it becomes our Scripture.[23]

Many Christians recognize that to embody the Bible cannot mean trying to replicate even one of the bygone eras represented in the canon. Taking the Bible seriously is not nostalgia for "the good old days." Indeed, if the Bible is to function as Scripture *for us,* fidelity to its witness cannot mean the repristination of its ancient worlds. Fidelity to the Bible requires its translation *into our world.*[24] To be so scripted by the Bible cannot be a matter of simply adopting New Testament practices any more than the imitation of Christ requires that we all become itinerant preachers. No Christian today abstains from eating meat that has been strangled or refrains from eating blood sausage, even though these activities are quite clearly proscribed in the New Testament (Acts 15:20). Christians some time ago interpreted that recommendation to be no longer applicable. Furthermore, anyone who digs deeply into the Bible cannot help but be struck by the diversity of practices—regarding personal wealth, for example—commended within the New Testament alone. The nature of the Bible itself necessitates its interpretation.

Whenever we claim the Bible as Scripture—as an authoritative source of moral wisdom for us—we are immediately and inevitably confronted by two questions. What controls our selection of texts? and what controls the interpretation of the texts we have selected? Hauerwas proposes, in a move more typically Roman Catholic than Protestant, that traditional Church teachings should be in control.

The Moral Ambiguity of Some Church Teachings

Protestant and Roman Catholic Christians divided (in part at any rate) precisely over this question about "the control" of the Bible. Thus many, Protestants especially, believed Hauerwas to be suggesting that they jump "from the frying pan into the fire," when he concluded that Christians should place their interpretations "under the authority" of the Church.[25] This may free the Bible from some of the distortions associated with the secularism rampant in the U.S. but, they argue, the Bible can be—indeed has been on occasion—held captive, not only by the civil ideologies that worry Hauerwas but also by errors (sometimes long-standing) on the part of the Church.

Church history displays the ambiguity of some of the Church's moral teachings and raises real questions about the trustworthiness of Christian traditions as interpretive frameworks. Few would contest the claim that the moral teachings of Christianity have changed over the centuries,[26] but there is vigorous debate (especially among Roman Catholics) about both (1) how to describe and (2) how to evaluate these changes. Without doubt, some changes in Church teachings are merely adjustments necessitated by changes in the moral situations faced by the faithful.[27] But others seem to represent more substantive developments, prompted by what John Henry Newman called in his classic "An Essay on the Development of Christian Doctrine" a "warfare of ideas."[28] This has resulted in much-needed corrections in the Church's moral teachings.[29]

Another question key to the biblical renewal of moral theology is therefore: on what basis should we evaluate developments in and challenges to traditional Church teachings? This is relatively easy to do in retrospect. Hindsight always seems to make moral discernment easier. But of course what we really need help with is assessing changes while they are being proposed. On what basis should we decide whether a proposed "development" represents a salutary renewal of the Church's teachings on a particular issue or the corruption of those teachings?

Initially (at any rate) the answer to this question seems clear enough: base one's assessment of the proposed development on whether or not it is biblically inspired, corroborated, or at least not contradicted! The Bible is for Christians a necessary and indispensable source of moral wisdom. Any proposed change in traditional Church teaching should in some at least minimal sense cohere with the witness preserved in the Bible. There is even broad ecumenical agreement about the significance for Christians of moral arguments based on the Scriptures. And yet, while all this is true, it leads us right back to the problem with which we started.

Reviewing the Hermeneutical Circle

When confronted with questions about the basis on which we ought to highlight and interpret biblical texts we reiterate the ancient conviction that Church teachings are better than secular ideologies as guiding frameworks for biblical interpretation. Yet while better overall, at least some of the Church's traditional teachings may need dramatic "development." The fact that some Church teachings are corroborated by the scriptural interpretations they frame while others are contradicted by commonplace accounts of biblical testimony does not in itself solve the problem with which we wrestle. A cursory review of the history of moral theology discloses that in both cases—either of corroboration or contradiction—one has no guarantee of having thereby discerned the living Tradition.

This gives rise to at least two important questions: first, should Church teachings, or some other sources of moral wisdom, be in control of the interpretative process? and second, given the promise of Christ that at least some Church teachings will be developed further, how do we determine which ones? Clearly, even when the Christian Scriptures and traditions are bound together in a hermeneutical partnership not all our ethical questions are answered. Yet there is no better alternative to this circular relationship. Clearly, leashing the Scriptures to secular ideologies would offer no more helpful interpretative framework. Furthermore, though potentially vicious, the hermeneutical circle between the Bible and Church teachings is most often illuminative.

The Church as a Deliberative Community for Biblical Interpretation and Moral Discernment

Taking the Bible seriously requires that Christians hold themselves accountable to an inclusive dialogue about the moral meaning of both the Bible and traditional Church teachings. Such work by definition is communal. Happily, it is to the Church as a whole that God has entrusted the Word and promised the Spirit. To argue that the Church is the proper context in which to read the Scriptures does not entail a triumphalist ecclesiology. No one knows where the Spirit might blow. Yet Christians ought to trust in the promised presence of the Spirit in the Church. This does not eliminate the possibility of individual insight into Scripture, or guarantee that official magisterial teachings will never be mistaken. To claim that the Church as a whole is the bearer of Scripture and tradition means that *all* the faithful—not just bishops, ministers, or theologians, with their advanced theological educations—have the privilege and call to wrestle with the Word of God. The questions and insights all people bring to text studies and moral deliberation out of their diverse contexts in the world contribute greatly to the illumination of the Word and moral discernment. The contributions of secular disciplines and the full range of human experience to the biblical renewal of moral theology are not just welcome but essential.

This of course is not anything like an endorsement of private interpretation. While the Bible is a resource for and open to all the faithful, the Church is the context within which to interpret the Bible according to Catholic teaching. When we practice "reading in communion" with one another, our sense of a text's meaning for the moral life is expanded by the diverse views we engage. Our interpretation is sometimes corroborated, other times corrected, often enriched. This is especially true if these "others" with whom we are reading are in some sense outsiders to our perspective. The biblical renewal of moral theology requires that the hermeneutical and discernment process be communal, inclusive of all the faithful, and cross-disciplinary.

DISCERNING THE LIVING TRADITION

While the ecclesial structures for authenticating Church teachings are not everywhere the same,[30] *every* Christian denomination must reckon with how theological disagreement contributes to the interrelated processes of interpreting various sources of moral wisdom and the discernment of the living Tradition.[31] If there is to be an authentic renewal of moral theology, then all Christian denominations must be open to and prepared for not only vigorous deliberation about how best to interpret the Scriptures, the conclusions of secular disciplines, and human experience, but also for disagreements with official denominational statements about those same deliberations. Some lay people, pastoral ministers, congregations, other Church-related institutions—as well as theologians—disagree with the traditional Christian endorsement of certain forms of heterosexism. When a "warfare of ideas" (to use the terms suggested by John Henry Newman) has been spawned by the interplay between theological, biblical, scientific, philosophical, pastoral, and experiential sources of moral insight—as this anthology makes clear is the case in regard to the ethical analysis of sexual diversity within Catholicism—then the integration of theological disagreement into our operative ecclesiology is part of the challenge of learning to be a community of moral deliberation as well as moral conviction.

The very possibility of an outcome such as this tempts some within the Church to shut down the kind of theological dialogue represented in this volume. For them loyalty to the Church mandates humble submission and silent *obedience.* In contrast many contributors to this volume believe that on occasion responsible disagreement alone can express the fidelity and *respect* the living Tradition warrants.

A RESPONSIBLE PUBLIC CONVERSATION

According to the late moral theologian Richard A. McCormick, traditional moral doctrines are authoritative in the sense that they enjoy the presumption of *truth.*[32] This means that those who would disagree carry the burden of proof. However, this *presumption* of truth remains simply that—a presumption. The credibility of official Church teachings on specific moral matters may be tested in terms of a variety of criteria: their coherence, elegance, comprehensiveness, etc. For example, the presumption of truth such teachings enjoy may eventually be judged strong or weak depending upon the extent and the degree to which all sources of moral wisdom relevant to particular issues have been explored in their formation. Whenever the hierarchical magisterium fails to adequately gather and assess all the moral wisdom available to it, the presumption in favor of its teachings is weakened. In such a case, faithfulness to the living Tradition may take the form of disagreement with a particular magisterial teaching. In this way neglected insights might be highlighted.

The theological discussions that ensue might yield progress, but such a result is not inevitable. Clearly theological debate can be conducted in ways that prove to be irresponsible. In their 1968 pastoral letter, "Human Life in Our Day," the U.S. bishops outlined three norms that ought to govern theological dissent. First, the reasons for it must be serious and well-founded. Second, the manner in which the criticism is developed must be such that it fosters respect for the teaching authority of the hierarchical *magisterium* in general. Third, it ought not give scandal.

Since not even the most conservative Catholic would deny that theological debate is legitimate under some circumstances, the important question is: when (if ever) should such disagreements be made *public*? In their 1968 pastoral letter the U.S. bishops called for a fruitful dialogue among bishops and theologians about precisely this issue. In its 1990 "Instruction on the Ecclesial Vocation of the Theologian" the CDF gave its views on the matter. The Vatican invites bishops and theologians into private conversations and encourages the exchange of personal correspondence on matters about which moral theologians argue. The Vatican acknowledges that the tradition will be strengthened by this testing. Through this "warfare of ideas" the Church will be better able to articulate the faith. In the long run such a dialogue will serve the search for moral truth within the Church.

However, the Instruction clearly warns against some forms of public theological dissent, especially those involving the "popular" press and mass media "campaigns." Explicitly unaddressed is the expression of theological disagreements in semi-public arenas, such as professional societies, scholarly conferences, academic journals, university-level lectures, and scholarly book series. Since it is precisely such theological writings that have been the primary focus of recent investigations of the CDF, it would not be paranoid to conclude that the expression of theological dissent even in such venues is implicitly forbidden. Indeed, this much about the thrust of the Instruction is clear: the Vatican would prefer theological debate in the Church to be conducted *sotto voce*, that is, in a "low voice" not intended to be overheard. Theological disagreements need not always be silenced, just muffled.

New theological views should be developed with care—and in venues like scholarly presses, which welcome the nuance that often accompanies such care. Furthermore, these lines of argument should be spoken "out loud," even though the ensuing moral deliberation may prove confusing, divisive, and costly to some in the Church. Only through public expression can these very ideas be critically tested. And such testing is part of the way that God's Word is authentically proclaimed; it is an expression of fidelity to the living Tradition when expressions of it, both new and old, are scrutinized.

Ultimately, however, moral deliberation must be conducted "out loud" because the very credibility of the Church's teachings depends in part upon their comprehensiveness. Their comprehensiveness in turn depends upon their formation in light of the full spectrum of sources of moral wisdom. Public deliberation facilitates the interplay of all the sources of moral wisdom promised to us and increases the magisterium's accessibility to them.

It is well known that many fertile Catholic spouses in North America practice artificial contraception. Many moral theologians believe that both developments in the scientific understanding of human sexuality and reproduction and the sexual, marital, and parental experience[33] of faithful lay people have not been adequately considered in the formation of official Church teaching regarding contraception. Hence many moral theologians in the U.S. publicly disagree with some of the conclusions of *Humanae Vitae*. From this perspective, the suppression of the public exploration of the full implications for sexual ethics of such scientific discoveries and experiences eliminates possible sources not only of confusion and error but also of theological correction and improvement as well. The proper interpretation of such data and experience should play an important role in the development of moral theology, along with the retrieval of traditional Church teachings and the proper interpretation of the biblical witness.

When the disciplinary and experiential expertise of all God's people is not included in the process of theological and moral discernment, then the Church cannot readily access the insights that might emerge from the work of the Spirit in the world, that is, in their lived experience of the faith and their "secular" disciplines and insights. Present discussion about the role of debate in the development of moral theology is not just about the role and responsibilities of bishops, priests, and theologians but also about the role and responsibilities of those with more secular vocations.

Furthermore, it is not coincidental that the flash points for this controversy are primarily issues in sexual ethics. Ethical problems concerning sexuality are issues with which most faithful lay people have considerable first-hand experience and to which they have given much prayer and thought. Some remain afraid that the laity will overhear, and subsequently be scandalized by, the discussions collected in this volume about what the Tradition, Bible, secular disciplines, and selected experiences of the faithful might have to say about sexual diversity because most of the views expressed "out loud" here respectfully question official

Church teaching. What this discussion about theological debate is ultimately about is the role of the laity in the Church, especially given the growing interest among faithful lay people in matters theological and moral.[34]

Many concur that public theological disagreements in regard to some noninfallible Church teachings run the risk of fostering confusion among some Catholic lay people.[35] As George B. Wilson notes, the magisterium is rightly concerned to protect the faithful from the heresy and sin associated with ill-formed consciences.[36] And as John Noonan writes, changes are not necessarily for the better; "the majority of mutations are harmful."[37] Yet while the Church as a whole cannot err in matters central to the faith, the premise, operative among many conservatives, that God could not allow the faithful to be led astray by false teachings for any length of time on noninfallible teachings is equally dangerous.

Bishops and theologians alike make prudential judgments about whether the risks that may be realistically associated with scholarly investigations such as this outweigh their potential contributions to the further development of moral theology and their educational benefits. They must consider in their calculus the dangers and costs associated with the stifling of all forms of *public* theological debate. In the United States most Catholic lay people, and certainly the secular world to which the Church is also called to bear witness, are confused and disturbed, indeed scandalized, by the sounds of enforced silence. The credibility of Church teachings is most surely eroded when scholarly arguments that foster honest inquiry into and respectful debate about them are not tolerated. All who gather together with the authors who contributed to this volume to "converse" about *Sexual Diversity and Catholicism* could do no better than to follow the instructions of St. Paul: "test everything and hold fast to what is good" (1 Thess 5:21).

NOTES: INTRODUCTION

[1] It is crucial that the extent of such violence not be underestimated. The much-publicized recent murders of Matthew Shepard and Billy Jack Gaither represent merely the tip of an apparently expanding iceberg. According to FBI Bias Crimes statistics hate crimes against gays doubled between 1990 and 1998. Because they both recognized that at least some forms of religious rhetoric were contributing to this rising rate of anti-gay violence, the Rev. Jerry Falwell and his gay friend and former ghost writer, Mel White, led a historic meeting between conservative and liberal, gay and straight Christians. These groups

gathered to search for common ground on which to stand against such fear and hatred. See the PBS Frontline episode, *Assault on Gay America: The Life and Death of Billy Jack.*

[2] Congregation for the Doctrine of the Faith (hereafter CDF), "Letter to the Bishops of the Catholic Church on the Pastoral Care of Homosexual Persons" (hereafter PCHP) (1986) 10.

[3] Bishops Joseph Charron and William Skylstad, "Statement on Same-Sex Unions," *Origins* 26/9 (August 1, 1996) 132–33.

[4] United States Catholic Conference (hereafter USCC), National Conference of Catholic Bishops (hereafter NCCB), "To Live in Christ Jesus" (1976) 52.

[5] USCC, NCCB, "Human Sexuality: A Catholic Perspective for Education and Lifelong Learning" (1991) 55, 56.

[6] CDF, PCHP (1986) 10.

[7] CDF, "Responding to Legislative Proposals on Discrimination Against Homosexuals" (hereafter SCC), revised text, *Origins* 20/10 (August 6, 1992) 173, 175–77.

[8] CDF, *Catechism of the Catholic Church* (Liberia Editrice Vaticana, 1994) 2358 (italics supplied).

[9] CDF, PCHP (1986) 10.

[10] Ibid. 9.

[11] Ibid. 17.

[12] CDF, SCC.

[13] In our culture getting married brings with it a social status rich in entitlements both informal and formal. Informally the public recognition of a marriage enables the community to support the spouses' efforts to cultivate their identity as married in order to maintain their covenant. On a more formal level society's refusal to license same sex marriages denies gay couples about two hundred benefits from and protections for their committed relationships. Included among such supports are: spousal immigration rights, the proxy privileges automatically attributed to "the next of kin" in regard to medical decisions and funeral arrangements, a variety of economic benefits (both direct and transferred) from Social Security, Medicare, veterans' and other pension plans, and the spousal benefits associated with life and health insurance policies. Because in most of the United States their committed relationships are not legally recognized, gay couples cannot file joint tax returns or automatically acquire joint home, auto, or health insurance policies. They do not receive the protection afforded heterosexual couples by custody, domestic abuse, divorce, child support, estate, and inheritance laws.

A change in our public policy in this regard is therefore not a matter merely of tolerance. It is important to be clear: the civil licensing of same sex marriages will express social approval for and the encouragement of steadfast and monogamous relationships among same sex people. By the same token, our present marriage laws—because they so powerfully privilege some citizens and so blatantly and seriously discriminate against others—must be able to demonstrate that they have a very compelling moral foundation. Otherwise they are patently unjust.

[14] Bishops Charron and Skylstad, *Origins* 26/9 (August, 1996) 133 [summary of their argument in the brackets is mine.]

[15] Stephen J. Pope, "Scientific and Natural Law Analyses of Homosexuality," *Journal of Religious Ethics* 25/1 (Spring 1997) 106.

[16] CDF, PCHP (1986) 5.

[17] Gen 1:27-28; 19:1-11; Lev 18:22; 20:13; 1 Cor 6:9; Rom 1:18-32; 1 Tim 1:10.

[18] The biblical renewal of moral theology is one part of the agenda for moral theology developed at the Second Vatican Council. Vatican II described the Bible as teaching "firmly, faithfully and without error the truth which God wanted put into the sacred writing for the sake of our salvation" (Dogmatic Constitution on Divine Revelation, *Dei Verbum*, 111). Just as the Bible should be "the soul of theology," so concluded the Council, moral theology "should be more thoroughly nourished by scriptural teaching" (Decree on Priestly Formation, *Optatum totius* 16, 452).

[19] Because recent Church teachings on this matter are discussed in this volume at some length in the chapter by Sidney Callahan, I would draw attention here only to the fact that, though such a claim in our present postmodern climate is unfashionable, arguably one of the twentieth century's most prominent scientists, operates with and argues for a similar epistemological vision. See Edward O. Wilson, *Consilience: The Unity of Knowledge* (New York: Alfred A. Knopf, 1998).

[20] Carolyn Osiek, R.S.C.J., "The New Handmaid: The Bible and Social Sciences," *Theological Studies* 50 (1989) 260–78; eadem, "The Social Sciences and the Second Testament: Problems and Challenges," *Biblical Theology Bulletin* 22 (Summer 1992) 88–95.

[21] CDF, PCHP (1986) 4.

[22] Stanley Hauerwas, *Unleashing the Scriptures* (Nashville: Abingdon, 1993) jacket.

[23] All of this is true of whatever functions as scripture for a person, whether that be the Bill of Rights, the *Sunday New York Times,* or the Bible. What is scripture is morally formative in a great variety of ways. It establishes certain behavioral boundaries, highlights certain features of (perhaps even creates) the landscape we roam, and nurtures in us certain habits of the heart. It weaves—

more or less successfully—various subplots into an integral whole. If we forget our master story, then like all who suffer amnesia we lose our sense of identity and our life disappears.

[24] Given the tremendous gaps between the concerns of ancient Israel and the early Church and the subplots of our world, translation may result in dramatic differences. Many recognize in the debates in recent decades about the dress codes for women religious translation questions quite similar to those faced by people striving to faithfully embody religious texts. In many cases the old habits adopted by religious orders signaled something about the priorities of their community, perhaps its solidarity with the poor. For example, at the time of the origin of their community most Franciscans were dressed in a manner indistinguishable from that of the poor of that day. Now, however, such garb may distance women and men religious from those with whom they wish to minister. It is reasonable to conclude that fidelity to such a habit might require a change in it or even the abandonment of it altogether! But life in a religious community—like life in biblically inspired communities—is quite complicated. Over the years religious costumes acquired additional meanings. In some communities they came to signal solidarity with other religious and commitment to life together. From this angle a change of habit might reasonably be interpreted as corrosive of community—analogous to the break signaled by the decision of a spouse to remove a wedding ring.

[25] Hauerwas, *Unleashing the Scriptures,* 15.

[26] The history of Church teaching reveals that even though Rome had spoken on an issue, the matter was often not closed. Pope Pius XII's nearly absolute condemnation of polygenism in *Humani generis* (1950) was quietly "dropped" shortly after its pronouncement, when theologians demonstrated that it did not threaten the doctrine of original sin. Though it took much longer, in 1992 Pope John Paul II admitted that Galileo had mistakenly been condemned for his support of the so-called Copernican revolution, and in June 1999 that same prelate praised directly the discoveries of his fellow Pole, Nicolaus Copernicus, whose theories had been denounced in 1616 as a "danger to the faith."

Any review of the development of moral doctrine surfaces similar points of discontinuity. For example, Walter Principe pointed out that the learning Church has changed its teachings on slavery, the termination of ectopic pregnancies, and torture ("When 'Authentic' Teachings Change," *The Ecumenist* 25/5 [July–August, 1987] 70–73). Similarly, John T. Noonan has pointed out that the Church's teachings on adultery, the death penalty, religious liberty (particularly the religious persecution—including torture—of heretics which had been required, but now is forbidden), and usury have all "developed" (John T. Noonan, Jr., "On the Development of Doctrine," *America* 180/11 (April 3, 1999) 6–8; see as well Noonan's "Experience and the Development of Moral

Doctrine," *CTSA Proceedings,* Michael Downey, ed., 54 (June 10–13, 1999) 43–56). Margaret A. Farley has demonstrated that analogous developments have occurred over the centuries in Church teachings on sexual ethics (in regard to pleasure, procreation, and love) with especially dramatic changes occurring in the twentieth century (Margaret A. Farley, "Same-Sex Relations: An Ethical Perspective," lecture presented at the New Ways Ministry Conference, Pittsburgh, 1997).

[27] In their book *The Abuse of Casuistry: A History of Moral Reasoning,* Albert R. Jonsen and Stephen Toulmin review in great detail several such changes in the moral teachings of the Christian West. For example, for most of Church history the practice of charging interest on loans was forbidden. This prohibition was linked to several biblical directives (such as Ps 15:5; Deut 23:19-20; Luke 6:35). In the economic worlds within which these texts were originally situated, and perhaps more importantly for many centuries in the economic worlds of their interpreters, loans functioned more or less as relief for the poor. Charging interest on money provided for such relief was viewed as the moral equivalent of stealing from the poor.

However, with the rise of capitalism the Church slowly came to recognize that loans could function in other ways. A loan could be a form of capital enterprise. Far from theft, charging a reasonable interest on this kind of loan is more like getting a fair price for the risk associated with investment and for the costs associated with administering the loan and losing the use of one's capital. (This of course leaves the question of the legitimacy of charging interest on IMF and World Bank relief loans wide open to debate.)

Though we don't feel the tension now, during the several centuries when this change in Church teaching evolved there was vigorous debate over how to interpret this development. Was it a prudent adjustment given the changes in the economic terrain, or was it an irresponsible moral compromise that not only accommodated but also contributed to the "unholy" rise of capitalism? In retrospect the answer seems fairly obvious: even those of us highly critical of capitalism would not commend a return to feudal economies. In any case for us today this particular question is moot. But the wider issue of how to interpret changes in the Church's moral teachings in the present is not.

[28] This essay of 1843 was discussed in Noonan's "On the Development of Doctrine," 6–7.

[29] Obviously, not every change is for the good, but at times renewal is clearly in order. Certainly Protestants at least in principle would be comfortable with such an assertion. Even while discussing the "tried and true" character of our common biblical heritage, reform theologian Max L. Stackhouse concedes the importance of testing not only the "new" but what is traditional as well. "We have to be critical of the evils of the past so that we do not perpetuate them in

the present" (Max L. Stackhouse, "Tradition and Revelation," *The Christian Century* 113/32 [November 6, 1996] 1061).

And at least since Vatican II a significant number of revisionist Roman Catholics are increasingly at home with an image of the Church as not only teaching but learning (Principe). The Council spoke often of the Church as the Pilgrim People of God. The Dogmatic Constitution on the Church (*Lumen gentium* 8) described it as a community both holy and "always in need of being purified."

[30] Christians are deeply divided over who in the Church is *ultimately* responsible for the interpretation of the Bible and Tradition. Whether the process of interpreting Church teachings, biblical texts, scientific studies, philosophical arguments, and human experience is defined as basically participatory or consultative will depend upon how the teaching office in any given communion has been defined. In some denominations this is the work of a church-wide assembly; in others it is essentially a congregational matter. For Roman Catholics this work belongs to the *magisterium*. The task of guiding, and when necessary arbitrating, the process of moral discernment is entrusted to all those commissioned to teaching ministries in the Church. Among these, bishops speak officially for the Roman Catholic Church.

[31] At sixty-two million, Roman Catholics comprise the vast majority of Christians in the United States, so moral arguments within Catholicism about this will be very significant. But this is not just a problem for Roman Catholics, as the many recent denominational disagreements about heterosexism and homosexuality indicate. It should be noted that the Georgia Baptist Convention (affiliated with the 15.7-million-strong Southern Baptist Convention) expelled two congregations for affirming gays in 2000. Similarly, four California congregations are threatened with expulsion by the American Baptist Church for welcoming sexual diversity. During their national conventions in 1999 and 2000 the United Methodist Church, the Presbyterian Church of the United States of America, the Reformed Church in America, the Episcopal Church, and the Evangelical Lutheran Church of America all devoted considerable time to the study and discussion of this issue.

[32] The discussion that follows is indebted to the helpful analyses of Richard A. McCormick, s.j., developed in "The Search for Truth in the Catholic Context," *America* 155/13 (November 8, 1986) 276–81 and in "Moral Doctrine: Stability and Development," *CTSA Preceedings* 54 (1999) 92–100. It should be noted that this language of presumption, however, was first employed in the National Catechetical Directory, *Sharing the Light of Faith* published first by the USCC in 1978.

[33] As in the case of any other source of moral wisdom, theologians are called to take the experience of the whole People of God seriously. Theologians are called to decipher such authentic "signs of the times." This includes evaluating

experience(s) critically, in light of the canons of reason and of Tradition and Scripture, and then giving voice to its wisdom in their debates. Why? Because the Holy Spirit dwells among and inspires all the People of God. This was recognized by the Second Vatican Council in its Declaration on Religious Liberty. The experience of ordinary Christian people with religious persecution proved to be an important factor in the (re)formation of the Church's teaching on this matter. It functioned as a source of moral wisdom or *locus theologicus* for the further development of the Church's moral teachings regarding religious liberty. Similarly, the experience of ordinary believers in regard to heterosexism and homosexuality will be an important source of moral wisdom for the Church.

[34] All parties to this debate recognize that because of this blossoming interest it is probably unrealistic to think that the popular press will not pick up on scholarly debates if the topic is "hot" enough. And it goes without saying that this volume addresses precisely such a "hot" topic. All concede that the popular press is not a medium ideally suited—even when it is so inclined—for the articulation of highly nuanced and complex theological arguments. All agree that both official Church teachings and divergent theological opinions can be and have been misrepresented by the press. When they are "popularized," the *status* of such theological opinions is often intentionally exaggerated by the media and consequently misperceived by the faithful, and most certainly by the wider public.

[35] Some may be confused by what they "overhear" in this scholarly volume. Such a disturbance could be an occasion of sin for them. Of course, this is far more likely to be true, and to remain true, if one views lay people as not only theologically illiterate but also as theologically uneducable. However, when lay people are seen as adults capable of and called to life-long learning about their faith, then even if they are theologically uneducated at present, this very same volume—and any media interest in it—could be an opportunity for further theological education and occasion conscience formation.

[36] George B. Wilson, "'Dissent' or Conversation among Adults?" *America* 180/8 (March 13, 1999) 8–12.

[37] Noonan, "On the Development of Doctrine," 7.

Part One:
Interpreting Church Teachings

1

A Call to Listen: The Church's Pastoral and Theological Response to Gays and Lesbians

Bishop Thomas J. Gumbleton

*T*hroughout many years of pastoral experience, I have come to a deeper understanding of what is meant by the words recorded by Matthew as the conclusion of the Sermon on the Mount: "You must be perfect as your Father in heaven is perfect" (Matt 5:48).

This is not a call to what is impossible. We are not expected to become "God." But just as God is fully and completely God in the fullness of what it means to be God, so each of us is called by God to be fully and completely the human person God has made us to be. Jesus is the model for us, not in his divinity, but in his humanity. Certainly Jesus came to reveal God to us. But he also came to reveal us to ourselves. Not only is he truly God, he is also truly human. By his presence among us, fully human, like us in every way except sin, Jesus shows us how the glory of God is revealed in us when we become fully alive, fully the human person we are called to be. Because Jesus was without sin, he was fully human, fully alive. Sin is the rejection of the truth of our humanity. Sin detracts from our fullness of life, from our being fully human. We are urged to become perfect, which means to be all God has made it possible for us to be.

Obviously, this does not happen at once. The original blessing of our creation has been diminished, sometimes to what seems an almost

3

unredeemable degree, by sin. It takes a long process of being healed, of being loved into a new fullness of humanness, by the God who first loved us into existence, into life.

We have various sources of guidance to help us grow into full human persons as we live out our time on earth. God's Word in the Old Testament and the New Testament, and especially in Jesus, is the first source for us to look to. The community of Jesus' disciples and its tradition is a second source. In addition, we have the insights of other human persons who have prayerfully and consistently pondered God's Word and who can share their insights in directing us. Finally, as the Second Vatican Council reminded us, we have the divine voice echoing in our own depth, within our own spirit as a law written by God in human hearts. This is the voice of individual conscience.

I intend this essay to be a way of showing that homosexual persons can be "perfect," just as heterosexual persons can be. They can be all God calls them to be as homosexual human beings, just as heterosexual persons can be fully human in their heterosexuality. There is extraordinary diversity in the ways that human creatures image God, in whose image and likeness they are created. I also intend to show that homosexual persons must struggle to reach as full a human development as possible by using the same resources of guidance God has given for all. As they do this, all of us must respect their honesty and integrity as they search for the way to their full humanness. At the outset I insist that they have the same right and obligation to use these sources of guidance that all of us have. And I am confident that the God who made them, and who knows them in the depths of their being, will bring them to an ever fuller sense of peace, love, and life as they move along in their struggle to be fully human.

We who watch, and perhaps help to guide, will be moved to awe at the amazing, even infinite diversity of the God who is imaged in every being loved into existence by this same God.

My awareness of the spiritual needs of homosexual persons and my ever deeper involvement in ministry to homosexual persons began in 1992. In March 1992 I was invited, along with two other bishops, to speak at a national meeting of New Ways Ministry. The three of us had been asked to serve as a panel of bishops offering a pastoral response to gay and lesbian persons in the Church.

Prior to the meeting each of us was contacted directly or indirectly by the papal nuncio, who suggested that we ought to withdraw from the program. However, after talking it over with each other we decided that our participation in the work of New Ways Ministry was an appropriate pastoral outreach to gay and lesbian people. I am very grateful that I went because it was a significant turning point in my own life. I thought very carefully about what I was going to say. In fact, I had two presentations prepared in my mind. I was thinking of a rather generic sort of presentation in which I would indicate how pleased I was to be there, how grateful I was for the invitation to speak, and how appropriate it seemed to me that bishops would engage in some fashion in this clearly identified ministry to the homosexual community within the Catholic Church. I would insist on the need for their full inclusion in the Church; on the need to eliminate all overt and subtle discrimination against homosexual people; how I as a bishop would be committed to this in my own personal attitude and actions; and how I would work for this in every way possible. I wanted to leave them with confidence that they would no longer have to hide their identity in order to be fully welcome in the Church, that a new era was opening up in the Church.

The other presentation would be much more personal. I would share my own "story" of confronting within myself a deep homophobia and working my way beyond it by having to deal with this pastoral problem, not in an academic or theoretical way, but within my own immediate family. Still debating within myself as I walked to the podium, and not sure if I was ready to do it, I said to myself, "I'm going to do it. I am going to tell my own story."

It is obviously very hard for gay and lesbian people to come out. First, there has to be a process of self-awareness, of coming to an understanding of their sexual identity. Then there is often a difficult struggle with self-acceptance. Very often, if not universally, homosexual people have been "programmed" into a deep self-hatred and a sense that they cannot even be loved by God. This must be overcome, even to the point of rejoicing in who they are and fully accepting their homosexuality as the way God is calling them to be. Then after self-acceptance there is still the risk of being rejected by others, especially by the most significant people in their lives—parents, siblings, the Church, teachers, friends, etc. Today it is encouraging that so many are coming to accept themselves and risking all that goes with "coming out."

Though it is not totally comparable, nevertheless it is also hard for those of us who are not gay or lesbian but who have in some cases a child, or in my case a brother, who is homosexual to publicly acknowledge this. I was hesitant because I was not sure how publicly acknowledging and affirming my brother would affect my own ministry or the public esteem accorded to bishops and their role in the Church. Obviously, my concern reflected my own ignorance and even fear of homosexual persons. This is an attitude that is often generically described as homophobic. It is very much present in our Church and our society. Rejecting any fear of this consequence, I told them my "story," together with an account of what has happened subsequently.

I grew up in a very Catholic family. I am the sixth of ten children— eight boys and two girls. We grew up during the hard times of the Depression, through the Second World War, and its aftermath when things got better economically. I went to parochial school and was very close to the Church. I followed the example of my parents who were very faithful Catholics. When I was just fourteen I went to Sacred Heart Seminary to begin high school and continue for four years of college. After that I spent four more years studying at St. John's Seminary.

I took to the seminary life very much. I enjoyed it; I did well; and I was very much influenced by the kind of training I had there. As I look back now, I realize how unprepared I was after my ordination in 1956 to be a pastoral minister to gay or lesbian people. To tell you the truth, I never knew what a homosexual person was until I got into theology. I was never prepared to minister adequately. I can remember hearing confessions for hours at a time. The very large parish where I was stationed in the 1950s had a heavy schedule of confessions. Spending hours and hours in the confessional, I would periodically have men come who were gay, even though I didn't know the term then. They would confess committing acts with other men. I remember how dogmatic I was and how decisive I was in telling them it was wrong and they would have to stop. My understanding was that it was a free choice, and just as with any other sin, the sinner must try to do something about it. I thought I was giving good advice by telling them to separate themselves from the places where it happened. In reality I had not even a minimum understanding of their situation. I never thought of it as sexual orientation. While I thought I was being very pastoral and helpful, I was actually being totally insensitive and, in many cases, very hurtful to people who came to me and to the Church for help. I was in no position to give it.

Much later I read an interview with Andrew Sullivan, a gay Catholic man, printed in *America* magazine in May 1993. It made me realize how inadequate and even hurtful my efforts were. A few paragraphs from the interview say it very well:

Natural law! Here is something [homosexuality] that seems to occur spontaneously in nature, in all societies and civilizations. Why not a teaching about the nature of homosexuality and what its good is? How can we be good? Teach us. How does one inform the moral lives of homosexuals? The church has an obligation to all its faithful to teach us how to live and how to be good—which is not merely dismissal, silence, embarrassment or a "unique" doctrine on one's inherent disorder. Explain it. How does God make this? Why does it occur? What should we do? How can the doctrine of Christian love be applied to homosexual people as well?

Now it may be this search will turn up all sorts of options and possibilities. There may be all sorts of notions and debate about the nature of this phenomenon and what its final end might be. But that it has a final end is important. The church has to understand—people in the church have to understand—what it must be to grow up loving God and wanting to live one's life well and truly, as a human being, able to love and contribute and believe, and yet having nothing.

I grew up with nothing. No one taught me anything except that this couldn't be mentioned. And as a result of the total lack of teaching, gay Catholics and gay people in general are in crisis. No wonder people's lives—many gay lives—are unhappy or distraught or in dysfunction, because there is no guidance at *all*. Here is a population within the church, and outside the church, desperately seeking spiritual health and values. And the church refuses to come to our aid, refuses to listen to this call.[1]

I was so clearly a part of the Church that "refuses to come to our aid, refuses to listen to this call."

As I look back now, I can see why. In my own Catholic family you just did what the Church said: follow the rules. And while one would hope that in the seminary you would get some understanding about something like sexuality, this was not the case. In fact, in these all-male institutions the training intensified the homophobia with which I was raised. We used to get a spiritual conference with the spiritual director every week. Three or four times a year there would be a talk about "particular friendships." At the time I did not even know what they were actually talking about. Only later did I realize they were warning us to be careful not to get into a relationship with another student. We were warned of being seen too often with the same person, chatting in the corridor, or having someone in our room. Once in a while a student would leave suddenly. Later, I could discern the reason. He was gay. But at the time it never dawned on me because no one ever spoke in open terms about this whole phenomenon of gay people.

I learned how to be a priest out of that experience: the narrowly Catholic cultural ghetto I grew up in and the closed seminary life that followed. My preparation to minister pastorally was based on my seminary training. I never got any real understanding of sexuality even as a part of my own psychological development. There were, of course, positive aspects of that training. But what should have been a major part of it was not there. For all practical purposes our training was very thorough in teaching us how to repress our sexuality in order to be faithful to our promise of celibacy. Questions of human intimacy and of healthy affectionate behavior were never raised. We were expected to cope with our sexuality in the best way we could. The goal was simply to avoid sin and eternal damnation. This resulted in serious underdevelopment for the majority of priests and made it almost impossible for us to minister effectively, especially in guiding people toward full acceptance of their sexuality and integration of that into their person, whether homosexual or heterosexual.

I have a younger brother, Dan, who was also in the seminary. As I look back I can see a pattern in his life that I didn't pay any attention to at the time. After a few years he was suddenly dropped from the seminary; there was no explanation, and he never said much about it to anybody. I called the provincial of the religious order, but he was very evasive. I had a suspicion why Dan was dropped, but I preferred not to explore further. He was gay, but not wanting to admit it even to himself; he got married and seemed to have a good relationship. He and his wife had four daughters, and they lived together for about fifteen years. But then they moved away, and again I can see that as part of the pattern. Not being able to tell anyone, gay men or lesbians often move away from where they are known. He and his wife moved to the West Coast. He was hiding who he really was, and his marriage really wasn't working out. It came to the point where he knew he had to be honest about who he really is. When his older kids were in their early teens, his marriage broke up. Fortunately for him, he and his wife were able to separate amicably, and their children are all still in a good relationship with Dan and his former wife. We were in contact all that time.

In the mid-1980s my brother sent a very lengthy and detailed letter to my mother and all of us siblings. The letter was his coming out, telling us he is gay, telling us his whole situation. By this time he was living with his partner in California and finally had a very humanly enriching life.

He had come to complete acceptance of himself as a gay man. He no longer had to deny his most basic identity. He no longer had to run away. He was at peace within himself, and he knew he was loved by God who, of course, had always known exactly who he was as a gay man. He had learned how to integrate his sexuality into his life in a psychologically healthy way.

When I got the letter, however, my reaction was very negative. I am not happy with myself for reacting this way, but at the time the letter made me angry. I knew he sent the letter, but I never read it. I threw aside my brother's most personal revelation because I was so angry. After I had been ordained a bishop in 1968 I was much more in the public arena in the diocese, and when I got involved in various movements I was a public figure in an even larger sphere. Part of my anger upon receiving my brother's letter was rooted in a selfish concern about myself. If my brother became known as a gay person, people in the Church would wonder about me, too, and what would that mean? Could I be publicly seen with my brother? Would I have to shun him? Would negative judgments be made about my family? Would people even wonder if I were gay? Would society's negative attitudes toward homosexual people be transferred to me?

It was more than I wanted to deal with. And so, even though I knew all of us got the same letter, I never spoke to my mother or any of my siblings about it. And the silence went on for about a year. But it was finally broken, at least indirectly, when one of Dan's daughters was going to be married. Some of us went to California for the wedding. We all acted very normally and by our actions we, in a way, said it was all right. We were accepting Dan as he is. We were still not going to discuss it and affirm him with our words. Although I presumed the whole family was now at peace about it, I was wrong. My mother was still having a very hard time. She had lived her whole life in the Church, which had never really been welcoming to those who were homosexual. In fact, she had simply understood that being homosexual meant you were a sinner and not able to be loved by God. She knew that she could accept Dan and that she would never stop loving him. But she also could not reject the Church or what she thought was the Church's teaching.

I discovered how much she was troubled by this conflict between her love for Dan and what she thought the Church was teaching about him when she raised the question to me. I used to stop and visit my mother about once a week because she lived in Detroit where I lived. If I had an event nearby I would stop by afterward and could always count on getting a bite to eat and visiting with her for a couple of hours. When my mother was in her upper eighties, only a couple of years before she died, she tried to make sure all of her children were taken care of. My oldest sister was in an institution from the time she was very young because of brain damage when she was born. That was one thing my mother was very concerned about—after she died what was going to happen to Loretta? We worked this out so mother was very much at peace with this situation.

But then one night as I was leaving, I stepped out the front door and she followed me out. We were chatting for a few minutes, and she then asked the question she had been struggling with: Is Dan going to hell? I knew what she was talking about. For her, someone who was gay was evil and was going to hell. And I'm sure she could not be at peace with that question on her mind. Even though I had not dealt with the whole thing very well myself, I had begun to explore my own feelings and had done much reading and reflection about all the issues concerning homosexuality and Church teaching. I knew that I had to answer her question truthfully. And I was ready. "No, of course not. God made Dan that way and God won't put him in hell because Dan is a gay person. Dan didn't choose it. That's the way Dan is; that's who he is. God doesn't send us to hell because of who we are." And so I said it. I brought it all into the open. I know it was very consoling to my mother, but when I said it, it wasn't just to be consoling. I was not trying to make her feel good so she could die in peace. I knew what I said was the truth.

My mother's question really opened my eyes about the pain and anguish that many, many people have and especially do experience in the Roman Catholic Church and other churches as well. It is precisely because of a very narrow, negative attitude toward homosexuals. For too long we have allowed prejudiced judgments, expressed in a variety of negative descriptive words and discriminatory actions, to go unchecked. As a mother of a lesbian woman described it in a published letter about her daughter, the Church "offered her condemnation instead of compassion. She fears the judgment of most of those who love her because they have been 'programmed' to perceive her real identity as being perverted . . ." And she goes on to say: "My daughter is still honest, charitable and loving and, I am certain, treasured by God who has always known her secret. I am filled with dismay that my church insists she is anything less, while it strives to convince others that she is a threat to society."[2]

I could experience my mother's anguish in everything this other mother felt about her daughter. And I knew that, as a pastoral minister in the Church, I had to act to change this.

The New Ways Ministry national meeting offered the first opportunity. Before this meeting I had not been public about my experience. In fact, I had not spoken to anyone about it. I decided it was time to speak publicly. It was time to say: I am a bishop, and I have a gay brother. He is still my brother. He is still part of our family. We fully accept him. And we believe God does also. As soon as I told the story, I realized how important it was to say this. It had an immediate and profound impact on all who heard it. Subsequently, what I said at the conference was written up in the *National Catholic Reporter* as a feature story. And, prior to the strike and lockout at the Detroit Newspapers, a *Detroit Free Press* journalist interviewed me and wrote a feature story for the Sunday paper, which is distributed throughout Michigan. I felt really good about that. Far from being angry with my brother, I came to admire him for the way he came to self-acceptance and a realization of God's love in his life. I also admired his courage in risking rejection in order to open the eyes of many others. I was proud of him. Now that I have become public about our family, and told my "story," a whole new area of ministry has opened up for me. I have been able to respond to a large number of people who contact me from the whole homosexual community and from their families. Where Andrew Sullivan found nothing in the Church, I have been able to put some compassionate listening and some careful guidance.

To me it has been a very enriching experience. I have heard from people who have gone through very, very hard times: gay people, lesbian people, parents, priests afraid to tell their bishop they are gay. They didn't know where to turn, but now they felt they could share their story with me. I have been able to listen sensitively and offer understanding to an extraordinary number of people. I have been able to guide many who were in much turmoil. And I have met many good people who helped me understand even better. It had been a struggle for me to reach this point, but when I did I discovered many beautiful people who are suffering a lot and who so much need good pastoral ministry. And now I also realize how important it is to reach out pastorally and to make the Church a truly welcoming and inclusive community.

At the end of the U.S. Bishops' pastoral letter "Always Our Children," we state:

To our homosexual brothers and sisters we offer a concluding word. This message has been an outstretched hand to your parents and families inviting them to accept God's grace present in their lives and to trust in the unfailing mercy of Jesus our Lord. Now we stretch out our hands and invite you to do the same. We are called to become one body, one spirit in Christ. We need one another if we are to ". . . grow in every way into him who is the head, Christ, from whom the whole body, joined and held together by every supporting ligament, with the proper functioning of each part brings about the body's growth and builds itself up in love" (Eph 4:15-16).

Though at times you may feel discouraged, hurt, or angry, do not walk away from your families, from the Christian community, from all those who love you. In you God's love is revealed. You are always our children.[3]

This genuine reaching out and the invitation to our homosexual brothers and sisters to respond by reaching back to us, and journeying with the whole community with an awareness that God's love is revealed in them as it is in all of us, is the first step in making our Church a truly inclusive Church.

Succeeding steps are also suggested in this pastoral letter. A couple of additional quotes make clear what these steps must be: (1) The teachings of the Church make it clear that the fundamental human rights of homosexual persons must be defended and that all of us must strive to eliminate any forms of injustice, oppression, or violence against them. (2) It is not sufficient only to avoid unjust discrimination. Homosexual persons "must be accepted with respect, compassion and sensitivity" (*Catechism of the Catholic Church* 2358). They, as is true of every human being, need to be nourished at many different levels simultaneously. This includes friendship, which is a way of loving and is essential to healthy human development. It is one of the richest possible human experiences. (3) More than twenty years ago we bishops stated that "Homosexuals . . . should have an active role in the Christian community."[3] What does this mean in practice? It means that all homosexual persons have a right to be welcomed into the community, to hear the word of God, and to receive pastoral care. (4) Nothing in the Bible or in Catholic teaching can be used to justify prejudicial or discriminatory attitudes and behaviors. We reiterate here what we said in an earlier statement: We call on all Christians and citizens of good will to confront their own fears about homosexuality and to curb the humor and discrimination that offend homosexual persons. We understand that having a homosexual orientation brings with it enough anxiety, pain, and issues related to self-acceptance without society bringing the additional prejudicial treatment.[4]

However, even with these position statements, we still need to do more. We need to face the reality that there is a basic incoherence in the Church's teaching on homosexuality. This is brought out very poignantly by Andrew Sullivan in the interview quoted previously. He, first of all, makes the point that, according to official Church teaching, homosexuality has no finality. He puts it this way: "It is bizarre that something can occur naturally and have no natural end. I think it's a unique doctrine. . . ."[5] He goes on to point out that the Church concedes in the *Catechism* "That homosexuality is, so far as one can tell, an involuntary condition. . . ." It is an orientation "and it is involuntary. Some people seem to be constitutively homosexual."[6]

But the contradiction or incoherence of the teaching arises with the expression of the condition, when one acts on what he or she is constitutively as a human person. As he puts it:

> Yet the expression of this condition, which is involuntary and therefore sinless—because if it is involuntary, obviously no sin attaches—is always and everywhere sinful! Well, I could rack my brains for an analogy in any other Catholic doctrine that would come up with such a notion. Philosophically, it is incoherent, fundamentally incoherent. People are born with all sorts of things. We are born with original sin, but that is in itself sinful—an involuntary condition but it is sin.
>
> The analogy might be thought to be disability, but at the core of what disabled human beings can be—which means their spiritual and emotional life—the church not only affirms the equal dignity of disabled people in that regard but encourages us to see it and to take away the prejudice of not believing a disabled person can lead a full and integrated human life even though they cannot walk or they experience some other disability.
>
> But the disability that we are asked to believe that we are about is fundamental to our integrity as emotional beings, as I understand it. Now, I have tried to understand what this doctrine is about because my life is at stake in it. I believe God thinks there is a final end for me and others that is related to our essence as images of God and as people who are called to love ourselves and others. I am drawn, in the natural way I think human beings are drawn, to love and care for another person. I agree with the church's teaching about natural law in that regard. I think we are called to commitment and to fidelity, and I see that all around me in the gay world. I see, as one was taught that one would see

something in natural law, self-evident activity leading toward this final
end, which is commitment and love: the need and desire and hunger for
that. That is the *sensus fidelium,* and there is no attempt within the
church right now even to bring that sense into the teaching or into the
discussion of the teaching.

You see it even in the documents. The documents will say, on the one
hand compassion, on the other hand objective disorder. A document
that can come up with this phrase, "not unjust discrimination," is con-
torted because the church is going in two different directions at once
with this doctrine. On the one hand, it is recognizing the humanity of
the individual being; on the other, it is not letting that human being be
fully human.[7]

The Catholic Church's teaching about moral questions regarding marriage and sexuality, questions of intimacy, of one person loving another,
has undergone enrichment over the centuries. This has happened especially in modern times when moral theology began to use the insights
drawn from the lived experience of married men and women. An example of early Church teaching on marriage, and specifically the place
of sex, is found in a directive from Pope Gregory I to St. Augustine, first
archbishop of Canterbury in the beginning of the seventh century,
"Since even the lawful intercourse of the wedded cannot take place
without pleasure of the flesh, entrance into a sacred place shall be ab-
stained from because the pleasure itself can by no means be without
sin."[8] Such a directive expresses a clearly negative attitude toward sex in
marriage and the pleasure to be found in married love. The Church was
teaching that it was sinful to enjoy and relish one's sexual love. It was
sinful and would preclude participation in the Eucharist. Today, we
have people writing moral theology textbooks and treatises who are lay
people, many of whom are in a married relationship, and many who are
women. This development offers opportunities for new perspectives. In
fact, Pope John Paul II has given us a document, a lyrical and beautiful
document about married life and married love, that totally transcends
what Pope Gregory said. And so we have evolved our teaching substantially in what we understand as morally good and morally healthy.

What God really wants for each of us is that we become as fully a
human person as possible and that we avoid those things that diminish
us and make us less than fully human. In this perspective we realize the
importance of integrating our sexuality into our development as a person. And we understand the struggle that everyone has in trying to integrate her/his sexuality in the framework of her/his life. As a celibate

person I have to discover the way I can be healthy psychologically, and know how to love other people, including having intimacy without physical sexual intimacy. I feel I am called to celibacy, that I have to struggle within that framework. Married people have to integrate their sexuality into their relationship with one another. Their coming together in sexual love must be in a way of total giving to one another. It must be a way for them to express their total communion of life, a sacrament bringing the presence of God who is Love into their relationship. Their physical love expresses what should be present in every aspect of their lives: complete and unconditional love. Obviously, the fullness of such love becomes realized only over years of married life. And as they grow in love they grow into full humanness.

Gay and lesbian persons must struggle to learn how to love also. They too must learn how to integrate their sexuality into genuine intimacy with another person. How to do this, when one has no call to celibacy, is something that moral theology has not grappled with to any extent. We do know what God wants for all of us. God wills that each one of us becomes a fully human person; fully developed as a human person and, therefore, a person who is at peace within oneself; one who develops the talents and skills that one is given. This will happen through our loving relationships. And for most people it will happen through a special relationship with another person in a very loving and nurturing way.

From this it seems clear that the most important way to judge what is morally right or wrong in our actions is to discern what makes us more or less a fully developed human person. This discernment is very important as we are drawn into sexual relationships, but also in any human relationship where we are trying to develop intimacy. What is morally right will always make us better persons. An early Church axiom put it this way: "The glory of God is the human being fully alive."[9] So the commandments or moral laws that we learn about are not just hoops that somehow God wants to make us jump through. That is not the point at all. God is trying to show us the way. And for a Christian, the way is Jesus who for us is the full revelation of God present in the world. He showed us the way to fullness of life—the only way—the way of Love.

In order to deepen our understanding of homosexual love we must listen to the experience of homosexual people as they struggle to become fully the person each is called to be. Just as moral theologians began to use the insights of married people in developing guidance for the living out of married love, so must moral theologians begin to draw from the experience of those who are called to integrate their homosexuality into their lives in a fully life-giving way. Once again I turn to Andrew Sullivan, who is Roman Catholic and gay. His own experience is very enlightening and serves as a concrete example of what I am suggesting:

> Being gay is not about sex as such. Fundamentally, it's about one's core emotional identity. Fundamentally, it's about how one loves ultimately and how that can make one a whole as a human being.
>
> The moral consequences, in my own life, of the refusal to allow myself to love another human being, were disastrous. They made me permanently frustrated and angry and bitter. It spilled into other areas of my life. Once that emotional blockage is removed, one's whole moral equilibrium can improve, just as a single person's moral equilibrium in a whole range of areas can improve with marriage, in many ways, because there is a kind of stability and security and rock upon which to build one's moral and emotional life. To deny this to gay people is not only incoherent and wrong from the Christian point of view. It is incredibly destructive of the moral quality of their lives in general.[10]

So we ask, does that make sense? Does it make sense to teach people to avoid loving, intimate relationships when the result is permanent frustration? anger? bitterness? That was his result. It affected his whole life including his relationship within his family, with his friends, and so forth. That was his experience in trying to live the way the Church had taught him to live. It was not healthy; it was not lifegiving. He was asked about the contradiction between trying to be Catholic and trying to be homosexual and active:

> There is a basic contradiction. I completely concede that, at one level. At another level—and I confronted this, actually, with my first boyfriend, who was also Roman Catholic. When we had a fight one day, he said: "Do you really believe that what we are doing is wrong? Because if you do, I can't go on with this. And yet you don't want to challenge the Church's teaching on this, or leave the Church." And of course I was forced to say I don't believe, at some level, I really do not believe that the love of one person for another and the commitment of one person to another, in the emotional construct which homosexuality dictates to us—I know in my heart of hearts that cannot be wrong. I know that there are many things within homosexual life that can be wrong—just as in heterosexual life they can be wrong. There are many things in my sexual and emotional

life that I do not believe are spiritually pure, in any way. It is fraught with moral danger, but at its deepest level it struck me as completely inconceivable—from my own moral experience, from a real honest attempt to understand that experience—that it was wrong.

I experienced coming out in exactly the way you would think. I didn't really express any homosexual emotions or commitments or relationships until I was in my early 20's, partly because of the strict religious upbringing I had, and my commitment to my faith. It was not something I blew off casually. I struggled enormously with it. But as soon as I actually explored the possibility of human contact within my emotional and sexual make-up, in other words, as soon as I allowed myself to love someone— all the constructs the Church had taught me about the inherent disorder seemed just so self-evidently wrong that I could no longer find it that problematic. Because my own moral sense was overwhelming, because I felt, through the experience of loving someone or being allowed to love someone, an enormous sense of the presence of God—for the first time in my life.[11]

In the Christian context, what he is saying comes from the Letter of John: "God is love, and where there is love, there is God" (1 John 4:16). He is saying: "When I really allowed myself to love and be loved, for the first time in my life I deeply experienced the presence of God because God is love!" But we have not listened to what gay/lesbian people tell us: that they find their relationships lifegiving, that their relationships have the potential to build them up, that they deepen their sense of the presence of God, and thus are sacramental.

But the really big problem for gay and lesbian people as they try to grow into full human persons is how to deal with the clear teaching of the Church. In the letter "Always Our Children" the U.S. bishops teach:

> To live and love chastely is to understand that "only within marriage does sexual intercourse fully symbolize the Creator's dual design, as an act of covenant love, with the potential of co-creating new human life" (United States Catholic Conference, "Human Sexuality: A Catholic Perspective for Education and Lifelong Learning," 1991, p. 55). This is a fundamental teaching of our Church about sexuality, rooted in the biblical account of man and woman created in the image of God and made for union with one another (Genesis 2–3).

Two conclusions follow. First, it is God's plan that sexual intercourse occur only within marriage between a man and a woman. Second, every act of intercourse must be open to the possible creation of human life. Homosexual intercourse cannot fulfill these two conditions. Therefore, the Church teaches that homogenital behavior is objectively immoral, while making the important distinction between this behavior and a homosexual orientation, which is not immoral in itself. It is also important to recognize that neither a homosexual orientation, nor a heterosexual one, leads inevitably to sexual activity. One's total personhood is not reducible to sexual orientation or behavior.[12]

This is clear Church teaching. But also there is within the Catholic tradition, a fundamental moral teaching that comes before anything else. It is the teaching regarding "primacy of conscience." That is to say, each of us has the responsibility to explore our conscience and make judgments regarding moral choices and to determine what is lifegiving or not. And that means that the judgment I make in my conscience is the final arbiter of what is right or wrong for me. It is a heavy responsibility and some people would rather not take it upon themselves. They would prefer that the Church just tell them if this or that is right or wrong. But we must accept this responsibility. We must say to ourselves, "I've got this responsibility. I've got to deal with this and come to a conclusion in my own conscience and I've got to stand before God with what I decide."

The Second Vatican Council speaks of this teaching. It describes one's conscience as the divine voice echoing in our own depth, within our own spirit as a law written by God in human hearts. In other words, we have been given this sense of what is good and what is bad. A person must always obey the certain judgment of his/her own conscience. And so when we are trying to discern what is right or wrong in the depth of our own hearts, we have to listen as deeply as we can to what God speaks in our hearts. We look within ourselves and try to determine what is our experience. We must reflect on this experience in the context of what has been revealed in Scripture. We must also consider Catholic tradition which for two thousand years has been reflecting on the teaching from this Word of God; we must take our experience into our communion with God in our own prayer. Finally, we discern with the help of another person, a spiritual guide who can provide counsel and direction for us. On the basis of this discernment we can come to a decision in conscience. That decision is what we must act on and that is what will make us grow spiritually and personally. Yes, we can lie to ourselves, but we also know when we are being honest with ourselves. Obviously, we can make a mistake, but if we are honest we will discover we made a mistake and can then move in a different direction.

Some may ask if this means there is no longer moral law and anything goes. But anyone who takes the concept of primacy of conscience seriously will quickly realize that it is a very challenging way to live. The goal is to make oneself a fully human person, living in peace and serenity within oneself. Such a peace and serenity is virtually impossible if one is being untrue to him/herself.

A clear example of the use of this teaching within the Church is found when we consider the moral question of the intent to use nuclear weapons. These are weapons of mass and indiscriminate destruction. Catholic moral teaching from the highest authoritative source, the Second Vatican Council, has condemned their use without exception:

> With these truths in mind, this most holy Synod makes its own the condemnations of total war already pronounced by recent Popes, and issues the following declaration: Any act of war aimed indiscriminately at the destruction of entire cities or of extensive areas along with their population is a crime against God and humankind. It merits unequivocal and unhesitating condemnation.[13]

The teaching is very clear. Yet no Catholic on a Trident submarine, or a Strategic Air Command plane, or based at a missile silo has ever been condemned for carrying out the U.S. policy of deterrence, which includes the clear intent to use such weapons. No Catholic in the whole military chain of command that obeys this policy has ever, to my knowledge, been refused the Eucharist because he or she is a public sinner. In fact, these persons in the military are provided with Catholic priest chaplains who provide them the full ministry of the Church.

Obviously, what is happening in this situation is an acceptance that each person is exercising his or her right to make a decision in conscience. That justifies, in their individual discernment, acting contrary to the clear teaching of the Church. In this particular moral question—probably the most grave moral question human beings have ever faced—I presume military chaplains clearly present this teaching in specific detail, in Sunday sermons at military bases and in individual pastoral counseling. The need to place conscience above the obligation to obey military commands is one of the most important moral challenges of our time. While individuals in the military carefully discern how their conscience directs them, the bishops, moral leaders in the Church, allow them full freedom to act as they determine is right for them. I presume the bishops hope that eventually they will discover that their actions are not morally acceptable and that they will refuse to continue acting contrary to clear Church teaching.

My expectation is that the Church, especially its bishop leaders, will act the same way toward homosexual people who may from their conscientious discernment determine to live in a way contrary to Church teaching. We will continue to present the teaching clearly. But at the same time we will respect the rights of conscience as every person struggles to find his or her way to God.

I am convinced that as our whole Church struggles to understand the phenomenon of homosexuality, gay and lesbian people can be an important resource for us as they struggle within their own consciences to discern how their sexuality is to be integrated into their own lives in the most humanly and spiritually enriching way possible to them. The Word of God, the tradition of the Church, their own deep prayer life and careful discernment with a director/spiritual guide, are all available to them. As they undertake their individual human journey we, as Church, need to develop a much more pastoral ministry so that the alienation and the hurt and the pain they have experienced will be eliminated, so that gay brothers and lesbian sisters, sons and daughters will know that they are fully welcome within our church communities. As we welcome them, love them, respect them, and deeply listen to them, we will come to be more manifestly the living presence of Jesus that his community of disciples is called to be.

Over the centuries a listening Church was enriched by a deeper understanding of married sexual love. Is it not possible that our gay and lesbian brothers and sisters will enrich all of us with a deeper understanding of homosexual love? We can hope for the day when the "Andrew Sullivans" of our Church will feel fully welcome and experience a ministry that is responsive to their needs.

NOTES: CHAPTER 1

[1] Thomas H. Stahel, "'I'm Here': An Interview with Andrew Sullivan," *America* 168:16 (May 8, 1993) 11.

[2] Letter to the Editor, *America* (October 17, 1992) 286.

[3] National Conference of Catholic Bishops (hereafter NCCB), "To Live in Christ Jesus: A Pastoral Reflection on the Moral Life" (Washington, D.C.: USCC, 1976) 19.

[4] NCCB, "Human Sexuality: A Catholic Perspective for Education and Lifelong Learning" (Washington, D.C.: USCC, 1991) 55.

[5] Stahel, "'I'm Here,'" 7.

[6] Ibid.

[7] Ibid.

[8] Pope Gregory I, Book 11, Epistle 64 in Migne, *Patrologia Latina,* 77:1196–97.

[9] Irenaeus of Lyons, *Against the Heresies,* 4.20. SC 7 (Paris: Cerf, 1965) 100/2:648–49. *Gloria Dei vivens homo.*

[10] Stahel, "'I'm Here,'" 8.

[11] Ibid. 6.

[12] USCC, *Always Our Children* (Washington, D.C.: September 10, 1997) 8.

[13] "Pastoral Constitution on the Church in the Modern World," *The Documents of Vatican II,* ed. Walter M. Abbott (New York: Guild Press, 1966) 80, 294.

2

Unitive and Procreative Meaning: The Inseparable Link

James P. Hanigan

I n articulating the position of the Roman Catholic Church on the
morality of using artificial means to regulate human conception,
Pope Paul VI, in his capacity as the supreme teacher of the Church,[1]
asserted that his teaching was "founded upon the inseparable connection, willed by God and unable to be broken by man on his own initiative, between the two meanings of the conjugal act: the unitive meaning
and the procreative meaning."[2] This was a new way of expressing the
foundational truth upon which official Roman Catholic teaching on the
ontological and moral meaning of human sexual activity is based. At
the same time the Pope endorsed a substantially new ecclesial understanding of human sexual activity in marriage as a participation in and
reflection of Divine Love.[3]

This newness of expression and substance in the encyclical was due
in large measure to the teaching of the Second Vatican Council.[4] The
novelty of this expression led to arguments over what, if anything, was
substantively new in the teaching and what the implications of that
newness might mean in practice.[5] Of crucial significance for interpreting the teaching was the insistence in the conciliar document, one repeated with careful qualification in *Humanae vitae*,[6] that "the actions
within marriage by which the couple are united intimately and chastely
are noble and worthy ones. Expressed in a manner which is truly human,

these actions signify and promote that mutual self-giving by which spouses enrich each other with a joyful and thankful will."[7] And the Council drew the conclusion that "marriage persists as a whole manner and communion of life, and maintains its value and indissolubility, even when offspring are lacking—despite, rather often, the very intense desire of the couple."[8]

Humanae vitae, therefore, when read in the light of *Gaudium et spes,* did two things. It first celebrated the goodness of marital sexual activity, even apart from any actual procreative intent or possibility on the part of the spouses, when "expressed in a manner which is truly human." Second, it insisted that such acts had both procreative and unitive meaning in the divine plan of creation and so should be done in such a way that they would truthfully express such meaning in the lives of the spouses. In proclaiming the existence of an inseparable connection between the unitive and procreative meanings of the act of sexual intercourse, Paul VI, in effect, provided Roman Catholic sexual ethics with a new fundamental basis for judgments about the morality of all specific sexual behaviors.

Among the kinds of sexual actions contrary to this fundamental criterion are all sexual acts between homosexual partners inasmuch as such acts cannot of their very nature have procreative significance, at least in the common, biological sense of the word procreative. But then sexual acts between spouses, at least one of whom is known, for whatever reason, to be infertile, would also not appear to have such procreative meaning. If the morality of sexual acts between same-sex partners is to be reevaluated in the Catholic tradition, then either this central claim of *Humanae vitae* must be called into question, or it must be interpreted to mean something other than what the author of the encyclical explicitly intended it to mean.[9]

It is not the intent of this essay to call Paul VI's assertion into question.[10] Instead I wish to inquire into the basis on which the claim rests, and more particularly to inquire into whether the authority of Scripture either supports or challenges the assertion. In carrying out this inquiry I hope to arrive at a clearer sense of what the claim actually means. The reasons for making such an inquiry are both ecumenical[11] and methodological.[12] The ecclesial warrant for the inquiry is the mandate of the Second Vatican Council in regard to the biblical renewal of moral theology.[13]

Humanae vitae itself made no pretense that its central teaching was directly based upon a reading of the scriptural texts. In stating his core teaching "that each and every marriage act must remain open to the transmission of life,"[14] Paul VI explained that he was "calling men back to the norms of the natural law"[15] as interpreted by the constant doctrine of the Church. He thought "that the men of our day are particularly capable of seizing the deeply reasonable and human character of this fundamental principle."[16] Hence his teaching on the inseparable connection between the unitive and procreative meanings of sexual intercourse did not appeal to the authority of Scripture as warrant for its truth, nor did he base its truth solely on the authority of the papal office.

Still, despite his appeal to the natural law as the foundation of his teaching, there are clear indications of theological and scriptural influences in how Paul VI read the natural law tradition. These indications are hinted at in one paragraph of the encyclical.[17] These hints are, first, that God is love and that conjugal love has its origin, and hence its specific nature and nobility, in reference to God; second, that marriage is of divine origin and is a way God has of realizing in human life his plan of love; third, that God is the author of life and human beings collaborate with God in both the generation and education of new life; and fourth, that marriage represents the union of Christ and the Church.

It was these scriptural hints—and others, to be sure—that Paul VI's successor, John Paul II, took up in response to his own challenge[18] to theologians to explore the scriptural foundations of the teaching of *Humanae vitae*. In the series of catechetical talks he began shortly after the 1980 Synod on the Family, John Paul II employed a profoundly philosophical exegesis of the creation accounts in Genesis to elaborate a theology of the body[19] and to develop such key notions as original solitude,[20] the nuptial meaning of the body,[21] and the significance of sexual complementarity.[22]

Basic to the teaching of both popes on the intrinsic connection between the two meanings of human sexual intercourse as rooted in the natural law are the Genesis creation accounts, how those accounts are related to the natural law, and how they are related to the rest of the scriptural witness. In order to pursue the purpose of this paper, namely, to examine whether the authority of Scripture supports or challenges the teaching about this inseparable link willed by God, I will proceed in three steps. First, I will examine the creation accounts in relation to the rest of Scripture to see how these accounts provide a narrative framework for an understanding of the natural law.[23] Second, I will relate this narrative framework to an understanding of human sexuality. Third, I will assess the papal claim about an inseparable link between the unitive and procreative meanings of human sexual activity in light of this narrative framework.

THE BIBLE AND NATURAL LAW

The import of the creation accounts in Genesis for Christian theology, especially for its normative understanding of human sexuality, is highlighted by a story in the synoptic gospels. In Mark 10:2-12 and its parallel Matt 19:3-9, Jesus, in response to the Pharisees' question about divorce, invokes the creation accounts in Genesis as revelatory of God's original creative purpose and draws from these accounts one normative implication. "But from the beginning of creation God made them male and female" (Mark 10:6). "So God created humankind in his image, in the image of God he created them; male and female he created them" (Gen 1:27). This divine creative act is the reason why a man leaves his father and mother and becomes one flesh with his wife. They are no longer two but one. According to the Jesus of the synoptic gospels, God, in creating them male and female, has intended this union of the man and the woman; hence no human being has the authority to dissolve it.

Furthermore, Jesus, in the two synoptic passages, attributes the Mosaic permission to divorce one's wife to a concession to human sinfulness, to the hardness of heart of the chosen people in their historical journey. "Because of your hardness of heart he wrote this commandment for you" (Mark 10:5). In the same way the story of the Fall in Genesis regarded painful childbirth and male domination of women (Gen 3:16), among other things, not as part of God's original creative intent, but as consequences of, and so punishment for, sin. In proclaiming his own teaching about divorce and remarriage as a form of adultery Jesus did not appeal to his own authority, but to the original natural order intended by God in creation, an order both the gospels and the Pauline epistles understand to be reestablished, and indeed also transcended, in Christ.

We find this same understanding of the relationship between creation (nature) and history in Paul's letter to the Romans. As Paul narrates the relationship, "what can be known about God is plain to them, because God has shown it to them. Ever since the creation of the world his eternal power and divine nature, invisible though they are, have been understood and seen through the things he has made" (Rom 1:19-20). But human sinfulness intervened in history as human beings preferred themselves to God and so "they became futile in their thinking, and their senseless minds were darkened. Claiming to be wise they became fools" (Rom 1:21-22). For Paul, human beings turned away from God with the consequence that they were left by God to their own sinful desires. This involved a turning away from the order established by God in creation, from the natural to what was unnatural, to the disorder of sin. This was a move, as Paul understood it, from the rational to the irrational, from divine wisdom to human folly that paraded itself as wisdom. Paul sums up this conflictual history and experience of sin quite simply and personally. "So then, with my mind I am a slave to the law of God, but with my flesh I am a slave to the law of sin" (Rom 7:25).

These texts, of course, as well as many others of a similar kind,[24] do not provide a developed theory of natural law any more than they serve as some kind of scriptural proof for the theory. What they do provide are the elements of a narrative framework, what Richard Hays has called a "symbolic world that creates the perceptual categories through which we interpret reality."[25] This symbolic world contains affirmations both about the activity and character of God and about the human condition and its possibilities. It is within this symbolic world that particular accounts of natural law first find not only plausibility but a persuasive intelligibility that further illumines the creation accounts in Genesis.[26] If we examine those accounts we discover the following significant points.

First, the uniqueness and the transcendental dignity of the human person have their original source and foundation in the gratuitous, loving creation of humankind, male and female, by God in God's own image and likeness, which God found to be very good. While all created beings are made by God, only human beings are, in virtue of their shared created nature, and not in virtue of their idiosyncratic characteristics, constituted in the divine image and likeness. All created beings come forth from the mind of God; that is to say, they participate in what Aquinas called the Eternal Law, but rational creatures, among whom we count the human creature, participate in the Eternal Law in a unique and special way.[27] Only human beings are given dominion over the earth and its great variety and multitude of creatures, and so, precisely in their humanity, they share in the divine providential care for the good of all creation. Only with human beings does God establish a personal dialogue, a relationship of mutual knowledge and love. It is only human beings, then, who are constituted as moral agents, who, as beings given to themselves and to one another as gift, have the attendant and inescapable moral responsibility of a knowing and free response to God and to other creatures. It is neither arbitrary reason nor fanciful exegesis, therefore, to see in the human potential for moral agency, in the human capacity to discover and freely choose the good of their own being as well as the good of other created beings as established by the Creator, the created basis of human dignity.[28] Human beings are made by God to accept the gift and act out the responsibility, and it is the reasonable and right thing for them to do, for only so will they find the fulfillment of what God has made them for, their good. That is a concise, narratively shaped way of speaking about the natural law.

Second, to make humans in the divine image and likeness God created them male and female. Human sexual duality, therefore, is an essential constituent of human nature and includes, but is more than, a mere physical difference in anatomical structure or biological function, for it is a primary feature of the creation of humankind in the divine image and likeness. In finding each other as given by God to one another, woman given to man, man given to woman, as mutual helpmates, the man and woman find themselves, find what it is to be human. That it is not good for the man to be alone cannot be read in a mere psychological or even sociological sense, *albeit* both may be true enough. At a deep metaphysical level, as well as a moral level, human nature is sexually dual, but not dualistic, and this sexual difference, to repeat, is not just a bodily or a physical difference, but an ontological one. The man and the woman are each in his and her own right fully human and made by God for God, but are ordered to and given to one another as mutual helpmates to constitute the human. Certainly other kinds of human relationships are possible and necessary and good in human life, but none of them has the primary significance accorded to the male/female relationship in the creation accounts and thereafter. And none of them has mutual sexual self-donation at its very center.

God's intentions for them and their life together as male and female are specified in Genesis in a number of ways. The most obvious is that they are commanded to be fruitful and multiply. Human beings are to have a family history, not just a personal story. The capacity to procreate, to become participants with God in the creation of new human life (Gen 4:1) is not an accidental or casual feature of human sexual duality, but a fundamental aspect of human sexual responsibility, of the human vocation as male and female.[29] They are instructed to exercise a shared dominion over the creatures of the earth, to take responsibility for their well-being; in turn they have a right to the use of them in accord with the nature of each kind of creature. Finally, they are called to be helpmates to each other, leaving father and mother and cleaving to one another in faithful loyalty. And they are to do all this in freedom under the sovereign authority of God. So God intended it from the beginning; so Jesus teaches in the synoptic gospels.

The prologue to the Gospel of John adds additional authority and substance to Jesus' teaching in the synoptics. For Jesus is the Word of God made flesh, the Word who was with God from the beginning and through whom all things were made. "All things came into being through him, and without him not one thing came into being" (John 1:3). Paul also advances this claim: "there is one God, the Father, from whom are all things and for whom we exist, and one Lord, Jesus Christ, through whom are all things and through whom we exist" (1 Cor 8:6). The Pauline letters to the Ephesians (Eph 1:9-23) and to the Colossians make the same point: "for in him all things in heaven and on earth were created, things visible and invisible . . . all things have been created through him and for him" (Col 1:16). Who better to speak of the divine intention in creation than the Word who was there from the beginning and through whom and for whom all was made?

These biblical affirmations about the creation of the world, its multitude of creatures and especially human beings, by God, and in and through and for Christ, speak about who and what human beings are, about human nature. In light of the biblical creation narratives and the narratives that follow it seems that human beings cannot be fully and properly understood as human apart from their origin and destiny, their nature and their end. These narratives provide the context of responsibility for the human person precisely as human. They proclaim what faith believes God to have revealed as the divine intention for man and woman to be and to become through employing the gifts with which God endowed human nature. The natural law, then, is intelligible in light of the creation accounts as the participation of the rational creature in the eternal plan of God.

But the natural law must also be seen by Christian theology, in light of the New Testament witness, as an aspect of the human journey to the God-man, Jesus Christ, in whom and for whom and through whom all things were made. When faith discovers that this Jesus is the Way, the Truth, and the Life, creation and the natural law are not set aside as irrelevant; still less are they negated in some way. For, as Josef Fuchs has pointed out:

> The will to believe in Christ and to adhere to him signifies, in fact and always, a moral decision that must logically be previous to faith in Christ.

Therefore it receives its objective expression in norms that are independent of this faith. The natural law indicates in what case and in whom we may believe and to whom one may or even must surrender oneself. Christ the Lord as the prototype and norm of man, represents a positive value for human nature; man's attitude towards this positive value is necessarily determined from the moral viewpoint by man's being. This is the natural law, even though its expression in natural terms remains hypothetical.[30]

One cannot, therefore, play Christ and the scriptural witness off against natural law, history against nature, creation against covenant, the individual against the community, human differences and plurality against human sameness and commonality. Nor does *Humanae vitae* do so. Rather the encyclical, I suggest, understands the natural law and its requirements in the context of the symbolic world of the Bible, the scriptural narrative of creation, sin, redemption, and eschatological destiny. In that light we may turn to the application of the natural law made in the encyclical to human sexuality.

SEXUALITY AND THE NATURAL LAW

Just how fundamental to human nature and to human sexual relationships and behavior is sexual duality? Is there some non-oppressive way to understand what John Paul II has been trying to elaborate in his language of sexual complementarity? Let me acknowledge at the outset the historic and contemporary misuses and abuses of the notions of sexual duality and complementarity. Perhaps the history of misuse and abuse is so deformed that the words and even the ideas the words express are beyond rehabilitation.[31] Unfortunately, I do not know any better words or phrases to employ here, and I can only try to insist that the terms point to a kind of male-female difference and mutuality that is different from the difference and mutuality we can experience in all other human relationships. "This at last is bone of my bones and flesh of my flesh; this one shall be called Woman, for out of Man this one was taken" (Gen 2:23).

About human sexuality Paul VI in *Humanae vitae* made several biblically based points to which we referred earlier. The first was that God is love and so all created reality is an expression and reflection of that love, is in its essential being good. This is emphatically true for what the Pope called conjugal love, the mutual acceptance of, shared delight in, the common life together of the man and the woman. Genesis presents the gift of sexuality in the creation of man and woman not simply as the gift of sexual pleasure or of physical intimacy, as one gift among many given by God to human beings for their delight, but as a cleaving together to become one flesh, as a relationship that has its nature and its goodness in reference to God and to the divine plan which already looks ahead to the story of Abraham and Sarah and the creation of the chosen people, and for Christian theology ultimately to the coming of Christ.

The second point made by Paul VI was that the cleaving together to become one flesh, the relationship we call marriage, which Jesus refers to in the synoptic gospels as intended by God to be faithful and exclusive, is one way God has of realizing in human history his plan of love "to gather up all things in him" (Eph 1:10). One could begin to trace in the biblical texts themselves the unfolding human understanding of the successes and failures of marriage in this plan of love, starting with Abraham and Sarah and the child of the covenantal promise, Isaac, then passing on through the turmoil and triumphs of the patriarchs and matriarchs, the judges and kings and prophets. At last one would arrive at the mystery of Mary, Virgin and Mother of Christ and of the Church, and the great Pauline analogy, a third point Paul VI made, of the marital union of male and female as the sacramental sign of the mystery of Christ's union with his bride, the Church. Despite failure and sin, marriage has taken the human family where God intended it to go.

In our present context it is proper to note that Paul VI refers to marriage, the union in sexual duality, as one way God has of realizing in human history the divine plan of love. That suggests there are other ways God has to achieve this plan. But conjugal union is the way that fully enacts human sexuality, that effects the reconciliation, the unity of that most fundamental, created difference, male and female, and establishes that most basic community of both Church and society, the family.

The fourth point made by Paul VI in *Humanae vitae* had to do with the mission, the work of the marital relationship, the command to the man and the woman to be fruitful and multiply, to cooperate with God in the procreation of and caring for new human lives as a fundamental aspect of their dominion over creation. This relationship of man and woman has attached to it a basic social significance, a procreative significance that, to be sure, does not exhaust the meaning of their relationship, but whose absence from the sexual relationship would render the creation accounts, the promises of the covenant, and the angelic annunciation to Mary, as we have them, unintelligible.

What we have in the Scripture, then, is not primarily a set of rules, or even basic moral principles[32] governing human sexual conduct, but a symbolic world, a narrative vision of the meaning of human sexuality and sexual behavior in the divine plan. This vision links together in a unified whole, and gives vocational significance to, the human goods of sexual activity which the Catholic tradition has historically called, following Augustine, the *bona prolis, fidelitatis et sacramenti*. More contemporary language has spoken about the unitive, procreative, and sacramental meanings of sexual relationships.[33] In less technical language, there is a unity of sex, love, marriage, children, and holiness. It would appear that Pope Paul VI was not without biblical support in making the claim for an inseparable connection willed by God between the unitive and procreative meanings of sexual intercourse.

ASSESSMENT

In his "Apostolic Exhortation on the Family" John Paul II pointed out that the Church knows two ways of living out one's sexuality in accord with the divine plan of love. "Christian revelation," he wrote, "recognizes two specific ways of realizing the vocation of the human person, in its entirety, to love: marriage and virginity or celibacy. Either one is in its own proper form an actuation of the most profound truth of man, of his being 'created in the image of God.'"[34] Both these ways of life are biblically informed, i.e., inspired by and shaped by the biblical narrative, as well as enjoying the benefit of the lived historical experience of the Church and the discernment of the Church's magisterium. That is to say, we can make rational, theological sense of them.

Marriage is, of course, a natural reality that requires no special revelation, no act of personal faith in the God of the Bible or in his Christ, for human beings to make basic rational, human sense out of it as a social institution, an interpersonal relationship, and a community of care for the future. We can recognize that marriage has the capability of fostering and promoting the human growth and happiness of spouses, children, and other family members, when lived with mutual respect, fidelity, and commitment. As a social institution it also contributes to the stability and development of society. Even if we were to embrace the practice of same-sex marriages, the human sense we would make of such relationships would have to be on the basis of some sort of loose analogy with heterosexual marriages.[35]

The rational understanding of consecrated virginity or celibacy transcends the natural law and requires the introduction of data from revelation accepted in faith. An understanding of the Kingdom of God, of the eschatological destiny of human beings called to eternal communion with the Triune God, where there is no marrying or giving in marriage, would be essential. Our further comprehension of the human meaning of consecrated celibacy is greatly helped by the paradigmatic examples of Jesus and Paul and a host of other saints in the tradition.

The heart of the matter for the Church, when considering both these ways of life, would seem to be the recognition that God has a purpose in creating human beings as God did, and so human sexuality, in its physical structure and biological consequence, in its erotic passion and energy, in the human desire for intimacy, and the human need for physical touch and interpersonal bonding, also has a purpose in God's plan. That purpose can be handily summarized in terms of holiness and service. That is to say, the scriptural vision associates sexuality with vocation and community, and historically the Church has been able to make sense of this association in the two vocations of marriage and consecrated celibacy, vocations that mutually support and illumine one another. We have been able to make both rational and religious sense of marriage as a freely chosen way of life whose basic structure or nature was established by God in the creation of them as male and female. We have also been able to make theological and personal sense of consecrated celibacy as a charismatic gift intended for the service of the Church, the People of God, and a way of life that bears witness to the fullness of the coming Kingdom of God.

The theological question we obviously face today in the Church in regard to human sexuality has, it seems to me, four dimensions,[36] only one of which concerns us here. What sexual and social sense, both theologically and rationally, can we make out of the situation of homosexual people for whom active heterosexual relationships are constitutionally unwelcome and personally unwise, but who also do not recognize a personal call to a life of consecrated celibacy? The argument of this paper has been that the intellectual framework provided by the larger biblical narrative that supports an understanding of the natural law is on solid ground when it claims an inseparable connection willed by God between the unitive and procreative meanings of human sexuality. Put negatively, the paper has argued that the biblical narrative does not enable us, indeed does not allow us, to make theological sense out of homosexual relationships and actions, precisely as sexual.[37] It should not be surprising, therefore, that the Church teaches that the homosexual orientation, insofar as it is an inclination to actions that are theologically unintelligible, is an objective disorder.[38]

In developing the application of this understanding of human sexuality to specific sexual behaviors, the Second Vatican Council, Pope Paul VI, and especially Pope John Paul II have embraced the contemporary personalist understanding of sexual relations. The official teachers of the Church have recognized that sex in its full human, moral dimension is an interpersonal relationship, not a relationship between body parts or sexual organs, not simply a biological function. They have spoken of sex as the mutual gift of one embodied person to another embodied person, a mutual gift in sign and promise of one's whole self to the other. The most problematic, most debated feature of the official teaching in application has been why every single marital act, and not just the marital relationship as a whole, must be open to the possibility of procreation, however unlikely.

This is not the place to argue for or against that specific application of the broader claim about the inseparable unity of the procreative and unitive meanings of sexual intercourse. What I wish to attend to here by way of conclusion is what is given and what is received in the reality of marriage. As John Paul II has been at some pains to point out, what is given in the act of interpersonal sexual union, in the gift of one's body to the other, if there is truthfulness to the gift, is the gift of oneself, and this includes the gift of one's fertility, of one's capacity for procreation. In giving his body, himself, to the woman, the man gives her the potential gift of motherhood; in giving her body, herself to the man, the woman gives him the potential gift of fatherhood. Together in their mutual giving and receiving they gift each other with the real possibility of that most extraordinary of human achievements, the procreation of a unique being who is flesh of their flesh and bone of their bone, made in the image and likeness of God, an achievement in the natural order so extraordinary that there is no gift and no responsibility to compare to it.

Because Catholic faith is incarnational to its roots—the Word truly became flesh and dwelt among us—the iconic significance of one's sexuality, one's maleness or femaleness in all its embodied reality, must be taken with full seriousness. Male sexuality is created to be spousal in that it is ordered to interpersonal union; it is not good for the man to be alone. But it is also paternal in its ordination to the maternal, to the female, and to the raising up of new life. Female sexuality is likewise spousal in that it too is ordered in its creation to interpersonal union; it is also not good for the woman to be alone. But it is also maternal in its ordination to the paternal, the male, and to the birthing and nurturing of new life.

This is the rational meaning of human sexuality as the created gift of the creator to human nature. In the mystery of sin and redemption that is human history, we are aware that the gift has been sorely abused and received and used very often with great irresponsibility. But it has also been taken up in Christ into the mystery of salvation and enabled to become both an occasion for and a means of holiness and service. This is the truth of human sexuality as the Church has come in its historical pilgrimage to understand it through the continuous reading of the narratives of Scripture and the rational analysis of human nature we call the natural law. This is an affirmation of both faith and reason about the truth of human beings as created by God at the ontological and moral levels. It is not an affirmation that is necessarily borne out by the psychological perceptions or social experiences of any one individual or group.

Our contemporary argument in the churches about the moral compatibility of homosexual acts and relationships with the Christian Gospel may well be an argument over whether and why the narratives of personal experience and the rationality of scientific interpretation can and do override the biblical narratives as read in the experience of the Church we call tradition and the rationality of human nature. The resolution of the argument requires that we overcome the false opposition between creation or nature and history, revelation and reason, human sameness and human diversity.

NOTES: CHAPTER 2

[1] Pope Paul VI, *Humanae vitae* 4–6, in Joseph Gremillion, *The Gospel of Peace and Justice: Catholic Social Teaching Since Pope John* (Maryknoll, N.Y.: Orbis, 1976) 429–30.

[2] Ibid. 12, 433.

[3] Ibid. 8, 430–31.

[4] *Gaudium et spes* (Pastoral Constitution on the Church in the Modern World) 49–50, Walter M. Abbott, s.j., ed., *The Documents of Vatican II* (New York: Crossroad, 1989) 252–55.

[5] Janet Smith, *Humanae Vitae a Generation Later* (Washington, D.C.: The Catholic University of America Press, 1991) 61–67; James P. Hanigan, *What Are They Saying About Sexual Morality?* (New York/Mahwah: Paulist, 1982) 30–37.

[6] *Humanae vitae* 11, 432.

[7] *Gaudium et spes* 49, 253.

[8] Ibid. 50, 255.

[9] *Humanae vitae* 14, 434.

[10] Bernard Haring, C.SS.R., "The Inseparability of the Unitive-Procreative Functions of the Marital Act," in Charles E. Curran and Richard A. McCormick, S.J., eds., *Readings in Moral Theology No. 8: Dialogue About Catholic Sexual Teaching* (New York/Mahwah: Paulist, 1993) 153–67, does call the assertion into question, even while arguing for a different but unspecified kind of unity between the two meanings.

[11] Issues of sexual morality, most especially homosexual acts, have become highly and passionately divisive both within and among Christian churches. See Kevin T. Kelly, *New Directions in Sexual Ethics: Moral Theology and the Challenge of AIDS* (London/Washington: Geoffrey Chapman, 1998) 22–39, 74–78; John J. Carey, ed., *The Sexuality Debate in North American Churches, 1988–1995* (Lewiston/Queenston/Lampeter: Edwin Mellen, 1995); Walter Wink, ed., *Homosexuality and Christian Faith: Questions of Conscience for the Churches* (Minneapolis: Fortress, 1999).

[12] John Paul II, *The Splendor of Truth (Veritatis splendor)* 4–5 (Washington, D.C.: United States Catholic Conference, 1993) 7–11.

[13] "Special attention needs to be given to the development of moral theology. Its scientific exposition should be more thoroughly nourished by scriptural teaching." *Optatam totius* (Decree on Priestly Formation) 16, in Abbott, *Documents*, 452.

[14] *Humanae vitae* 11, 433.

[15] Ibid.

[16] Ibid. 12, 433.

[17] Ibid. 8, 430–31.

[18] John Paul II, *Familiaris consortio* (The Apostolic Exhortation on the Family) 31, in *Origins* 11, 28/29 (December 24, 1981) 447.

[19] Richard Greco, "Recent Ecclesiastical Teaching," in Charles E. Curran and Richard A. McCormick, S.J., eds., *John Paul II and Moral Theology: Readings in Moral Theology No. 10* (New York/Mahwah: Paulist, 1998) 137. John Paul II has developed his theology of the body in three stages, corresponding to which are the volumes *Original Unity of Man and Woman: Catechesis on the Book of Genesis* (Boston: St. Paul Books & Media, 1981), a series of talks dealing with the beginning or the past for which the key biblical texts are Gen 1:27 and 2:23-24, and Matt 19:36; *Blessed Are the Pure of Heart* (Boston: St. Paul Books & Media, 1983), dealing with historical existence, the present, where the key biblical texts are Matt 5:27-28, 1 John 2:16-17, and Gal 5:15-21; *The Theology of Marriage*

and Celibacy (Boston: St. Paul Books & Media, 1986), focusing on eschatological destiny, the future, for which the key biblical texts are Mark 12:18-27 (and parallels Matt 22:23-33, Luke 20:27-40, and Eph 5:22-33).

[20] Mary Shivanandan, *Crossing the Threshold of Love: A New Vision of Marriage* (Washington, D.C.: The Catholic University of America Press, 1999); also eadem, *Original Solitude: Its Meaning in Contemporary Marriage,* unpublished doctoral dissertation (Ann Arbor, Mich.: UMI Dissertation Series, 1996) 15–43.

[21] John Paul II, *Original Unity of Man and Woman* 106–22.

[22] John Paul II, "Letter to Women," *Origins* 25, 9 (July 27, 1994); also Prudence Allen, "Integral Sex Complementarity and the Theology of Communion," *Communio* XVII, 4 (Winter 1990) 523–44.

[23] Pamela M. Hall, *Narrative and the Natural Law: An Interpretation of Thomistic Ethics* (Notre Dame, Ind.: University of Notre Dame Press, 1995).

[24] The Psalms and the rest of the wisdom literature would yield a number of such texts.

[25] Richard B. Hays, *The Moral Vision of the New Testament: A Contemporary Introduction to New Testament Ethics* (San Francisco: Harper Collins, 1996) 209.

[26] This notion of mutual illumination, first of reason by faith and then of faith by reason, is the argument of Pope John Paul II, *Fides et ratio,* especially 16–48, *Origins* 28, 19 (October 22, 1998) 323–31.

[27] This is, of course, Thomas's simplest definition of the natural law. He also relates this participation to divine providence. *Summa Theologiae* Ia IIae, q.91, a.2.

[28] *Gaudium et spes* 16, Abbott, *Documents,* 213. "In the depths of his conscience, man detects a law which he does not impose upon himself, but which holds him to obedience. . . . For man has in his heart a law written by God. To obey it is the very dignity of man; according to it he will be judged."

[29] Janet E. Smith, "The *Munus* of Transmitting Human Life: A New Approach to *Humanae Vitae,*" *The Thomist* 54, 3 (July 1990) 385–427; also Smith, *Humanae Vitae: A Generation Later,* 136–48.

[30] Josef Fuchs, S.J., *Natural Law: A Theological Investigation,* trans. Helmut Reckter, S.J., and John A. Dowling (New York: Sheed and Ward, 1965) 74.

[31] Kelly, *New Directions in Sexual Ethics,* 50–54.

[32] Hays, *The Moral Vision of the New Testament* 291–312. I am agreeing here with those who argue that the question of homosexual activity and the Bible is not settled by the citation of the seven scriptural passages commonly understood to condemn homosexual activity. See Robin Scroggs, *The New Testament and Homosexuality* (Philadelphia: Fortress, 1983). Whether one interprets

these passages as absolute rules or, as seems more common today, demonstrates through historical-critical method their inapplicability to our contemporary question as Scroggs does—see also Walter Wink, "Homosexuality and the Bible," *Homosexuality and Christian Faith* 33–49—the normative contribution of Scripture to the Christian moral life is shortchanged. I am more impressed by the approach of Hays, *Moral Vision* 379–406, though his approach cries out for additional natural law reflections.

[33] Lisa Sowle Cahill, "Marriage: Institution, Relationship, Sacrament," in John A. Coleman, s.j., ed., *One Hundred Years of Catholic Social Thought: Celebration and Challenge* (Maryknoll, N.Y.: Orbis, 1991) 111, has described this complex of goods as sex, love, and procreation. Official Church teaching always speaks about conjugal love in this complex of goods or values in the attempt to distinguish it clearly from simple sexual attraction and romantic love.

[34] John Paul II, *Familiaris consortio* 11.

[35] Joseph Monti, *Arguing About Sex: The Rhetoric of Christian Sexual Morality* (Albany, N.Y.: State University of New York Press, 1995) 197–255.

[36] In addition to the problem of making rational, theological sense out of the sexuality of gay, lesbian, and bisexual people, the three other dimensions would require us to do the same for single people of any sexual orientation, for divorced people unable to have their marriages annulled, and how to speak to people's sexuality in an increasingly individualistic culture that routinely associates sexual activity and marriage with emotional and physical satisfactions and nothing else.

[37] Mary E. Hunt, *Fierce Tenderness: A Feminist Theology of Friendship* (New York: Continuum, 1991) has offered friendship rather than family as a way of understanding such relationships. For reasons mentioned in the text, as well as the nature of friendship itself, I do not think her argument works.

[38] Congregation for the Doctrine of the Faith, "Letter to the Bishops of the Catholic Church on the Pastoral Care of Homosexual Persons" 3, *Origins* 16, 22 (November 13, 1986) 379. "Although the particular inclination of the homosexual person is not a sin, it is a more or less strong tendency ordered toward an intrinsic evil and thus the inclination must be seen as an objective disorder." In so far as that description fits what a homosexual orientation is, and I know of no reason to think that it is an adequate description or account of such an orientation, the theological issue is the inability to give same-sex activities vocational and ecclesial meaning. John Paul II never directly addresses the issue of homosexuality, but in his "Letter to Families" 17, *Origins* 23, 37 (March 3, 1994) 651, he warns against the public recognition of "other interpersonal unions" which do not meet the procreative criterion as a "threat to the future of the family and of society itself." Such a claim is altogether implausible if it is taken to mean, as seems common in many quarters, that heterosexual people will rush off into homosexual relationships. It is not implausible if it is

understood to mean that public recognition of same-sex unions that lack theological meaning threatens to alter the cultural and theological meaning of heterosexual relationships.

3

The Bridegroom and the Bride: The Theological Anthropology of John Paul II and Its Relation to the Bible and Homosexuality

Susan A. Ross

ecent Vatican actions and statements have made it quite clear that the Church's teaching on the moral status of homosexuality is not likely to change any time soon. The removal of Sr. Jeannine Gramick and Fr. Robert Nugent from their work in New Ways Ministries in the summer of 1999 illustrates the seriousness with which the Vatican takes this issue. Gramick and Nugent's failure to emphasize strongly enough the sinful character of homosexual acts and the "disordered" nature of homosexual orientation appears to be the reason for the Vatican's action.[1] As it is usually presented, the Church's official teaching on homosexuality is based on its interpretation of certain key biblical passages (Gen 19:1-11; Lev 18:22; 1 Cor 6:9; Rom 1:18-32; 1 Tim 1:10, in the Vatican's 1986 statement) along with its understanding of the tradition. Discussion among moral theologians is usually carried on in reference to the Catholic natural law tradition as well as the Bible.[2]

Notwithstanding the centrality of these biblical passages and of natural law, I will argue here that there is another crucial factor to be taken into account in understanding the Church's official teaching, especially as it has been developed and expressed under the papacy of John Paul II. This is the "nuptial metaphor": the image that expresses the understanding that God and humanity, and men and women, exist together as Bridegroom and Bride. This relationship is one of "gender complementarity": that is, sexuality is an intrinsic dimension of the person, there are "essential" characteristics that accompany maleness and femaleness, and these differences "complete" men and women in relation to each other.[3] Moreover, the nuptial metaphor is developed largely through meditations based on Scripture. I will show that Mary, the mother of Jesus, is central to this understanding of the nuptial metaphor, and that John Paul II's theological anthropology is, in some crucial ways, more mariological than christological. Needless to say, homosexuality does not find a place in this schema. My focus on complementarity and the Bridegroom-Bride relationship is intended to provide essential background to the more direct discussion of homosexuality covered by other essays in this collection.

A further issue is the adequacy of this metaphor as the basis for a contemporary theological anthropology. While it is clear that homosexual relationships are ruled out in this understanding, this anthropology is problematic for heterosexual relationships as well, in that it presents an asymmetrical picture of relationships that at best suggests a benevolent paternalism and at worst implies that men's dominance over women is justified by the Bible and the tradition.

GENDER COMPLEMENTARITY

Gender complementarity refers to a conception of men and women as (a) essentially different and (b) "complete" only in relation to each other. According to this understanding maleness and femaleness constitute the original dimorphic condition of humanity as intended by God and as evidenced in the two creation narratives in Genesis. In John Paul II's understanding, however, gender complementarity has also come to include a definition of what is "essential" to being male and female. A certain form of "essentialism" has long been a part of official Vatican teaching on womanhood, but it has taken on enhanced importance in the writings of John Paul II.[4] The characteristics of femaleness have received particular attention from John Paul II: receptivity and maternal nurturing emerge as central. Maleness in turn is often described in terms of initiation and activity.[5]

Gender complementarity has been used in arguments against women's ordination by using the analogy of the role of the (male) priest and Christ with the Bridegroom, and with the Church and women as the Bride.[6] Against those who would argue for the issue of ordination being primarily a question of justice, advocates of male-only ordination claim that sexuality has a significance that goes far deeper than race or ethnic difference.[7] True justice cannot contradict one's "essential nature." From this perspective maleness and femaleness are not, as Rosemary Radford Ruether has said, "reproductive role specializations," but are rather "essential" to (that is, having to do with the "essence" of) human personhood.[8]

In an earlier work I argued that the nuptial metaphor for the Church and for male-female relations has come to assume a significance that it did not have prior to debates regarding women's ordination.[9] The Church's "feminine" character—as well as that of women human beings—has come to be emphasized far more than it had been before women's ordination became contentious, and when other metaphors, such as People of God, the field of God, the edifice of God, the sheepfold, etc., were used more frequently.[10] The nuptial metaphor has been used frequently in the Christian spiritual and mystical tradition and it has most often illustrated intimacy and love between the partners. It has not, for the most part, served as a prescriptive model for gender roles. In my view this is because the issue of gender roles was not in question.[11] In medieval literature, for example, men wrote frequently about themselves as the Bride of Christ, and suckled at the breast of Jesus.[12] But in the present femininity no longer has the more fluid meaning that was associated with it in the medieval period. The nuptial metaphor is now defined consciously and purposefully to prescribe gender roles—particularly in relation to the hierarchy and male priesthood—and implicitly to proscribe homosexual relations.

This view of sexuality pays little if any attention to the natural and social sciences, nor does it draw sufficiently on accounts by men and women of their own sexuality.[13] Its main source is an aesthetic and typological interpretation of the Bible that itself already assumes gender complementarity. Mary is central in this interpretation as she models both humanity and womanhood. Indeed, Mary's role is in some ways more central for theological anthropology than is that of Jesus.

In the case of the "distinct character" of womanhood, papal writings draw quite freely on the Bible, and the interpretation of both masculinity and femininity that emerges from this particular reading has little explicit connection with historical-critical interpretation. In dealing with homosexuality papal writings seem at first more concerned to establish the historical (and thus more literal) character of biblical condemnations of homosexuality, but these writings still return to a reading of the Scriptures that is less historical-critical than typological. Such a selective use of Scripture to make theological and moral arguments is not unusual in the Roman Catholic tradition, given its reliance on reason and natural law as well as Scripture. Yet this particular use of typology is problematic in that it proceeds without sufficient consultation or coherence with reason and natural law.

Feminist and other liberation theologians have argued cogently over the last forty years that traditional theological models have often served to perpetuate injustice, have hidden their indebtedness to a narrow construal of experience, and thus need to be revised by a more critical approach to the use of traditional sources, including the Bible.[14] In particular, attention to historical-critical methods in biblical interpretation is important because these methods are able to place biblical statements and models within their particular historical, social, and political contexts, and thus relativize their claims to timeless truth. Since my expertise is not in biblical interpretation but in systematic theology, I cannot address the issue of the adequacy of John Paul II's interpretation of biblical passages. But I can suggest that inattention to such methods runs the risk of making the kinds of interpretations that feminist and other liberation theologies warn against: that is, interpretations that ignore historical context and that elevate a particular and contextual interpretation to the level of divine revelation.

MARY AND "WOMANHOOD" IN PAPAL WRITINGS

Anyone familiar with the writings of John Paul II knows that Mary, the mother of Jesus, occupies a central role in his theology and spirituality. Mary constitutes the essence of womanhood, and indeed of humanity as well, in her receptivity and openness to God. There was some discussion in the mid-1990s that John Paul II was on the verge of naming Mary "Co-Redemptrix" of the human race, but such a statement has not yet come forth from the Vatican. Even a cursory reading of the Pope's Marian writings, however, will show why such a statement was thought to be imminent. In any case, Mary's role is much more than that of being the mother of Jesus. Mary is the archetype of humanity, and the consequence of this is that there is a definite "metaphysical" gender complementarity to the pope's theological anthropology that distinguishes it from anthropologies that rely more on christology.[15]

In *Mulieris dignitatem* (hereafter *MD*) John Paul II presents an extended meditation on womanhood and on humanity itself as grounded in Mary. This meditation is itself based in what can only be called a spiritual elaboration of certain biblical passages. Beginning with the "protoevangelium" of Gen 3:15 ("I will put enmity between you and the woman") and linking this with Paul's statement in Gal 4:4 ("When the time had fully come, God sent forth his Son, born of a woman"), John Paul II argues that "woman" (Mary) is central to human salvation: "This event is realized in her and through her" (*MD* 3). Shortly after, John Paul II notes that "A woman is to be found at the center of this salvific event" (*MD* 3). He goes on to highlight the significance of Mary for all humanity:

> From this point of view, the "woman" is the representative and the archetype of the whole human race. She represents the humanity which belongs to all human beings, both men and women (*MD* 4).

In the next section of the encyclical the Pope's language becomes even stronger in its reference to the significance of Mary. This passage is worth quoting at length:

> Thus, by considering the reality "woman-mother of God," we enter in a very appropriate way into this Marian year meditation. This reality also determines the essential horizon of reflection on the dignity and the vocation of women. In anything we think, say or do concerning the dignity and the vocation of women, our thoughts, hearts, and actions must not become detached from this horizon. *The dignity of every human being and the vocation corresponding to that dignity find their definitive measure in union with God. Mary, the woman of the Bible, is the most complete expression of this dignity and vocation. For no human being, male or female, created in the image and likeness of God, can in any way attain fulfillment apart from this image and likeness* (*MD* 5; emphasis supplied).

The striking nature of this language cannot go unnoticed. The Pope's understanding of what it means to be human is derived here not primarily from christology but rather from mariology. It is possible, of course, to argue that mariology is necessarily derivative from christology. But Mary's role, in John Paul II's thinking, has a distinctness all its own. Not surprisingly, when discussing the role of Jesus he relies on a rather "high" christology: "At all times Christ [John Paul II seldom uses the name Jesus] is aware of being 'the servant of the Lord' . . . which includes the essential content of his messianic mission, namely, his awareness of being the redeemer of the world" (*MD* 5). The result is what I am calling a cosmic vision of human redemption based on God's active relationship with the receptive Mary, and Mary's receptive relationship with her active Son ("Mary takes her place within Christ's messianic service" [*MD* 5]). Human redemption is initiated with Mary's response to God.

Humanity's position in relation to God is one of receptivity. Humanity is the Bride in relation to God the Bridegroom. In a very profound sense humanity is "essentially" feminine. Mary's "yes" is the model for the human response to God. Because Christ is God made present in human form, Mary's "yes" to God is also a "yes" to her Son and so the divine/human relationship is further illustrated in Mary's relationship to her Son. There is, then, both an ontological priority of the divine over the human in the person of Jesus Christ and an ontological necessity of God's becoming human in the form of a male.

Such a "high" christology (that is, a christology that begins with the "descent" of God into human form, not with "ascent" of the human Jesus to union with God) relies more on Johannine and Pauline texts than "low" christologies that rely more on the synoptic gospels. John Paul II is clearly orthodox in his understanding of the union of the divine and human natures in Christ. Yet since Christ is *both* God and man, his humanity *per se* cannot be separated from his divinity. Therefore Mary's *pure* humanity becomes the model for the human rather than Christ's unique (human and divine) personhood. Mary's humanity is then the prototype for all of humanity.

When it comes to relationships between human beings John Paul II returns to Genesis, with a reading of the creation narrative that elides both the P (Priestly) and the J (Jahwist) stories, and that is also read through his understanding of the Trinity's role. Male and female are understood to be fully equal, and rationality is identified as humanity's highest quality (*MD* 6). Yet what emerges as even more significant than rationality is the need for human beings to be in relationship (*MD* 6). The relationship of man and woman is analogous to the relationship between God and Mary (humanity): "The image and likeness of God in man, created as man and woman (in the analogy that can be presumed between Creator and creature), thus also expresses the 'unity of the two' in a common humanity. This 'unity of the two,' which is a sign of interpersonal communion, shows that the creation of man [sic] is also marked by a certain likeness to the divine communion *('communio')*" (*MD* 7).

John Paul II's encyclical letter on Mary, *Redemptoris Mater* (published in 1987, a year before *MD*) develops many of the same themes, although its emphasis is more on Mary herself. Here again the language is striking. Mary's role is central to salvation, although it is always dependent on her son. In one passage John Paul II describes her "pre-existence": "In the mystery of Christ she is present 'even before the creation of the world,' as one whom the Father 'has chosen' as Mother of his Son in the Incarnation" (*RM* 8). The language of Mary's "election" is also frequent (*RM* 9, 11). Throughout the encyclical Mary is described as the one who affirms and assents to God's initiatory call; indeed, she is "obedient" to this call (*RM* 13), and her "fiat" ("let it be done to me") is compared with Abraham's obedient response to God's call. She "accepts fully" (*RM* 14, 20), is obedient (*RM* 13), and "abandons herself" (*RM* 15) to God's call. In one significant passage her "journey of faith" is described in words familiar to theologians everywhere: she offered to God the Father "the full submission of intellect and will" and "abandon[ed] herself totally to God through 'the obedience of faith'" (*RM* 26). Mary is the "first to believe" (*RM* 26) and is therefore the first member of the Church. Her motherhood goes beyond biological motherhood (John 19:25-27, the passage in which Christ commends the Beloved Disciple and his mother to each other is cited) to nurturing care for all. In Mary's dependence on God and on her son she is "the most perfect image of freedom and of the liberation of humanity and of the universe" (*RM* 37). She is "subordinate" to her Son (*RM* 38) and is a model of "total self-giving to God" (*RM* 39). Throughout the encyclical she is described as "the Mother of the Son of God" in relation to God's Fatherhood (see especially *RM* 21). Mary was an "exceptional witness" to Christ's work, but she "did not directly receive this apostolic mission" (the mission of evangelization given to the apostles; *RM* 26).

A great deal can be said about the implications for relations between men and women that derive from John Paul II's interpretation of the creation narratives and of passages concerning Mary.[16] My point here, however, is that gender complementarity, at least as John Paul II understands it, goes far beyond a reading of natural law and even beyond a straightforward reading of the creation narratives. (Indeed, one wonders where natural law even is.) In other words, John Paul II is not so much arguing that human beings were created by God and intended to be male and female, as we can see in the natural world (although this is an implied part of his argument), but rather that creation and redemption correspond to a divine plan in which the Creator establishes a spousal relationship with His creation. This relationship is initiated by God, and humanity responds. Human spousal relationships then correspond to this order in which one (God, the man) initiates and the other (humanity, the woman) answers. Indeed, toward the end of *MD* the Pope writes: "The bridegroom is the one who loves. The bride is loved; It is she who receives love, in order to love in return" (*MD* 29) and later, again a passage worth quoting at length:

> Unless we refer to this order and primacy, we cannot give a complete and adequate answer to the question about women's dignity and vocation. When we say that the woman is the one who receives love in order to love in return, this refers not only or above all to the specific spousal relationship of marriage, *it means something more universal, based on the fact of her being a woman within all the interpersonal relationships which, in the most varied ways, shape society and structure the interaction between all persons—men and women* (*MD* 29; emphasis supplied).

The Pope concludes his meditation on the spousal relationship here with another reference to Mary and claims that woman's unique gift is that of loving others: "Woman can only find herself by giving love to others" (*MD* 30), a love that she has first received from her spouse and therefore from God.

SOME PRELIMINARY IMPLICATIONS

What conclusions can we draw from John Paul II's meditation on Mary and on womanhood? What are the implications for homosexuality and the biblical renewal of moral theology? First, it is clear that, for John Paul II, historical-critical method is but one method among others that can be used (but is not necessary) to interpret the significance of these texts. Indeed, one could well say that historical-critical method is not even at the top of the list of methods to be used, and there is no reference at all to historical-critical biblical scholarship on Mary. Like the theologian he so admires, Hans Urs von Balthasar, John Paul II reads Scripture through the long tradition of allegorical and typological interpretation going back to the early Christian Fathers.[17] In this school of interpretation the literal (or historical) meaning is only the surface meaning and must be plumbed more deeply for more profound levels of meaning. The early Fathers of the Church provide examples and direction for this type of interpretation. Irenaeus and Bernard of Clair-vaux are frequently cited for their own Marian meditations.

A second implication is that gender has to do with far more than human relationships. Gender, for John Paul II, is not just a physical category; it is a metaphysical and theological category that corresponds to the entire "order of creation." Indeed, God's relationship with humanity, as seen in his calling Mary to be the mother of God, is itself a gendered relationship, with God as the Bridegroom (in Christ) and Mary as the Bride (in humanity). Human relationships are to model this primal and cosmic relationship, in which maleness and femaleness correspond to the relationship between God and humanity. While the language never goes so far as to identify Mary with the divine, Mary's existence nevertheless is predetermined and elected by God, and Mary's status as having been preserved from original sin and assumed bodily into heaven assures the reader that this is no ordinary human being.

Third, the kind of relationship that is so ordered by God is one of complementarity, in which each gender has distinct roles and character-istics that pertain to its "essence." John Paul II does say that "generation" is a quality that pertains to both mothers and fathers (*MD* 8). But the fact that the initiation of love comes from the Bridegroom, and there-fore the male, means that generation, in some profound cosmic ways, is more male than female. Human love, like divine love, is generative and life-giving as well as receptive and nurturing; for both, love must consist of "mutual self-giving."[18] As the model of womanhood and of human-ity, Mary exemplifies this receptive, accepting, self-giving, affirming character, which human beings, and particularly women, are to imitate.

Homosexual relationships, therefore, while not explicitly addressed here, do not have a place in this cosmic drama. In fact, according to official teaching they go counter to the roles that were intended for all men and women.[19] Human life is truly a drama in which there are ap-pointed parts for each role and where we are all expected to play our individual parts. Homosexuality represents a type of human relation-ship that not only challenges but perverts these roles. It is a profoundly disordered way of living in relationship with others.

THE MARRIAGE METAPHOR AND THEOLOGICAL METHOD

One could ask at this point whether we dealing here with a simple incommensurability of approaches, where the allegorical-typological

approach of the Pope and the historical-critical approach of the contemporary biblical critic have practically nothing to say to each other.
And we could ask what is the place of spiritual/typological interpretation when it comes to moral questions. But one might also argue that,
in accord with Roman Catholic understandings of theological method,
historical-critical interpretation and judicious consultation of natural
and social sciences and of accounts of human experience are also necessary.

My concern with John Paul II's interpretation is that it is deriving
both moral norms and prescriptive models for human relationships
from a "spiritual" reading of the Bible. Seeing the nuptial relationship in
the creation narratives is indeed one possible way of understanding·
biblical passages, and it has a long history in the spiritual and mystical
tradition. Even historical-critical scholarship on its own, in fact, may not
shed sufficient light on male-female relationships or same-sex relationships. Biblical interpretations need to be supplemented by and correlated with other sources of human wisdom and experience, as they have
always been in the Roman Catholic tradition. In this case the tradition,
as it has understood sexuality, is largely in accord with the interpretation
of John Paul II. But it is at this point that one must ask about the theologian's obligation to engage in historical-critical scholarship, if only to
continue to test the adequacy of traditional interpretations, as well as
the obligation to consult other sources of human knowledge and wisdom.

If one were to rely only on the Bible it would be difficult to characterize biblical marital relationships as largely, or even remotely, equal.
While the Song of Songs is one description of a "spousal" relationship
in which there is something resembling equality—indeed, a number of
authors have speculated that the author of this book is a woman[20]—
most descriptions of nuptial relationships in the Bible are, if anything,
characterized by their asymmetrical power.[21] Wives often have little say
in their choice of marriage partner (e.g., Rachel) and their basic value
consists in their reproductive capacities (e.g., Sarah). Yet these examples
do not necessarily mean that no marriage can possibly be a mutual and
egalitarian one. The narrative of Genesis 2–3 expresses the need that
human beings have for each other; the mutuality of the first couple's
relationship was destroyed by sin.[22] Even Christian writers—Paul, for
example—argue for mutuality in terms of sexuality, although the social
situation of his time was not an egalitarian one.

The nuptial relationship that John Paul II idealizes can certainly be
described as a patriarchal one, in that the Bride is dependent upon the

Bridegroom in a way that the Bridegroom is not dependent upon the Bride. It is not without reason that some gay and lesbian writers have asked whether marriage is the best metaphor for gay and lesbian egalitarian relationships.[23] Their answer is that friendship offers a better model for mutual and egalitarian relationships. Yet I would be reluctant to agree too readily with the dismissal of marriage as an appropriate model for heterosexual relationships, given its endurance over time, its ability to adapt to changing situations, and the lack of other models for raising children.[24] My point here is not so much to question the adequacy of marriage itself but the particular way in which the marital relationship is understood in John Paul II's theology.

A number of contemporary theologians have argued for a reconstruction of the theology of marriage given the changes in the situation of women and society. Lisa Sowle Cahill and Bonnie Miller-McLemore, for example, have both argued *for* procreative marriage as a primary model for human relationships.[25] Both also recognize the compelling need to reassess the roles of men as well as women in the present. For these two theologians the Bible is an important resource for theology but it needs to be put into a critical correlation with accounts of human experiences and the findings of the natural and social sciences. My point here is that John Paul II's use of the Bible as a resource for reflection on human relationships does not take into account such experiences.

It may not be entirely fair to compare *Redemptoris Mater* and *Mulieris dignitatem* to the Vatican's "Statement on the Pastoral Care of Homosexual Persons" of October 1986, since the statement is not an encyclical and is not under the direct authorship of the Pope. But a few observations may be helpful in understanding the role of Scripture in all three documents. The 1986 statement criticizes a "new exegesis of scripture" that at minimum relativizes and at most dismisses the relevance of particular biblical passages to the issue of homosexuality (#4). Further, the statement argues for a "clear consistency within the scriptures themselves on the moral issue of homosexual behavior" (5) and that Scripture cannot be interpreted "in a way which contradicts the Church's living Tradition" (5).

The statement affirms human creation by God and also asserts that "in the complementarity of the sexes, they [human beings] are called to reflect the inner unity of the Creator" (6). The "spousal significance" of the human body remains after original sin, but it is "now clouded" (6). The statement goes on to identify certain biblical passages as confirming this "clouding" by sin (see 6). In 7, however, the statement specifically mentions the importance of symbolism in human creation: "To choose someone of the same sex for one's sexual activity is *to annul the rich symbolism and meaning, not to mention the goals, of the Creator's sexual design*" (7; my emphasis). Moreover, even though homosexual persons may be "generous and giving of themselves," homosexual activity is *"essentially self-indulgent"* (7; my emphasis). Because human actions are always embodied, and because this embodiment is more than functional, even the intention of self-gift and of mutuality in a same-sex relationship would be nullified, in the thinking of the Vatican, by the very fact that the persons engaged in the sexual act are the same sex.

There is an even more pointed statement in this paragraph that tends to reduce self-giving to the physical ability to transmit life: "Homosexual activity is not a complementary union, able to transmit life; and so it thwarts the call to a life of that form of self-giving which the Gospel says is the essence of Christian living" (7). The statement seems to be saying that the "gift of self" to the other in heterosexual intercourse embodies something distinctly Christian. For the Vatican, gender complementarity is the visible embodiment of "self-gift," which therefore cannot occur in same-sex relations. Later the statement argues that homosexual persons should follow the example of the cross by denying their sexual desires. This self-denial is "in service to the will of God himself who makes life come from death and empowers those who trust in him to practice virtue in place of vice" (12). A parallel can be found in *RM* 39, where Mary's example of perpetual virginity is a "result of her total self-giving to God." Human beings are called to emulate Mary, and so the decision to live without a genital sexual life, as did Mary, would be the ideal.

In this statement "self-indulgence" is described in contrast to "self-giving." And in a homosexual context, self-indulgence seems to be equated with self-pleasure. One must ask, as a number of feminist theologians have, whether John Paul II's emphasis on self-giving, particularly for women, is not problematic on a number of counts.[26] Moreover, the statement also conveys a distrust of pleasure for its own sake. From a feminist perspective, then, a conception of human virtue that elevates self-giving and is suspicious of self-pleasure is problematic at least. It may well be appropriate in our consumer-oriented, materialist culture to urge that we all be more self-giving. But the call for self-gift must be attentive, as liberation theologians argue, to the context: *who* is expected to be self-giving? Do concerns for self-gift take justice into account?

Further, statements about "self-indulgence" need to be balanced with a recognition of the tradition's historical suspicion of sexual pleasure.[27] Not all pleasure is self-indulgent or sinful.

The point of this brief comparison of documents on Mary with the statement on homosexuality is to show a consistency in their reliance on a "symbolic" or "typological" reading of Scripture and to emphasize that any position critical of the Vatican's statements on homosexuality must take into account what I am calling here a "metaphysical gender complementarity" that sees God as "essentially" male and Mary and humanity as "essentially" female. This understanding of human sexuality and its "essential" characteristics arises out of a particular phenomenological and personalist interpretation of the human person.[28] Yet, as feminist moral theologians have demonstrated, this interpretation of sexuality lacks a critical understanding of experience.[29] The "fact" of woman's "receptivity" in particular but also of the "natural complementarity" between the sexes is asserted but not empirically established. Thus, while the Vatican is in many ways consistent with the tradition in not reading Scripture more or less literally, its reliance in the case of womanhood and also of homosexuality on a spiritual, allegorical reading of Scripture without at the same time taking account of some empirical evidence does not do justice to the historical tradition's careful balance between revelation and reason.

In the case of gender complementarity, the example of Mary drawn from a meditative reading of Scripture forms the basis of John Paul II's theological anthropology. Those familiar with John Paul II's moral theology, as he develops it in *Veritatis splendor*, for example, know that he relies less on a traditional natural law approach than he does on a personalist reading of Scripture. Cristina L. H. Traina sums it up when she says: ". . . in *Veritatis splendor* natural reason does not supply even knowledge of minimal requirements [for the demands of the natural law]."[30] By excluding the natural and social sciences from having a significant role in his theology and also from influencing his scriptural interpretation, John Paul II ends up basing his understanding of the human person on a theological aesthetics.

While I would not want to separate entirely the aesthetic and the moral, I would argue that it is imperative to examine the potential moral dimension of the aesthetic. Theological aesthetics can play an important role in theology, as even liberation theologians are recently exploring, but there is a need for some connection with experience and some way of adjudicating different pictures of experience.[31]

CONCLUDING REFLECTIONS

By way of conclusion let me reiterate and expand on some issues involved in this nuptial interpretation of divine-human and human-human relationships:

1. *The role of the body in the nuptial metaphor.* In John Paul II's writings, nearly all of the focus is on the bodies of women; far less is said about male embodiment. The lack of any reference to empirical studies or even the social sciences makes the Pope's understanding of "natural receptivity" as well as natural male activity in need of much more justification. While I think it is more than possible to develop a mariology that emphasizes the choices that Mary had to make and her willingness to live with the consequences of these choices, as well as her role as the "first among the faithful," the characterization of both the body and psyche of "woman" as essentially receptive undermines the full subjectivity of women. Such a characterization seems to undermine women's full moral agency. The tradition is rife with examples of women's moral subjectivity carrying little if any weight in its moral deliberations. Moreover, the ecclesiological implications for the Church as the body of Christ having an almost wholly receptive role are obvious.[32]

When it comes to same-sex relationships, since there is no complementarity there is no modeling of the divine-human relationship. Symbolically, according to the Vatican, same-sex relationships model human-human relationships. Interestingly, the Vatican characterizes these relationships as not so much sterile as "self-indulgent." One is pleasing *oneself* (as one sees oneself in another) and not someone who is really "other." Therefore this love is not "self-giving," which is the ultimate model of love in Christianity. Such a construal of self-gift seems to reduce activity and receptivity to biology. But this symbolic modeling of relationship also pushes the question of the role of "sameness" and "difference" in human relationships. What kind of theological anthropology grounds same-sex relationships? And what is the role of the body in same-sex relationships?

I would suggest that theological reflection on relationships take into account a much wider modeling of relational possibilities, as we see, for example, in Margaret Farley's book *Personal Commitments.*[33] My own argument in *Extravagant Affections* was that the nuptial model hardly accounts for all the possibilities of human relationships: parent-child, sibling-sibling, friend-friend, etc. A broader familial model, I argued there, that takes into account the diverse relationships that human beings engage in during their lives, would offer greater possibilities for conceiving of just and fulfilling personal relationships within a Christian context. Moreover, sexual differentiation among human beings is far more complex than is usually recognized.[34] While heterosexual relationships remain the privileged place for procreation, human sexuality is ordered not only for procreation but also for pleasure. The kind of attention that Christine E. Gudorf has paid to the importance of pleasure is important.[35]

2. *The nature of the nuptial relationship.* As I argue elsewhere, John Paul II's understanding of the spousal relationship is that it is a completely dyadic one in which the multiplicity of roles in human relationships is not given enough attention or credit.[36] While the Vatican writings refer to the Trinity and thus suggest a community (of more than two) as the basis for relationship, the fact is that real-life marital relationships involve a complex nexus of extended families, friends, often children, and the world of work. This is also true of same-sex couples. While it is important for married couples, and for persons in committed relationships, to develop *a* complementarity in their relationship (and to argue for this would take a whole book on marriage, which I cannot do in this space)—that is, to develop a way of living with each other in which each person's distinctive gifts as well as weaknesses in the relationship can be honored as well as compensated for—to suggest that men must always take the leadership role in marriage is to write a prescription for multiple abuses of power. Such are the examples that drive Hunt, Heyward, and Stuart to argue *against* marriage as a model for egalitarian same-sex relationships. Such a reconstructed complementarity would emphasize an interdependence in which persons could grow and mature together rather than an asymmetrical and codependent relationship.[37]

What kinds of models of relationships between God and humanity might ground an argument for same-sex relationships? Certainly friendship has emerged as one of the most promising models so far. But I would caution against an overuse of mutual human relationships as the only analogies for the divine-human relationship. A focus on divine transcendence and mystery, thus far insufficiently explored by feminist theologians, may prove to be even more promising than images of God the Mother. All too often, human beings, feminists included, anthropomorphize God into an image that neatly coincides with their own concerns. A greater emphasis on God's mystery and ineffability suggests that humans would do well to be careful before assuming they know what God's will for them is to be, or before assuming that they know the contours of divine-human relationships. The deep mystery of the human relationship with God might invite a greater respect for how mysterious humans are to each other.

3. *The idea of Mary's womanhood and femininity.* This understanding of Mary needs further attention on the part of historical theologians. It would be important to chart historically when and how this theme has developed and how the status of women in societies has paralleled this idea.[38] Further, the ways that men have seen themselves in the feminine role also bear some significance for the issue of homosexuality. How, if at all, has "femininity" functioned as an ideal for *both* men and women in the long tradition of spiritual writing? And what has this femininity meant, in different contexts? When men assume the role of the Bride in relation to Christ, or see themselves in relation to Jesus as Mother, during a time when the femininity of the soul is a given, what are the implications for gender complementarity? My own thinking is that, historically, gender roles have been more fluid, with the medieval period serving as a model for such variability. The struggle for women's rights in the last century has, in my judgment, resulted in a much more rigid attitude on the part of the Church to variability in gender roles. But it is clear that more scholarship on Mary is necessary on this important point.

There is much more than can be said here about the role of the feminine in Christian theology. More than one Protestant author has commented on how their tradition has, in some ways, "deprived" both women and men of a possible way of envisioning the transcendent in more than male terms.[39] While the construction of "femininity" continues to be a controversial topic among feminist writers there is, in my view, a need to develop an understanding of womanhood that is neither that of a "female man" nor of the "virgin bride"/"total woman." Such an understanding needs to be attentive both to the findings of the natural and social sciences and to critical approaches to human knowledge.[40]

4. *The role of aesthetics in biblical interpretation.* That John Paul II's writings echo many of the themes of Hans Urs von Balthasar's theological aesthetics has been observed by a number of scholars.[41] Von Balthasar

is concerned—and I think there is some justification for his concern—that historical-critical biblical interpretation trumps any other kind of interpretation, particularly "spiritual" readings of Scripture.[42] This observation, however, raises further questions. Surely the Bible has been and will continue to be a text that inspires people privately as well as one that continues to raise crucial historical-critical questions. I would not want to argue against aesthetic interpretations of the Bible, but I would question using such aesthetic interpretations to make moral judgments without placing them in critical correlation with other sources of human knowledge and wisdom.

With the nuptial metaphor we have a case of a particular "type" or model of relationship between God and humanity, and between human beings themselves, being carried to the next level as the model for *all* relationships. Given that this relationship is also asymmetrical in terms of power, one must ask whether there is a morally problematic dimension to this understanding of the beautiful. Without the kind of experiential grounding that characterizes the Roman Catholic moral tradition (and, I would argue, the systematic tradition as well), such a reading risks not only alienation from experience but also injustice.

In addition, troubling questions emerge about relationships in human society. If all human beings are receptive, what is this to say about human roles in self-governance, in dealing with moral conflicts, in adjudicating issues of power?[43] And with the divine-human relationship, what does this model say about God's power and the role of human beings as co-creators? If one were to argue that this relationship is based in the scriptural tradition, then one would need some careful historical-critical work to decipher and explore further the nature of marriage relationships in the Hebrew and early Christian traditions.

In sum, the nuptial metaphor is central to John Paul II's theological anthropology. Human beings are the Bride in relation to God the Bridegroom. Homosexual relationships are not only immoral on the grounds of the Bible's testimony, tradition, and natural law, they also "annul the rich symbolism . . . of the Creator's sexual design." While this chapter has focused more on the ways in which this clearly heterosexual relationship is described, the implications are quite clear for homosexual relationships. This chapter is, of course, only an initial sketch of the implications of this theology, but my hope is that reflection on the nuptial metaphor might initiate further investigation of these and related issues.

NOTES: CHAPTER 3

[1] "Notification regarding Sr. Jeannine Gramick, S.S.N.D., and Fr. Robert Nugent, S.D.S.," Congregation for the Doctrine of the Faith, July 13, 1999.

[2] See, for example, Charles E. Curran, *Critical Concerns in Moral Theology* (Notre Dame, Ind.: University of Notre Dame Press, 1984), Richard A. McCormick, *The Critical Calling: Reflections on Moral Dilemmas Since Vatican II* (Washington, D.C.: Georgetown University Press, 1989), Lisa Sowle Cahill, *Sex, Gender and Christian Ethics* (Cambridge: Cambridge University Press, 1996).

[3] For one of the earliest statements of John Paul II's thinking on sexuality, see *Love and Responsibility,* trans. H. T. Willetts (New York: Farrar, Strauss, and Giroux, 1981 [1960]).

[4] See, for example, Pius XI, *Casti Connubii,* 1930.

[5] See *Inter Insigniores,* the Vatican "Statement on the Question of the Admission of Women to the Ministerial Priesthood," in Leonard Swidler and Arlene Swidler, eds., *Women Priests: A Catholic Commentary on the Vatican Declaration* (New York: Paulist, 1977) 30; John Paul II, *Mulieris Dignitatem.* It is worth noting here that the distinction between "sex" (as biological) and "gender" (as socially conditioned) that is central to feminist thought is almost completely absent from Vatican discussions on complementarity. Sex and gender are seen as roughly identical.

[6] See *Inter Insigniores,* 29.

[7] Ibid. 31.

[8] Rosemary Radford Ruether, *Sexism and God-Talk: Toward a Feminist Theology* (Boston: Beacon, 1983) 111; for a criticism of this view see Francis Martin, *The Feminist Question: Feminist Theology in the Light of Christian Tradition* (Grand Rapids, Mich.: Eerdmans, 1984).

[9] See Susan A. Ross, *Extravagant Affections: A Feminist Sacramental Theology* (New York: Continuum, 1998), especially ch. 4.

[10] These descriptions of the Church are drawn from *Lumen Gentium,* The Dogmatic Constitution on the Church, in *Vatican II: The Conciliar and Post-Conciliar Documents,* ed. Austin Flannery, O.P. (Northport, N.Y.: Costello Publishing Co., 1980).

[11] See Carroll Stuhlmueller, "Bridegroom: A Biblical Symbol of Union, not Separation," in Swidler and Swidler, eds., *Women Priests,* 278–83. But see also Renita Weems, *Battered Love: Marriage, Sex, and Violence in the Hebrew Prophets* (Nashville: Abingdon, 1993), who argues that the metaphor draws on the experience of patriarchal marriage in the ancient Israelite world. Weems shows how the prophets used the image of the "harlot wife" as an example of Israel's failure to keep its covenant with God.

[12] See Caroline Walker Bynum, *Jesus as Mother: Studies in the Spirituality of the High Middle Ages* (Berkeley: University of California Press, 1982).

[13] This is a point made by Lisa Sowle Cahill in both *Between the Sexes: Foundations for a Christian Ethic of Sexuality* (Philadelphia: Fortress; New York: Paulist, 1985) and in *Sex, Gender, and Christian Ethics*.

[14] Gustavo Gutierrez, *A Theology of Liberation: History, Politics, and Salvation*, trans. and ed. by Sister Caridad Inda and John Eagleson (Maryknoll, N.Y.: Orbis, 1988 [1973]); James H. Cone, *The God of the Oppressed* (New York: Seabury, 1975); Elisabeth Schüssler Fiorenza, *In Memory of Her: A Feminist Critical Reconstruction of Christian Origins* (New York: Crossroad, 1982), are but three prominent examples of liberation theology done from Latin American, African-American, and feminist-liberation perspectives respectively.

[15] Liberation theology would be an example of a theological anthropology that is christological in its understanding of the human, deriving from an understanding of Jesus' actions. See, for example, Leonardo Boff, *Jesus Christ Liberator: A Critical Christology for Our Times*, trans. Patrick Hughes (Maryknoll, N.Y.: Orbis, 1978).

[16] See Ross, *Extravagant Affections*, especially ch. 4.

[17] For Hans Urs von Balthasar's understanding of the limitations of the contributions of historical-critical interpretation of the Bible to theology see *The Glory of the Lord: A Theological Aesthetics*, vol. 1, *Seeing the Form*, trans. Erasmo Leiva-Merikakis and edited by Joseph Fessio and John Riches (San Francisco: Ignatius Press; New York: Crossroad, 1982).

[18] See John Paul II, "Letter to Families," February 2, 1994.

[19] I deliberately use the term "drama" to suggest the reliance on the thought of von Balthasar that is so strongly present in John Paul II. The third part of von Balthasar's theological project is termed a "Theo-Drama." See Hans Urs von Balthasar, *Theo-Drama: Theological Dramatic Theory*, trans. Graham Harrison (San Francisco: Ignatius Press, 1990 [1988]).

[20] See, e.g., Andre LaCoque in the volume co-authored with Paul Ricoeur, *Thinking Biblically: Exegetical and Hermeneutical Studies* (Chicago: University of Chicago Press, 1998). But note that LaCoque argues, and cites others in support of his point, that this "subversive" relationship is outside the social order of marriage.

[21] See Renita Weems, *Battered Love* (n. 11 above). This is a fascinating study of the prophets' use of the "marriage metaphor" to characterize the relationship Israel has with God. By drawing on this metaphor, and particularly that of the straying, or harlot, wife, the prophets were able to shape the thinking of the Israelite leaders in relation to women.

²² See Phyllis Trible, "Eve and Adam: Genesis 2–3 Reread," in Carol Christ and Judith Plaskow, eds., *Womanspirit Rising: A Feminist Reader in Religion* (San Francisco: Harper and Row, 1979) 74–83.

²³ See Carter Heyward, *Staying Power: Reflections on Gender, Justice, and Compassion* (Cleveland: Pilgrim Press, 1995); idem, *Touching Our Strength: The Erotic as Power and the Love of God* (San Francisco: Harper and Row, 1989); Mary E. Hunt, *Fierce Tenderness: A Feminist Theology of Friendship* (New York: Crossroad, 1991); Elizabeth Stuart, *Just Good Friends: Towards a Lesbian and Gay Theology of Friendship* (London and New York: Mowbray, 1995).

²⁴ I am indebted to the work of Lisa Sowle Cahill, particularly in *Sex, Gender, and Christian Ethics.*

²⁵ See Lisa Sowle Cahill, *Sex, Gender and Christian Ethics;* Bonnie Miller-McLemore, *Also a Mother: Work and Family as Theological Dilemma* (Nashville: Abingdon, 1994).

²⁶ See Valerie Saiving, "The Human Situation: A Feminine View," in Christ and Plaskow, eds., *Womanspirit Rising;* Barbara Hilkert Andolsen, "Agape in Feminist Ethics," in Lois K. Daly, ed., *Feminist Theological Ethics: A Reader* (Louisville: Westminster John Knox, 1994); Miller-McLemore, *Also a Mother.*

²⁷ See John Mahoney, *The Making of Moral Theology: A Study of the Roman Catholic Tradition* (Oxford: Clarendon Press, 1987).

²⁸ See John Paul II, *Love and Responsibility,* for a more extended treatment of this subject.

²⁹ See in particular Lisa Sowle Cahill, *Sex, Gender, and Christian Ethics,* and Cristina L.H. Traina, *Feminist Ethics and Natural Law: The End of the Anathemas* (Washington, D.C.: Georgetown University Press, 1999).

³⁰ Traina, *Feminist Ethics,* 125.

³¹ For one perspective on the role of aesthetics in liberation theology see Roberto Goizueta, *Caminémos con Jésus: Toward a Hispanic/Latino Theology of Accompaniment* (Maryknoll, N.Y.: Orbis, 1995) especially chs. 4–5.

³² See Susan A. Ross, "The Bride of Christ and the Body Politic: Body and Gender in Pre-Vatican II Marriage Theology," *Journal of Religion* 71 (July 1991) 345–61.

³³ Margaret A. Farley, *Personal Commitments: Making, Keeping, Breaking* (San Francisco: Harper and Row, 1986).

³⁴ See Natalie Angier, *Woman: An Intimate Geography* (New York: Random House, 1999); Judith Lorber, *Paradoxes of Gender* (New Haven: Yale University Press, 1994).

³⁵ See Christine E. Gudorf, *Body, Sex, and Pleasure: Reconstructing Christian Sexual Ethics* (Cleveland: Pilgrim Press, 1994).

³⁶ Ross, *Extravagant Affections,* ch. 4.

[37] I am grateful to Patricia Jung for suggesting this reconstruction of complementarity.

[38] See Marina Warner, *Alone of All Her Sex: The Myth and Cult of the Virgin Mary* (New York: Knopf, 1976).

[39] See, e.g., Miller-McLemore, *Also a Mother.*

[40] For example, the work of Sarah Blaffer Hrdy is important to note when considering the human "drive" or "instinct" for motherhood. See her *Mother Nature: A History of Mothers, Infants, and Natural Selection* (New York: Pantheon, 1999); see also Angier, *Woman.*

[41] See, e.g., Edward T. Oakes, *Pattern of Redemption: The Theology of Hans Urs von Balthasar* (New York: Continuum, 1994).

[42] See von Balthasar, *Seeing the Form,* 31ff.

[43] See Ross, "The Bride of Christ."

4

The Church and Homosexuality: A Lonerganian Approach

Jon Nilson

INTRODUCTION

*I*magine that a Catholic could travel back in time to December 8, 1965, the solemn conclusion of the Second Vatican Council. Imagine too that this Catholic could tell one of the bishops who had just signed the Council's "Pastoral Constitution on the Church in the Modern World" (*Gaudium et spes;* hereafter *GS*) that fundamental questions about the origins and implications of homosexuality would soon arise within the Church. The bishop would imagine the discussions and debates unfolding in a particular way because his vision would be shaped by the Council's portrait of a Church renewed.

This Church's life would be primarily a communion or *koinonia,* a web of mutually illuminating and invigorating relationships among the People of God gifted by the Holy Spirit. Moreover, this Church would no longer operate like a fortress defended against outsiders. Instead, it would be both in and of the world, sharing the "joy and hope, the griefs and anxieties" (*GS* 1) of all people, Catholic or not. The council even affirmed a kind of communion between this Church and the world, highlighting the ways in which each has benefited the other. It went so far as to say that the Church needs the world (*GS* 44). Thus, it declared, "conversation" *(colloquium)* on problems of common concern was "the most eloquent proof of [the Church's] solidarity with the human family" (*GS* 3). As the council itself took up this conversation it described the Church's distinctive approach to these problems as one shaped by the "light of the Gospel and *human experience*" (*GS* 46; emphasis added).

Naturally, then, our bishop would envision the pope and his fellow bishops deeply involved in discernment, i.e., consulting biologists, sociologists and psychologists; reading moral theologians and historians of theology; meeting with individuals and groups of homosexual persons, as well as with their families and friends. The Church's teachers would listen and contribute to the discussions and debates in order to discover the content and appropriate language for the Church's official teaching on homosexuality. If they were pressed for answers before their discernment was complete, they would reply, "We aren't finished with our inquiry yet—and, please, don't think that we have all the answers all the time to every question. After all, it's not easy 'to hear, distinguish, and interpret the many voices of our age, and to judge them in light of the divine Word.'" (*GS* 44)

In the matter of homosexuality, however, the Church's practice and teaching has not developed according to the conciliar scenario portrayed above. The most recent and dramatic evidence for this is the judgment of the Congregation for the Doctrine of the Faith (hereafter referred to as CDF) against Sr. Jeannine Gramick and Fr. Robert Nugent in the summer of 1999. According to the CDF their ministry was not only ambiguous about the intrinsic evil of homosexual acts but it also presented the official teaching of the Church as simply one of a number of legitimate moral options "and also open to fundamental change" in the future. Thus, said the Congregation, "the positions advanced by Sr. Jeannine Gramick and Fr. Robert Nugent regarding the intrinsic evil of homosexual acts and the objective disorder of the homosexual inclination are doctrinally unacceptable because they do not faithfully convey the clear and constant teaching of the Catholic Church in this area."[1]

This summary sentence capsulizes the official teaching: homosexuality constitutes a deviation from the order of nature according to which humans are created male and female by God; moral norms based on the truth of human nature are unchangeable since "human nature" is complete and finished; sexuality is complementary, and the two dimensions of sexual activity, unitive and procreative, may not be "unnaturally" separated. Thus the giving and receiving of sexual pleasure by homosexual persons, whether lovingly and permanently committed to one another or not, is contrary to the divine will. There are no conceivable circumstances that would warrant change in this teaching of the Church.

This paper seeks to clarify the meaning, motive, and effect of this teaching by responding to three questions. First, how does it relate to the content of the Gospel? Second, what explains the rhetoric and repetition of the teaching by the pope and the CDF? Third, might the content and style of the current teaching weaken the Church?

HOW DOES THIS TEACHING RELATE TO THE GOSPEL?

The content of a particular teaching and its importance are two distinct issues. Thus Vatican II reminded Catholic theologians "engaged in ecumenical dialogue" that a "hierarchy of truths" exists in Catholic teachings because the truths "vary in their relationship to the foundation of the Christian faith [i.e., Jesus Christ]" ("Decree on Ecumenism" *[Unitatis redintegratio]* 11; hereafter *UR*). The Council affirmed that papal "judgments" are not to be understood and accepted uniformly, but instead "according to his [the Pope's] manifest mind and will . . . [which] may be known chiefly either from the character of the documents, from his frequent repetition of the same doctrine, or from his manner of speaking" ("Dogmatic Constitution on the Church" *[Lumen gentium]* 25; hereafter *LG*). Taken out of its full context, the official teaching on homosexuality could be misconstrued as part of the essential and constitutive content of the Church's faith and, as such, to preclude not only dissent but also disagreement. But certain aspects of this teaching's context need to be recalled, lest it be taken to be more or less weighty than it actually is.

First, the Church's official teachers are themselves uncertain about the origins of homosexuality. As a result, the official text of the *Catechism of the Catholic Church,* which, according to Pope John Paul II in his 1993 encyclical on moral norms, *Veritatis splendor* 5 (hereafter *VS*), contains "a complete and systematic exposition of Christian moral teaching," has been changed. The original version of the *Catechism* had stated that those who have "deep-seated homosexual tendencies . . . do not choose their condition." In September 1997, however, this acknowledgment of their lack of choice was replaced with the statement that the homosexual "inclination . . . [is] objectively disordered" (*Catechism of the Catholic Church* 2358; hereafter *CCC*).

Cardinal Ratzinger, prefect of the CDF, explained the change: "'One objection was that we made people think that homosexual tendency was innate, that it was already present at the moment of birth or conception of the person. Many competent experts said this has not been proven.' Others, he said, thought the catechism left the origin—*and therefore the basis for a moral judgment*—of homosexuality too open."[2]

The Cardinal also said, "The origin of homosexual tendency is under discussion" and it "is not simply a matter of choice or will." He said that the *Catechism* must not presume to have the answer to the question of the origin of the homosexual tendency.[3] Thus the text reads: "Its psychological genesis remains largely unexplained" (*CCC* 2357).

Second, the structure and teaching of the *Catechism* show that certain disagreements over specific moral norms call for toleration of differing views and careful discernment in the current situation. It is clear from the text that not every moral norm belongs to the content of the apostolic faith.[4] According to the Holy Father the object of faith is the "Christian mystery" unfolded in Part One, which is organized according to the Apostles' Creed, a "faithful summary of the apostles' faith" (194). Part One does not deal with specific moral precepts because they do not belong to the fundamental, essential, and distinctive content of the Christian faith. This faith "enlightens and sustains the children of God in their actions (third part) . . ."; their actions are "expressions of faith."[5] Consistent with this approach, the *Catechism* maintains that the unity of the Church requires "visible bonds of communion" (815), but does not specify a uniform set of moral norms as one of these bonds. Furthermore, the elimination of moral disagreements is not listed as one of the "certain things . . . required . . ." to respond adequately to the call of the Spirit toward unity of the Christian churches (821).

In Part Three on morals, "Life in Christ," the negative judgment of homosexual acts is restrained in contrast to other judgments. Since sexuality is ingredient to personal identity and profoundly affects one's ability to love and to enter into close relationships with others (2332), the *Catechism* urges everyone to acknowledge and accept their sexual identity (2333). Thus chastity is developed, "the successful integration of sexuality within the person" (2337). Yet "sexuality" here means "heterosexuality" since it is complementary and ordered to marriage and family life (2333).

Homosexuality refers to "relations between men or between women who experience an exclusive or predominant sexual attraction toward persons of the same sex" (2357). This formulation suggests that the homosexual "tendency" is somehow not ingredient to personal identity. Although its "psychological genesis remains largely unexplained" (2357), this ignorance is not morally relevant. Homosexual acts are still "intrinsically disordered" (2357) because, as Ratzinger said, "they do not correspond to the fundamental tendency of sexuality which between a man and a woman is ordered toward the birth of children."[6] Thus, says the *Catechism,* homosexual acts are "contrary to the natural law" because "they close the sexual act to the gift of life. They do not proceed from a genuine affective and sexual complementarity" (2357). Therefore, "under no circumstances can [homosexual acts] be approved" (2357).

By contrast with this one, other judgments of the *Catechism* are much stronger. For example, withholding approval from "intrinsically disordered" acts is a far cry from the "gravely sinful" character of direct, intentional killing (2268). Direct abortion is "gravely contrary to the moral law . . . abortion and infanticide are abominable crimes" (2271), and abortion incurs excommunication (2272). Euthanasia is "morally unacceptable"; it constitutes murder (2277). The evil of adultery occupies two full paragraphs, 2380–2381. Pornography is a "grave offense" (2354), prostitution always gravely sinful (2355), artificial contraception is "intrinsically evil," and rape is "always an intrinsically evil act" (2356). The *Catechism* judges homosexual acts far more lightly than it does many others.

Third, the Church's eucharistic practice shows that the teaching does not belong to the essential content of the Gospel.

Although Vatican II described the Eucharist as both a sign and an instrument of the unity of the Church (see *UR* 2; also *LG* 7), Roman Catholic policy, as a general rule, restricts the reception of the Eucharist to Roman Catholics since the Eucharist must signify and actualize the very fullness of faith.[7]

Despite their positions on homosexuality and homosexual acts, however, neither Fr. Nugent nor (in a similar case) Fr. Charles E. Curran, whose position on homosexuality was one of the reasons for his dismissal from The Catholic University of America, has been forbidden to preach and preside at the Eucharist, the sign and instrument of the Church's unity in faith. While Curran could no longer function as an "official" Roman Catholic theologian, he and Nugent continue to preside at the celebration that unsurpassably actualizes and manifests the unity of the Catholic faith. If the teaching of the intrinsic evil of homosexual acts and the objective disorder of homosexuality itself belonged to the essential substance of the apostolic faith, they would have been forbidden to do this.

Fourth, "reception" is emerging as an important element in contemporary ecclesiology.

Until the Council of Nicaea and its decisions subsequently won wide acceptance, an orthodox Christian could still be uncertain, ambiguous, and even dead wrong concerning the divinity of Jesus. There is a less significant but definite parallel today with homosexuality. Granted that the notion of "reception" of magisterial teaching is still being developed by theologians, it is still clear that, despite the statements of the *Catechism, Veritatis splendor,* and the three documents of the CDF (*Persona Humana* ["Declaration on Certain Questions Concerning Sexual Ethics"], 1975; *Homosexualitatis problema* ["Letter to the Bishops of the Catholic Church on the Pastoral Care of Homosexual Persons"], 1986, and the Notification concerning Gramick and Nugent), the official teaching has not so far been "received" by many of the faithful as an expression of their faith.[8] The current situation is thus quite different from the one described by *LG* 25, where the assent of the Church is always given to infallible teaching since the same Holy Spirit illumines both the teachers and the taught.

Fifth, papal "judgments" are to be accepted "according to his [the pope's] manifest mind and will . . . known chiefly either from the character of the documents, from his frequent repetition of the same doctrine, or from his manner of speaking" (*LG* 25).

Undeniably, John Paul II has taught that there is an "intrinsic and unbreakable bond between faith and morality" (see *VS* 88–89). The Gospel includes certain clear moral norms that are universal and exceptionless. In *VS* he forcefully rejects the notion that Church membership and communion are compatible with some kinds of pluralism in moral opinions and behaviors (4, 25, 88). On the contrary, revelation includes a "specific and determined moral content, universally valid and permanent" (37). For John Paul II the Catholic tradition holds certain acts to be intrinsically evil and they cannot become virtuous or even neutral by a good intention or circumstances.

Yet his teaching has to be understood in its full context; that is, "the character of the documents [and] . . . his manner of speaking," among other factors. Though the Holy Father has spoken repeatedly and firmly about the intrinsic evil of contraception, he has not pointed to the difference between the Roman Catholic Church and the other churches on this issue as an "insuperable obstacle to reconciliation" of the churches.[9]

In his 1995 encyclical on Church unity, *Ut unum sint* ("That They May Be One"; hereafter *UUS*), which appeared less than two years after *VS* and less than two months after his second encyclical on moral issues, *Evangelium vitae* ("The Gospel of Life"; hereafter *EV*), John Paul II insists, as he has repeatedly done, that "the unity willed by God can be attained only by the adherence of all to the content of revealed faith in its entirety" (18). Later, he names the issues still standing in the way of "a true consensus of faith": the relationship between Scripture and tradition, the Eucharist, ordination, the magisterium, and the Virgin Mary (79). Moral disagreements are not on this list.

Such disagreements surely impair communion, but they do not necessarily break it. In *UUS* the Pope recalls that Vatican II put moral issues on the ecumenical agenda because "There are many Christians who do not always understand the Gospel in the same way as Catholics." Thus, he concludes, "there is much room for dialogue concerning the moral principles of the Gospel and their implications" (68).

This dialogue is not primarily intended to secure the unity of faith necessary for reconciliation but to enable the churches better to serve society in an age of moral relativism. The second Anglican-Roman Catholic International Commission had said, "Painful and perplexing as they [i.e., disagreements on moral matters] are, *they do not reveal a fundamental divergence in our understanding of the moral implications of the Gospel*."[10] Speaking at an ecumenical prayer service with the Archbishop of Canterbury, John Paul II outlined the difficulties created by moral disagreements:

> . . . if Christians cannot agree over the claims which the Gospel makes on their lives, far from giving common witness, they may actually contribute to society's moral confusion and loss of bearings. The recent statement . . . "Life in Christ" [published by the Anglican-Roman Catholic International Commission in 1994) is a timely encouragement to Anglicans and Roman Catholics to engage in further theological reflection about the moral life so as to resolve existing divergences and ensure that new areas of divergence do not arise, and *in order to establish a firmer basis for joint witness before the many moral dilemmas facing men and women today*.[11]

As we have seen, there are good reasons to place the Church's teaching on homosexuality and homosexual acts rather lower on the scale of the "hierarchy of truths" than the repetition and rhetoric of that teaching would suggest. Still, what accounts for the contrast between the rhetoric and the authority of this teaching? The Pope's remark points to the most plausible explanation for the contrast.

WHAT EXPLAINS THE RHETORIC AND REPETITION OF THE OFFICIAL TEACHING?

The principles underlying both the Church's stand on homosexuality and the CDF's intolerance of the purported ambiguities in Gramick's and Nugent's ministry are the unchanging moral norms that arise from a vision of the complementary nature of sexuality and its ordering towards procreation. For many, however, the credibility of this teaching is substantially weakened by questionable exegesis, a problematic interpretation of Tradition, and inadequate attention to the perspectives of social science and homosexual experience. Yet there are continued repetitions of the teaching coupled with appeals to the Spirit's guidance of the Church's teaching authority as its basic warrant.

It is important to understand what is behind the Pope's statement about the importance of the churches' "joint witness before many moral dilemmas today." This motive is highlighted in "Homosexuality and Gospel Truth: Towards Effective Pastoral Care" by Fr. Robert A. Gahl, Jr., which appeared in the same issue of *L'Osservatore Romano* that carried the CDF's Notification. Gahl does not refer to the Notification or even mention Gramick and Nugent, but his article is clearly the Vatican counterpoint to their now officially discredited approach.

Gahl breaks no new ground. His language and arguments mirror the official position of institutional Catholicism, as we have seen it here. He does not address or even acknowledge the philosophical, theological, and exegetical questions that have made the official teaching problematic, nor does he take cognizance of the experiences of lesbians and gays, and their families and friends.

He does, however, point to the real motive for the Church's stand that has received too little attention: the conviction that the Church's teaching is not merely helpful but practically necessary to society if it is to accomplish its proper purposes. In Gahl's words, "By 'rejecting erroneous opinions regarding homosexuality,' the Church 'defends personal freedom and dignity.' Social harmony depends, in part, on the proper living out of the mutual support and complementarity between the two sexes, which is why the Church cannot support civil legislation protecting 'behaviour to which no one has any conceivable right.'"[12] And again,

"Pastoral programmes, when undertaken in conformity with the truth of revelation, contribute to the human and spiritual benefit of homo-sexual persons, and to the integrity of society."[13]

John Paul II himself has already developed this theme with greater detail and emphasis in *VS*, especially in 95–101. The mind is clouded by sin. The forces of materialism and secularism are potent and pervasive. Thus humanity needs a clear, constant, and consistent set of norms that reflect God's will for individual and communal life. Otherwise there is the prospect of "a headlong plunge into the most dangerous crisis which can afflict man [sic]: the confusion between good and evil, which makes it impossible to build up and to preserve the moral order of indi-viduals and communities" (*VS* 93). Only the magisterium, enlightened by the Holy Spirit, can teach reliably these necessary norms. The Church's proclamation of moral truth through its divinely guided teachers (i.e., the pope and the bishops teaching in communion with him) provide a critical contribution to the well-being and harmony of society. Those moral theologians whose teaching conforms to magister-ial teaching also serve society by making the official moral doctrines more comprehensible and persuasive (*VS* 111).

Central to Roman Catholic social teaching is the axiom that the family is the foundation of society. Not only does the family provide society with new members but it also forms those members to take up their own responsibilities and make their own contributions to the wel-fare of others.[14] But the integrity and harmony of marriage and family life require the right understanding and ordering of sexuality.[15] There-fore, at its best, the reason for the Church's focus on sexual issues is not the prurient fascination of frustrated celibates, homophobia, or sexism, as some allege, but its authentic concern for the welfare of humanity, which depends decisively on the welfare of the family.

The problem is not with the Church's motive, then, but with the ways in which it expresses its concern for human well-being when it comes to homosexuality. The content and rhetoric of the official teach-ing are simply repeated whenever a serious challenge seems put to it. The findings, however tentative, of exegetes, psychologists, sociologists, moral philosophers, and theologians and the experience of gays and les-bians and their families seem to have no impact whatsoever. As a result, the gap between the magisterium on one side, and the people and many moral theologians on the other side, grows dangerously wider and wider as their mutual trust breaks down.

IS THE TEACHING WEAKENING THE CHURCH?

There is an intelligible, though unfortunate, pattern to the exercise of Church authority when it comes to homosexuality. Its structural dynamics are outlined in the work of Bernard Lonergan (d. 1984). In a study not published during his lifetime[16] entitled "Moral Theology and the Human Sciences," Lonergan sketches situations in which moral theologians must either collaborate with or draw upon the human sciences.

This necessity complicates moral theology in a number of ways, not least because it calls for dialectical analyses whenever differences are discovered among the conclusions of scientists and/or between the scientific consensus and theological or ecclesiastical conclusions. For a more detailed treatment of such conflict Lonergan refers the reader to his *Insight: A Study of Human Understanding*,[17] and, in particular, to the themes of bias, scotosis, scotoma, repression, and decline.

Bias, argues Lonergan, is a "love of darkness," and scotosis is the resulting process of resisting insight. Scotosis is "prior to conscious advertence and . . . regard[s] directly not how we are to behave but what we are to understand" (192-193). It involves "repressing from consciousness a scheme that would suggest the [unwanted] insight . . . prevent[ing] the emergence into consciousness of perspectives that would give rise to unwanted insights . . ." (192). "To exclude an insight," however, "is also to exclude the further questions that would arise from it and the complementary insights that would carry it towards a rounded and balanced viewpoint. To lack that fuller view results in behaviour that generates misunderstanding both in ourselves and in others" (191). Lonergan calls the blind spot that results a "scotoma."

He notes that there is a process analogous to scotosis at the social level:

> In each stage of the historical process, the facts are the social situation produced by the practical intelligence of the previous situation. Again, in each stage, practical intelligence is engaged in grasping the concrete intelligibility and the immediate potentialities immanent in the facts. *Finally, at each stage of the process, the general bias of common sense involves the disregard of timely and fruitful ideas; and this disregard not only excludes their implementation but also deprives subsequent stages both of the further ideas, to which they would give rise, and of the correction that they and their retinue would bring to the ideas that are implemented* (228–29; emphasis added).

Three features mark the ensuing decline of a community that suffers scotosis. While Lonergan is describing the deterioration of an entire society, his descriptions are also applicable to the social organization that is the Roman Catholic Church, as will be clear in what follows.

First, "the social situation deteriorates cumulatively" (229). It is characterized by anomalies, increasing conflict, and spreading stagnation. Finally, the only "intelligibility" in the social situation is a standoff of conflicting powers and pressures. Lonergan's prognostication seems confirmed as the "credibility gap" widens between Rome and the ordinary faithful when it comes to sexual issues, as centralization of teaching and governing authority in the Vatican (see, e.g., the 1998 papal directives *Ad tuendam fidem* ["To Protect the Faith"] and *Apostolos suos* ["On the Theological and Juridical Nature of Episcopal Conferences"]) increases, and the status and powers of the ordained are emphasized without developing structures for consulting representative and competent laity.[18]

Second, genuine understanding becomes increasingly irrelevant to a social body shot through with anomalies. Lonergan observes that "Intelligence can easily link culture, religion, philosophy to the realm of concrete living only if the latter is intelligible" (229). But the realm of concrete living that is the Church lacks intelligibility to the extent that its teachings and policies have little or no discernible relation to the experiences of the faithful and the investigations of exegetes, ethicists, systematic and pastoral theologians, and social scientists.

It is important to note here that bias, scotosis, and repression are always defended in terms of some particular good. Bias develops an "ingenious, plausible, self-adapting resistance" (230) to efforts that would unmask and disarm it. In this case, resistance to new data and perspectives on homosexuality is "ingenious, plausible, self-adapting resistance" insofar as it is framed as a necessary service to society where individualistic and nontraditional views of gender and sexuality appear now to threaten the vitality of the family, society's foundation and heart and core. Yet this is a complex claim that requires an empirical basis and empirical confirmation. As yet, there is insufficient evidence that any empirical data have materially affected the official teaching.

Third, the "major surrender" of "the normative significance of detached and disinterested intelligence" (230) leaves the understanding no way to discriminate between "social achievement and the social surd" (230–31). Some of the signs of this surrender in today's Church are the control of the membership, topics, and discussion methods within the Synods of Bishops; the insistence upon canonical mandates for all theologians; the redefinition of the role of the theologian as one of defending and explaining the official teaching, even those teachings for which infallibility is not claimed; and the demands for internal assent of moral theologians to particular teachings (*VS* 110). The "social surd," which is constituted by ignoring data and perspectives relevant to homosexuality (*VS* 112), is then framed as the "social achievement" of saving humanity from "a headlong plunge into the most dangerous crisis . . . the confusion between good and evil . . ." (*VS* 93).

Yet, says Lonergan,

> . . . there is such a thing as progress and its principle is liberty. There is progress, because practical intelligence grasps ideas in data, guides activity by the ideas, and reaches fuller and more accurate ideas through the situations produced by the activity. The principle of progress is liberty, for the ideas occur to the man (sic) on the spot, their only satisfactory expression is their implementation, their only adequate correction is the emergence of further insights; *on the other hand, one might as well declare openly that all new ideas are taboo, as require that they be examined, evaluated and approved by some hierarchy of officials and bureaucrats; for members of this hierarchy possess authority and power in inverse ratio to their familiarity with the concrete situations in which the new ideas emerge; they never know whether or not the new idea will work; much less can they divine how it might be corrected or developed; and since the one thing they dread is making a mistake, they devote their energies to paper work and postpone decisions* (*Insight*, 234–35; emphasis added).

Vatican II intended to inaugurate a cautious rapprochement with the contemporary world, after nearly two centuries of condemning it and fleeing from it. It offered guidelines for a new collaborative and constructive relationship. This is a risky enterprise, as the Council itself acknowledged. Many assumptions, convictions, experiences and perspectives in today's world call into question, if not dissolve, traditional moral norms.

Yet the magisterium has apparently terminated the effort toward rapprochement on questions related to the family. Today its response to these complex moral issues, including homosexuality, is not that conversation urged by Vatican II as the "most eloquent proof of the Church's solidarity with the human family." Instead, contemporary experiences and perspectives on sexuality are taken as *prima facie* erroneous. In place of a conversation between Church and world there is the clear, consistent, and unchanging moral teaching.

Despite some short-term gains, the costs of this strategy are very high: theological incoherence, the appearance of arrogance in seeming to dismiss the tentative findings of the social sciences (*VS* 112), and dismissal of the testimony of its own homosexual members and even marginalizing them (as well as their families and friends) by the claim that their sexual inclination, unlike that of their heterosexual sisters and brothers, is "objectively disordered," and the resulting loss of credibility by the Church's teaching authority.

John Paul II echoes Vatican II's theme of "conversation" when he underlines the necessity of sincere exchange with everyone about the basic issues of human life (see *EV* 95). But conversation cannot be genuine nor can exchange be mutual in face of the claims that the magisterium already possesses and teaches the truths necessary for human life. The Church sincerely desires to serve humanity. But until and unless it is evident that "The Roman Pontiff and the bishops, in conformity with their duty and as befits the gravity of the matter, strive painstakingly and by appropriate means to inquire properly into that revelation and to give apt expression to its contents" (*LG* 25), their service is likely to be construed simply as fear masked by arrogance.

NOTES: CHAPTER 4

[1] *Origins* (July 29, 1999) 136.

[2] Catholic News Service, "Catechism takes harder line on death penalty," *National Catholic Reporter* (September 19, 1997) 12 (emphasis added).

[3] *Origins* (September 25, 1997) 242. Cardinal Ratzinger is not the only Christian struggling with the issues of homosexuality. Consider the Presbyterian Church U.S.A.'s debates and votes on the so-called Chastity Amendment, the United Methodists' arguments over the blessings of same-sex unions by Jimmy Creech and Gary Bell, the trial of Episcopal bishop Walter Righter for ordaining a noncelibate homosexual man to the diaconate, and the debates prior to, during, and after the Anglican Communion's Lambeth Conference in the summer of 1998.

[4] The *Catechism* is a key text for this discussion, given the importance ascribed to it by John Paul II. Not only is it said to contain "a complete and systematic exposition of Christian moral teaching" (*VS* 5) but he also describes it as "a sure norm, a valid and legitimate instrument for ecclesial communion. . . . [and] meant to support ecumenical efforts that are moved by the holy desire for the unity of all Christians . . ." See his Apostolic Constitution *Fidei depositum* ["The Deposit of Faith"] 3, printed as an Introduction to the *Catechism*.

[5] Ibid. 2.

[6] "Catechism takes harder line," 12.

[7] See *UR* 8 and the Code of Canon Law, 844.1.

[8] Among the more recent and accessible supporting data for this claim see tables 3, 5, 7, and 9 in "NCR Survey," *National Catholic Reporter,* October 29, 1999.

[9] I am grateful to Francis A. Sullivan, S.J., for calling this to my attention.

[10] "Life in Christ: Morals, Communion, and the Church," 101 (emphasis added). Text in Jeffrey Gros et al., eds., *Common Witness to the Gospel: Documents on Anglican-Roman Catholic Relations 1983–1995* (Washington, D.C.: United States Catholic Conference, 1997) 185–216.

[11] *Origins* (December 19, 1996) 439 (emphasis added).

[12] *Origins* (July 29, 1999) 138. His quotations are drawn from the CDF's *Homosexualitatis Problema,* October 1986.

[13] Ibid. 139.

[14] See, *inter alia, GS* 47, 52; see also the U.S. Bishops' Pastoral Message "Follow the Way of Love" for a "translation" of these ideas (Washington, D.C.: National Conference of Catholic Bishops, 1994).

[15] See John Paul II, "Apostolic Exhortation on the Role of the Christian Family in the Modern World" *(Familiaris consortio)* December 15, 1981, 37.

[16] Originally it was a working paper for the International Theological Commission.

[17] Quotations from *Insight* are taken from Frederick E. Crowe and Robert M. Doran, eds., *Collected Works of Bernard Lonergan,* vol. 3 (Toronto: University of Toronto Press, 1992).

[18] See various Vatican dicasteries' "Some Questions Regarding Collaboration of Nonordained Faithful in Priests' Sacred Ministry," *Origins* (September 27, 1997) 397, 399–409.

Part Two:
Interpreting the Bible

5

The Promise of Postmodern Hermeneutics for the Biblical Renewal of Moral Theology

Patricia Beattie Jung

INTRODUCTION

For the Bible to be a source of renewal for moral theology, ethicists must explicitly and critically weave into their arguments insights that spring from the proper interpretation of Scripture. Some Christian ethicists find worrisome the admittedly circular, and hence potentially vicious, hermeneutical partnership between Scripture and various traditions. This is especially true when the traditions are secular, but it applies at least potentially to traditional Church teachings as well. Given this hermeneutical circle, the Bible cannot provide the sort of "objective" foundation for ethical arguments most moral theologians prize.

The claim, frequently associated with Evangelical Protestantism today,[1] that the Bible is not just *an* authoritative source and norm for ethical reflection, but is rather the *only* source of moral wisdom for Christians, is not a very helpful "solution" to this problem. However tempting its rhetoric, it does not provide a real alternative to the problems posed by tradition-bound hermeneutical circles. This is so because no written text—not even the Bible—can be the only source of moral

wisdom for Christians. By their very nature, texts require interpretation, and interpretation is inescapably contextual. Furthermore, many
reasonable interpretations of both what a text meant and what it means
are possible. As the practice of preaching on biblical texts makes clear,
Christians have known for a long time that the scriptural witness is
beyond a singular meaning.[2]

Even more importantly, what a text meant should not control what
it means. This does not mean that careful exegetical work is not important to the hermeneutical process. Historical arguments are helpful in
many respects. They can help us "hear" what we may find challenging.
But historical-critical arguments alone cannot establish whether there is
or is not a biblical foundation for any particular moral viewpoint, including that under examination in this volume, heterocentrism. Such
an interpretative judgment requires the interplay of multiple sources of
wisdom: theological, pastoral, scientific, philosophical, and literary, as
well as socio-historical. The postmodern framework for interpretation
promises to foster precisely the required sort of interdisciplinary, inclusive conversation.

THE DREAM BEHIND HISTORICAL CRITICISM

Many biblical theologians still naïvely hope that modern methods
of historical criticism will yield an "objective" account of a text's meaning and thus resolve moral debates among Christians. But this Enlightenment dream is misleading. While they remain useful, historical
arguments cannot provide the much-longed-for, tradition-independent
foundation for interpretative judgments with which any reasonable
person would agree.

For our purposes what is important to note is that for a few significant decades in the middle of this century there was a remarkable ecumenical consensus about how to establish the truthfulness of a particular
biblical interpretation. Not so very long ago both Roman Catholic and
Protestant biblical scholars thought they knew how to adjudicate between all conflicting interpretations. In his 1943 encyclical "By the Inspiration of the Divine Spirit" *(Divino afflante Spiritu)*, Pope Pius XII
not only officially approved the historical study of the Scriptures but
declared that the pursuit of the "mind of the author" should have the
greatest priority among Catholic exegetes.[3] It was widely assumed in
most, if not all, instances that what a text originally meant could be "objectively" determined, and furthermore, that what it meant should con-

trol what the text means for us today. Historical criticism was thought to uncover the world behind the text from which it arose. Initially it was presumed that, as historians, biblical scholars could approach texts objectively and simply peer through these literary windows onto the past, like disinterested spectators or uninvolved reporters. The text, it was assumed, did not mediate the past, but instead provided the scholar direct access to it.

These illusions accompanied the transmission of historical methods even though, as ethicist William Schweiker notes, early in this century "Albert Schweitzer observed that biblical scholars had peered down into the deep well of history only to see themselves."[4] Still biblical theologians were confident that increased dedication to the canons of critical reasoning would eventually pay off and unmask all their heretofore hidden interests. Many interpreters believed that historical-critical methods would eventually enable them to avoid eisegesis completely. The canons of reason would enable scholars not to read ideas into a text. Only when the "control" of the interpretation of texts was removed from the particular traditions of specific communities—whether gendered, sexual, ethnic, national, or denominational—and given over to this "higher criticism" would the "real" meaning be discovered. The dream was that historical-critical methods would yield an "objective" account of a text's meaning that would prove compelling to all reasonable persons. And so it was, as Allen D. Verhey has succinctly put it, that reason "displaced tradition and community as the test for interpretation."[5]

Even so, a more sober estimation of the contributions of historical criticism to the hermeneutical process has been in the making for decades. Daniel J. Harrington, S.J., reports that over "thirty years ago there was a lively debate about whether presuppositionless exegesis was possible" among scholars.[6] The answer, even then, was a resounding "No." Belief in historical positivism among biblical scholars should have died. Everyone agreed: no scholar works from a transcendent, tradition-neutral perspective, free from all prejudice. But good dreams die hard, and this one is no exception. While conceding its theoretical impossibility, many biblical scholars, even yet, strive to put aside as many of their presuppositions as possible. While absolutely context-independent interpretation is deemed illusory, many scholars continue to approach texts as if they could have only one truly valid meaning.

Enthusiasm for the modern historical-critical approach remained strong during the Second Vatican Council. Still, both the "Dogmatic Constitution on Divine Revelation"[7] and later the *Catechism of the*

Catholic Church[8] clearly maintain a distinction between what the biblical author(s) may have intended and what God wants to reveal to us by their words. These Church teachings suggest that what a text meant may overlap with what it means, but not necessarily so.

Similarly, the exact role of the "original" meaning of a biblical text is ambiguous in the 1993 document, "The Interpretation of the Bible in the Church," developed by the Pontifical Biblical Commission (hereafter PBC).[9] Here the PBC emphasized what it called the literal sense of Scripture, that is, what "has been expressed directly," associating this meaning with the historical-critical method.[10] Early in the document the PBC argues that this interpretative approach is "indispensable," and that respect for the human aspects of Scripture (its incarnation) "not only admits the use of this method but actually requires it."[11] In his comments on this document Pope John Paul II suggests the neglect or denial of this method reflects a kind of exegetical docetism. With the basic thrust of such claims I have little difficulty, as is evidenced in the section on the "new historicism" toward the end of this chapter.

Yet at other junctures the PBC seems to go far beyond this claim, giving this literal sense at least a kind of directional priority over other meanings.[12] Given the confusion this has evoked, it is perhaps worth quoting the document on this point at some length:

> Historical-critical exegesis has too often tended to limit the meaning of texts by tying it too rigidly to precise historical circumstances. It should seek rather to determine the direction of thought expressed by the text; this direction, far from working toward a limitation of meaning, will on the contrary dispose the exegete to perceive extensions of it. . . . The literal sense is, from the start, open to further developments, which are produced though the "rereadings" *("relectures")* of texts in new contexts. . . . (But) one must reject as unauthentic every interpretation alien to the meaning expressed by the human authors in their written text.[13]

At the heart of the matter, of course, is what counts as alien. Wisely, the PBC wishes to set some boundaries around the interpretive process: precluding both "wholly subjective" and overly historical interpretations. The latter might exclude "all possibility of higher fulfillment," evoked by the ongoing "influence of the Holy Spirit."[14] Further interpretive criteria are not given by the PBC, but it is clear decisions about what is alien rest with the official magisterium. Whether all traditional Church teachings are part of the living tradition and how the Holy

Spirit is actively guiding the development of moral wisdom in the Church are two issues that will surface as we examine the adequacy of this "answer" to the questions raised about hermeneutical methods.

What is important to understand is that the Enlightenment quest for an "objective" interpretative account has proven to be not only illusory, but dangerous as well. This approach simply leaves masked, and consequently unexamined, whole sets of highly influential—potentially, though not necessarily, dangerous—assumptions. The sometimes tragic repercussions of these hidden agendas are quite evident in the current debate about heterocentrism. While Church teachings may often, even normally, illumine the biblical witness, sometimes a traditional lens can shroud the Scriptures in misinterpretation.

Consider, for example, the commonly held heterocentric interpretation of the story of Sodom (Gen 19:1-11), reasserted in 1986 by the Vatican. Speaking of this biblical passage, the Congregation for the Doctrine of Faith (hereafter CDF) concludes "there can be no doubt of the moral judgment made there against homosexual relations."[15] Rome proclaims: there is "no doubt." Yet, many biblical scholars—including profoundly conservative advocates of heterocentrism like Richard B. Hays[16]—believe this particular passage does not even speak of—let alone against— same-sex activity *per se,* just as a parallel story about another-sex gang rape in Judges 19 does not reveal God's judgment about, or against, other-sex activity *per se.* Instead of illuminating the text, the Church's tradition of heterocentrism has obscured the witness of this passage against sexual violence in general, and against same-sex gang rape in particular.

This is a classic illustration of the dangers associated with any interpretative strategy that does not force open its contextual premises to critical analysis. All interpreters bring convictions to the text that impact their interpretation of it. And like heterocentric traditions, queer and gay traditions can unduly influence the selection and interpretation of biblical texts used in arguments against heterosexism. Though certainly an inevitable risk, especially when they remain hidden, my point is not simply to demonstrate that gender politics can lead to the misinterpretation of the Bible. Arguments from both sides of the debate amply illustrate this. Such ideological frameworks are ingredient to— indeed, create the very possibility of—every interpretation of the Bible. The question, as ethicist Stanley Hauerwas puts it, is not *whether* but *which* traditions will frame our reading of Scripture.[17]

The Church's traditions are as a whole more trustworthy interpretative filters than any of the other master stories available to us in the new millennium. But the tendency of some to treat each and every one of the Church's specific moral teachings as if they were a part of this living tradition, and hence absolutely beyond suspicion, is a serious problem. Why? For nearly fourteen hundred years what the Church commonly taught about slave rebellion was wrong, as was what it didn't teach about slavery *per se*. What Christianity did teach about slavery over the centuries was deeply rooted in fairly cogent (mis)interpretations of the testimonies given by many biblical authors and communities. So there is good reason to be morally suspicious not only of Christian moral traditions but of certain traditional (mis)interpretations of biblical testimonies as well. Yet if the question truly is *not whether but which* traditions will frame biblical interpretation, then it certainly seems reasonable enough to argue that *Christian* traditions should organize the various ethnic, national, class, gender, and sexual interests brought by Christian interpreters to biblical texts.

THE PLOT THICKENS

Church history indicates that it is not all that unusual to find some Church teachings in tension, if not in irreconcilable conflict, with at least some interpretations of the biblical witness. When coupled with the polemics of the period, this situation convinced many Protestants by the seventeenth century of the need to wrestle the control of biblical interpretation away not only from the magisterium as defined by Rome but from the control of many traditional teachings as well. Even today this is in large part what many Protestant Christians mean when they claim that the Bible is morally authoritative for them.[18] But the Bible cannot be an exclusive source of moral wisdom for Christians, whether they want it to be or not. The sort of tradition-independent interpretation presumed possible by some of today's advocates of this view simply cannot be accomplished. Extrabiblical sources of moral wisdom are *always* involved in our reading of Scripture, whether we acknowledge and critically assess them or not.

If reading the Bible is inescapably tradition-dependent, then other, more pertinent questions arise. If the Bible is inspired, should it be given *a priori* primacy among other, admittedly indispensable sources? Or should such primacy be given *a priori* to the teachings of the ordinary magisterium, also presumed both inspired and indispensable, at least by Roman Catholics?

The biblical renewal of moral theology will eventually prove to be a surprising source of ecclesial reform for all parties to these disputes, and postmodern hermeneutical theory carries with it some fruitful insights into this hermeneutical partnership. As a way into those arguments let us review the contemporary Roman Catholic approach to the partnership between the Bible and the Church's traditional moral teachings.

THE BIBLE AND TRADITION:
A CATHOLIC PERSPECTIVE

In an extraordinary break from the disputes that have divided Christians in the West, the Second Vatican Council chose to leave behind more polemical approaches to this partnership. The Council offered no rule of thumb to follow in the discernment process when a conflict between a Church teaching and a biblical interpretation surfaces. Instead, since the Bible and these traditions spring from the same divine Source, Vatican II insisted that there could never be any real conflict between them. Any tensions could only be apparent. This is part of what was at stake in the Council's decision not to adopt so-called "two-font" language when describing this partnership. Ultimately, the bishops argued, the problem will prove illusory: either the "traditional" teaching or practice under question will prove not to be part of the living tradition, or the particular biblical interpretation under debate will prove to be distortive of the Gospel. There can be no enduring rivalry between these sources of moral wisdom.

While reasonable enough in theory, this response seems to beg the question of how we should determine in practice what belongs to the living tradition and what belongs to sound biblical interpretation. Thankfully, the Council did not duck the problem altogether. It explicitly rejected the claim that the Bible should be treated as either the only or the primary source of wisdom. And the Council refused to teach that such a status should instead be given to magisterial teachings. Indeed, when the key phrase "all that she has" was deleted from its description of the living tradition, the Second Vatican Council, indirectly at any rate, recognized the fact that some of what has been taught by the Church over the centuries has not been part of the living tradition.

What this means for the contemporary ethical debate about any moral problem among Roman Catholics is this: when a traditional Church teaching, say about homosexuality, and the best of contemporary biblical scholarship collide, there are *in theory* at least two possible ways for the Church to respond. On the one hand, the Church could judge the new biblical interpretations to be erroneous, and this is precisely the judgment the Church has made about many recent reinterpretations of the biblical passages that speak about homoerotic activity.[19] On the other hand, there is the possibility for the Church to reform its moral teaching in light of compelling new developments in biblical interpretation. While this has been possible, as a matter of principle at any rate, since the Second Vatican Council, it must be conceded that so far most of the warnings issued from the Vatican have focused on the dangers of tendentious or confusing biblical interpretations rather than misleading Church teachings.

A MODEST THESIS

There was wisdom in leaving the question of the relative authority of various sources of moral wisdom *in principle* unresolved. It is my contention that the fundamental unity of the many sources of wisdom that comprise the living tradition can be seen only in their interplay. Perhaps it is wise not to give an interpretation of Scripture priority over a practice rooted in tradition ahead of that interplay. Similarly, perhaps it is wise not to give priority to a traditional teaching ahead of its interplay with the biblical readings that might challenge it. Christians will flourish only when their Scripture(s) and traditions stand in a mutually normative relationship. Why?

THE MORAL AMBIVALENCE OF THE BIBLE

There is *good* reason not to grant the Bible primacy *a priori* over traditional Church teachings, because the testimonies of some biblical communities might best be interpreted as morally mistaken.[20] Yet many Christians do not think of the Bible as really human, that is, as completely historical and culturally conditioned. Therefore the assertion that certain testimonies are best interpreted as morally suspect implicates God in error, if not evil. Yet, as biblical scholar Sandra M. Schneiders recognizes, thinking of the Bible as really human opens "up the theological possibility of acknowledging the limitations and mistakes, even the untruths and the oppressiveness in the text, without attributing these shortcomings to God or investing them with divine authority."[21] Inspiration is not properly understood when it is reduced to a claim about the accuracy—whether historical, scientific, moral, or theological—of any particular interpretation of any biblical passage. To say the Bible is inspired is to say something about God. As inspired, the Bible has the power to draw our lives—indeed to draw the world—into God's embrace. When the truly human character of the entire Bible is uncoupled from its character as inspired, then the faithful are not able to rest in the assurance that God has provided what the cosmos needs for salvation.

The Bible is simultaneously and completely both divinely inspired and fully human. Everything about the Bible—from the processes whereby it was formed to present-day interpretations—is both Word of God and subject to all the exigencies of finitude, even to the complicities of sin. Christians have no assurances of biblical inerrancy—*even in matters moral and theological*[22]—unless they are matters central to the deposit of faith. The PBC recognizes that "the writings of the Old Testament contain certain 'imperfect and provisional' (*Dei Verbum*, 15)" moral positions regarding slavery, divorce, and extermination in war, and that "the New Testament is not easy to interpret in the area of morality."[23]

Many think this controversial claim hinges on biblical interpretations about which there is little consensus. For example, there is no consensus that the patriarchal texts within the Bible are morally suspect. Though Christian feminists judge their testimony suspect, many other Christians still believe, at least in regard to gender roles, that the so-called "love patriarchalism" testified to in the New Testament is authorized by God. Many still believe these are precisely the scripts men and women should follow.[24]

More of us might agree that the anti-Semitism that spots the New Testament should not be embodied in our lives. In light of the Holocaust it seems appropriate to be cautious about letting certain biblical passages morally form our lives. Of this particular concern the PBC has written: "Particular attention is necessary, according to the spirit of the Second Vatican Council (*Nostra aetate*, 4), to avoid absolutely any actualization of certain texts of the New Testament which could provoke or reinforce unfavorable attitudes to the Jewish people."[25] Yet others have argued that anti-Semitism does not infect these texts, but rather has been imposed on it from outside by prejudiced interpreters.[26] Hence, they argue, it is not the original meaning of these texts that is morally problematic, but rather it is their subsequent biased misinterpretation that needs correction.

SLAVERY: A USEFUL DIGRESSION

Such debates—about sexism, anti-Semitism, and of course about the dispute that is the focus of this volume, heterocentrism—are today very divisive for Christians. The heat they generate, however, detracts from our ability to reflect on the deliberative process. Though admittedly a lengthy digression, a review of the slavery debate will prove fruitful because it is no longer "too hot for us to handle."[27]

It is distressing to realize the number of Christian cultures that not only legally permitted the practice of slavery but were constructed so that such subjugation was essential to their economies right up to the twentieth century. However, there is now consensus among Christians about both (1) the immorality of slavery, and (2) the need not to let certain portions of the biblical witness about slavery continue to function in morally formative ways for us.[28] As theologian Elizabeth A. Johnson puts it, clearly certain texts should "no longer guide Christian discourse and behavior, for rather than contribute to the good news of salvation, they long sustained a genuinely evil social institution."[29] Virtually no Christian today thinks of the biblical texts interpreted in the past as "pro-slavery" as revelatory of moral paradigms for our behavior. But this has not always been the case. Whether there is a biblical basis for slavery was hotly debated among Christians for a long time. Just a century and a half ago this debate proved tragically divisive in the U.S., especially among Protestants.[30]

There is a diverse witness in the Scriptures about slavery.[31] But *when they are properly interpreted as morally mistaken,* the so-called "pro-slavery" texts cannot be used to make a Christian case for, or to justify biblically, any form of slavery. It is, however, important to understand that many Southerners, Protestant and Catholic alike, who fought and died in the Civil War believed the Bible offered a religious rationale for their defense of chattel slavery.[32]

As they saw it, slavery was part of a broad social order established by God both as a punishment and remedy for sin. This way of life was revealed in the Bible. It is clear from their arguments that they saw themselves as soldiers defending God's Will against those unfaithful to it. All their justifications for slavery—most of which were scripturally supported arguments—rooted the subjugation of slaves to masters, and of blacks to whites, in the foundational subordination of women to men. Thus, as in the debates today about homosexuality and heterosexism, much was at stake in their battle over slavery. The very structure of their households and the wider social order based on "the family" were contested. Ours is by far not the first culture war over "family values" in the U.S.

Ideally, within this version of "love patriarchalism" masters were to protect, nurture, educate, and sanction the marriages of slaves, as well as appropriately "discipline" them and "supervise" their work. Of course, the reality of slavery was far from this ideal. Recognizing this, many of the preachers who defended slavery as an institution nonetheless called for the cruel treatment of slaves to be stopped, and for abusive, unjust masters to be punished.[33] But slavery itself was not viewed as inherently sinful. It was a part of the hierarchical pattern of social organization they believed ordained by God and revealed as "normative" in the Bible. Indeed, slavery's protection as an institution warranted their pastoral blessing. In 1840 Bishop John England of Charleston, South Carolina, argued publicly (without rebuttal by his brother bishops) that Pope Gregory XVI's apostolic letter of 1839 was not abolitionist in sentiment, and that it condemned outright only the international slave trade. In 1843, Bishop Patrick Kendrick of Philadelphia publicly argued against the abolition of slavery.[34] "As late as 1866 the Holy Office ruled that the buying and selling of slaves was not contrary to natural law."[35]

Catholics today would do well to "go to school" on the history of this moral debate, as they wrestle with the question of whether or not there is a biblical foundation for heterocentrism. What is important to understand here is that the many Catholics who sought to preserve slavery were deeply committed Christians. Those who fought sacrificed their lives for a cause they perceived (erroneously, but not unreasonably) to be God's Will as revealed in the Bible.[36] In hindsight it is easy for us to see that even when they were willing to wrestle with the *entire* biblical witness regarding slavery they tended to spiritualize the texts interpreted by their adversaries as "anti-slavery," so they would harmonize with the picture of God's Will that their interpretation of the "pro-slavery" texts had reinforced. Like armchair quarterbacks, we are quick to yell "interference!" But when we examine more closely just how it is *we* interpret, and the fact that we do not treat the so-called "pro-slavery" texts as morally authoritative for us, we recognize that some form of "interference" is unavoidable.

As our now commonplace treatment of the so-called "pro-slavery" texts illustrates, historical criticism does not settle the question of what a text should mean to us today. While understanding both what a text meant to its author(s) and audience and how it was traditionally interpreted over the centuries is very useful, it ought not necessarily be decisive for or hegemonic in the interpretative process. Today we know a lot about what "pro-slavery" texts meant, both originally and through the centuries, and yet we judge them morally suspect. In the case of slavery this judgment is reinforced by the "anti-slavery" testimonies also found in the Bible.[37] "Pro-slavery" passages are judged mistaken in the light of an intrabiblical "anti-slavery" canon.

Of course what we select as our "canon within the canon" ultimately depends upon what we bring to the text. The selection of what is to be privileged is based on what we understand to be at the heart of the Gospel. But such broad theological parameters contribute little to the resolution of ethical debates among us about the Christian life.[38]

In sum, whether they were conscious of it or not, both sides in the debate about slavery interpreted various biblical texts in light of a "canon within the canon." Jewish scholar Judith Plaskow states the issue succinctly. "Claiming the authority of a specific strand then is not a matter of identifying the essential and authentic voice of a particular faith. Rather, it is part of a contest . . . over who has the right to speak for tradition."[39] The creation of a "canon within the canon" in itself is not problematic. If one seriously wrestles with the Bible in all its diversity, then such an interpretative strategy will prove inescapable.[40] However, the question of how to justify what is selected for this "canon within the canon" is problematic.[41]

There is nothing in "anti-slavery" texts to suggest that we should assume them to be morally absolute. Likewise there is nothing in the "pro-slavery" texts to suggest that we should not assume each of them to be Scripture for us, and Plaskow is wise to remind us that "the troublesome aspects of the tradition do not disappear, however, simply because we ignore them, but they are left to shape consciousness and affect hearts and minds."[42] The selection of a "canon within the canon" is rooted in moral wisdom harvested outside the Bible. These insights may be corroborated and confirmed by portions of the Scripture, but ultimately the decision about which texts to privilege, and how to interpret them, is always made on an extrabiblical basis.

Note: it is not just the *inescapability* of eisegesis that proves so disturbing. What is so disquieting about the case of slavery is that for over fourteen hundred years many of the traditions—both ecclesial and secular—through which Christians interpreted the Bible corroborated, rather than challenged, the "pro-slavery" reading that dominated in the West.[43] Widely accepted patterns of biblical interpretation and traditional moral teachings were closely interwoven into an interpretive partnership. In this case, what they reinforced in each other was a vicious error of tragic proportion.

In regard to slavery, many Christians see the tremendous risks associated with the hermeneutical circle. As Barbara Kingsolver's novel *The Poisonwood Bible* dramatizes, the Bible can be deadly in many contexts. In his commentary on her postcolonial treatment of mission activity in Africa, Frederick J. Gaiser summarizes this point. "We can and do use the Bible against one another, use God to enforce our own wills, use religion to protect ourselves from the vulnerability of coming into contact with a God who can kill and make alive. . . ."[44] Many progressive Catholics worry that precisely this same sort of dangerously circular reasoning informs the Church's heterocentric sexual ethic and subsequent endorsement of some forms of heterosexism. GLBT people speak often of their experience of "Bible bullets" being fired at them. The Bible certainly has been, and might well be, interpreted in deadly ways. Yet, when correctly interpreted within the stream of the living tradition under the guidance of the magisterium (to use Catholic language),[45] such "false paths" can be avoided. Rightly preached (to use Protestant language), the Bible brings good news of a God who seeks only life for the world, indeed, life abundant. It is from these dual vantage points that we must evaluate the postmodern approach to biblical interpretation: from the edge of this ethical specter and the need it underscores for minimizing the harm the Church might do in the name of the Bible and our moral traditions, and from our call to faithfully proclaim God's gospel of life that we must interpret.

DANCING BEYOND THE BIFURCATION OF SUSPICION AND APPRECIATION

We know that some of the traditions we bring to the Bible—including not only many secular, but also some Christian traditions—have legitimated practices we now discern to be morally abominable. Therefore we recognize the need for an interpretative strategy that will expose—and lay open to challenge whenever appropriate—the particular

interests expressed in our interpretative frameworks. We need a hermeneutical strategy that will force us to wrestle with texts our framework
renders obscure, even offensive to us (like the "pro-slavery" texts), so
that if and when necessary the Bible may speak to us a Word we are not
inclined to hear. But if some biblical texts can be reasonably interpreted
in ways that sanctify evil, and were so even under the guidance of the
magisterium, as my digression illustrated, we also need an interpretative
strategy that will expose—and lay open to challenge whenever appropriate—the particular interests expressed in every biblical text.

It is precisely the faithful *appreciation* of and reliance on both the
Bible and Church traditions as inspired sources of wisdom that invites
us to take up a hermeneutic of *suspicion* in their regard. Given the
morally suspect character of portions of both the Bible and the Church's
moral traditions, we need an interpretative strategy that enables them
to mutually interrogate one another during their interplay. This is only
possible if we do not privilege *a priori* either source of wisdom. When
the relationships between these sources are truly dialogical, their interplay introduces the possibility of reciprocal correction.[46] Hence on the
one hand the Bible may challenge traditional Church teachings, the best
of human reason, and/or our experience of the ongoing work of God
among us. On the other hand, this interplay may lead beyond the biblical testimony regarding a moral matter to the proclamation of a new
Word.[47]

Biblical scholars argue that the Bible itself invites the faithful into
such a process and provides us with many precedents for such activity.
Frederick J. Gaiser notes that these include not only the occasions when
Jesus spoke a new Word (e.g., Matt. 5:21, 38-39), but also the welcoming
of foreigners and eunuchs in third Isaiah, and at certain points perhaps
the proclamations of Peter and Paul in the primitive Church (e.g., Acts
10:9; Gal 3:28; 5:6).[48] Luke Timothy Johnson makes a similar point
when he argues that biblical "texts authorize a certain freedom in interpretation by presenting a model of how Torah was reinterpreted in the
light of new experiences."[49] Both men make these methodological comments in the context of wrestling with the question of whether interpretations of texts traditionally thought to endorse heterosexism should be
revised.

For the promise of this interplay to be realized, it is essential that
neither Scripture nor traditional Church teachings be muted. For their
"dialogue" to be potentially both mutually corrective and/or mutually
corroborative, an interpretative strategy must be adopted that is both

open-ended and highly participatory. This is exactly what is reinforced by the postmodern approach to biblical interpretation, and why it holds such promise for the renewal of moral theology.

POSTMODERN CRITICISM

In recent decades the probability of not one but many legitimate interpretations became evident as the Bible became increasingly the subject of literary approaches. It was this realization that ushered much of biblical scholarship into a postmodern approach to textual analysis. When the world of the text interacts with that of the reader, a new world of meaning "in front of the text" (as Hans-Georg Gadamer located it) is forged. Therefore what the text means is always in this sense contextual.[50] The result is that the distinction between exegesis and eisegesis no longer makes much sense.[51]

Note, however, that the acceptance of such epistemological non-foundationalism does not mandate the acceptance of ontological non-foundationalism. Most (even postmodern) people remain convinced that the religious and moral convictions for which we lay down our lives are worthy of such commitment only if they serve realities that transcend in some sense the partiality and perspectivalism of such subjective and communal perspectives. From an ethical point of view individuals are obliged to test, as well as follow, the dictates of their consciences. As People of God, the Church is obliged to learn as well as teach. Ethical discernment, therefore, must be a dialogical enterprise in which we test our commitments "out loud" in conversation with others who will challenge us and to whom we are accountable.

If indeed it is wise for Christians to approach any weaving of the Bible and traditional Church teachings with both appreciation and suspicion, then it is also important to foster between these sources a mutually interrogatory exchange. This can only occur when a plurality of readings is welcomed. It is the genius of the postmodern perspective to focus on the benefits rather than the liabilities of the fact that readers contribute to the meaning of texts. From this point of view the fact that texts function at least as much like mirrors as they do windows is a matter to be celebrated, not a risk to be bemoaned or a danger to be avoided. Perspectivalism is not only a limitation to be overcome but also a power to be celebrated, precisely because it creates the possibility of the plurality of readings requisite for mutual interrogation.

By refusing to put the lid on the interpretative process—that is, by refusing to assert that there is just one valid meaning in the text—postmodern interpreters invite a plurality of readings. Like any hermeneutical strategy, this one simply tries to establish ground rules that will foster fair argument about the meaning of the text. The open-ended nature of the postmodern strategy, however, guarantees that there will always be room for the voices of those who have been or might be harmed by traditional interpretations. This hermeneutical strategy makes room in the conversation for people with perspectives on the text frequently left out of the interpretative loop. It enables those so inclined to incorporate into the interpretative conversation voices that previously may have been marginalized or repressed. These other readings rooted in differences of gender, orientation, ethnicity, class, discipline, and culture enliven the interplay.

This is no mean accomplishment from an ethical point of view, but neither is it a magical guarantee that a better interpretation will follow. The emergence of interpretations congruent with the gospel is ultimately a matter of inspired intuition. Such discernment is mysterious but not private. It is both personal and communal. Meeks argues that "one job of Christian moral formation is to create practices and occasions that will nurture" what George Eliot called the intuitions that accompany such fellow feeling.[52] This is precisely what a postmodern approach to biblical interpretation does.

A PLACE FOR THE "NEW HISTORICISM"

According to biblical theologian Duane A. Priebe it is precisely in terms of this context—of the epistemological significance of transcending the limitations of one's own point of view by attending to the voices of others—that the issue of the "abiding contribution of historical methodologies" is best considered.[53] The question, notes moral theologian Lisa Sowle Cahill, is whether it is "possible to generalize some definite and necessary role that historical criticism will have in the development of any ethical (or theological) perspective."[54] My answer is "Yes." In the last decade a new strategy has emerged among secular literary critics that appears to blend concern for historical meaning with literary techniques. This hermeneutical approach seems to have originated around 1983 with the work of Stephen J. Greenblatt.[55]

This "new historicism" treats the text not as a window through which one discovers the past, but rather as itself a cultural artifact on the basis of which one might hypothesize about the past. Admittedly subjective values enter into every phase of this descriptive inquiry. For example, whether a reader operates with structural, functional, or conflictual models of social interaction will color his or her hypotheses of the text's relationship to its own context. However, these historical reconstructions do not merely mirror present and /or traditional value configurations. There can be striking moments of disjunction between ancient texts and the contemporary interpretative context, that is, between the "strange" values represented in the textual object of one's study and one's own premises.

According to Priebe, while historical reconstructions "cannot control the scope of a text's potential for meaning," such work provides the text with some protection, distancing it (as it were) from the coopting power of contemporary agendas.[56] Credible accounts of a text's original meaning—like any other interpretations of the text—may challenge some of the previously unexamined, perhaps parochial assumptions we bring to it. What is of enduring value about historical criticism is that it "allows the text to have its say in its distance" from us.[57] I agree with Bruce Malina when he argues that considerate readers will make the effort to learn what the text meant, so as not to twist the words of that witness.[58]

Still, there is no basis—theological or otherwise—for the veneration of any past meaning of a text—including its original meaning. This is not the same thing as saying every interpretation is equally valid, or that there cannot or should not be any family resemblance between the moral worlds constructed by Christian communities across a wide scope of time and range of cultures.

However, some biblical scholars are not satisfied with this minimalist account of the enduring value of historical work. They argue that the meaning associated with the author's intention and the historical context out of which the text originated, despite the fact that this may differ even from the text's final literary form and canonical context, should determine the scope of interpretations judged legitimate today. For example, in apparent concurrence with Elisabeth Schüssler Fiorenza, Lisa Sowle Cahill argues that—to the extent we are able to reconstruct them—at least some moral outlooks of at least some biblical communities should control the scope of legitimate interpretations. They would function not as timeless archetypes but as historical prototypes for the Church today. Fidelity to these inspired worlds requires that we form morally analogous communities. In this way an admittedly subjective reconstruction of the original meaning of the text limits "the number of interpretations that can credibly be offered for a text."[59] Otherwise, these theologians fear, the postmodern strategy simply leaves us stranded in a "wilderness of mirrors." Whatever its assets, the liabilities of what we used to call "eisegesis" remain clear. The postmodern approach to the interpretive process seems—to them at any rate—completely out of control.

But this need not be the case. All classic texts provide interpreters with some boundaries. Schneiders brought this point close to home by noting that the meaning of the word "men," in the phrase "all men are created equal," has changed over the last two hundred years.[60] As best we can tell, this phrase in the U.S. Constitution originally meant adult, white, property-owning, free males. Its meaning has expanded to include others as the context of its readers changed over the years. Thus, while there may be no single meaning to any text, there is some denotative integrity to them. The meaning of "men" is not likely ever to include insect life, though some might argue that nonhuman forms of sapient life (such as dolphins) might one day also be routinely connoted by the term. Consider the word "sexism." It denotes discrimination based on gender. In our patriarchal world it connotes prejudice against women. There is the possibility of a quite different meaning emerging in a matriarchal world. There it would connote prejudice against men. There is no single right interpretation of it; like all words it can embrace multiple meanings. But there is some stability about the line or range of meaning properly associated with it. Some imaginable meanings are simply wrong and should be discarded as such. Insects are not men; sexism is not racism, etc.

Paul Ricoeur has noted frequently that written texts, unlike more improvisational forms of communication, have a stability that enables them to exist apart from the control of their author's intention. It is this autonomy that enables written texts to travel across historical and cultural boundaries, evoking necessarily different interpretations. And it is precisely this integrity that puts some parameters around the interpretative process. Reading remains always contextual. But readers do not endow a text with all its meaning, as if it were created "out of nothing." They simply contribute to it. Note: not "any ol' interpretation" can be justified. A textual case cannot be made that 1 Tim 6:1-6 underwrites slave rebellion. Such an interpretation can and should be discarded as manifestly wrong on the basis that it has no warrant in the text. Yet this call to submissive obedience should certainly be interpreted as mistaken.

In contrast, some postmodern theorists, more radical than I, believe that interpreters have the power not merely to contribute to meaning but to create it. For them it is not enough to say that people contribute to the construction of meaning and therefore that there are many meanings in a text. No one has more succinctly traced the ethical implications of this view than William Schweiker. In what he aptly labels this "overly politicized" account, texts themselves are seen as empty. Interpreters are portrayed as "sovereign creators of meaning," and no reading can be judged out of bounds.[61] When they insist that "a radical diversity of meanings (can be) worked at the will of interpretative communities,"[62] rather than insisting on an authentic plurality, they truly do leave those who turn to the Bible "empty handed" in a "wilderness of mirrors." Any study of the exegetical history of texts demonstrates that this wilderness can be both rich in diversity and also terrifying in its consequences. Some interpretations have had a tremendously negative impact: they have underwritten practices like slavery, anti-Semitism, gay-bashing, etc.

COMMUNAL DELIBERATION

The task of faithfully embracing the biblical witness goes well beyond its blind transmission or passive reception. It includes its proper interpretation and embodiment in our lives. Because the postmodern strategy is inclusive, it is inconclusive. It leaves us with no single certain interpretation about which there is a consensus on the basis of which to make our decision. Some find this dysfunctional from an ethical point of view. What possible good could come from the vigorous engagement of several plausible takes on a text? Such a conversation might indeed render overt what both heterocentric and queer people bring to the text, but might such an open-ended strategy also leave both sides to the debate at least temporarily immobilized? Won't it leave those who participate in such an interplay wondering about the comparative merits of their interpretation and the moral policies it suggests?

It probably will. And perhaps such humility is precisely what the doctor ordered. Clearly the Church needs to be a community of moral conviction, but it also needs to be a community of ongoing and inclusive moral conversation. Christians need to be concerned about not harming one another and/or the world in the name of God. Against this hazard, there is safety in numbers. A postmodern approach seems well suited to the character of the mutually interrogatory interplay that fidelity to the Bible and to traditional Church teachings about homo-sexuality requires. One fruit of the biblical renewal of moral theology will be tentative, reformable moral teachings conscious of their roots in an ongoing, communal process of moral discernment.

This is a strategy that both depends upon and will build up the Church as a community of moral deliberation. It is a strategy for dealing with bitter disputes with deep biblical roots. John R. Donahue, S.J., argues that such an inclusive, deliberative process is what Paul commends in Romans 14–15 to those embroiled at that time in debates about dietary customs.[63] Paul does not tell those divided in Rome to abandon their deeply held convictions, nor does he impose his view. He does tell them (three times) to "welcome each other," "just as Christ has welcomed you, for the glory of God" (Rom 15:7).

NOTES: CHAPTER 5

[1] Though certainly believers in the perspicuity and sufficiency of Scripture, neither Martin Luther nor John Calvin claimed that the Bible was the sole, in the sense of exclusive or only, normative source for Christian faith and practice. It would be historically wrong to construe their conflict with Catholicism as pitting the Bible against tradition or Church, though perhaps such a view might accurately be linked with the so-called "Radical" end of the Reformation. Luther's agenda, at least initially, was simply to bring certain ecclesial and sacramental traditions under the arbitrating authority of the Scripture. For more detail on these and related concerns see D. H. Williams, "The Search for *Sola Scriptura* in the Early Church," *Interpretation* 52/4 (October 1998) 354–66.

[2] In his work, *The Analogical Imagination: Christian Theology and the Culture of Pluralism* (New York: Crossroad, 1981), David Tracy characterized "classic" texts as having both an "excess of meaning" and a transcendent voice, that is, the ability to speak beyond a particular time and place. My argument in this essay hinges significantly on the claim that the Bible is in this sense a "classic" text. That language can function this way at all—that it can have many meanings—is a seriously contested matter. For a blistering attack on this axiom see the review essay, "The Bible: Witness or Warrant: Reflections on Daniel Patte's *Ethics of Biblical Interpretation*" by Bruce J. Malina, a contributor to this volume with whom I delighted to argue the point and from whom I learned much. His essay can be found in the *Biblical Theology Bulletin* 26/2 (Summer 1996) 82–87.

[3] In 1893 Pope Leo XIII gave a cautious nod to some forms of historical criticism, but the impact of this tentative acceptance was blunted by the subse-

quent resistance both Pope Pius X and Pope Benedict XV had to modernity in general, and to historical-critical approaches to the Bible in particular.

[4] For a very helpful analysis of two important books on the subject of this essay see the review of *The Ethics of Biblical Interpretation* by Daniel Patte and *The Politics of Biblical Interpretation* by David Penchansky written by William Schweiker in *The Journal of Religion* 76/2 (April 1996) 355–57.

[5] Allen D. Verhey, "The Holy Bible and Sanctified Sexuality: An Evangelical Approach to Scriptural and Sexual Ethics," *Interpretation* 49/1 (January 1995) 31–45.

[6] Daniel J. Harrington, s.j., "Catholic Interpretation of Scripture," in Kenneth Hagen, ed., *The Bible in the Churches* (Milwaukee: Marquette University Press, 1994) 51.

[7] Also known as *Dei Verbum* (1965) 12, 1.

[8] "Sacred Scripture," *Catechism of the Catholic Church* (Washington, D.C.: USCC, 1994) 101–41, especially 109.

[9] Pontifical Biblical Commission, "The Interpretation of the Bible in the Church," *Origins* 23/29 (January 6, 1994) front p., 499–524.

[10] Ibid. 512.

[11] Ibid. 500.

[12] For an interesting analysis of these and related points see Lewis Ayres and Stephen E. Fowl, "(Mis)reading the Face of God: *The Interpretation of the Bible in the Church*," *Theological Studies* 60/3 (1999) 513–27. In the end I think their analysis of the PBC document flawed on several counts, but most especially because they, like the PBC itself, fail to take sufficient note of the distinction between arguing that historical-critical methods are indispensable and giving them priority over other interpretive approaches.

[13] Ibid. 512, English parentheticals and emphasis mine.

[14] Ibid.

[15] Congregation for the Doctrine of Faith (hereafter CDF), "Letter on the Pastoral Care of Homosexual Persons" (hereafter PCHP) (1986) 6.

[16] Richard B. Hays, "Awaiting the Redemption of Our Bodies," *Sojourners* 20/6 (July 1991) 17–21, in particular 18.

[17] Stanley Hauerwas, *Unleashing the Scriptures* (Nashville: Abingdon, 1993) 15.

[18] Again, for more detail on these matters see Williams, "Search for *Sola Scriptura*."

[19] CDF, PCHP, no. 4.

[20] This possibility of moral error is readily admitted by the PBC in "Interpretation," 519.

[21] Sandra M. Schneiders, "The Bible and Feminism," in Catherine Mowry LaCugna, ed., *Freeing Theology* (San Francisco: Harper, 1993) 40.

[22] While my primary focus in this essay is on the moral life, let me be clear that I do not think that every theological portrayal of God is trustworthy. The abusive images of God in the stories of the sacrifice of Isaac and in the opening chapters of the book of Hosea are cases in point. But examples of questionable images of God abound. Elsewhere in the Bible God is portrayed as trucking in the wholesale slaughter of Israel's enemies. Of course, when we evaluate what the Bible says about God we risk painting God in our own image, but the very diversity of images in the canon makes such risky discernment necessary. The Bible itself testifies to the appropriateness of questioning and challenging various portrayals of God. Abraham (Gen 18:25), Moses (Exod 32:1-14), and Job put some tough questions to God. This essay aims to address the methodological issues contemporary theologians face while continuing this faithful work.

[23] PBC, "Interpretation," 519.

[24] As Schneiders points out, not all Christians agree that the deutero-Pauline text that limits the participation of women, found in 1 Cor 14:34-36, establishes female subordination in the Church for all time. Why? Because some now *see,* that is, interpret, the silencing of women as a "text of terror," and others do not. Schneiders puts it this way: "How various parts of the text are revelatory depends on our understanding of what a text is and therefore how it is to be engaged." ("Living Word or Dead(ly) Letter: The Encounter between the New Testament and Contemporary Experience," *The Catholic Theological Society of American Proceedings of the Forty-Seventh Annual Convention* [Santa Clara: Santa Clara University, 1992] Paul Crowley, ed. [Pittsburgh: CTSA, 1992] 45–60, 59.)

Consider these examples. Virtually everyone agrees that the story told in Judges 19—in which a woman is handed over as a surrogate victim to be gang raped and subsequently dismembered by the one for whom she served as surrogate—is not revelatory of an eternally valid example of moral behavior. As is also evidenced in Genesis 34 and 2 Samuel 13, this text presumes that women can be disposed of as their masters deem fit and that their personal welfare is unimportant compared to those the hospitality code prioritizes. All these texts call for revenge, but the injury to be avenged was to the male master "harmed" by the crime. The terrifying presumption about the expendability of women that underpins these stories violates the ideals of *both* feminism and "benevolent" paternalism.

Still there is no consensus about how to interpret the texts that call for the silencing of women in Church. Yet *both* kinds of texts—both Judges 19 and 1 Corinthians 14—are Scripture for us. They were both inspired by God and written for our edification. But to what do they witness? And what do they warrant? It is my belief that in *both* cases these texts witness to the depth of our bondage to sin, and that they *both* challenge us to go and do differently. Neither is a paradigm for moral behavior. Of course, not everyone shares this interpretation, and these texts have not always been so interpreted.

[25] PBC, "Interpretation," 521. Note: The term "actualization" would suggest in this context that what the text originally meant might now best be interpreted as morally mistaken.

[26] This is certainly the implication of the highly controversial claims made by the Commission for Religious Relations with the Jews, under the direction of the Pontifical Council for Promoting Christian Unity, in its 1998 document "We Remember: A Reflection on the Shoah." Incredibly, this document characterizes not just Nazism, but anti-Semitism, as thoroughly modern ideas with pagan roots completely outside Christianity.

[27] Some would argue that there are too many differences between what the Bible has to say about slavery and its testimony about homosexuality to make a comparison of these debates useful. Admittedly there are important differences between texts that directly prohibit, tacitly endorse, or sanction behaviors. But remember, slave rebellion, just like homoerotic behavior, was directly prohibited, and Paul attributes the former to Jesus directly.

[28] It is important not to conclude from this review that slavery is a dead issue. An enormous slave trade continues today all over the world, including the abduction and trafficking in women and children for sexual slavery in the U.S. See the CIA's "International Trafficking in Women to the United States: A Contemporary Manifestation of Slavery" (November 1999), an analysis of the problem involving an estimated fifty thousand victims annually. Modern ethical debates among Christians in this regard, however, focus on the long-term consequences of strategies like "slave redemption" in the Sudan and relocation efforts in the U.S.

[29] Elizabeth A. Johnson, *She Who Is* (New York: Crossroad, 1993) 79.

[30] As a southern minority eager to establish their credentials as "good Americans," the Catholic Church in the eighteenth and nineteenth centuries was largely uninvolved in the national debate over slavery. The Church condemned the abuses associated with slavery and advocated more humane treatment for slaves, including their recognition as human beings with souls, in need of religious instruction and the sacraments, and their right to have families and be sold as family units. (Note: This stance challenged those Christians who refused to baptize African slaves on the grounds that they were not human.) Yet, while most favored a policy of gradual emancipation, accompanied by the repatriation of those freed and willing to return to their "homeland" in Africa (or to the "mission" established by the Church for such in Liberia), Catholics virtually never agitated to end slavery. Indeed, at this time many religious congregations (including the Jesuits of the Maryland Province), bishops, priests, and lay people were themselves slaveholders.

Abolitionists were practically all Protestant in background. The Quakers were the first Christian denomination to condemn the institution of slavery *per se* (though Gregory of Nyssa preached a sermon against the practice as early as 365 C.E., and the international slave trade was condemned in 1482 by Pope Pius II.) But it was a small group of New England evangelicals, "Bible-thumping" defectors from the major denominations, who first pressed for the immediate abolition of slavery. As Kenneth J. Zanca notes in his brief commentary on the primary documents he has collected for his anthology, *American Catholics and Slavery: 1789–1866* (Lanham, Md.: University Press of America, 1994) 36, "Catholics saw abolitionists as interpreting the bible in ways they couldn't accept. . . . Only the Church was given the authority to interpret the scriptures, and it had done so over the centuries, finding in favor of the slave holder."

³¹ See Willard M. Swartley, *Slavery, Sabbath, War and Women: Case Issues in Biblical Interpretation* (Scottsdale, Penn.: Herald Press, 1983).

³² Elizabeth Fox-Genovese and Eugene D. Genovese, "The Divine Sanction of Social Order: Religious Foundations of the Southern Slaveholders' World View," *JAAR* 55/2 (Summer 1987) 211–33.

³³ The condemnation of the mistreatment at least of "household" slaves was not uniquely Christian. Even ancient Romans linked such cruelty with weakness of character.

³⁴ Their interpretation of this papal document is certainly convenient, since the importation of slaves was made illegal in the U.S. by federal law in 1808, triggering a dramatic decline in international slave trade and a concomitant rise in the domestic slave market. However, their interpretation was not unreasonable either. Nowhere does the apostolic letter condemn slavery *per se* or call for its abolition as an institution in the Americas or Africa. After noting the implicit endorsement of slavery by the first apostles, Pope Gregory XVI recalls those biblical texts that invite Christians to regard their slaves as brothers, arguing that Christian masters should be more inclined "to free those who merited it." This is what led over several centuries, he continues, to the eventual demise of slave economies in most Christian nations. Greed, he argues, triggered the resurgence of slave trading during the colonial era; then he joins a long line of popes who as early as the fifteenth century condemned such international commerce, warning that no one in the future should support or engage in such trafficking.

³⁵ John T. Noonan, Jr., "Experience and the Development of Moral Doctrine," *CTSA Proceedings* 54, Michael Downey, ed. (1999) 53. Noonan cites here a letter from the Holy Office to the Vicar Apostolic of the Galle Tribe in Ethiopia, dated June 20, 1866, *Collectanea S.C. de Propaganda Fide* 1, 1293.

³⁶ Though it was not a slave economy, several forms of slavery were taken for granted in ancient Israel, including the sale of children for debt (2 Kings 4:1). Rules regulating these activities thereby implicitly endorsed them. For ex-

ample, in Exod 20:10; 23:12 slaves are commanded to keep holy the Lord's day and rest on the Sabbath. Leviticus 19:20-22 specifies the punishment for sexual activity with one's female slave if she is betrothed to another. In other passages slavery is more directly sanctioned. Deuteronomy 20:10-14, along with 1 Sam 17:9, permits Jews to take slaves as war booty. In Gen 24:35 the Lord is described as blessing Abraham by multiplying his slaves. In Gen 16:9 God's angel commands the slave Hagar to return to Sarah, her mistress. Though normally Jews were prohibited from making other Jews slaves (Lev 25:39-46), in Deut 15:16-17 God requires that such slavery become a lifelong arrangement, even among Jews, if, for example, the bondman is unwilling to abandon his wife and children (Exod 21:1-6, especially 5, 6).

In the West the first true slave economy was constructed in Greece. There is evidence of it in the writings of Plato; it finds classic expression in Aristotle. This way of ordering an economy and defining household obligations did not originate with Christianity. Furthermore, according to the review provided by biblical scholar Carolyn Osiek, in the Greco-Roman world there were at least two types of slavery. One was basically penal, most aptly associated with being worked to death in agricultural chain gangs, mines, and/or the galleys of ships, or with execution either by crucifixion or in an amphitheatre by wild beasts. The other form of slavery was most aptly associated with the management of the household and might entail menial domestic tasks, the guardianship and education of children, and/or the administration of important business affairs. See Osiek, "Slavery in the Second Testament World," *Biblical Theology Bulletin* 22 (Winter 1992) 175.

Slaves of the latter type were frequently mentioned in the gospel parables, though translators tend to disguise this reality by calling them stewards or servants. Wayne A. Meeks notes that at the heart of the "pro-slavery" arguments in eighteenth- and nineteenth-century America was the claim that "if slavery were 'evil in itself,' God would have forbidden it, not given rules for its practice" ("The *'Haustafeln'* and American Slavery: A Hermeneutical Challenge," in Eugene H. Lovering, Jr., and Jerry L. Sumney, eds., *Theology and Ethics in Paul and His Interpreters: Essays in Honor of Victor Paul Furnish* (Nashville: Abingdon, 1996) 236. Instead the apostles regulate, and thereby approve, slavery *per se.* Indeed, they call slaves to hearty obedience and enjoin them repeatedly to be subject, even to suffer wrongfully in imitation of Christ (Eph 6:5-8; 1 Cor 7:20-24; Col 3:22-25; 4:1; Titus 2:9-10; Philemon; 1 Pet 2:18-19). In 1 Tim 6:1-6, Paul declares that his call for the submissive obedience of slaves is based directly on the words of Jesus.

In her essay "Paul and the African American Community," C. Michelle Venable-Ridley explores why much of the Pauline corpus is viewed as suspect, if not held in contempt, by many in the black community (in Emile M. Townes, ed., *Embracing the Spirit: Womanist Perspectives on Hope, Salvation and Transformation* [Maryknoll, N.Y.: Orbis, 1997] 213). This portion of the Bible was frequently interpreted so that it accomodated and enforced slavery. Venable-Ridley opens her essay with the following story, originally recorded by Howard Thurman about his grandmother. "With a feeling of great temerity I asked her one day why it was that she would not let me read any of the Pauline letters. What she told me I shall never forget. 'During the days of slavery,' she said, 'the master's minister would occasionally hold services for the slaves. Old man McGee was so mean that he would not let a Negro minister preach to his slaves. Always the white minister used as his text: "Slaves be obedient to them that are your master . . . , as unto Christ." . . . I promised my Maker that if I ever learned to read and if freedom ever came, I would not read that part of the Bible.'"

[37] Today Christians interpret the Exodus account—the story of God's deliverance of Israel from slavery in Egypt—as revealing that God hates and condemns slavery. We accept the invitation of the Exodus account to identify with those in bondage and with those who cry out for freedom. We highlight Deut 23:15-16, which forbids returning runaway slaves. We now interpret Paul's requests (1) that slaves be treated justly (Col 4:1; Eph 6:9), and (2) that Philemon take back the fugitive slave Onesimus, and that he receive Onesimus as a brother (not a slave) *in the flesh as well as in the Lord* (v. 16) as exhortations the trajectories of which at least invite the dismantling of slavery. These texts (along with others) have become a kind of lens through which we now critically interpret the "pro-slavery" texts.

[38] As moral theologian Margaret Farley has repeatedly noted, love is the starting point for, not the conclusion of, Christian ethical reflection. No doubt some among both Christian abolitionists and love patriarchalists believed that their quite divergent convictions about slavery were life-giving and truly liberating. Neither may have perceived their prescriptions to be oppressive or death-dealing. Both might have claimed as their own starting point the great commandment: to love one another as oneself. The same, of course, is true for many of the Christian participants in the present debate about heterosexism and homosexuality. What should be at issue for Christians in their moral deliberations about heterosexism is precisely what it means to love gay, lesbian, bisexual, and transgendered (hereafter GLBT) people.

[39] Judith Plaskow, "Thinking about Thinking about Good Sex," in Patricia Beattie Jung, Mary Hunt, Radhika Balakrishnan, eds., *Good Sex: Feminist Perspectives from the World's Religions* (New Brunswick, N.J.: Rutgers University Press, 2001).

[40] Traditionally, of course, Christians assumed that individual parts of the canon were always basically compatible. The plurality within the moral witness was thought to reflect different but basically complementary perspectives on a common tradition. It was thought possible to "harmonize" the various passages—one with another.

In contrast, today, many interpreters no longer assume the testimony of various biblical communities to be so complementary. The scriptural witness on some moral issues is recognized to be truly diverse and conflictual, if not contradictory. Canonical diversity is assumed to be as true of the Bible as is canonical coherence.

It should be noted, however, that some contemporary ethicists continue to make efforts to harmonize truly diverse passages by arguing that they referred to forms of slavery quite different from and much less heinous than what we know as institutional slavery now. It is true that slavery has been constructed differently in different cultural contexts. Though not herself engaged in an effort to "harmonize" such passages, Carolyn Osiek notes that "ancient slavery was neither race-specific nor racist (which is not to deny that racism existed in the culture); there was no necessary assumption of natural inferiority; and manumission or the acquisition of freedom was quite common" (See Osiek, "Slavery," 174).

However, all slavery, regardless of its local construction, is terrible. In virtually every case, slaves are treated as property (even when also recognized as persons) and are subject to coercion. It has been argued compellingly that in the searing light of the Holocaust we should offer no interpretation of texts in the New Testament infected with anti-Semitism that could not be proclaimed in the presence of burning Jewish children. I believe that the same hermeneutical principle should apply in this analogous case: no interpretation of "pro-slavery" texts should be offered that could not be taught in the presence of children pirated for sexual slavery, in ancient or present times. Like the prayers we offer, what we preach and teach on the basis of the Bible is proclaimed in the presence of the entire communion of saints: both slave and free.

Others try to harmonize such passages by arguing that they are directed to different individuals (in the overall economy of the Church), or apply only to certain time periods in the lives of individuals or in the history of the Church. In my judgment all such efforts to harmonize these conflicting testimonies ultimately prove to be unfaithful both to the particular texts involved and to the biblical witness in general.

[41] Some argue that the selection of this "inner" canon can be based on the "special" nature of certain texts themselves. Among those who are conscious of this as their methodology three rationales frequently surface. Each explanation is problematic.

(1) Some privilege words attributed to Jesus. This approach is evident in *red letter* editions of the Bible. They defend this selection by arguing that the words attributed directly to Jesus should have "special" status because the source of these words is not merely inspired but divine. However, the identification of the authentic sayings of Jesus is a matter of considerable controversy. Furthermore, those who would privilege these sayings should remember that they were mediated by ordinary human communities. We do not have access

(except perhaps in one instance) to Jesus' Aramaic words; we have access only to Greek translations of them that sometimes conflict. Fully fallible human communities remembered, translated into Greek, preserved, contextualized, canonized, translated them into English, and interpreted them. While this entire process of mediation is truly inspired, it is also fully human, finite, and faulted.

(2) Others suggest we should privilege what is counter-cultural. They assume that counter-cultural texts are less likely to be distorted by their *Sitz im Leben,* or by particular historical concerns or cultural biases. For example, Phyllis Trible claims that the Yahwist account of creation in Genesis 2–3 is a text about the proper role and status of women in the light of which other texts should be evaluated. Trible argues that this depatriarchalizing text should be privileged because historically it was profoundly counter-cultural. However, it must be recognized that even a counter-cultural text is conditioned by the culture it criticizes. It is as much a product of the cultural polarity it reflects as is the *status quo.* It is not intrinsically less perspectival, limited, or culturally bound, only differently so.

(3) Finally, some suggest we should privilege texts that speak of "originating revelatory events" or "foundational events" for the community. They should be privileged (it is argued) because they are either (a) more pristine given their historical proximity to the events they describe or (b) essential to the community's sense of identity. (3a) However, the fact that a text dates from close to the time of the occurrence of an event does not in itself guarantee its moral superiority. For example, Wayne Meeks notes that many liberation theologians argue that the "*Haustafeln*" are second-generation, compromising reactions to earlier, presumably more authentic, egalitarian impulses. However, such reconstructions of a "Golden Age" are at best probabilistic, and ignore the rightful claim of later texts to full canonical status (Meeks, "'*Haustafeln*,'" 247–49).

(3b) The foundational status of a text is not self-evident. We have considerable consensus that Jesus' crucifixion and resurrection are events foundational to Christian identity, yet some choose to focus on the cross and others on the empty tomb as keys to that identity. Again Meeks's review of this hermeneutical challenge and of the shortcomings of the strategies adopted in response to it is useful. The search within Protestant liberalism for "immutable principles"of interpretation is doomed. Meeks reminds his readers of Karl Barth's response to Rudolph Bultmann's objection that he (Barth) failed to distinguish in his commentary on Romans between the Spirit of Christ and other spirits evident in Paul's letter. "Barth replied: ALL the words of Scripture are voices of those other spirits—'the Word must be discerned in, through and against them!'" (Meeks, "'*Haustafeln*,'" 246).

[42] Plaskow, "Thinking about Thinking."

[43] Largely rehearsing the Pauline directives, the *Didache* (4:9-11) exhorts slaves to obey their masters, and masters reciprocally to treat their slaves justly.

Sts. Ignatius of Antioch (c. 107 C.E.), John Chrysostom (c. 400 C.E.), and Gregory the Great (c. 589 C.E.), all accepted slavery *per se,* while advocating the humane treatment of slaves and the practice of manumission. The claim that the institution was a consequence of the Fall was a rationale for slavery first fully articulated by St. Augustine of Hippo in *The City of God* (chs. 15–16).

In *Slavery and the Catholic Tradition: Rights in the Balance* (New York: Peter Lang, 1994) Stephen F. Brett notes that St. Thomas Aquinas (c. 1265 C.E.) qualified Aristotle's argument that those more gifted should rule by arguing that such authority was not attached to the person's essence, but should be exercised instead only in relation to specific arenas of life in service to a particular end. While domination *per se* is not a consequence of sin *(Summa Theologica II/II: 10.10),* it must be providential to be authentic. Furthermore, Thomas Aquinas argued that slavery runs counter to the primary intention of nature, though not its secondary intention. It was a punishment for sin that was justified if it served its purpose (the good of the slave, the good of the master, the common good). Given the reality of medieval slavery, Aquinas concluded it was no sin to own slaves. He did not condemn slavery as an institution.

However, Brett argues convincingly that if they had been properly applied, Thomistic principles could not have justified the brutal, race-based slavery of Spanish colonialism. The focus on the individual rights of slaves promoted by Francisco de Vitoria and his disciple Domingo de Soto in the sixteenth century may have benefited slaves, but it also had the tragic consequence of leaving unexamined the question of whether such a form of slavery could ever be justified.

[44] Frederick J. Gaiser, "God as Evil?" *Word and World* 19/4 (Fall 1999) 336.

[45] PBC, "Interpretation," 521.

[46] This process should be coherent with the broader theological method of "mutually critical correlation" developed by David Tracy on the basis of the inevitability of interpretation and the commitment to respectfully converse with the tradition.

[47] Though perhaps it is more comfortable for Catholics to reach, this is not a distinctively Roman Catholic conclusion. Luther himself recognized that if we have Christ, then the Church could easily establish new decalogues. He recognized that this new Word might challenge both tradition and the Scriptures.

[48] Frederick J. Gaiser, "A New Word on Homosexuality? Isaiah 56:1-8 as Case Study," *Word and World* 14/3 (Summer 1994) 280–93.

[49] Luke Timothy Johnson, "Debate and Discernment," *Commonweal* 121/2 (January 28, 1994) 11.

[50] Schneiders (in "The Bible and Feminism," 47) makes it clear that reading is never a matter of discovering, and then consuming or passing on, a text's real meaning. Instead, meaning is born of an interactive process like making music. Neither the score alone nor the musician's sensitivities alone culminates in

music. Only in the interactive event known as a performance is music made. We discern what a classic text means similarly.

The contextual character of interpretation was made most evident to me on one occasion when I was rehearsing, as I had dozens of times before in the U.S., the debate between Christian feminists and "love patriarchalists" about how to interpret the household codes in the Pastorals. Do they represent, as Elisabeth Schüssler Fiorenza has argued, tragic corruptions of the "discipleship of equals" that marked earlier Christian communities? Or do they sanctify that form of life known as "love patriarchalism"?

Though most were polite, not one of my students wanted to engage this debate. Instead, they wanted to talk about Schüssler Fiorenza's portrayal of later New Testament communities as divided over questions of compromise and martyrdom. For them, martyrdom was not *obviously* morally superior to survival and compromise. These seminarians were Chinese, and my classroom was in Hong Kong. What surfaced for them in those texts mirrored not a culture war over gender roles, but the issues of martyrdom, accommodation, and the survival of the Church under persecution. These issues were very real to them as Christians in Hong Kong facing into the events of 1997. Even what comes to the foreground in a text is highly contextual.

[51] Hauerwas, *Unleashing the Scriptures,* 151.

[52] Meeks, *"Haustafeln,"* 252.

[53] Duane A. Priebe, "A Holy God, an Idolatrous People and Religious Pluralism: Hosea 1–3," *Currents* 23/2 (April 1996) 126.

[54] Lisa Sowle Cahill, "Scripture, Moral Community and Social Criticism," in Paul Scervish, ed., *Wealth in Western Thought: The Case For and Against Riches* (Westport, Conn.: Praeger, 1994) 215.

[55] My summary of these developments is indebted to the review of this new historicism developed by John R. Donahue, s.j., in "The Literary Turn and New Testament Theology: Detour or New Direction," *The Journal of Religion* 76/2 (April 1996) 250–75. Also of interest to those who seek to understand in greater detail the roots of this strategy is Michael Groden's *The Johns Hopkins Guide to Literary Theory and Criticism* (Baltimore: Johns Hopkins University Press, 1994).

[56] Priebe, "A Holy God," 127.

[57] Ibid.

[58] Malina, "The Bible" (see n. 2 above) 84.

[59] Cahill, "Scripture," 215. NB: The basis on which these selections would be made remains unclear. These same limits could make it impossible to judge slavery *per se* wrong.

[60] Schneiders, "The Bible and Feminism" 48.

[61] Schweiker, book review of Patte and Penchansky (see n. 4 above) 357.

[62] Those who operate with this "overly politicized" view of postmodernism, notes Schweiker, recognize that there must be some control placed "on the agenda of the interpretative community" (Ibid.). So they attempt to address this concern by appealing to the good will of interpretative communities. They remind biblical scholars of their obligations to serve justice in general, and of their responsibilities in regard to the interests of others in particular. There are at least two problems with such appeals. In the first place, they are dangerously optimistic and place a lot of trust in human goodness, both individual and communal. In the second place, they are vague. This is not surprising since postmodernists have argued that a definitive account of what the moral agenda of biblical interpreters should be is precisely the sort of normative judgment that cannot be justified.

[63] John R. Donahue, S.J., "Breaking Down the Dividing Wall of Hostility: A Biblical Mandate for the New Millennium," *The Santa Clara Lectures* 4/2 (February 8, 1998) 1–21.

6

Questions about the Construction of (Homo)sexuality: Same-Sex Relations in the Hebrew Bible

Robert A. Di Vito

*I*n the 1986 "Letter to the Bishops of the Catholic Church on the Pastoral Care of Homosexual Persons," issued by the Congregation for the Doctrine of the Faith, "a new exegesis of Sacred Scripture" is identified as one of the causes of confusion regarding the Church's teaching.[1] By this the letter means an exegesis that tacitly approves of homosexuality, either by asserting that the Bible has nothing to say on the subject of homosexuality or by contending that its statements are so culturally and historically conditioned that they are no longer applicable to life today.

The goal of this paper, within a historical-critical framework, is to articulate one way in which the Old Testament (hereafter OT)[2] might contribute to the contemporary discussion of homosexuality, particularly within the context of moral theology. Without ignoring how the biblical text has often served the purposes of those responsible for unspeakable suffering to gays and lesbians, my effort here is to seek a way beyond the obvious impasse that comes from simply juxtaposing the biblical prohibitions to contemporary sexual norms and practices. I hope to find that way by asking, not for the retreat of one of the parties, but what, if any, insight emerges from a respectful confrontation and lively clash of the biblical text with contemporary constructions of sexuality.

To accomplish this the paper will investigate four topics essential to a responsible interpretation of the biblical text. These are: (1) the limitations of the biblical texts as these bear on the contemporary discussion of homosexuality; (2) biblical legislation on same-sex relations prior to its incorporation within Leviticus and against the background of the ancient Near East; (3) the placement of this legislation within the levitical Code of Holiness; and (4) the implications of this contextualization for the perspective of the OT on same-sex relations. It is my hope that this perspective might be useful in the current discussion of homosexuality in moral theology to the extent that it can provide a way to mediate between the traditional teaching of the Church on homosexuality and those very challenges it faces today.

DEFINING THE LIMITS OF THE BIBLICAL TEXT IN THE CURRENT DISCUSSION OF HOMOSEXUALITY

Basic to historical-critical thinking is the effort to establish the actual relevance of OT data to the question being addressed to the Bible today, even in those cases where lexical correspondences suggest that one is dealing with comparable phenomena. This becomes still more important when the answer to the question will inform one's moral judgments and presumably affect the lives and loves of people in dramatic ways. The issue of homosexuality is one such question, and it is one where the limitations of the biblical data impose certain restraints on the applicability of the Bible's evaluations to contemporary discussions of homosexuality's morality and to their use as a support for the Church's traditional teaching.

First among the limitations of the biblical data is the striking lack of explicit textual reference to same-sex relations in the OT. Individual lists of relevant passages vary, but there is broad consensus only regarding Lev 18:22 and 20:13, with perhaps some debate on the usefulness of passages such as Gen 19:1-11 and Judg 19:22-30. While John Boswell's attempt to eliminate the relevance of Genesis 19 to the discussion by explaining away the idiomatic usage there of Hebrew *yādaᶜ*, "to know," is obviously misguided,[3] in both Genesis and Judges we are dealing with attempts to gang rape the guests of individuals who were themselves resident aliens. This—and not homosexuality or the attempt at homosexual relations—is the crime of the Sodomites and the Gibeahites which is the immediate provocation in the stories for their destruction. It is a crime all the more heinous because of their sheer contempt for the obligations of hospitality. In fact, that the men of the town demand "to know" Lot's male visitors, and the Gibeahites the Levite, rather than women underlines the outrage insofar as the gang rape of a male represents—sorry to say, even in our day as seen in the recent gang rape by New York policemen of an Ethiopian detainee—the ultimate means to attack the manly honor of the victim and deprive him of his dignity. As such it has absolutely nothing to do with one's being a homosexual or with the illegitimacy of same-sex relations. If one supposes that Gen 19:1-11 can be used as the basis for condemning homosexuality today, one should also probably conclude that the outcome of the story in Judges (the Levite's concubine is handed over to the townsmen as a substitute for the Levite) implies for its part that heterosexual relations are objectionable.[4]

This leaves only Lev 18:22 and 20:13, where of course we have no comprehensive statements about homosexual relations but in each case a brief, one-verse prohibition regarding same-sex male relations. As part of the same literary source, a literary source within Leviticus composed primarily of legal material and known today as the Holiness Code or Holiness Source (hereafter H), each text is included in a list of prohibitions which are largely sexual in nature. But since neither the principle of selection nor the sequence of ordering is obvious, the immediate context provides little support for the specific interpretation of either text or of their original meaning outside their present placement in H. Unfortunately, even the prohibitions themselves are not straightforward in their meaning, since both texts employ an idiom otherwise unattested in the Hebrew Bible, namely *miškĕbê ʾiššâ*, "the lying(s) down of a woman," whose precise meaning is fraught with a considerable variety of philological and interpretative problems. Moreover, since Lev 20:13 probably was composed on the basis of 18:22, along with most of the rest of the material in chapter 20,[5] this means one has a very narrow textual base from which to interpret the original content of the prohibition and the specific transgression it has in view.

All in all, the relative lack of attention to the matter of same-sex relations in the OT—especially when comparison is made to the other sexual transgressions listed in Leviticus 18 and 20—can only provoke speculation about the degree to which homosexuality is an issue of real practical concern. Since the topic of same-sex relations occurs in the

Middle Assyrian Laws—although not in the Codes of Eshnunna and Hammurapi—could its inclusion in Leviticus be accounted for by the inheritance of a legal tradition dependent on Mesopotamia? If so, what we have in the legislation of Leviticus is more in the nature of a theoretical case rather than legislation based on Israel's lived experience.[6]

Besides the scarcity of biblical material relating to the topic, another limitation on the applicability of the Bible to the contemporary discussion of homosexuality is the lack of any corresponding terminology to describe same-sex relations. It is generally recognized, for example, that there is no single Hebrew word that even remotely expresses the substance of what is covered by the contemporary term "homosexuality." The latter term is, in fact, of comparatively recent origin, having been introduced into English circa 1892 to render the German neologism that had itself appeared in print for the first time in 1869.[7] Before then there was, as David Halperin has said, no homosexuality, only sexual inversion.[8] While "inversion" referred to a broad range of pathologies in which one has "inverted" his/her proper sex roles, the term "homosexuality" implied a whole new conceptualization of human sexuality: where

> sexual identity was thus polarized around a central opposition defined by the binary play of sameness and difference in the sexes of the sexual partners; people belonged henceforward to one or the other of two exclusive categories, and much ingenuity was lavished on the multiplication of techniques for deciphering what a person's sexual orientation "really" was—independent, that is, of beguiling appearances.[9]

Where previously one's homosexual acts, just like one's heterosexual acts, stood on their own to be evaluated as discrete acts suggestive perhaps of no more than an acquired habit or an individual taste, now they were seen as expressions of one's deeper sexuality. They spoke now of who one was at a level not ascertainable by the recognition of one's biological sex, an isolable center within oneself that governed one's sexual behavior and was constitutive of who one was in a way that one's choice in wines or in clothes was not. In short, the emergence of the language of homosexuality meant that people no longer shared basically the same set of sexual appetites and desires whose exercise could be reckoned as more or less normal along some hypothetical behavioral spectrum; instead people were to be distinguished at a level constitutive of who they were according to what type of sexuality they had, by whether their orientation was to partners of the same sex or the opposite.[10]

This change in the language and conceptualization surrounding sexuality underlines the fact that same-sex interaction within the Bible cannot be taken at face value but has to be viewed within the broader context of its construction of gender roles and personal identity, something that is as much historically and culturally conditioned as ours. From that vantage point, the OT's construal of sexuality in terms of discrete acts occasions no surprise. As I have developed elsewhere,[11] it goes hand-in-hand with the OT's innocence with respect to significant aspects of modern selfhood, particularly its affirmation of the human person as autonomous, self-sufficient, disengaged from its social location, and someone for whom there is an "inside" as opposed to an "outside," a world that holds the key to our "true" selves. In other words, where salient aspects of modern identity are grounded in modernity's location of the self in the "inner depths" of one's own interiority, a certain sense of *inwardness* as Charles Taylor has put it,[12] the OT locates the self in its social roles and public relations. In its pages one finds a self that—in sharp contrast to modernity's emphasis on individuals—is deeply embedded in an all-enveloping web of family relations that precludes self-sufficiency and self-responsibility and constitutes the basic mode of personal identification and selfhood (cf. Josh 7:14-18). As such, the individual Israelite, disengaged from membership in family and community, is not a "self" about whom one can meaningfully speak or whose actions one could meaningfully evaluate. The only reality is the socially "embedded self"; the only morality, that which is given by the social roles and practices of the group, which both define who one is and determine the full extent of one's obligations and duties. In the OT our language must be of a moral community before it is that of a moral person.

In the context of the present discussion concerning the modern concept of homosexuality, the OT's construction of personal identity needs emphasis. Without the West's developed sense of inwardness, which has for its precondition Plato's localization of human thought and feeling in "soul" or "mind,"[13] one does *not* find a domain or center in the psychology of the Hebrew corresponding to the modern notion of sexuality; nor is there, more generally, anything corresponding to the modern sense of "self" as an organizing center of the person, or even corresponding to the traditional metaphysical notion of "soul" as the seat of human faculties and the center from which its activity organically flows.[14] The kind of centering within the person implied in the modern notion of sexual orientation simply finds no resonance in the

OT, where one's sexuality neither unfolds nor becomes the object of a personal quest.

One of the most striking features of modern identity is the conviction that each individual has an "inner depth" that marks the individual as unique. It is the task of every person to discover this realm, since it provides the key to one's true self and functions as the only legitimate standard by which one can judge oneself or be judged by others. Of course this is, as we have already suggested, quite foreign to the OT, where in a way quite unknown to modernity one simply is one's social role and does not merely "play" a role distinct from who one really is on the inside. On the contrary, one's real self is the public self, given with one's social role and status, and apart from the place one occupies in society there is no marker of personal identity, no "inner depths" to discover on a personal search. To that extent, apart from instances of outright deception, the self is transparent, and one really is one's behavior, if one is anything at all. And so, too, one is one's body, to such an extent that physical defects are sufficient to disqualify individuals from certain activities, such as exercise of the priesthood or entrance into the covenant community (Lev 21:16-24). Rather than suggesting an empty formalism or externalism, these kinds of prohibitions regarding the lame or the blind simply highlight the absence of "inner depths" in the Hebrew psychology that could function effectively, as they do in modern identity, as the focal point of self-definition and personal identity. Without the modern language of "interiority," inevitably the priority in the OT is given to a person's acts over his/her "intent" or "motivation." Action does not manifest a self, nor is it an expression of soul; rather it belongs to personal identity in the same way as heart or spirit or soul.[15]

Enough has been said here to suggest some of the ways in which the distinctive anthropology of the OT might bear on the application of the Levitical prohibitions to the discussion of homosexuality in moral theology today. The differences between the OT's construction of personal identity and modernity's are indeed profound, so much so that one might argue—quite apart from any conviction about the Church's traditional teaching—for taking the OT out of the discussion altogether, as having no more significance for the contemporary Christian than its dietary laws. But if modernity's construction of personal identity, including one's sexuality, is, dare we say it, every bit as much a construct as the Bible's, such a move may be premature. To equate the Bible's potential contribution to the present discussion merely with the viability of its explicit pronouncements smacks of a propositional fundamentalism of a kind rejected already long ago by Augustine in *De Doctrina Christiana*, when he insisted on an interpretation of the Bible that did not consist simply in the restatement of the literal sense of a passage but tied a faithful interpretation to the order of charity (even when that entailed an interpretation that went against the literal sense of Scripture).[16] Turning the Bible into a book of prescriptions fails to recognize that the Bible's timelessness lies in its capacity to challenge the Christian by putting the whole of his/her life existentially in question.

THE BIBLICAL LEGISLATION IN
HISTORICAL PERSPECTIVE

> And with a male you shall not have (lit., "lie") the lying down of a woman *(miškěbê 'iššâ)*; it is an abomination *(tô'ēbâ)* (Lev 18:22).
>
> And as for a man who has (lit., "lies") with a male the lying down of a woman *(miškěbê 'iššâ)*—the two of them have committed an abomination *(tô'ēbâ)*; they will surely be put to death; their blood (guilt) is upon them (Lev 20:13).

Except for the otherwise unattested phrase *miškěbê 'iššâ* "the lying(s) down of a woman" shared by the two passages, the translation is relatively straightforward. The two verses obviously stand in a close relationship to each other, Lev 20:13 being apparently a recasting of Lev 18:22, which develops the earlier law in significant ways. While the prohibition of Lev 18:22 is cast in the second person masculine singular and formulated in what is frequently called the apodictic style ("You shall not . . ."),[17] Lev 20:13 is developed casuistically. After opening with a *casus pendens*-clause that takes up the case of a man who has sexual relations with another man precisely in the terms of the prohibition of Lev 18:20, it is framed objectively in the third person plural and makes the point that *both* parties—and not just the addressee of Lev 18:20—have done what is abhorrent. Therefore both come under the commination of the death penalty and both bear responsibility. As in 18:20, no mention is made of a woman in a same-sex relationship.[18]

The verb *šākab*, lit. "to lie," in these texts represents an idiom well known in the context of heterosexual relations specifically for sexual intercourse (e.g., Gen 20:15, 16; Exod 22:15; 2 Sam 11:4; 12:24), normally with the male partner as the subject of the verb but also with the female partner as the subject (Gen 19:33, 35). Copulation also seems to be indicated here, not only by the common usage but also from the context provided by Leviticus 18, where what all the prohibitions have in common is the (proper) disposition of a male Israelite's semen/"seed."[19] Thus one may reasonably suppose that anal intercourse is the action proscribed, particularly in view of the idiom *miškěbê ʾiššâ*, "the lying down of a woman."[20] The latter appears to introduce a division of roles into the prohibition's construction of intercourse specifically along the lines of gender.

This idiom *miškěbê ʾiššâ* is attested nowhere else in the OT, but one may get some indication of its meaning from the similarly framed idiom *miškab zākār*, lit. "the lying down of a male" (Num 31:17, 19, and 35; Judg 21:11 and 12). As the context makes clear, this latter idiom must mean vaginal penetration by the male, since it is used to define a virgin as opposed to a non-virgin. If so, it also suggests that *miškěbê ʾiššâ*, "the lying(s) down of a woman," should mean something akin, presumably vaginal receptivity. This distinction between penetration and being penetrated is certainly plausible and it may be supported by the contrasting *nomen rectums* "male" and "woman."

But can we circumscribe the meaning of this idiom even more, to distinguish further *miškab zākār* from *miškěbê ʾiššâ*? Perhaps Saul Olyan goes too far here when he takes *miškab zākār* to mean what a woman knows in vaginal intercourse and *miškěbê ʾiššâ* a male partner's experience of vaginal receptivity, based on his connection of the two idioms as an opposing word-pair. But strictly speaking, as in English, in Hebrew *zākār* "male" and *ʾiššâ* "woman" are not word-pairs, even if their meanings overlap. If "male" and "woman" are not an opposing word-pair in Hebrew, logically one cannot argue that the usage of one idiom is strictly differentiated from the other. In fact, the evidence suggests otherwise, for while *miškab zākār* is indeed used in the Bible to describe what a woman "knows" in intercourse (e.g., Judg 21:11, *ʾiššâ yōdaʿat miškab zākār*, "a woman knowing the lying down of a male"), Olyan himself points out that in 1QSᵃ 1:10 the same idiom is used to describe what a male experiences in intercourse.[21] So, it is not a question— at least necessarily—in these idioms of a woman's experience of vaginal penetration *(miškab zākār)* versus a man's experience of vaginal receptivity *(miškěbê ʾiššâ)*. Given the uniqueness of the idiom *miškěbê ʾiššâ* and the ambiguity of *miškab zākār*, the best we can conclude, conservatively speaking, is that *miškěbê ʾiššâ* is equivalent to vaginal receptivity, corresponding to a hypothetical *miškěbê ʾîš*, "the lying of a man," for vaginal penetration (i.e., parallel to *miškab zākār*).

As we shall see, all of this has important implications for under-standing the OT's construction of sexual activity. For it is important to note that this construction of intercourse does not immediately suggest the active-passive/domination-subordination structure Nissinen seems to assume informs the OT's construal of sexual intercourse, one ob-served in classical Greece and Rome, as well as perhaps ancient Assyria.[22] This difference in the OT's construction of intercourse is, in fact, what we expect. In the same way that the English word "intercourse" is gender neutral, in the Hebrew idiom for intercourse "to know" (*yādaʿ*), a man may "know" a woman (Gen 4:1) just as a woman may "know" a man (Gen 19:8) or the men of Sodom may demand to "know" Lot's male visitors (Gen 19:5); similarly, for the idiom "to lie" *(šākab)*, a man may "lie" with a woman as a woman may "lie" with a man.[23] There is also much that the active-passive structure when applied to the biblical record leaves unexplained. After all, in Lev 18:22 and 20:13 why should the "active" partner be condemned if the active-passive distinction rep-resents the basic structure of all sexual activity? And if activity-passivity represents the basic structure of the sexual act, just how does it work in the prohibition of bestiality (18:23), where not only men but also women are included in the prohibition?

If the active-passive/domination-subordination structure does not provide a clue about what motivates the prohibition, the idiom in 18:22 and 20:13 does provide the reader with an indication. It does not seem too adventurous to suppose that what finally is at issue is a violation of role expectations and to that extent a boundary violation between the sexes, apparently the willing or unwilling assumption of vaginal recep-tivity by a male. In other words, it is not the quality or kind of sexual conduct that is at issue but the violation of roles as such.[24] For even if the terminology for intercourse we have examined is not hierarchical, it is scripted exclusively for men and women (cf. 18:23). In fact, the very absoluteness of the prohibition underlines the gender expectations for intercourse—namely, a man and a woman—even as it entertains no other considerations, including status. (Consequently, in Lev 20:13, where punishment is stipulated for the offense, both participants are fi-nally held accountable, with no distinction made between the insertive partner and the receptive partner.[25]) This is not to deny that status en-ters into the construction of gender in ancient Israel; nor is it to deny the jurisdiction of the male over a woman's reproductive capacity and sexual function, implicit in the Levitical designation for the female partner "the nakedness of" (a specific male), *ʿerwat* PN (Lev 18:8b, 10,

14, 16b).[26] But where—according to David Halperin—power is at issue in the symmetry of the sexual act in classical Greece, here the essential consideration is gender.[27] Its violation renders the act abhorrent, an "abomination."[28] In short, sexual intercourse here, while scripted for gender, does not include in that script a difference in status for man and woman.[29]

If one allows for the different intents behind the lists of prohibitions in Leviticus 18 and 20 and Mesopotamian legal texts,[30] legislation from the *Middle Assyrian Laws* (hereafter *MAL*) provides an instructive comparison. In the context of laws addressing crimes against married women, and immediately following upon a law concerned with a false accusation of male prostitution (repeated acts of apparently voluntary receptive intercourse),[31] *MAL* A 20 addresses the case of intercourse between two men of the same rank (or less likely two neighbors):[32] "If a man has sex with his comrade *(tappāšu inīk)* and they prove the charges against him and find him guilty, they shall have sex with him and they shall turn him into a eunuch *(inikkūš ana ša rēšen utarrūš).*"[33] Strikingly, only the initiator (subject) of the action and presumably insertive partner is punished, albeit with less severity than in the Bible or even than could be expected in cases of adultery (*MAL* A 12-13; cf. *MAL* A 15). His punishment has two aspects: (1) application of the *lex talionis* ("they have sex with him") to shame him; and (2) castration to prevent further incidents. But the latter punishment also effects a change in his gender role, as if to suggest again what is at the heart of the crime. Presumably, at issue here is sex forced upon another man—his equal in status ("comrade")—which has the effect of imposing upon that individual a woman's role of receptivity. Given the punishment and the fact that only the subject is punished, the law does not seem to concern itself with consensual sex; and even more, it does not speak to the issue of sex between men of different statuses. By highlighting that the victim is a *tappû* (a social equal) the law suggests that were the act perpetrated on one of lower status (e.g., a citizen imposing himself on a non-citizen), it would not be punishable. It would not be punishable because the act of intercourse was structured along lines of domination and subordination. In sum, *MAL* A 20 does not prohibit same-sex relations between men without qualification: it suggests instead that the status of the coerced partner is decisive.

The relative importance of status in *MAL* stands in sharp contrast to the absoluteness of the biblical prohibition, which admits of no qualification for status, age, or even mutual consent, even as it provides no

explanation or justification for the prohibition. This complete absence
of qualification in the biblical prohibitions, combined with the drastic
nature of the punishment, which finally is specified only in Lev 20:13,
does not suggest in fact a formulation that has as its goal the exploration and application of legal principle. Instead these formulations,
particularly the direct prohibition of Lev 18:22 with its "You shall not
. . . ," suggest a kind of sermonic rhetoric that in the context of a con-
fessing community has as its goal admonition. Even if these prohibitions have their origins elsewhere, catechesis and instruction intent on
the demarcation and consolidation of the community are now responsible for their present shape.[34]

THE PLACEMENT OF THE PROHIBITIONS
IN THE HOLINESS CODE

The impression that the formulation of the individual prohibitions
in Lev 18:22 and 20:13 reflects a catechetical/instructional intent rather
than jurisprudence is reinforced when one examines the context in
which they are found, namely, the lists of prohibitions that comprise
Leviticus 18 and 20 of H. Olyan is probably correct about the lack of
any necessary and original connection between these prohibitions of
male sexual relations and the various prohibitions now surrounding
them concerning incest (Lev 18:6-18; 20:11-12, 14, 17, 19-21), adultery
(Lev 18:20; 20:10), bestiality (Lev 18:23; 20:15-16), and child sacrifice
(Lev 18:21; 20:1-5), all of which in contrast to 18:22 and 20:13 find
parallels elsewhere in the OT.[35] It thus comes as no surprise that commentators have been preoccupied with trying to determine what motivated the tradents of these chapters to make the association here and how
this shapes the reader's understanding of the proscribed behavior.

Despite repeated attempts to find a single overarching principle
(e.g., association with idolatry, the wasting of a man's "seed," mixing of
defiling fluids, conformity to a class),[36] no consensus has yet emerged
on the unspoken rationale governing the association of all these varied
proscriptions. As we have already seen, no explicit reason is offered for
the ban on male-male sexual relations in 18:22 or 20:13 or for what
amounts to its condemnation, "It is an abomination *(tôʿēbâ)*" (18:22b;
cf. 20:13a). The usage of *tôʿēbâ* is simply too broad to be of much help
even if all of the prohibited acts preceding the redactional frame of vv.
26-30 are also called such. Olyan is probably correct when he observes

on the basis of *tôʿēbâ*'s appearance only in 18:22 that its use here was original and that it was subsequently generalized in the framing material of 18:26-30.[37] But an explanation of sorts is also precisely what is provided by the didactic frames H creates for the lists in Leviticus 18 and 20 (18:1-5, 24-30; 20:7-8, 22-26).

Considerations of uncleanness, or impurity—absent from the individual prohibitions—now become paramount in 18:24-30 and 20:22-24, 26. The forbidden practices bring defilement upon those who do them as well as upon the land. They are in fact the very kinds of things done by the nations *(haggôyîm)* whom God is casting out, and whom, even more, the defiled land, now personified, vomits out (18:25; 20:23). So Israel must take care not to follow in their ways or the land will vomit Israel out, too (18:28; 20:22). Israel must be holy (20:7, 26) for her God is YHWH, who is holy (19:2), and has set Israel apart from other peoples (20:24, 26).[38]

This linkage of the prohibitions of same sex-relations in 18:22 and 20:13 with the purity concerns of the H tradents has been widely remarked upon. Indeed it is precisely this linkage that has led many to conclude that H's concern in prohibiting same-sex relations is "merely" ritual purity, of the same order as the dietary restrictions alluded to, for example, in 20:25. As Boswell puts it, the author of Leviticus did not regard homosexual conduct as intrinsically evil, like rape or theft, but "ritually unclean for Jews, like eating pork or engaging in intercourse during menstruation."[39] Boswell bases this interpretation on his understanding of the word *tôʿēbâ*, "abomination," and its association in his mind with Gentile practices and with what is ritually unclean. Therefore when Lev 18:22 uses the term in reference to same-sex relations between males it is actually urging Jews to avoid what is associated with "ethnic contamination or idolatry"—in this case, temple prostitution. As such, Lev 18:22 and 20:13 are valid only for ancient Israel and have no relationship to modern homosexuality, which is not in any case connected to idolatry.

Boswell's understanding of the term *tôʿēbâ* along with its distinction between intrinsically evil acts and mere ritual violations has been thoroughly rejected as foreign to the book of Leviticus and requires no further comment here.[40] As Greenberg has said, everything prohibited by God is wrong for the authors of Leviticus, including violations of the menstrual taboo or of the dietary laws. But what has not been sufficiently noted in response to those who, like Boswell, dismiss H's purity concerns in the framing of the prohibitions is the nature of the distinction between moral purity and ritual purity and the fact that same-sex relations are clearly associated in the H redaction with a concern for the former and not the latter. Note that according to the H framing materials in Lev 18:26, the prohibition of same-sex relations in Leviticus—far from being something simply of concern to the Israelites in the land—applies unequivocally to all who reside in the land, even as it had applied to those who preceded the Israelites.

The distinction between moral purity and ritual purity has been recently reviewed by Jonathan Klawans, and this discussion depends upon his analysis of the biblical data.[41] The starting point is the recognition that certain sins defile in a way that is different from but just as real as the bodily defilements described in Leviticus 11–15 and Numbers 19. On the one hand, so-called "ritual defilement" is the consequence of direct or secondary contact with a variety of purely natural processes, among them childbirth (Lev 12:1-8), an infectious scaly disease (Lev 13:1–14:32), various genital discharges (Lev 15:1-33), carcasses of animals (Lev 11:1-47), and human corpses (Num 19:10-22). The duration of the impurity in each case may vary, and how one cleanses himself or herself may also vary. But the essential characteristics of this kind of impurity or uncleanness, as summarized by Klawans, are clear: "it is natural, more or less unavoidable, generally not sinful, and typically impermanent."[42] "As far as the biblical law is concerned, the leper is ritually impure, but the leper is not guilty. Thus the following claim still stands: it is not sinful to be ritually impure, and ritual impurity does not result from sin."[43]

Quite different, on the other hand, is moral impurity. Here certain acts—among them various sexual transgressions such as incest or same-sex intercourse between males (Lev 18:6-29), idolatry (19:31), child-sacrifice to Moloch (20:1-3), and bloodshed (Num 35:34-35)—are considered so serious that they are thought to defile. But significantly, while these acts result in moral impurity on the sinner (Lev 18:24), the land (18:25; Ezek 36:7), and the sanctuary (Lev 20:3; Ezek 5:11), *they do not result in ritual defilement.* There is no defilement of those proximate to the sinner nor is there the threat of contagion found in ritual impurity. As a result, one does not have to bathe subsequent to contact with an idolater, a murderer, or someone guilty of sexual transgression. Instead of a purification rite, moral purity is restored by the punishment imposed upon the sinner or the sinner's atonement.[44]

There is no suggestion, moreover, that the land, which has been defiled by these sorts of transgressions, is only ritually impure. Rather it suffers what Klawans calls "a non-contagious degradation," a kind of shameful degradation, the ultimate result of which if unchecked is the exile of the land's inhabitants (Lev 18:24-29; Ezekiel 36; Isaiah 24).[45] Even if different from ritual defilement, the degradation is substantial and no mere figure of speech, leading as it does to tangible consequences for the sinner or those who are complicit. Of course, that is what the language of defilement itself suggests: the moral impurity represents a change in the condition of the infected party or object no less real for not being visible, coming upon a person or thing from without as an external threat, like a disease, rather than simply a kind of projection or manifestation of some subjective or interior state.

Modern legal systems in talking about wrongful conduct that is harmful distinguish between "torts" and "crimes." Where torts are viewed as purely personal wrongs against the victim and generally of a lower moral culpability, where the initiative for proceeding against the guilty party is in the hands of the victim and the state's interest is limited to the victim's compensation, a crime is a wrong against society itself. As such, the initiative to proceed belongs to the state, regardless of whether there is a specific victim or not, and without regard to the victim's own wishes, for the purpose of the state's intervention is not to compensate the victim but to punish the offender.[46]

Ancient Near Eastern codes, however, evidence three categories of wrongs, albeit with a considerable degree of overlap, the second and third of which correspond to crime in the modern sense. These three categories are: (1) harmful acts with a low level of culpability comparable to modern torts; (2) acts with a high level of moral culpability (incest or blasphemy) Westbrook calls "public offenses," thought to bring down divine wrath on the whole society in the form of plagues or military disasters, by means of a pollution which it was society's responsibility to rid itself of; and (3) acts Westbrook calls "private offenses," which make up the prime examples of crimes today (e.g., homicide, rape, theft, etc.).[47]

According to this scheme, then, by its inclusion in the list of sexual transgressions, the intercourse between males prohibited in Lev 18:22 and 20:13 is, for the H tradents of this material, at least, regarded as public offense, implicating the whole of society and of sufficient seriousness to warrant divine sanctions against that society (Lev 18:24-28; 20:22-23). While an immediate conclusion about the morality of same-sex relations today on the basis of this judgment is unwarranted, the point to be made here is that for H a violation of the prohibition of same-sex relations is not "merely" a matter of ritual purity, on the order of an infraction of the dietary rules as claimed by Boswell and others, but an issue of moral purity, a public "crime," if you will, that implicates not only the offender and his/her immediate circle but in fact the whole of Israelite society.

THE IMPLICATIONS OF THE H REDACTION
FOR THE OT PERSPECTIVE AND ITS CONTRIBUTION
TO THE CURRENT DISCUSSION

The cautions expressed above about the usefulness of the Bible in contemporary discussions of homosexuality make it clear that the Bible's prohibition of same-sex relations in Leviticus cannot be immediately translated into a norm for today without significant interpretation. Yet just as in cases where experience and reflection in the light of the Gospel have rendered explicit OT interdictions and commands non-binding for Christians (e.g., prohibitions against sexual relations with a menstruant woman, Lev 18:19) or even morally repugnant (e.g., the extermination of the Canaanites, Deut 7:1-5), so here too what is decisive finally is the claim the biblical text makes on the reader to grapple with the questions to which it responds and the process of reflection it inspires. For those who find in the Bible God's word addressed to them for today this remains the heart of obedience.

In that spirit a significant issue emerges from the foregoing study of Lev 18:22 and 20:13 for the contemporary Christian construction of (homo)sexuality, especially in light of H's shaping of these prohibitives. As already intimated, this has to do with what might be called the "public" character of same-sex relations in the OT in the face of contemporary society's insistence on sexual behavior as what is most inward, individual, and private, the personal expression of some unique sexuality.[48] This perspective comes out in several ways, including initially the very manner in which H in its framing materials (e.g., Lev 18:1-5; 20:7-8, 23-24, 26) takes conformity to its norms in this area as a way of expressing the distinctive character of the Israelite *community*. "Do not follow the customs of the nations (*gôyîm*) which I am casting out before you . . . ," (20:23) says the Lord through Moses to the assembled Israelite men; and H's rhetoric here is designed to consolidate the post-exilic Jewish community by a strategy of separation and exclusion. What moderns take as most intimate and personal here becomes a question of national self-definition.

It is striking, too, that for H the consequence of a violation of the ban on same-sex relations in Lev 18:22 and 20:13 is specifically "defilement," an "archaic conception of fault" conceived of symbolically in the guise of a quasi-physical stain or blemish infecting a person from without and pointing to a "quasi-moral unworthiness" (Ricoeur).[49] In other words, the consequences avowed by H are conceived, albeit primitively, as in some sense exterior and objective, as if to suggest that what one does with one's sexuality is inevitably drawn into webs of sociality that comprise one's individual identity. Sexual behavior is not in some sense an issue simply of sexuality, and for H the interdiction on same-sex relations occurs, as we have seen, in a list of prohibitions comprised of those offenses that might be called "public" as opposed to "private." Sex involves role-playing, and the roles are those determined by one's place in society, which in ancient Israel is based in good part, if not primarily, on the physiologically grounded taxonomy of male and female.[50]

As a symbol, there can be no question of completely elucidating the nature of the "defilement" envisioned by the H tradents. Defilement for the ancients adheres to everything that is terrifying, dangerous, or unusual.[51] For its part, the text itself offers nothing that might explain the motivation behind the taboo. All that is clear is that the "trigger" for the defilement occasioned by same-sex relations is some transgression of the physiologically determined gender structure that insists on sexual relations being reserved for a man and a woman. The roles of men and women are clear and distinct, and the prohibitions of Lev 18:22 and 20:13 eliminate the possibility of slippage resulting from men's assuming, or being subjected to, the role of a woman. Essentially, they enforce an isomorphic relationship between one's identity as male or female and gender roles (the latter being cultural constructions of the former), with no "space" left for an individual's unique "sexuality" to compete with or challenge the resulting construction.

To the extent that a gender role is the basis of an individual's larger role in society this restriction on the construction of gender roles brings the performance of sexual acts essentially within the public arena rather than confining it to the personal and private world of the individual. Sexual acts, in other words, are for the OT manifestations of sociality rather than of what is most intimate and personal to the individual sexual performer. As such, the morality of sexual acts is established by their conformity to the expectations that accompany gender roles, and this analysis, to be complete, hinges upon an evaluation of the overall contribution these gender roles make to the social life of the community.

Paul Ricoeur has remarked that there is probably no taboo in which "there does not dwell some reverence, some veneration of order."[52] If so, can we say more about the order promoted by the prohibitions of Lev 18:22 and 20:13? Sara Melcher, for example, has suggested that all these laws in chapters 18 and 20 seem to be aimed at the protection of pure patrilineal inheritance, noting that if the system of land tenure fails, the "sons of Israel will find themselves literally landless."[53] There is much to be said for this, given H's framing of the laws. All the same, it is difficult, as Melcher admits, to reduce these complex texts to one factor alone, and it is hard to see how the interdiction of male intercourse is essential to preserve the lines of descent.[54] So, might the motivation simply be the preservation and enhancement of the patriarchal system itself? Certainly, the apparent effort to enforce the strict separation of gender roles would argue in favor of such an understanding, at least to the extent that these gender roles also carry status claims with them. Yet even so it is not clear that a ban on male (anal) intercourse necessarily promotes patriarchy, if to some extent, at least, sexual interaction can be a mechanism for social bonding (e.g., inter-generationally, as in classical Athens), and when in classical Athens, where pederasty was institutionalized and same-sex relations tolerated within limits, the position of women was arguably more severely restricted than in ancient Israel. Indeed, the pederastic ideal, as practiced in classical Greece, seems in good part to have been motivated by a considerable distrust of women's spiritual and intellectual resources.[55]

Rather than patriarchal institutions as such being fostered by the Levitical ban, perhaps all we can say is that the insistence on gendering sexual acts represents more generally simply one strategy—among many others—for clearly subordinating the goals and aspirations of the individual sexual performer to the goals of the community to which he or she belongs, and promoting social solidarity. This comes through the insistence on the individual's identification, to the extent possible, with the role assigned by one's place in the family and the larger communal structures founded upon it. As already suggested, in the absence of a conception of the person having "inner depths" that are the genuine source of one's personal identity, one simply is one's social role and does not simply play a role distinct from who one is publicly. So sexual intercourse truly is a social act, a manifestation of socially constructed gender roles rather than simply an expression of one's sexuality. The comments of David Halperin on the essentially social determination of sexual life in classical Athens are largely relevant here as well:

If there is a lesson that historians should draw from this picture of ancient sexual attitudes and behaviors, it is that we need to de-center *sexuality* from the focus of the interpretation of sexual experience. Just because modern bourgeois Westerners are so obsessed with sexuality, so convinced that it holds the key to the hermeneutics of the self (and, hence to social psychology as an object of historical study), we ought not therefore to conclude that everyone has always considered sexuality a basic and irreducible element in, or a central feature of, human life. On the contrary . . . it seems that many ancients conceived of sexuality in non-sexual terms: what was fundamental to their experience of sex was not anything *we* would regard as essentially sexual; rather, it was something essentially social—namely, the modality of power relations that informed and structured the sexual act. Instead of viewing public and political life as a dramatization of individual sexual psychology, as we often tend to do, they saw sexual behavior as an expression of the dominant themes in contemporary social relations.[56]

Whatever the differences in the construction of sexual experience between ancient Israel and classical Greece, the essential point is the social determination of the sexual experience. As such, it stands in sharp contrast to the contemporary Western view of sexual identity as a private and personal realm, at once individual and autonomous, where a larger society's interests have no place not granted it by the individual.

This fundamental contrast between the modern West and the OT, however, reveals more than the distance we stand from ancient Israel. It also lays bare the fact of choice and decision. If, with Kluckhohn, we may say that all societies share more or less the same basic stock of values, to the extent that what we call values represent "solutions" to common human problems, then the contrast we are sketching here is only relative and not an absolute dichotomy.[57] Put differently, if every society struggles with how to order individual needs and goals with the interests of society and the larger communities to which we belong, where we and biblical Israel differ in our attitudes to sexual experience is in the ranking of certain values associated with it and in the degree of our explicitness about these values.

Biblical Israel and the modern West seem to be at opposite ends of a spectrum when it comes to how we view sexual experience and the goals of sexual life. As such, the OT's construction of sexuality becomes a kind of mirror in which we can recognize those elements or dimensions of sexuality we tend to suppress in an insistence on sex as essentially private and personal. We must, as David Halperin concludes, "be willing to admit that what seem to be our most inward, authentic, and private experiences are actually, in Adrienne Rich's admirable phrase, 'shared, unnecessary / and political.'"[58] Particularly within the Catholic tradition, where notions of the common good and community have always played a role in moral discernment, the analysis of sexuality, including the critical evaluation of gender constructs as well as specific erotic behaviors and sexual lifestyles, cannot be confined to the realm of what is merely private and personal but needs to be carried out also within the framework of a comprehensive social ethics.

This is a challenge the OT's construal of sexuality offers to contemporary constructions—whether heterosexual or homosexual—and for all people, sexually active or not, including celibates. At some level one's sexuality is not one's own but manifests, and should indeed manifest, a social and communal dimension. Procreation, traditionally understood in the Catholic Church as one of the ends of sexual relations, is one, but certainly not the only way for this social and communal dimension to come out. This dimension is expressed in the traditional upholding of the unitive or love-making purpose of sexual activity as well. The bonding of people into intimate partnerships serves the common good by providing people with mutual support and companionship, as well as by creating stable households in which children and/or aged parents and others might be nurtured well.

As evident for those who are infertile, single, or celibate, even the command given in Gen 1:28 to multiply cannot be fulfilled in the same way, even if all of us—gay or straight—stand under the same obligation.[59] Perhaps only in a society characterized by "mechanical solidarity," in Durkheim's phrasing, such as biblical Israel, would one want to insist on a univocal response to one's obligations to the community in the area of sexual life. But in the complex, now global society in which we live, there may well be multiple ways of embodying these values. While not every imaginable gender construction serves the commonweal, fidelity to the biblical witness does not require that our inter- and intra-generational obligations play themselves out in the same, univocal way they did in ancient Israel.

If through the claim that the OT makes on a Christian today the goods of society need to be rediscovered in discussions of sexuality, this does not mean that those in the Church who condemn homosexuality in the name of the Church's traditional teaching can rest self-satisfied that their proscription enjoys incontestable biblical warrant. The perspective that the OT opens up, even in its harsh prohibitions of same-sex relations in Leviticus, ought to be a word of challenge to all the faithful. In this sense the Bible needs to function as a kind of "common ground" for liberal and conservative alike. The Church, especially its teachers, needs to actively listen to the gay community's own articulation of its sexual experience. It needs to hear how gays and lesbians see the expression of their sexuality in the service of specific and concrete social goals.[60] The gay community, especially the Christians therein, needs to listen to this biblical word about the communal and public character of sexuality. The claim of the OT, including its prohibitions, will be honored in the end only when all those addressed by it seriously grapple with the subject matter and in that sense experience again the very questionableness of their own most precious convictions.

NOTES: CHAPTER 6

In addition to the comments and suggestions of members of my working group contributing to this volume, especially Mary E. Hunt and Cristina L. H. Traina, I wish to acknowledge in particular the contribution of my graduate research assistant, Patricia Walters, and, of course, Patricia Beattie Jung and Joseph Coray for organizing the project and seeing this volume to its completion.

[1] Congregation for the Doctrine of the Faith, "On the Pastoral Care of Homosexual Persons," *Origins* 16 (November 13, 1986) 379.

[2] Although the Roman Catholic canon of the Old Testament goes beyond the bounds of the traditional Hebrew (and Aramaic) Bible and therefore would include, in particular, the Wisdom of Solomon, a book potentially relevant to this investigation, this study will limit itself to those books that comprise the protocanonical books of the Old Testament.

[3] John Boswell, *Christianity, Social Tolerance and Homosexuality: Gay People in Western Europe from the Beginning of the Christian Era to the Fourteenth Century* (Chicago: University of Chicago Press, 1980) 93–96. Boswell attempts to argue that "to know" means in Gen 19:1-11 only "to get acquainted" and that the crime of the Sodomites is the violation of the guests' rights to privacy in accordance with the laws of hospitality. For a full treatment of this problem see Lynne C. Boughton, "Biblical Texts and Homosexuality: A Response to John Boswell," *Irish Theological Quarterly* 58 (1992) 142–43.

[4] Martti Nissinen, *Homoeroticism in the Biblical World: A Historical Perspective,* trans. Kirsi Stjerna (Minneapolis: Fortress, 1998) 51.

[5] Erhard S. Gerstenberger, *Leviticus: A Commentary,* The Old Testament Library (Louisville: Westminster John Knox, 1996) 288–89; Nissinen, *Homoeroticism in the Biblical World,* 37–38.

[6] Raymond Westbrook, "Punishments and Crimes," *Anchor Bible Dictionary,* ed. David N. Freedman (New York: Doubleday, 1992) 5:546–47.

[7] David M. Halperin, "Sex Before Sexuality: Pederasty, Politics, and Power in Classical Athens," in John Corvino, ed., *Same Sex: Debating the Ethics, Science, and Culture of Homosexuality* (Lanham, Md.: Rowman & Littlefield, 1997) 203–4; Gerstenberger, *Leviticus,* 288–89. According to Halperin (367, n. 1) the English use is most likely wrongly attributed by the *OED* to Charles Gilbert Chaddock. The German original was produced apparently by the translator and *littérateur* Karl Maria Kertbeny (367, n. 2). For its part, the term "heterosexuality" appears in English eight years after "homosexuality" (206).

[8] Halperin, "Sex Before Sexuality," 204.

[9] Ibid. 205.

[10] Ibid. 207–8.

[11] Robert Di Vito, "Here One Need Not Be Oneself: The Concept of 'Self' in the Hebrew Scriptures," in David Aune and John McCarthy, eds., *The Whole and Divided Self* (New York: Crossroad, 1997) 49–88, especially 52. See also my "Old Testament Anthropology and the Construction of Personal Identity," *CBQ* 61 (1999) 220.

[12] Charles Taylor, *Sources of the Self: The Making of the Modern Identity* (Cambridge, Mass.: Harvard University Press, 1989) 4.

[13] Ibid. 111–26.

[14] Di Vito, "Here One Need Not Be Oneself," 59–60. The closest Hebrew *nepeš* ever gets to acquiring this status is in a usage that extends its basic meaning of "throat" and its characteristic activity "need," or "desire," but none of the emotions associated with this usage are *nepeš*-specific.

[15] Di Vito, "Here One Need Not Be Oneself," 63–71.

[16] Augustine, *De Doctrina Christiana,* III xv–xvi.

[17] On the so-called apodictic law style see Gerstenberger, *Leviticus,* 264–65.

[18] Insofar as the text was written (presumably) by men for men, one explanation of the fact that women are not included in a similarly-framed prohibition about lesbianism here—or, for that matter, anywhere in the Hebrew Bible —may be simple ignorance on the part of men about what was going on. But more may be implied. See below.

[19] This also applies to v. 21 which concerns the sacrifice of one's offspring (lit. "seed") to Molech.

[20] Oral sex, however, cannot be excluded. If the idiom "the lying down of a woman" refers to (vaginal) intercourse (see below), then its use to describe homosexual relations can only be analogous.

[21] Further, since the idiom used in Lev 18:20 and 20:13 occurs nowhere else and is never used in the same context with the idiom *miškab zākār*, one has little basis for calling the two idioms a word-pair, especially when one does not expect, as Olyan acknowledges, the pairing of *ʾiššâ* with *zākār*, but *ʾîš*.

[22] Nissinen, *Homoeroticism in the Biblical World*, 43–44. Although he provides no discussion, note, however, that in connection with the interpretation of *MAL* 20, Westbrook observes that the distinction between "active and passive sodomy, the latter being the lot of the lower orders of society . . . finds no echo in the biblical law." See Westbrook, "Punishments and Crimes," 549.

[23] Here I take obvious issue with Nissinen's interpretation of the term's significance as a window onto the actual structure of the act of intercourse in ancient Israel; cf. Nissinen, *Homoeroticism in the Biblical World*, 43–44.

[24] For the significance the issue of boundary violation has in Paul's thought see, for example, Bernadette Brooten, *Love Between Women: Early Christian Responses to Female Homoeroticism* (Chicago: University of Chicago Press, 1996) 209, 213, 275–76, 298.

[25] If, as Olyan asserts, the shift to the plural subject in 20:13 "they" (following upon the *casus pendens*; cf. 18:22, singular "you") is awkward, this suggests that this stipulation of punishment for both parties is the result of redactional work. In the original formulation of prohibition—prior to its present placement—Lev 20:13 mandated punishment for only the insertive partner, even as 18:22 is addressed only to him. See Saul M. Olyan, "'And with a Male You Shall Not Lie the Lying Down of a Woman': On the Meaning and Significance of Leviticus 18:22 and 20:13," in Gary David Comstock and Susan E. Henking, eds., *Que(e)Rying Religion* (New York: Continuum, 1997) 401–2.

[26] On the significance of the idiom see Sarah J. Melcher, "The Holiness Code and Human Sexuality," in Robert L. Brawley, ed., *Biblical Ethics and Homosexuality* (Louisville: Westminster John Knox, 1996) 94–95. But Melcher also notes in 20:17 a usage that represents an apparent exception to the pattern in ch. 18, remarking that this verse is exceptional in portraying the woman as an equal partner in the prohibited sexual act.

[27] Halperin, "Sex Before Sexuality," 215–17.

[28] See here Olyan, "'And with a Male You Shall not Lie,'" 514, n. 3. Note, contra Boswell, *Christianity, Social Tolerance, and Homosexuality*, 100, that while

the usage of the term *tô'ēbâ* is open to some interpretation, it does not indicate that the character of the offense here is "merely" cultic.

[29] It is perhaps noteworthy—given the thoroughly patriarchal character of ancient Israel—that, nonetheless, in Lev 20:9 the prohibition of cursing applies to both the mother and the father.

[30] On the differences between Mesopotamia's legal texts and modern legislation see Westbrook, "Punishments and Crimes," 546–47. On the catechetical and instructional intent behind the lists of prohibitions in Leviticus 18 and 20 see Gerstenberger, *Leviticus*, 261–64.

[31] Nissinen, *Homoeroticism in the Biblical World*, 25. The discussion that follows is heavily indebted to the analysis of Nissinen, ibid. 24–28.

[32] On the meaning of the term *tappā'u*, see J. Bottéro and H. Petschow, "Homosexualität," *Reallexikon der Assyriologie* (Berlin: de Gruyter, 1972–1975) 4:461–62; *Akkadisches Handwörterbuch*, Wolfram von Soden, ed., 3 vols. (Wiesbaden: Otto Harrassowitz, 1965–1981) 1321–22; Olyan, "'And with a Male You Shall not Lie,'" 405.

[33] For the English translation see Nissinen, *Homoeroticism in the Biblical World*, 25.

[34] Gerstenberger, *Leviticus*, 302–4.

[35] Olyan, "'And with a Male You Shall Not Lie,'" 398–99.

[36] For a summary of recent proposals see Olyan, "'And with a Male You Shall not Lie,'" 408–12. Olyan's own proposal involves a variation of a ban on mixing defiling fluids.

[37] See Olyan, "'And with a Male You Shall Not Lie,'" 514, n. 3.

[38] It is striking that there is not a single reference here in the H redactional framework to the structure of creation (Gen 1:27) or to the divine command to procreate (Gen 1:28) as a possible argument in favor of a number of the prohibitions regarding particular kinds of sexual relations.

[39] Boswell, *Christianity, Social Tolerance, and Homosexuality*, 100–1.

[40] See, among others, David F. Greenberg, *The Construction of Homosexuality* (Chicago: University of Chicago Press, 1988) 195–96.

[41] Jonathan Klawans, "The Impurity of Immorality in Ancient Judaism," *Journal of Jewish Studies* 48.1 (1997) 1–16.

[42] Of course, to refuse to purify oneself or to contact the holy while in a condition of impurity may very well be sinful (Lev 7:20-21; 15:31; 22:3-7); Klawans, "The Impurity of Immorality," 2.

[43] Klawans, "The Impurity of Immorality," 3.

[44] According to Klawans ("The Impurity of Immorality," 8) in the Dead Sea Scrolls one sees the association between moral purity and ritual purity carried a step further: now "all sin, in and of itself, renders the sinner ritually defiling —even without any outward manifestation of a ritual defilement. . . . For the Qumran sectarian, there is not merely an association between ritual and moral impurity, there is a nearly complete identification of ritual and moral impurity."

[45] Klawans, "The Impurity of Immorality," 5.

[46] Westbrook, "Punishments and Crimes," 548.

[47] Ibid.

[48] For a similar point of view from a lesbian feminist perspective see the discussion in this volume by Mary E. Hunt, "Catholic Lesbian Feminist Theology: A Sketch for a Portrait."

[49] Paul Ricoeur, *The Symbolism of Evil*, trans. Emerson Buchana (Boston: Beacon, 1967) 35. It points to "quasi-moral unworthiness" for Ricoeur because the distinction between the pure and the impure in its most general terms embraces the division of the physical and the ethical and does not fundamentally distinguish at this level between the misfortune which happens to one and the evil one does (26–27).

[50] As noted by Herman C. Waetjen ("Same-Sex Sexual Relations in Antiquity and Sexuality and Sexual Identity in Contemporary American Society," in Robert L. Brawley, ed., *Biblical Ethics and Homosexuality* [Louisville: Westminster John Knox, 1996] 104), in Genesis 1–2 "creation and its cosmic order do not originate from a primordial struggle between the binary realities of male and female, nor are women identified with nature while men are representative of culture. Nevertheless, gender differentiation is a structural reality of creation and is therefore determinative of life in society."

[51] Ricoeur, *Symbolism of Evil*, 12.

[52] Ricoeur, *Symbolism of Evil*, 43.

[53] Melcher, "The Holiness Code and Human Sexuality," 98–99.

[54] This has been noted also by Tikva Frymer-Kensky, "Law and Philosophy: The Case of Sex in the Bible," *Semeia* 45 (1989) 96–97.

[55] Nissinen, *Homoeroticism in the Biblical World*, 58–69.

[56] Halperin, "Sex Before Sexuality," 218.

[57] Florence Rockwood Kluckhohn and Fred L. Strodtbeck, *Variations in Value Orientations* (Evanston, Ill.: Row, Peterson and Company, 1961) 1–10.

[58] Halperin, "Sex Before Sexuality," 219.

[59] Choon-Leong Seow, "Textual Orientation," in Robert L. Brawley, ed., *Biblical Ethics and Homosexuality* (Louisville: Westminster John Knox, 1996) 10.

[60] See here, for example, Hunt, "Catholic Lesbian Feminist Theology."

7

Romans 1:26-27: The Claim that Homosexuality Is Unnatural

Leland J. White

*Leviticus says, "A man shall not lie with a man as with a woman."
No man does that. When a man lies with a man, he lies about how
much sex he's had. When a man lies with a woman, he lies about
how much money he makes.*

Jerry Seinfeld (1998), a talk-show comment

*The texts we study are, for the most part, rather like men's coffee-
house talk. Their legislative intent contains a fair amount of bluff,
of saving face: they regularly lay down laws which are belied by the
jokes those same men will later tell. What we do not have written
down are the stage directions (as it were) for those texts—the
crossed fingers, the knowing nods of conspiratorial agreement.*

John J. Winkler (1990) 70

*The belief that the hostility of the Christian Scriptures to homo-
sexuality caused Western society to turn against it should not require
any elaborate refutation. The very same books which are thought to
condemn homosexual acts condemn hypocrisy in the most strident
terms, and on greater authority: and yet Western society did not
create any social taboos against hypocrisy, did not claim that*

hypocrites were "unnatural," did not segregate them into an oppressed minority, did not enact laws punishing their sin with castration or death. No Christian state, in fact, has passed laws against hypocrisy per se, despite its continual and explicit condemnation by Jesus and the church. In the very same list which has been claimed to exclude from the kingdom of heaven those guilty of homosexual practices, the greedy are also excluded. And yet no medieval states burned the greedy at the stake. Obviously some factors beyond biblical precedent were at work in late medieval states which licensed prostitutes . . . but burned gay people: by any objective standard, there is far more objuration of prostitution in the New Testament than of homosexuality. Biblical strictures have been employed with great selectivity by all Christian states, and in a historical context what determines the selection is clearly the crucial issue.

John Boswell (1980) 7

I will take up Seinfeld and Winkler in due course. John Boswell may focus discussion on the role Rom 1:26-27 has played in the tragedy of Church teaching on sexual ethics in general and homosexual ethics in particular. I cite Boswell not to exonerate the Church—and by Church I mean not only the pastoral and academic magisteria, but all its members—of heterosexist, if not homophobic, teaching and acts. Indeed, secular forces unleashed by the Enlightenment, I insist, set the agenda on the dignity of gay people just as they did on other issues of human dignity such as slavery, totalitarianism, and feminism, to cite but a few recent examples. The Church inevitably arrives on the scene, in Lonergan's memorable words, "late and out of breath."

Every time a text, a message is sent to a target audience, Boswell reminds us, the meaning, significance, and scope of the text will be determined more by the target than by the source. The skillful speaker or considerate writer so far as possible anticipates the effect, conspiring, as Winkler observes, with the target. But even the most skillful and considerate writer fails remote and unanticipated targets unless those remote, unanticipated targets know the protocols[1] governing the construction of the text. The Bible and subsequent traditional Mediterranean sources were not produced by considerate writers because traditional Mediterranean discourse is high-context in nature, which means that writers expected targeted readers to share the context of the writers. Biblical writers did not anticipate twentieth-century Americans who would be unfamiliar with the traditional Mediterranean context, where social protocols corresponding to textual protocols governed.

The present study elaborates a model of the social protocol governing Rom 1:26-27, a text often cited as biblical support for the proposition that homosexuality is unnatural. Comprehensive, hence relatively abstract cultural models are designed to allow testable conclusions about what a text means (see Carney, 1975). Call such models macromodels, if you like: they look beyond a supposed intent of, or direct influence on the author to uncover unacknowledged presuppositions generally at work on what might be called a culture continent, such as traditional Mediterranean society (Gilmore, 1987). Still more abstract models of cultural patterns tracking, for instance, collectivism or individualism also provide testable insight. In the case at hand, φύσις, traditionally translated as "nature," fits within a model of traditional Mediterranean perceptions, judgments, and statements on bodies, social hierarchy, and gender, each of which will be elaborated and tested in terms of Rom 1:26-27.

CULTURAL CONTEXTUALIZATION OF ROMANS 1:26-27

The text of Rom 1:26-27 reads:

> For this reason God gave them up to dishonorable passions. Their women exchanged *natural* [φυσικὴν] [Vulgate *naturalem*] relations [χρῆσιν] for *unnatural* [παρὰ φύσιν] [Vulgate *contra naturam*],[27] and the men likewise gave up *natural* [φυσικὴν] [Vulgate *naturali*] relations [χρῆσιν] with women and were consumed with passion for one another, men committing shameless acts with men and receiving in their own persons the due penalty for their error *(emphasis added)*.

What did Paul mean? Trapped in the quicksand tagged intentional fallacy, any answer to this question is suspect, even Paul's own answer, were it available. The RSV, following Vulgate precedent, translates the key words "natural" and "unnatural." How were these words construed in the world of medieval scholastics such as Aquinas, or the later neo-Thomists who shaped pre-Vatican II moral theology? That is a question for another study. Traditional exegetes were content to do pretty much what Jerome did with the text, substitute the words of their own language for the Greek words.

Biblical scholars awakened by historical criticism have accustomed us to contextualize the text by reconstructing the history of verbal usage, construing words as symbols representing ideas, to be accurately deciphered by recreating the history of the ideas. More recently biblicists and historians have expanded their understanding of history to embrace social history. In each of these cases, in principle, the task of the translator/interpreter is to identify the idea in the target world that corresponds to the idea in the source world and substitute one symbol, one word for the other. Both Boswell and his critics very largely approached Rom 1:26-27 in this manner (White, 1993). Boswell correctly asked why this text was so largely isolated from other proscriptions in the Bible, why it alone, rather than, along with it, proscriptions of such acts as hypocrisy, murder, and adultery, would become a basis for establishing an unmentionable crime.

Sociolinguists, however, reach beyond philology and the history of ideas. Words do not, according to sociolinguists, refer to ideas, least of all to ideas shared by all humans. They refer to realities and the interactions among realities in the social system of those who use them. The shot fired to signal the beginning of a race, or to mark the death of a leader, does not refer to the same social institution as the shot fired by the executioner or the hit man. The semantic fields differ. The more comprehensive our understanding of the social system the better our ability to translate or interpret individual symbols, i.e., words, within a social system. Beyond social institutions are cultures, which embrace not only institutional systems but, more significantly, symbolic systems.

Symbolic systems, cultures, provide overarching frameworks of meaning for individual symbols and institutions. In a word, social systems are micro-social worlds within the macro-social world of a culture. For example, medicine and law occupy micro-social worlds within U.S. culture. Each also might exist within other cultures. If a U.S. lawyer needs to interpret a U.S. doctor's text, familiarity with the contemporary medical lexicon and social context of contemporary medicine is prerequisite. United States professionals largely share and may take for granted the same overarching symbolic system of U.S. culture. Not so other cultures: the contemporary U.S. lawyer and doctor alike, in order to interpret an ancient medical text, require, and must acquire, knowledge not only of ancient medicine but of the much broader social system from which terms such as "health," "disease," etc. derive their meaning. This broader social system, culture, contains clues critical to the interpretation of each of the artifacts produced within it.

Increasingly historians, historical critics of the Bible among them, intuitively appreciate the relevance of cultural difference in reconstructing past meanings. But they often rely on intuitive analysis rather than on macro-social, cross-cultural modeling. Not surprisingly, intuitive contextualization is often inadequate. Even when it is adequate, historians, even social historians, have no basis for replicating or testing the intuitively derived context. More abstract, higher level cultural models are critical for the cross-cultural testing that lends a measured, i.e. social scientific, probability to conclusions about context and meaning.

Social science criticism of the Bible has developed over the last two or three decades to fill the gap between intuitive understanding and testable interpretation. Cultural anthropologists, sociologists, and other social scientists have elaborated and tested models that scholars such as Norman Gottwald (1979), Bruce Malina (1993), and John Elliott (1987) have applied to the social worlds in which biblical texts were composed, heard, and applied. This is not the place to lay out the whole theoretical underpinning of the social science approach. Suffice it to say that it answers a distinctly different question than do other efforts to establish textual context. Its question is not, for example, "Did Paul know how Philo used this or that term?" or, "Did Paul expect his readers to be familiar with Philo's use?" Instead, its question is more like the following: "What was commonly presupposed by the inhabitants of Paul's traditional Mediterranean social world to such a pervasive extent that neither he nor other Mediterraneans had to express them, if in fact they were conscious of them?"

Presuppositions about the body, social hierarchy, and gender are significant elements of the macro-social world that sometimes consciously, but more often subconsciously, may have shaped the sense of "nature" or "natural" not only for Paul but for traditional Mediterraneans who shared his culture.

For example, except for certain specifically sex-related purposes contemporary Americans do not as a matter of rule categorize individuals by gender. Indeed, the rule is so much to the contrary that when it is breached we cry "foul." A great delicacy in South Carolina's Charleston, my home town, is labeled "She-Crab Soup." I have often had to explain to non-Charlestonians that the label is not sexist; the recipe requires a female crab to provide roe, an indispensable ingredient in this lightly sherried delicacy. By way of contrast, only non-Mediterraneans like ourselves would wonder why Mediterraneans will invariably speak of "boy babies" and "girl babies" rather than simply "children" (Malina 1989, 134), why Mediterranean inheritance follows paternal but not maternal descent (or in some cases the reverse), why the Vatican apparently cannot imagine female priests. The purity lines between the genders are always clear because they derive from *social,* not sexual identity (see Nissinen 1998, 60).

Contemporary Americans, focusing on the individual from a psychological perspective, tend to reduce gender to sexual identity. Sexual identity indicates little about social role, and efforts to justify social discrimination based on sexual identity appear as arbitrary as similar justifications of discrimination based on other physical or psychological characteristics such as left-handedness, racial or ethnic or religious background. The gay rights movement, like the feminist movement, is rooted in the Enlightenment protocol that social discrimination on non-instrumental grounds is illegitimate. To state the protocol: All persons physically and mentally able to engage in an activity have a right to do so under similar conditions and circumstances. Being gay or female are individual variations, either beyond choice or legitimately chosen. In either case Americans see little or no social significance where traditional Mediterraneans found it critical to focus on social identity.

"NATURE" (φύσις): WHAT IT INCLUDES

Grasping what "nature" (φύσις) meant to traditional Mediterraneans is difficult. One factor in the difficulty is the fact that we live with categories that govern us as effectively as the Mediterranean categories of male and female. At least from the time of Descartes we have assumed that the categories of nature and spirit, body and soul are mutually exclusive (see Martin 1995, 4). The Cartesian view shapes our lives morally as well as intellectually. In Catholic universities, for example, the "natural" sciences can no longer be imagined to threaten theology. It goes without saying that whatever evolutionary hypotheses may be advanced about the universe, they apply only to the "physical" universe. To theistic believers the "Big Bang" theory explains only the physical effect of a divine will to create. Knowing or investigating an ultimate cause is beyond the realm of the natural sciences.[2] Cartesian dualism differs from even "the most dualistic of ancient philosophers"(Martin 1995, 12), Plato, precisely because Cartesian dualism is ontological, stemming from "two radically different realms of reality" (Martin 1995, 6).[3]

What Cartesian (and modern religious) sensibilities would see in terms of ontological dichotomies, ancient Mediterraneans would see in terms of hierarchy, notably a hierarchy of essence or being. The difference between ancient and Cartesian perspectives may be marked even in the seemingly minor linguistic shift from "hierarchy of being" to "hierarchy of beings." For the ancients hierarchy bespoke a continuum or spectrum rather than one entity or type of entity subordinated to another. This point is exemplified in Hierocles' description of the human self or soul:

> The human being is formed in pregnancy by the seed drawing *hylē* [matter] from the mother's body and with it fashioning the embryo. He speaks of the growing entity throughout as physis (a "piece of nature"? "physique"?) and pneuma ("breath" or "spirit"). "In the early stages, the physique is breath of a rather dense kind and considerably distant from soul; but later, when it is close to birth, it becomes finer . . . So when it passes outside, it is adequate for the environment, with the result that, having been hardened thereby, it is capable of changing into soul." [Hierocles, *Elements of Ethics* I. 5-33, 4.38-53 (HP 53B) cited in Martin 1995, 254 n. 21] *By the gradual process of gestation, physis has become psyche in a progression along a continuous spectrum of what we, but not they, would call matter* (Martin 1995, 10) *(emphasis added).*

Along the continuum that was the hierarchy of being, the elements, *pneuma* notably included, were distributed in different measures so that the human self was not *like*, but *was* a microcosm of the universe at large (Martin 1995, 16). Whether ancients were speaking of medicine or optics, external *pneuma zōtikon* passed through bodily orifices into the arteries, nerves, and inner passageways to provide life to various parts of the body, and it was refined to nourish the *pneuma psychikon*. In short, what would later be categorized as "natural" or "material" differed in degree, not kind, from what we call "supernatural" or "spiritual." Their universe was monistic, differentiated only by the spectrum of refinement along which its one principle occurred.

HIERARCHY AND SOCIAL ORDER

Assume that humans require order. Having constructed a monistic universe, ancient Mediterraneans created meaning, i.e., a sense of place for themselves and for all the features of their universe, by means of a social grid that was *replicated* in their relationship to all the elements of their universe, whether gods or lesser beings.

Replicating cultural patterns across a wide range of activities and relationships is common. Thus, for example, the U.S. value of instrumental mastery, which dictates that each individual person secure the means to control his or her existence, is replicated in child-rearing patterns, choice of work and relationships, access to services, and even security in sickness and retirement. United States lives are ordered by individual choice. Needless to say, no protocol of instrumental mastery obtains in traditional Mediterranean culture. There the group is the arbiter of order, assigning places for all members within two basic collectivist schemes, collateral and lineal (Kluckhohn and Strodtbeck, 1961). United States interpreters sometimes perceive collateral collectivists as egalitarian and non-coercive, if not indeed democratic.

This collateral collectivist pattern is typical of groups lacking social status and power vis-à-vis a dominant surrounding society. The perception by individualist American observers of egalitarian non-coercion in collateral collectivism is largely an illusion. The observer equates lack of control with lack of structure. Romantic portraits of the early Jesus movement phase of Christianity fail to see that maintenance of group boundaries severely circumscribes personal choice. Indeed, structure, for example in the form of patriarchal family control, is not so much lacking as rather unpredictable, owing to the lack of reinforcement by external authorities.[4]

As the Pauline enterprise advanced across the empire toward its Constantinian arrangement it absorbed the lineal collectivism of the empire. Its perspective became increasingly hierarchical, conforming generally to pervasively hierarchical upper-class Mediterranean culture. In the monistic cosmos every facet and element of the universe was perceived in hierarchical terms, and hierarchical social structure was likewise a given. As Mary Douglas insists, "The social body constrains the way the physical body is perceived" (1973, 93). Moreover, bearing in mind that the physical body is a microcosm of the universe, it should not be surprising that the distribution of the elements of the universe, earth, water, fire, air, and *aithēr* among humans accounts for their hierarchical relationships to one another and to all other beings. Earth and water are heavier, lower elements and passive, while fire and air are lighter, capable of causing movement and thus passive or active, while *aithēr* is always in the same condition and active. The body is classed with earth and water, the soul with the last three elements. The soul relates to the body as master to slave. Among humans, in Aristotle's familiar description, women are incomplete males because their bodies do not achieve the degree of dryness, heat, and solidity that males do. A hot, dry womb produces males, while cold, wet wombs issue females.

Hippocrates theorized that female fetuses take forty-two days to form, while the male fetuses take thirty because the female embryo is derived from thinner seed, weaker, and more fluid than the male. So also the male fetus moves at three months, the female at four (*On Generation* 18.1, cited in McLaren 1990, 31).

Much has been made of the fact that traditional Mediterranean sexual relations were characterized by inequality between the parties, making them exercises in domination and submission. For a male to submit to sexual penetration by another male may shame[5] the one submitting, if it does not rob him of his status as a man while exploiting him for the penetrator's benefit.[6] Without questioning that one's status is always a factor, we note that what is immediately relevant appears to be social status rather than one's status in the cosmic order. Thus the following, according to Seneca, are *contra naturam:* hot baths, potted plants, and banquets after sunset (because they cause wakefulness at night and daytime sleep, both unnatural acts). Speaking of sex between males, he condemns men dressing as women or making themselves look youthful (because they indicate that a man wishes to be the sexual object of a man). Contrary to nature, for Seneca in his attack on luxury, is what is contrary to the "simplicity of the unadorned life" or makes one depart from one's place in the social hierarchy (Winkler 1990, 21).

Likewise Dio Chrysostom judged non-reproductive sex unnatural (*Oration* 7, 134–36, 149, cited in Winkler 1990, 21), again not because it violates the cosmic order but because it is "self-indulgent, luxurious and exceedingly appealing" (Winkler 1990, 22). His concern is urban prostitution that provides a luxury market of boys and women, encouraging men to reach out to ever more refined forms of satisfaction, so that they progress from prostitutes to seducing honorable women with money, and finally to young men of good families on the brink of public office. What is contrary to nature is self-indulgence and treating future leaders as if they were slaves in a brothel. The offense is not in the sexual act *per se,* but in the willingness to ignore social hierarchy. It is not a sexual offense, but an offense against class.

A final example from Philo, who follows other moralists who turned to animals for examples, is very telling:

> Not only among animals domesticated and reared by us but also among the other species there are those which appear to have self-restraint. When the Egyptian crocodile . . . is inclined to copulate, he diverts the female to the bank and turns her over, it being natural to approach her

[when she is] lying on her back. After copulating, he turns her over with his forearms. But when she senses the copulation and the impregnation, she becomes malicious in purpose and pretends to desire copulation once more, displaying a harlot-like affection and assuming the usual position for copulation. So he immediately comes to ascertain, either by scent or other means, whether the invitation is genuine or merely pretense. By nature he is alert to hidden things. When the intent of the action is fully established by their looking into each other's eyes, he claws her guts and consumes them, for they are tender. And then unhindered by armored skin or hard and pointed spines, he tears her flesh apart. But enough about self-restraint (Winkler 1990, 23, citing Terian, 89–90).

Does this reveal nature or is it the observer's culture? The male crocodile takes the initiative, takes control, conforms to the missionary position (Winkler 1990, 23 asks if missionaries taught the crocodiles); female desire is wanton, harlot-like. In a fitting exercise of patriarchal duty the male crocodile inflicts "condign punishment" on the spot, tolerating no female self-indulgence, a lesson for all men.

GENDER

The pattern of perceiving the individual as a microcosm of the universe with each including the same elements as all the rest is replicated in Mediterranean perspective with regard to gender, which is not a matter so much of males and females as of masculine and feminine elements, again along a spectrum, both elements being found in both male and female persons.[7] Quoting the Pseudo-Aristotelian *Physiognomy*, Martin points to the "low-spirited man":

"His face is wrinkled, his eyes are dry and weak, but at the same time weakness of the eye signifies two things, softness *[malakos]* and effeminacy *[thēlu]* on the one hand, depression and lack of spirit on the other. He is stooping *[tapeinos]* in figure and feeble *[apēgoreukōs]* in his movements" (808a9-13). The man's weak eye is linked to softness of flesh and hence to the feminine. Contrary to modern heterosexist ideology, be it noted, effeminacy has no relation to homosexuality. The same text explains how to recognize men categorized as "charitable" types: they are "delicate-looking, pale-complexioned and bright-eyed; their nostrils are wrinkled and they are prone to tears. These characters are fond of women and inclined to have female children: they are amorous *(erōtikoi)* by nature, inclined to be reminiscent, of good dispositions and warm hearts" (808a34-38) . . . (1995, 33).

Within this framework boys, closer to the feminine in physique, weaker than the mature males, were more feminine and thus appropriate for passive sexual roles with men (Martin 1995, 34). Schematically, hierarchy dictating male over female, strength over weakness, superior over inferior, each body could be located along the spectrum and thus occupy its proper place in society and nature.

Gender as a matter of social identity distinct from sexual identity or desire means that one plays the masculine role. Masculinity should not be reduced to being active rather than passive. Masculinity means readiness to act honorably, in the public interest, unencumbered by the controls of a master, whether the master is another person or desire for personal gain. Men of honor will control themselves, as they do others, so that the patrimony they hold for their sons, the goods they hold for the state, will not be used merely to gain an object of personal desire. Prostitution is dishonorable because it may represent loss of the control necessary to act freely, not because of sexual acts with other men or with women (see Winkler 1990, 54–64).

A notable inconsistency in Mediterranean ideology, apparent to non-Mediterranean observers, is this: they believed character is set at birth, evidenced in bodily appearance, and yet they employed elaborate procedures to ensure that young bodies were formed in accordance with the aesthetics of their class. Manuals prescribed how women should behave during pregnancy, that they should be sober during intercourse to avoid strange fantasies that might be imprinted on any fetus produced. Examples of after-birth care for the nurse are more detailed: hold the infant upside down by the ankles to straighten the body, giving the spine the right curves; model every body part manually, hollowing out the buttocks, massaging the skull into proper proportions; shape the nose so that it was neither too flat nor too aquiline, etc. Males were of prime concern: genitals were to be manipulated, like other body parts; if the penis appeared to have no foreskin the nurse was to "draw the tip of the foreskin forward or even hold it together with a strand of wool to fasten it . . . [so that it may keep] *natural* good shape" (Martin 1995, 27–28 [emphasis added], quoting Soranus, *Gynecology* 2.16.34 [103]). Martin observes, "What is 'natural' is the body that conforms to the esthetic expectations of the upper class. One must, therefore, gently coerce the body into its 'natural' state" (1995, 28).

The manipulation of the young male body continued through adolescence, its goal being a body neither too soft nor too thick. According to Galen, it should not be exposed to a cold bath until about age twenty-five, at which point a detailed regimen prescribes a series of cold baths administered on successive days, along with anointings, massages, and exercises, all with the purpose of masculinizing the young body (Martin 1995, 28–29). In all these directions a concern to establish a favorable relationship of the body to the environment is evident. Ironically, while a human was a microcosm of the universe, ideal humanity had to be prepared to ward off imbalanced proportions of the elements it shared with the macrocosm.

Sexual identity, then, the critical element in the modern Western category of homosexuality, appears never to be acknowledged in traditional Mediterranean discussions of sexual activity, focused as they are on issues of social status. Gender identity is pervasive, yet scarcely fixed. Both male and female persons have elements of masculinity and femininity, which wax and wane over the course of one's life, and are sufficiently plastic that they might be and were deliberately cultivated. Traditional Mediterranean culture had, therefore, no basis for judging acts between persons of the same sex in the abstract.

Moreover, traditional Mediterranean criteria for judging activities between persons modern Americans would describe as "of the same sex" lead to conclusions profoundly disturbing to us. Where superior age is equated with superior status, for example, pederasty may be not only acceptable but idealized. As Americans, who equate superior age with power (a problematic, if not negative, category for Americans) and superior responsibility, we condemn pederasty as molestation.[8]

INTERPRETING ROMANS 1:26-27

When Paul writes of women and men engaging in relations contrary to nature, modern Western interpreters need to take into account a number of points. First, nature in traditional Mediterranean accounts was organically one. Second, distinctions within nature were drawn on a hierarchical basis, and hierarchy itself was rooted in social status. Third, "women" and "men" differ in social, not psycho-biological identity. Finally, the interpreter has to consider the reason the accusations are made.

According to the androcentric social protocol an accusation that "their women" were out of control condemned the male who should have been in charge, who was potentially deprived of the benefits accruing from possession of a wife, female slave, or daughter (bride price). Males having intercourse with other males were portrayed as lacking appropriate objects, being reduced to the social status of boys or women, or being out of control of themselves, to give only a few of the many possible inferences to be drawn from this behavior.

In addition to the social protocols referred to in the text, there is also the communication protocol that governs the text. What would a writer like Paul have reasonably expected to be the effect of his statement? Of course, the U.S. Bible reader and neo-Thomist moralist both think they know: Paul for them is referring to or possibly articulating an ethical judgment. The Letter to the Romans to the moralist, American or Catholic, is a source for moral theology, a manual of ethics. This presupposition is unconvincing. After all, Paul's attack is on what Romans *other* than those addressed are doing, not the Church in Rome, who would have been the recipients of his moral admonition. It is outsiders, those taken up in idolatry, who are shown to be subject to shameful passions. There is likewise no hint of a corresponding, slippery slope argument that might be stated: if you lust after men, you will end up in idolatry. No, we have an argument against idolatry.

If Paul is not addressing the idolaters, why does he argue against idolatry? It seems to be a case of preaching to the choir. More generally, the protocol that governs this communication is a variation of what we might call coffee-house talk, conversations among men posturing and bluffing among themselves. Perusing accounts Mediterranean males give of their relationships to their wives, especially their apparent delight in making the point of female inferiority and submission, modern Western readers—especially those of the female persuasion—may wonder why these men went off in groups to talk about it rather than staying home where they could have all the immediate benefits of kingship. What actually transpired when they did go home we shall never know because the books we read do not represent the whole picture. They give only the male's story. More significantly, perhaps, they present only that portion of the male's story that a male might tell to other males. As Jerry Seinfeld observes, men lie to men about sex, and to women about what they earned all day long when they were out "at work."

Few, if any, people lie for no reason. Quite often the reason is good enough that the lie is unrecognized even by the liar. Describe the Gospels and Letters to ordinary lay people as early Christian propaganda, which of course they are, and the effect is more often than not devastating. It is devastating because fair-minded Americans see propaganda and advertising as deceptive and manipulative. The same audience of fair-minded Americans in Lake Wobegon will applaud those who say "Lake Wobegon, where all the women are strong, all the men are good-looking, and all the children are above average." We like to live with the conviction that the game of life is stacked in our favor. We differ from traditional Mediterraneans like Paul on a major communication proto-col. Our protocol excludes negative advertising. Life is not for us a zero-sum game of honor. Running down the other side or other groups may destroy the other; among us it will just as certainly injure the one who does it. On the other hand, the communication protocol in Romans reflects the limited good, zero-sum social protocols of traditional Mediterranean life. If John could say, "He must increase. I must de-crease," how likely is Paul or any other traditional Mediterranean spokesman to go negative and personal against outsiders to their move-ment to assert the superior honor of their movement?

Is it possible that embedded in this in-group cheerleading pro-nouncement there is an implied prescription? Of course, anything is possible. Nonetheless, the writer may have thought that the conventions the text references in the attack on idolaters were prescriptive for fol-lowers in Rome. But how is that implication to be tested? Moreover, if they are implicitly prescriptive, with what force do the prescriptions apply? Are the prescriptions public fictions, akin to legislation serving symbolic rather than practical purposes? And how would such pre-scriptions be received or obeyed—a consideration the serious lawgiver must raise—"like homicide laws (almost universally), like traffic regula-tions (when the police are watching), or like Vatican pronouncements (in Italy, not at all)" (Winkler 1990, 51)?

REFERENCES

Balch, David L. (1998) "Romans 1:24-27, Science, and Homosexuality," *Cur-rents in Theology and Mission* 25/6:433–40.

Boswell, John. (1980) *Christianity, Social Tolerance and Homosexuality. Gay People in Western Europe from the Beginning of the Christian Era to the Fourteenth Century.* Chicago: University of Chicago Press.

Carney, T. F. (1975) *The Shape of the Past.* Lawrence, Kan.: Coronado Press.

Douglas, Mary. (1973) *Rules and Meanings: The Anthropology of Everyday Knowledge: Selected Readings.* New York: Penguin.

Elliott, John H. (1986) "Social Scientific Criticism of the New Testament: More on Methods and Models," *Semeia* 35:1–33.

Gilmore, David D., ed. (1987) *Honor and Shame and the Unity of the Mediter-ranean.* Washington, D.C.: American Anthropological Association.

Gottwald, Norman K. (1979) *The Tribes of Yahweh: A Sociology of the Religion of Liberated Israel 1250–1050 B.C.E.* Maryknoll, N.Y.: Orbis.

Kluckhohn, Florence Rockwood, and Fred L. Strodtbeck. (1961) *Variations in Value Orientation.* Evanston, Ill.: Row, Peterson & Co.

Malina, Bruce J. (1989) "Dealing with Biblical (Mediterranean) Characters: A Guide for U.S. Consumers," *Biblical Theology Bulletin* 19/4:127–41.

_____. (1993) *The New Testament World: Insights from Cultural Anthropology.* Revised Edition. Louisville: Westminster/John Knox.

Martin, Dale B. (1995) *The Corinthian Body.* New Haven: Yale University Press.

McLaren, Angus. (1990) *A History of Contraception: From Antiquity to the Present Day.* Oxford: Basil Blackwell.

Moore, Stephen D., and Janice Capel Anderson. (1998) "Taking It Like a Man: Masculinity in 4 Maccabees," *Journal of Biblical Literature* 117:249–73.

Nissinen, Martti. (1998) *Homoeroticism in the Biblical World.* Minneapolis: Fortress.

Terian, Alexander. (1981) *Philonis Alexandrini de animalibus, The Armenian Text with an Introduction, Translation and Commentary.* Studies in Hellenistic Judaism 1. Chico: Scholars.

Ward, Roy Bowen. (1997) "Why Unnatural? The Tradition behind Romans 1:26-27," *Harvard Theological Review* 90/3:263–84.

White, Leland J. (1993) "Biblical Texts and Contemporary Gay People: A Response to Boswell and Boughton," *Irish Theological Quarterly* 59/4:286–301.

_____. (1995) "Does the Bible Speak about Gays or Same-Sex Orientation?" *Biblical Theology Bulletin* 25/1:14–23.

Winkler, John J. (1990) *The Constraints of Desire: The Anthropology of Sex and Gender in Ancient Greece.* New York: Routledge.

NOTES: CHAPTER 7

[1] By protocol I mean a fixed, long-established code prescribing procedures regarded as due and correct. A protocol is regarded as non-negotiable, but nonetheless "an utterly conventional arrangement, not a natural order" (Winkler 1990, 4–5). Protocols can be precise because they govern a limited range of communications within a determined arena, generally communication in public, not private situations, in a segment, not in the entirety of social life.

[2] Martin (1995) argues that Descartes wished to study the world without threatening the Church's claim to exclusive jurisdiction over religious matters, inventing for the purpose the category of nature "as a closed, self-contained system, over against which he could oppose mind, soul, the spiritual, the psychological, and the divine."

³ Martin concludes:

> Descartes's importance for our purposes is his construction of that dualism as
> an ontological dualism (that is, his notion that these two things by their very
> substances partook of radically different realms of reality) and his linking of it
> to a larger dichotomous system that includes several other categories. On the
> one side were body, matter, nature, and the physical; on the other were soul or
> mind, nonmatter, the supernatural, and the spiritual or psychological. Though
> it still influences many modern minds, this was a system of which the ancients
> knew nothing (1995, 6).

⁴ This situation should make us wary of arguments based on Jesus' words
and actions in the Gospels that seem less controlling than the later Church. If
the accounts of Jesus' words and actions stem largely from the earliest phases of
movement activity it is as reasonable to conclude that silence on or even recognition of women as leaders reflected the group's marginal status as that it indicated openness on the issue. Likewise, the fact that no word attributed to Jesus
refers to homosexuality is non-probative if the movement had no need to consider it. That Jesus interprets Genesis 19 within the context of hospitality to his
disciples only establishes an alternative, albeit possibly more common, reading.
The alternative reading may or may not be exclusive.

⁵ I say "may shame" because honor and shame are determined in the public
arena. The shameful act must be known. What is alleged or acknowledged to or
by one's peers is significant. To use an anachronistic term, acts carried out "in the
closet" do not register. Again social status is the issue, not the sexual act per se.

⁶ Winkler (1990, 210–16) appends a translation of illustrations of the significance of penetrating another that appear in Artemidoros of Daldis' *Dream
Analysis*. Artemidoros classifies a series of sexual dreams in terms of intercourse (1) according to nature *[kata phusin]* and convention *[nomos]*, (2) contrary to convention, (3) contrary to nature. Among many dreams given, in the
first category the dream of a man manipulating his penis, the dreamer is characterized as penetrating "his male slave or female slave, because the hands
applied to his penis are serving him" (I, 78.I). The dream of a man who is out
of the country having sex with a son is good because it signifies reunion with
the son (a benefit), while the dream of a man at home having sex with a son is
bad, signifying a coming separation (a loss) because "the intercourse of men
for the most part takes place by one turning his back on the other." Both
dreams are of intercourse contrary to convention (I, 78.ii). Intercourse contrary to nature includes a rich man having sex with himself (which foretells
loss of substance), having sex with a god or goddess (for a sick man this foretells death where one mingles with the gods), having sex with an animal in
which he penetrates the animal (foretelling benefit to come from the beast),
and having sex in which he is penetrated by the animal (foretelling possible
death because the experience is violent). In these and the many other examples
of sexual dreams recounted, the sexual activity is invariably a matter of one

person penetrating another, even of "a woman [who] penetrates a woman" (I, 80). Further, the penetrator will always look to possible benefit from the penetrated. At no point is the issue of procreative or other biologically determined purpose raised.

[7] A recent *précis* of 4 Maccabees makes this case strikingly:

> Eleazar and the boys outman Antiochus Epiphanes, who has them tortured to death for their faithfulness to their ancestral religion. That a physically feeble old man (cf 7:13) and a small group of boys should overcome an elite [252]male in his prime challenges the hegemonic concept of masculinity, as we shall show. What is even more striking, however, is that the (similarly unnamed) mother of the seven boys also "takes it like a man." The exemplary self-mastery the boys demonstrate proves them worthy of the designation "men" (14:11), but so does the even greater self-mastery displayed by their elderly, widowed mother (15:23, 28-30; 16:14), who endures still greater agonies (14:11; cf. 16:2). Paradoxically, as we shall see, the prime exemplar of masculinity in 4 Maccabees is a woman (Moore and Anderson 1998, 251–52).

[8] In the *Laws* (835B–842A) Plato considers as a pipe dream a proposal to return to a social order conforming to nature as known before Oidipous' father Laios invented pederasty. The legislator saw that common belief and practice would have to be reconstructed to equate it with incest—an unimaginable (for him) achievement. The proposition was a thought-experiment comparable to the idea of censoring the poets (Winkler 1990, 18).

Different sensitivities about the moral significance of age differences possibly account for different responses to molestation by clerics in the U.S. and in the Vatican. However reprehensibly slow their response, U.S. bishops acted more quickly and decisively, perhaps more aware that molestation of minors was more than sexual sin.

8

The New Testament and Homosexuality?

Bruce J. Malina

INTRODUCTION

*T*he question mark in the title is intended to express both surprise and puzzlement. The surprise derives from the realization that any historically-minded person in the twenty-first century would expect to find anything at all about homosexuality in the New Testament. After all, the terms "homosexuality," "heterosexuality," and "bisexuality" are nineteenth-century inventions meant to label the dawning nineteenth-century awareness of persons as subjective, psychological centers of awareness, as individualistic. Individualism, in the sense we use the term in the U.S. today, is the outcome of that rearrangement of human perceptions and experience called Romanticism (also known as Postmodernism today).[1] Homosexuality describes a more or less permanent psychological state entailing the sexual orientation of individuals toward persons of the same biological gender. The nineteenth-century awareness that some persons were homosexual is, indeed, something new since before that period all evidence indicates that persons were anti-introspective and not psychologically minded at all. That means that even if persons were "homosexual," the same-gender sexual orientation would be ascribed to ethnic custom, popular custom, traditional convention, or some other group-specific social practice.[2] This was surely the case for the world of Jesus and the world of Paul.

Consider an experience we would consider most subjective, personal, and psychological—dreams. An early-second-century book of dream analysis, the *Oneirocritica* by Artemidoros of Daldis, shows no evidence of interest in internal, psychological states at all. "The significant messages from the Artemidoran soul concern external matters of fact, not internal feelings, whereas the Freudian soul is trying to talk about suppressed wishes" (Winkler 1990, 26). This lack of concern for the psychological is equally evident in biblical dreams (e.g., the many dreams in Genesis or Matthew 2; see Pilch 1997).

Some would argue that, human nature being what it is, there must have been homosexuals in the ancient world for Paul to condemn their behavior in Romans 1. If human nature means that dimension of human beings that is entirely the same for all human beings, such as anatomy, biological processes, and the subjects studied by the "natural" sciences of chemistry, biology, and physics, then one would have to admit that such human nature existed in the first-century Mediterranean world. Human nature in the sense of nature studied in the natural sciences refers to how human beings are entirely the same through time and over space. Social interpretations of human nature, however, take this entirely-the-same dimension of human beings and endow it with specific meanings and feelings within a well-defined social system. For example, all human beings the world over are females or males; but the meanings attached to being female or male are quite different in specific social groups. And all human beings the world over have offspring; but the significance of a first child over against other children, of male babies over against female babies, is quite distinct in different human societies. The area covering the way human groups interpret identical human nature is called the social or the cultural. While human beings might be the same the world over according to the perspectives of the natural sciences, what counts as proper human behavior can be explained in radically different ways according to the perspectives of specific cultures.

Human beings as we find them across time and space are entirely the same (nature), entirely different (unique personality, a Romantic concept), and somewhat the same and somewhat different (cultural interpretation of specific groups) at the same time (see Malina 1993). All social "isms" involve the identification of human nature with a specific culture or dimension of that culture (e.g., racism, sexism, feminism, etc.). Perhaps this is the underlying cause of the difficulties attending the evaluation of homosexuality in contemporary Roman Catholic moral theology. Is homosexuality a cultural perception specific to one or another society? Is the assessment of sexual orientation inbuilt in the nature of human beings (demonstrable by natural sciences) or the result of enculturation within a specific social system?

To appreciate what Paul meant by his statement in Romans 1 about same-gender sexual relations, one must look at the social system within which and from which his statements had meaning (see Halliday 1978; Malina 1991; 1996).

WHAT DID PAUL MEAN?

Language expresses meanings from a social system. Roman Catholic biblical interpreters have been directed more than once to discover what an author said and meant to a specific audience in a specific time and culture (*Dei Verbum* 12; "Interpreting the Bible in the Church"). Paul's statements were directed to a first-century Mediterranean audience, composed largely of Judeans.[3] His mode of argument, use of Israel's Scripture, concerns about his own *ethnos* (people), and his typical Israelite ethnocentrism all point to a Judean social context. This is surely the case for the document known as the Letter to the Romans. While Paul addresses "all God's beloved in Rome" (1:7), not once does he mention "Romans." Rather the letter is directed to Judeans, ethnic Israelites in Rome, who have accepted Jesus of Nazareth as Israel's Messiah soon to come. There are a few non-Israelites in the group (Rom 11:13: Paul is an apostle to Judeans in Gentile regions; the view of Eph 3:6 is post-Pauline). But they are not Paul's major concern. Rather the letter made sense to Israelite emigrés forming the rather small Jesus groups found largely in the Judean immigrant quarter (Trastevere) of first-century Rome. From a Judean ethnocentric perspective what characterized Gentiles—a word meaning everybody but Israelites—was idolatry. Non-Israelites behaved as they did because of their idolatry. Judeans might be anything, but it was a matter of ethnic pride not to waver in allegiance to the deity of the ethnic group, the God of Israel. The Judean focal value, a value espoused by Jesus-group members as well, was no mixture with outsiders.[4] With this value in mind, Paul addresses his fellow Israelite Jesus-group members in Rome.

After finishing the introductory niceties of the letter with its theological thematic (1:1-17), Paul launches into what seem to be standard Judean accusations against Gentile idolatry. The "us" against "them" language indicates this:

For the wrath of God is revealed from heaven against all ungodliness and wickedness of those who by their wickedness suppress the truth. For what can be known about God is plain to them, because God has shown it to them. Ever since the creation of the world his eternal power and divine nature, invisible though they are, have been understood and seen through the things he has made. So they are without excuse; for though they knew God, they did not honor him as God or give thanks to him, but they became futile in their thinking, and their senseless minds were darkened. Claiming to be wise, they became fools; and they exchanged the glory of the immortal God for images resembling a mortal human being or birds or four-footed animals or reptiles (Rom 1:18-23).

What is wrong with non-Israelites is that they do not worship the God of Israel, whom Judeans claim created the world (with Israel and Jerusalem at its center). Paul now moves on to describe the behavior typical of these idolaters, presumably not found among Israelites. It is this line of behavior that reveals them as idolaters since their behavior is a direct tit-for-tat (God "gave them up" to it: 1:24, 26, 28) outcome of idolatry:

Therefore *God gave them up* in the lusts of their hearts to impurity, to the degrading of their bodies among themselves, because they exchanged the truth about God for a lie and worshiped and served the creature rather than the Creator, who is blessed forever! Amen. For this reason *God gave them up* to degrading passions. Their women exchanged natural intercourse for unnatural, and in the same way also the men, giving up natural intercourse with women, were consumed with passion for one another. Men committed shameless acts with men and received in their own persons the due penalty for their error. And since they did not see fit to acknowledge God, *God gave them up* to a debased mind and to things that should not be done. They were filled with every kind of wickedness, evil, covetousness, malice. Full of envy, murder, strife, deceit, craftiness, they are gossips, slanderers, God-haters, insolent, haughty, boastful, inventors of evil, rebellious toward parents, foolish, faithless, heartless, ruthless. They know God's decree, that those who practice such things deserve to die— yet they not only do them but even applaud others who practice them. (Rom 1:24-32).

The "degrading" passions[5] to which idolaters have been delivered by God include: (1) females *(thēleiai)* exchanging natural *(physikē)* sexual intercourse for what is against nature *(para physin);* and males *(arsenes),* giving up natural sexual *(physikē)* intercourse with females, are consumed with passion for one another and receive in themselves their due penalty for their error; (2) debased minds, revealed in a list of deviant behaviors (recent treatments of this passage include Hasitschka 1998; Stegemann 1998; Tiedemann 1998; for the Bible in general Nissinen 1998; popular presentations: Helminiak 1994; Penna 1997).

Paul's opening categorization of persons on the basis of gender was typical of the ancient Mediterranean, where the self was defined in terms of gender, genealogy, and geography (see Malina and Neyrey 1996). Gender derives from biological birth determined by God and fixed by God's creation. Genealogy derives from the kin group into which one was born, a fact determined by God in a structural arrangement fixed by God. Geography derives from the location of the social group of persons to which one's kin group belonged. Social groups included their physical environment, their sky, land, air, and water, all intimately bound together. Thus self, status, and social group defined who one was in antiquity.

For all Mediterraneans of antiquity the gendered self was essentially either male or female, each with nature-given, distinctive, gender-based social expectations (see Malina 1990; 1994):

MALE	FEMALE
active	passive
dominant by nature	subordinate by nature[6]
controlling	controlled
penetrating	penetrated
seed bearing	field, seed receiving
concern for family honor	concern for family shame
honor symboled by phallus	shame symboled by hymen
represents family to the outside	represents family to the inside
like father like son	like mother like daughter

While these gender expectations were common in the ancient Mediterranean world, here in Romans 1 Paul is concerned with the behavior of females and males specifically in idolatrous societies, that is, outside Israelite society. Interpretations of his specific concerns often hinge on the word "natural." Females exchange natural intercourse for what is against nature, as do males. What does "nature" *(physis)* mean in first-century Hellenistic Greek? (There is no such term in Hebrew.) Perhaps it is best to begin with what it does not mean. It does not mean the area of concern of the "natural" sciences, the 100 percent sameness of all reality known through experimentation and laws of "nature" in physics, chemistry, biology, and by analogy in sociology and psychology. This is "nature" as conceived by Descartes and the "new science" of Bacon and Vico. This perspective separated the empirical from the personal or spiritual. Laws of nature were the regularities of the empirical world, observable and testable and formulated, if possible, in the univocal language of mathematics.

For first-century Mediterraneans nature *(physis)* referred, first of all, to what was customary and usual: either for a given *ethnos* or people, a given species of animals, or even a given person or animal. In this sense the natural stood opposed to the conventional or legal, the behavior decided upon by a person or group with legal power. The term also referred to what was usual in the qualities of all that existed, all creation—what is instinctive, species-specific. What happened customarily and recurrently was natural, traceable to origins, to creation. Planets naturally moved erratically. Honey naturally tasted sweet. The word also referred to the genitals, male or female, and at times to the anal orifice (see Liddell-Scott *ad verbum,* Winkler 1990, 217–20).

With reference to sexual relations there is an interesting passage in Artemidoros's *Oneirocritica* that offers a set of categories typical of early second-century Hellenism, perhaps earlier as well:

> In the section on sexual intercourse *(sunousia),* the best method of arrangement will be to consider firstly examples of sexual intercourse that is natural *(kata physin),* legal *(kata nomon)* and customary *(kat'ethos);* secondly examples of sexual intercourse that is illegal *(para nomon);* and thirdly examples of sexual intercourse that is unnatural *(para physin).* (*Oneirocritica* I.78, White 58).

The groupings are pertinent since in Romans Paul begins his categories with intercourse against nature followed by a list of behaviors, including intercourse, against law, here the law of Israel. What would such intercourse against nature include? While Paul specifies only two instances, Artemidoros observes that the sexual intercourse that is against nature is any sexual position apart from the frontal position, which is the only one "taught them (humans) by nature" *(to de sygchrōta monon hypo tēs physeōs didachthentes).* The reason for this is that all species have a sexual position proper to themselves, and "humans have the frontal position as their proper one *(anthrōpous to men oikeion schēma to proschrōta echein);* they have devised the others when they gave in to insolence, dissipation and debauchery"(*Oneirocritica* I.79, White 63).

Thus a female's sexual intercourse against nature, as Artemidorus notes, includes all other positions, specifically those in which the female role is not passive *(loc. cit.)*. This is in line with the Mediterranean gender concern that males are active and forceful, while females are passive and controlled. In this perspective, since males cannot engage in the frontal position with each other, their sexual relations have to be against nature.

If we follow Artemidoros, intercourse against convention or law *(para nomon)* is essentially incest of various types. Similarly oral sex is considered "doing the unmentionable" *(arretopoiesthai)*. The Hellenistic sensibility was that persons doing oral sex cannot "share mouths," i.e., kiss or eat together *(loc. cit.,* White 63–64). Paul too knows an unmentionable sexual relation, that of a male who marries his father's wife (1 Cor 5:1-2).

From where did anomalies such as females behaving like males or males behaving like females come? An explanation in Phaedrus's *Fables* (4.15), cited by Boyarin, accounts for "tribadic females and effeminate males" by recounting that Prometheus got drunk when making human beings and attached some male genitals to female people and some female genitals to male people by mistake. He concludes:

> To me it seems quite patent that the purport of the fable is that tribads are the men who got female genitals by mistake, and the *molles* are the women with male genitals attached to them. This actually provides beautiful evidence for Halperin's definition of sexuality as that modern cultural entity whose chief conceptual function "is to distinguish, once and for all, sexual identity from matters of gender—to decouple, as it were, *kinds* of sexual predilection from *degrees* of masculinity and femininity" (Halperin 1990, 25). For Phaedrus it was impossible to imagine a woman loving women, so a lesbian must "really" be a man in a woman's body "by mistake," and this was, in one version or another, the most common way in Euro-America of accounting for same sex eroticism until the early twentieth century. Even Krafft-Ebing toward the end of the nineteenth century still conceived of lesbians as men with female bodies, i.e., as male souls in bodies with female genitalia (Boyarin 1995, 345 n. 29).

Philo offers the view that, apart from boys used in pederasty, the passive partners in male sexual relations are actually androgynous persons who got that way either by birth or by continual same-gender sexual relations to the point of castrating themselves (*Special Laws* III.7.37-42). These passive partners demean male honor. For Greeks and Romans of the period it was precisely this demeaning of male honor, the denigration of male status, that made the passive male partner reprehensible (see Veyne 1998).

Paul, in turn, shares a similar view, although he explicitly ascribes same-gender sexual relations to idolatry. For while Paul may have shared Hellenistic sensibilities, his *ethnos* (people) had its own *ethos* (customs) that supported the "us" against "them" boundary that controlled Paul and that Paul articulates. It seems this was the common viewpoint of first-century Israelites.

ISRAELITE TRADITION

For any first-century Israelite, whether Judean, Galilean, Perean, or emigré, there would be little doubt concerning the center of the inhabited earth. Israelite orientation was focused on the central place of the land of Israel, Jerusalem. And even more sharply, the central focus of Jerusalem was the Temple of the God of Israel. Traditional Israelite ideology was pivoted on the awareness of the holiness of the God of Israel. Holiness here means social exclusivity, and the God of Israel demanded such exclusivity from the people whom he had chosen to be exclusively his—or so went Israel's story line.

While the sacred has to do with what was exclusive to the deity, the profane or non-exclusive to the deity consists of all creation categorized in terms of a system that would allow everything and everyone a certain meaning-endowing, sense-making situation or place. This is the purity system of Israel, providing a place for everyone/thing, and expecting everyone/thing in its place. Again this purity system derives from the God of Israel who created all that exists, and in that act of creation set up the system of categories into which all created beings properly fit (Gen 1:1–2:4a). Thus Israel's purity laws are in fact natural laws established by the creator himself (this was the prevailing, Priestly view; however, in Genesis 2 Adam sets up the initial categories, a feature noted in Rabbinism; see Eilberg-Schwartz 1990, 202–6, 226). It was up to Israel, as a sacred people, to live in purity. And it was notably up to the sacred attendants of the deity, Israel's priestly tribe, as God's divinely chosen retainers, to see to the observance of purity rules, both for themselves and the people at large. To approach the sacred, one had to be sacred and pure. To approach the sanctuary in general, one had to be pure.

As for morality, if Israelites are to be exclusive as their God is exclusive, they too will have to behave in a manner befitting their exclusivity over against the rest of humankind. This exclusivity includes living according to the categories established by Israel's God when the God of Israel created the world. It is these categories that serve as the matrix for Israelite definitions of what is in place (pure, clean) and what is out of place (impure, unclean). With purity a condition for access to the exclusive, only the clean can approach the God of Israel with any hope of success in the interaction (for an excellent summary see Frymer-Kensky 1983).

Thus the orientational map of Israel consists of two major category sets: the holy and profane (exclusive and non-exclusive) and the pure/clean and impure/unclean (in its proper place/out of place). These category sets cut through the five major classifications typical of all societies: self, others, animate and inanimate creatures, time, space. Temple arrangements point to the application of these category sets to space and to selves permitted in this space.

However, there are some categories of behavior that fall outside Israel's God-given purity system. These are the prohibitions that are simply anomalous. Those who perform actions prohibited by the God of Israel must be punished; their actions are irrevocable and irretrievable.

These are crimes prohibited by God and expressed in Israel's conventions and customs. Such crimes are full of danger consisting in a permanently applicable divine sanction for the deed. As a rule the culprit cannot exonerate him/her self.

The divinely ordained sanction will be applied, and this in one of two ways: either by God or by the Israelite community. The *sanctions applied by God* include the collection of *karet* (being cut off), penalties for persons defiling the sacred and thus violating the distinctions between sacred and profane, the foundational category for the whole system of meaning. Since God is exclusive (sacred) like the realms God marks off as exclusive, so too Israel is an exclusive people and must observe the boundaries of the sacred (Lev 11:44, 45; 19:2; 20:7, 26). "The violator is therefore expected to incur the *karet* penalty; in other words, his deed is expected to result in calamity to his entire lineage through the direct intervention of God ("automatically") and without necessitating societal action. This belief in automatic retribution protects the realm of the sacred by deterring acts which would encroach upon it" (Frymer-Kensky 1983, 406).

However, crimes whose sanction is the *death penalty to be applied by society* fall outside the boundaries of behavior controlled by *karet*. These include the behaviors prohibited by the Ten Commandments. The first set of prohibitions covers crimes that dishonor the God of Israel to such an extent that the requirement for satisfaction of honor is irreversible and irrevocable, including Sabbath observance. Then come crimes against parents, and finally crimes that dishonor a male's family honor, requiring vengeance and resulting in feuding.[7] As Josephus observes: "Now the greatest part of offenses with us are capital, as if anyone be guilty of adultery; if anyone force a virgin; if anyone be so impudent as to attempt sodomy with a male; or if, upon another's making an attempt upon him, he submits to be so used. There is also a law for slaves of the like nature that can never be avoided" (*Against Apion* 2.215, Whiston).

Significantly for Romans 1, the Torah prohibition of males lying with males as with a woman is found in the passage running from Leviticus 18–20, in a subset of crimes judged to be typical of non-Israelite behavior. In Israel such crimes deserve the death penalty, to be applied by Israelite society as explicitly commanded in the Torah: "You shall not do as they do in the land of Egypt, where you dwelt, and you shall not do as they do in the land of Canaan, to which I am bringing you" (Lev 18:3). Hence these are behaviors typical of the non-Israelites that Israel knew. Here for Paul they are typical of the non-Israelites Paul knows as well. The listing of behaviors in Leviticus 18 is outfitted with penalties in the parallel Leviticus 20; actions requiring the death penalty, should they be found in Israel, include: offering children to Molech (Lev 20:2), cursing father or mother (Lev 20:9), adultery (20:10), incest with mother/mother-in-law (Lev 20:11) or daughter-in-law (20:12), a male lying with a male as with a woman (Lev 20:13), male or female lying with a beast (Lev 20:15-16, and the earlier Exod 22:19: "Whoever lies with a beast shall be put to death"), acting as medium or wizard (20:27). While some of these behaviors are found elsewhere in the Torah, the prohibition of a male lying with a male as with a women is found only here (Lev 18:22 and 20:13; see especially Olyan 1994; Satlow 1994; Boyarin 1995; Halperin 1993). Such acts are said to pollute the land of Israel and the pollution of the land cannot be rectified by ritual purification.

It seems that Paul's categories in Romans, "according to nature" *(kata physin)* and "contrary to nature" *(para physin)*, are a Hellenistic Judean appropriation of traditional Israelite categories, as follows:

a. according to nature = according to the conventions *(nomos)* and customs *(ethos)* of Israel, i.e., holy and pure behavior as well as clean and unclean behaviors that can be "naturally" purified.

b. against nature = prohibitions in the conventions and customs of Israel sanctioned by a communal death penalty or direct divine punishment. Thus:

Israelite according to nature:

Exclusive (holy, sacred)

Non-exclusive (profane) $\left\{ \begin{array}{l} \text{In place (clean, pure)} \\ \text{Out of place (unclean, impure)} \end{array} \right.$

Israelite contrary to nature:

No place (anomalous) $\left\{ \begin{array}{l} \text{To be eradicated (death penalty)} \\ \text{To be left to God (divine penalty)} \end{array} \right.$

JUDEAN TRADITION

Aside from the prohibition of bestiality there is little in the first-century Judean tradition about "unnatural" behavior of women directed to women. Josephus notes that Israelite law only allows for sexual intercourse "according to nature with one's wife and for the procreation of children" (*Against Apion* 2.24.199). This presumably is the frontal position mentioned by Artemidoros, "according to nature." There is a rabbinic anecdote, dating to the period of the beginnings of the Jewish religion (fifth century C.E.), that is relevant here. Boyarin writes:

> Further evidence for the absence of a category of the "homosexual" in talmudic culture may be found in (the admittedly very rare) discussions of female same-sex genital practices, for instance, Babylonian Talmud *Yevamoth* 76a:
>
>> Rav Huna said: "Women who rub each other may not marry priests," but even Rabbi Eliezer who said that "an unmarried man who has intercourse with an unmarried woman without intending to marry her makes her a *zonah* [and thus unfit to marry a high priest]," his words only apply to a man [who lies with a woman] but as for a woman [who lies with a woman], it is mere lasciviousness." Also Babylonian Talmud *Shabbat* 65a-b: Shmuel's father did not allow his daughters to lie with each other. . . . Shall we say that this supports the view of Rav Huna, for Rav Huna said: "Women who rub each other may not marry priests"? No, he forbade it in order that they should not learn [the feel] of another body [and they would then lust to lie with men (Rashi)].

The only reason, according to this text, that unmarried women should not excite each other sexually is because it might lead to immorality, that is, sex with men (Boyarin 1995, 339).

It seems that female to female sexual orientation is omitted in the Torah tradition because women cannot "spill the seed." Female sexual stimulation by rubbing the genitals (i.e., tribadism, from Greek *tribein*) does not result in loss of seed, hence is not really sexual intercourse!

However, there are a number of passages in Judean documents more or less contemporary with Paul concerning "unnatural" behavior of men, and the type of male-to-male gender contact specified seems to refer to what Paul intimates. Consider Philo's observations in his running commentary on Leviticus 18, under the heading of the commandment, "you shall not commit adultery":

Moreover, another evil, much greater than that which we have already mentioned, has made its way among and been let loose upon cities, namely, the love of boys, which formerly was accounted a great infamy even to be spoken of, but which sin is a subject of boasting not only to those who practise it, but even to those who suffer it, and who, being accustomed to bearing the affliction of being treated like women, waste away as to both their souls and bodies, not bearing about them a single spark of a manly character to be kindled into a flame, but having even the hair of their heads conspicuously curled and adorned, and having their faces smeared with vermilion, and paint, and things of that kind, and having their eyes pencilled beneath, and having their skins anointed with fragrant perfumes (for in such persons as these a sweet smell is a most seductive quality), and being well appointed in everything that tends to beauty or elegance, are not ashamed to devote their constant study and endeavors to the task of changing their manly character into an effeminate one. And it is natural for those who obey the law to consider such persons worthy of death, since the law commands that the man-woman who adulterates the precious coinage of his nature shall die without redemption, not allowing him to live a single day, or even a single hour, as he is a disgrace to himself, and to his family, and to his country, and to the whole race of mankind. And let the man who is devoted to the love of boys submit to the same punishment, since he pursues that pleasure which is contrary to nature, and since, as far as depends upon him, he would make the cities desolate, and void, and empty of all inhabitants, wasting his power of propagating his species, and moreover, being a guide and teacher of those greatest of all evils, unmanliness and effeminate lust, stripping young men of the flower of their beauty, and wasting their prime of life in effeminacy, which he ought rather on the other hand to train to vigour and acts of courage; and last of all, because, like a worthless husbandman, he allows fertile and productive lands to lie fallow, contriving that they shall continue barren, and labours night and day at cultivating that soil from which he never expects any produce at all. And I imagine that the cause of this is that among many nations there are actually rewards given for intemperance and effeminacy. At all events one may see men-women continually strutting through the market place at midday, and leading the processions in festivals; and, impious men as they are, having received by lot the charge of the temple, and beginning the sacred and initiating rites, and concerned even in the holy mysteries of Ceres. And some of these persons have even carried their admiration of these delicate pleasures of youth so far that they have desired wholly to change their condition for that of women, and have castrated themselves and have clothed themselves in purple robes, like those who, having been the cause of great blessings to their native land, walk about attended by body-guards, pushing down every one whom they meet. But if there was a general indignation against those who venture to do such things, such as was felt by our lawgiver, and if such men were destroyed without any chance of escape as the common curse and pollution of their country, then many other persons would be warned and corrected by their example. For the punishments of those persons who have been already condemned cannot be averted by entreaty, and therefore cause no slight check to those persons who are ambitious of distinguishing themselves by the same pursuits (*Spec. Laws.* III.7.37-42, Yonge).

I cite this passage at length to demonstrate that for Philo males engaging in same-gender sexual relations are actually "heterosexuals" or "bisexuals," not what we would call "homosexuals." Furthermore, his "bisexuals" are males with physical male and female sexual characteristics, that is, androgynous persons, hermaphrodites, what physicians call "intersexed" persons today. This seems to be the common view. Given the fact that the ancients were anti-introspective and not psychologically-minded, it would be totally anachronistic to consider the human beings in question as persons with stable male and female gender or sexual orientations rooted in their personality or psychological makeup. The main reason why male same-gender sexual contact is wrong is that individuals who participate in it are "not only seeking to violate the marriage bed of others, but lusting unnaturally, and seeking to deface the manly character of the nature of man, and to change it into a woman-like appearance, for the sake of the gratification of his own polluted and accursed passions" (*Special Laws* II.14.50, Yonge).

What is immoral, then, is mixture, crossing same-gender boundaries and thereby dishonoring the male. We find a similar perspective in Philo's explanation of the types of persons found in ancient Sodom, persons worse than the Greeks and barbarians of his day:

> And what is signified by this is indicated in a most evident and careful manner by the events which ensued. The country of the Sodomites was a district of the land of Canaan, which the Syrians afterwards called Palestine, a country full of innumerable iniquities, and especially of gluttony and debauchery, and all the great and numerous pleasures of other kinds which have been built up by men as a fortress, on which account it had been already condemned by the Judge of the whole world. And the cause of its excessive and immoderate intemperance was the unlimited abundance of supplies of all kinds which its inhabitants enjoyed. For the land was one with a deep soil, and well watered, and as such produced abundant crops of every kind of fruit every year. And he was a wise man and spoke truly who said—"The greatest cause of all iniquity is found in overmuch prosperity." As men, being unable to bear discreetly a satiety of these things, get restive like cattle, and become stiff-necked, and discard the laws of nature, pursuing a great and intemperate indulgence of gluttony, and drinking, and unlawful connections; for not only did they go mad after women, and defile the marriage bed of others, but also those who were men lusted after one another, doing unseemly things, and not regarding or respecting their common nature, and though eager for children, they were convicted by having only an abortive offspring; but the conviction produced no advantage, since they were overcome by violent desire; and so, by degrees, the men became accustomed to be treated like women, and in this way engendered among themselves the disease of females, and intolerable evil; for they not only, as to effeminacy and delicacy, became like women in their persons, but they made also their souls most ignoble, corrupting in this way the whole race of man, as far as depended on them. At all events, if the Greeks and barbarians were to have agreed together, and to have adopted the commerce of the citizens of this city, their cities one after another would have become desolate, as if they had been emptied by a pestilence (*On Abraham* 26.133–36, Yonge).

Once more the problem is treating males as though they were females. This, of course, is changing the order of nature set out in Genesis. Note the explanation in *Testament of Naphtali:* "But you shall not be so, my children, recognizing in the firmament, in the earth, and in the sea, and in all created things, the Lord who made all things, that you become not as Sodom, which changed the order of nature. In like manner, the

Watchers also changed the order of their nature whom the Lord cursed at the flood, on whose account He made the earth without inhabitants and fruitless" (3:4-5, Charles). The Watchers crossed boundaries from their celestial being to have sexual relations with human females (Gen 6:1-4), thus "defiling themselves with women" (Rev 14:4). Philo equally makes reference to the wasting of the seed in such relations (and others as well, e.g., marrying a barren woman; Philo, *Special Laws* III *passim*). In this discussion it is perhaps useful to recall what the male ejaculate was for these learned ancients. Seneca explains:

> Whether the world is an animated being, or a body governed by nature, like trees and plants, there is incorporated in it from its beginning to its end everything it must do or undergo. In the semen there is contained the entire record of the man to be, and the not-yet-born infant has the laws governing a beard and grey hair. The features of the entire body and its successive phases are there, in a tiny and hidden form (*Naturales Quaestiones* 3, 29, 3 LCL).

Human seed, which only males have, are much like Russian nesting dolls or Chinese boxes, each containing the whole of forthcoming humankind. As Philo explains: "But we must be well assured that humans have from all eternity sprung from other humans in constant succession, the male implanting the seed in the female as in a field, and the female receiving the seed so as to preserve it" (*On the Eternity of the World* 13.69, Yonge). Thus all Arabs and Hebrews were to be found in Abraham's seed, just as Jesus was (Gal 3:16-18). To spill the seed, to "waste their seed of one's own deliberate purpose" (Philo, *Special Laws* III.6.34, Yonge) is tantamount to killing microhuman beings and more. Again Philo, addressing a male who would spill his seed:

> You will put an end to the honor due to parents, the attention of a wife, the education of children, the blameless services of servants, the management of a house, the government of a city, the firm establishment of laws, the guardianship of morals, reverence to one's elders, the habit of speaking well of the dead, good fellowship with the living, piety towards God as shown both in words and in deeds: for you are overturning and throwing into confusion all these things, sowing seed for yourself alone, and nursing up pleasure, that gluttonous intemperate origin of all evil (*On the Posterity of Cain* 53.181, Yonge).

Since only males had this seed, the crimes Philo lists are obviously male-specific.

MEANINGS AVAILABLE TO PAUL

Romans 1

From Philo, Artemidoros, Josephus, and other Hellenistic documents it seems the meanings available to Paul about some sexual behavior being against nature included the following. For females, sexual relations against nature essentially meant taking control in sexual relations and employing sexual positions other than frontal. For males sexual relations against nature included pederasty, bisexuality, and above all male-adopted androgyny. It is androgyny that Paul seems to have in mind when he speaks of males exchanging their male nature, perhaps by a life dedicated to acting like a female through castrations. As Philo explains, the real problem of such male-male sexual behavior is that it confuses male gender lines, thus dishonoring the male. Sexual relations were intended "by nature" to be between genders; same-gender sexual relations, like cross-dressing or cross-marriage, are against nature. Since females had no seed and could not penetrate, they really could not perform sexual relations with other females, but tribadism did make females prone to unlawful sexual relations with males.

Furthermore, any consideration of the list of prohibitions in Leviticus 18 and 20 sanctioned by the death penalty, such as male-male sexual intercourse, should also take note of the first-century Israelite appropriation of the command not to offer one's children to Molech. At the time of Paul, Israelites were believed to offer their children to Molech if they allowed them to intermarry with non-Israelites, i.e., mixed marriage. For example, "And if there is any man who wishes in Israel to give his daughter or his sister to any man who is of the seed of the Gentiles he shall surely die, and they shall stone him with stones; for he hath wrought shame in Israel; and they shall burn the woman with fire, because she has dishonored the name of the house of her father, and she shall be rooted out of Israel" (*Jub* 30:7-8, Charles).

Similarly, "Again Moses commands, do not either form a connection of marriage with one of another nation, and do not be seduced into complying with customs inconsistent with your own, and do not stray from the right way and forget the path which leads to piety, turning into a road which is no road" (Philo, *Special Laws* III.5.29, Yonge). Outside Israel presumably God himself will deliver up such perpetrators to some proper punishment.

Ten Commandment Lists

After demonstrating how God is dishonored by non-Israelites because of their "unnatural" sexual behavior contrary to Israel's conventions and customs revealed in the Torah, Paul goes on to list typical non-Israelite wickedness that likewise dishonors God as follows:

> They were filled with all manner of wickedness: (1) evil, covetousness, (2) malice, envy, (3) murder, strife, (4) deceit, malignity, (5) gossips, slanderers, (6) haters of God, (7) insolent, haughty, (8) boastful inventors of evil, disobedient to parents, (9) foolish, faithless, (10) heartless, ruthless (Rom 1:29-32).

The list is simply a disguised listing of the Ten Commandments of Israelite tradition. Josephus reports that in the Israel of his day, just as it was forbidden to utter the sacred Tetragrammaton, YHWH, the most sacred name of the God of Israel, so too it was forbidden to utter the "Ten Words" given on Sinai to Israel. While these are the very Ten Words "which Moses has left inscribed on the two tables," yet "these words it is not permitted us to state explicitly, to the letter." Nevertheless, Josephus indicates their "power" *[hous ou themiton estin hemin legein phanerōs pros lexin, tas de dynameis auton dēlōsomen]* (Ant 3.90 LCL). After all, these very words, "the ten commandments which God himself gave to his people without employing the agency of any prophet or interpreter" (Philo, *Special Laws* III, 2, 7) were the direct words of the God of Israel, hence full of power. They must not be repeated verbatim.[8]

While it was forbidden to recite the Ten Words in the exact wording and order found in the Torah passage recounting the Sinai incident, first-century Israelites did not refrain from quoting them. They simply disguised them or reordered them. In the synoptic tradition, for example, Jesus offers a listing to the Greedy Young Man as follows: "You shall not kill, You shall not commit adultery, You shall not steal, You shall not bear false witness, Honor your father and mother, and, You shall love your neighbor as yourself" (Matt 19:18-19; Mark 10:19 omits love of neighbor as does Luke 18:20, who inverts adultery and killing). Romans 1:29-32, in turn, is a disguised version. The same is true of lists in 1 Cor 6:9-11 and 1 Tim 1:9-11.

These lists collocate males who lie with males as with a woman *(arsenokoitai)* and those taking the woman's place *(malakoi)* with adulterers (Philo does the same thing in *Special Laws* 3); they impugn the honor of the male (see Malina 1993, 143–46).[9] What is distinctive of

Israel is that breaches of the Ten Commandments, aside from coveting (i.e., stealing property), all require the death penalty. Yet as Paul describes it, outside Israel such behaviors are dealt with by God.

CONCLUSIONS

Paul offers two sets of behavior to demonstrate the appropriateness of the wrath of God toward non-Israelites for their culpable idolatry. His argument is tit for tat. If human beings exchange non-gods for the God of Israel (known simply as "God") even though they know God, God delivers them up to exchanging female passivity for activity even though females know femininity, and maleness for femaleness even though they know maleness. God, then, delivers them up to their own wickedness in a set of behaviors that produces social disharmony due to the non-observance of God's Ten Commandments for Israel.

1. In Israel same-gender sexual relations are ascribed to alien ethnic custom, alien popular custom, alien traditional convention, or some other group-specific social practice. It did not belong in Israel and was forbidden as non-Israelite behavior bound up with non-Israelite idolatry. Same-gender sexual relations are a manifestation of idolatry.

2. The exchange of roles indicates the demeaning and dishonoring of roles according to nature and revealed in Torah, just as idolatry indicates the demeaning and dishonoring of God.

3. Idolatry, with the demeaning of God and God's entitlements, in the first part of Paul's argument makes the idolater worthy of death. Further, the demeaning of male roles, male entitlements, as well as disrespect for females and switch in female roles fall under the listings of prohibited behaviors deserving death in the Ten Commandments. This is the reason for the second part of the argument with Paul's listing of wickednesses.

4. There is perhaps an unexpressed concern about wasting seed. As a rule this is a concern with Israelite seed, not that of outsiders. What bothered Judean authors about male same-gender sexual relations in Israel was that it wasted seed that traced back to Abraham himself and was quite limited in amount.

5. All same-(usually male) gender sexual relations are contrary to nature largely because what Paul does, and perhaps what Hellenistic Judaism did before him, that is, subsume the category "contrary to

nature" to cover all those behaviors in Israel that are anomalous and punishable by death at the hands of the community (for Israelites) or by God in God's own way. The scenario here depicts the latter.

6. The insertion of same-gender sexual contact under the category of adultery, taken from the very Ten Commandments uttered directly to Israelites on Mount Sinai, means that behavior is viewed, like adultery, as dishonoring a male. Presumably same-gender sexual relations can only lead to social disorder and disturb social harmony. From the viewpoint of Israel's covenant with God, it breaks the covenant stipulations required by God. And from the perspective of Israel's purity rules it is an anomaly, a confusion of gender boundaries that lie at the basis of self-definition (like cross dressing, cross-ethnic marriage). What is distinctive in Paul's argument in Romans is that idolatry among non-Israelites is being punished by God. Israelites need not kill non-Israelites for their idolatry since these idolaters are handed over to their punishment by God. The implied punishment, in Philo at least, is lack of offspring with a resulting diminishing of population in city and ethnic territory!

POSTSCRIPT

If we return to the twenty-first century after this excursion into the first century we can see that Paul's perspectives, if taken consistently, simply do not make sense. Paul's teaching is rooted in Israel's creation story, with purity laws grounded in the nature described in that creation story. We who live in a relatively uncentered universe presumably controlled by regularities of physics and chemistry have a different creation story. Most would not take Israel's purity rule to be natural law itself, rooted in creation. Paul's viewpoint derives from his being immersed in Israel's boundary markers, between the Israelite ingroup and the non-Israelite outgroup. We no longer share this sort of ethnocentrism as a principle of morality. Paul's teaching is based on a biology in which males have seed containing veritable *homunculi,* while females offer only nourishment to the seed in the formation of humans. We explain the process of human generation quite differently today, since we believe both male and female parents equally contribute genetic material to their offspring.

Then, if we follow Israel's conception of nature in the Ten Commandments, any breach of these prohibitions (aside from coveting, i.e., stealing) requires the death penalty, and this death penalty cannot be waived, under penalty from God! It is curious that people today are little concerned about breaches of the Sabbath, about waiving the death penalty for murder, adultery, kidnapping, or perjury, yet have great emotional concern about "homosexuality"—something not envisioned in our terms by biblical authors.

Finally, and rather interestingly, Paul intimates that the presence of non-Israelites in Jesus groups is contrary to nature (*para physin,* Rom 11:24, the same phrase as in Rom 1:26). Their presence, of course, is a form of social bonding not unlike that involved in handing over one's children to Molech, wedding Israel with non-Israelites. Such behavior was punishable by death. This is perhaps one reason why Paul and his Jesus-group members were in conflict with their fellow Israelites. Be that as it may, Paul clearly is redefining Israelite purity rules. In this he is not unlike those Pharisees who countered the Priestly natural law of Genesis 1 with Adam's, i.e., human determination of purity rules in Gen 2:19-20.

REFERENCES

Artemidoros. *Onirocriticon Libri V.* Ed. Roger A. Pack. Leipzig: Tuebner, 1963.

_____. *The Interpretation of Dreams: Oneirocritica.* Trans. Robert J. White. Park Ridge, N.J.: Noyes Press, 1975.

Boyarin, Daniel. "Are There Any Jews in 'The History of Sexuality'?" *Journal of the History of Sexuality* 5/3 (1995) 333–55.

Bryant, Joseph M. *Moral Codes and Social Structure in Ancient Greece.* Albany, N.Y.: SUNY Press, 1996.

Charles, R. H., ed. *The Apocrypha and Pseudepigrapha of the Old Testament. Vol. II. Pseudepigrapha.* Oxford: Clarendon Press, 1913.

Eilberg-Schwartz, Howard. *The Savage in Judaism: An Anthropology of Israelite Religion and Ancient Judaism.* Bloomington, Ind.: Indiana University Press, 1990.

Frymer-Kensky, Tikva. "Pollution, Purification, and Purgation in Biblical Israel," in Carol L. Meyers and Michael P. O'Connor, eds., *The Word of the Lord Shall Go Forth: Essays in Honor of David Noel Freedman.* Winona Lake, Ind.: Eisenbrauns, 1983, 399–414.

Gilmore, David D. "The Shame of Dishonor," in idem, ed., *Honor and Shame and the Unity of the Mediterranean.* Special Publication of the American Anthropological Association 22. Washington: American Anthropological Association, 1987, 2–21.

Giovannini, Maureen J. "Chastity Codes in the Circum-Mediterranean: Comparative Perspectives," ibid. 61–74.

Greenblatt, Stephen. "Fiction and Friction," in Thomas C. Heller, Morton Sosna, and David E. Wellbery, eds., *Reconstructing Individualism: Autonomy, Individuality and the Self in Western Thought.* Stanford, Calif.: Stanford University Press, 1986, 30–52, 329–32.

Halliday, Michael A. K. *Language as Social Semiotic: The Social Interpretation of Language and Meaning.* Baltimore: University Park Press, 1978.

Halperin, David M. *One Hundred Years of Homosexuality and Other Essays on Greek Love.* New York and London: Routledge, 1990.

_____. "Is There a History of Sexuality?" in Henry Abelove, Michèle Aina Barale, and David M. Halperin, eds., *The Lesbian and Gay Studies Reader.* New York and London: Routledge, 1993, 416–31.

Hasitschka, Martin. "Homosexualität—eine Frage der Schöpfungsordnung," *Zeitschrift für Neues Testament* 1/2 (1998) 54–60.

Helminiak, Daniel A. *What the Bible Really Says about Homosexuality.* San Francisco: Alamo Square, 1994.

Josephus, Flavius. *The Works of Josephus: New Updated Edition.* Trans. William Whiston. Peabody, Mass.: Hendrickson, 1987.

Malina, Bruce J. *Christian Origins and Cultural Anthropology: Practical Models for Biblical Interpretation.* Atlanta: John Knox, 1986.

_____. "Mary—Woman of the Mediterranean: Mother and Son," *Biblical Theology Bulletin* 20 (1990) 54–64.

_____. "Reading Theory Perspective: Reading Luke-Acts," in Jerome H. Neyrey, ed., *The Social World of Luke-Acts: Models for Interpretation.* Peabody, Mass.: Hendrickson, 1991, 3–23.

_____. *The New Testament World: Insights from Cultural Anthropology.* 2nd revised edition. Louisville: Westminster John Knox, 1993.

_____. "'Let Him Deny Himself' (Mark 8:34//): A Social Psychological Model of Self-Denial," *Biblical Theology Bulletin* 24 (1994) 106–19.

_____. *The Social World of Jesus and the Gospels.* London and New York: Routledge, 1996.

Malina, Bruce J., and Jerome H. Neyrey. *Calling Jesus Names: The Social Value of Labels in Matthew.* Sonoma, Calif.: Polebridge Press, 1988.

_____. "Honor and Shame in Luke-Acts: Pivotal Values of the Mediterranean World," in Jerome H. Neyrey, ed., *The Social World of Luke-Acts: Models for Interpretation.* Peabody, Mass.: Hendrickson, 1991, 25–65.

_____. *Portraits of Paul: An Archaeology of Ancient Personality.* Louisville: Westminster John Knox, 1996.

Malina, Bruce J., and Richard L. Rohrbaugh. *Social-Science Commentary on the Synoptic Gospels.* Minneapolis: Fortress, 1992.

Neyrey, Jerome H. *Honor and Shame in the Gospel of Matthew.* Louisville: Westminster John Knox, 1998.

Nissinen, Martti. *Homoeroticism in the Biblical World: A Historical Perspective.* Minneapolis: Fortress, 1998.

Olyan, Saul M. "'And with a Male You Shall Not Lie the Lying Down of a Woman': On the Meaning and Significance of Leviticus 18:22 and 20:13," *Journal of the History of Sexuality* 5/2 (1994) 179–206.

Penna, Romano. "Christian Anthropology and Homosexuality—4: Homosexuality and the New Testament," *Osservatore Romano* March 12, 1997, 5. (sic – www.ewtn.com)

Philo, *The Works of Philo: New Updated Edition.* Trans. C. D. Yonge. Peabody, Mass.: Hendrickson, 1993.

Pilch, John J., "Psychological and Psychoanalytical Approaches to Interpreting the Bible in Social-Scientific Context (BTB Readers Guide)," *Biblical Theology Bulletin* 27 (1997) 112–16.

_____. *Healing in the New Testament: Insights from Medical and Mediterranean Anthropology.* Minneapolis: Fortress, 2000.

Satlow, Michael L. "'They Abused Him Like a Woman': Homoeroticism, Gender Blurring, and the Rabbis in Late Antiquity," *Journal of the History of Sexuality* 5/1 (1994) 1–25.

Stegemann, Wolfgang. "Homosexualität—ein modernes Konzept," *Zeitschrift für Neues Testament* 1/2 (1998) 61–68.

Tiedemann, Holger. "Das Gesetz in den Gliedern—Paulus und das sexuelle Begehren," *Zeitschrift für Neues Testament* 1/2 (1998) 18–28.

Triandis, Harry C. "Cross-Cultural Studies of Individualism and Collectivism," in John J. Berman, ed., *Nebraska Symposium on Motivation 1989: Cross-Cultural Perspectives.* Lincoln, Neb.: University of Nebraska Press, 1990, 41–133.

Vatican Documents: http://clawww.lmu.edu/faculty/fjust/fjust.html.

Veyne, Paul. "Rome: Une Société d'hommes," *L'Histoire* 221 (May 1998) 37.

Winkler, John J. *The Constraints of Desire: The Anthropology of Sex and Gender in Ancient Greece.* New York and London: Routledge, 1990.

NOTES: CHAPTER 8

[1] Homosexuality, that is, same-gender sexual orientation, was not of concern in antiquity. It is of recent vintage, emerging with the rise of economics as focal social institution and the changes in lifestyle brought on by the Industrial Revolution and Romanticism. With social interest turning to persons as individuals and their individualism, sexual orientation was disjoined from gender. "Though the term 'individualism' is relatively recent, a nineteenth-century coinage, the existence of individuals has long seemed to be a constitutive, universal element in the natural structure of human experience and hence more the basis than the object of historical investigation. But the belatedness of the general term for the phenomenon of individuals should make us wary of

assuming the stable existence of individualism as a category of human life
. . ." (Greenblatt 1986, 32, cited by Halperin 1990, 159). For the recent individualistic cultural script in comparison with majority collective societies in
the world today see Malina 1986; 1994; Triandis 1990.

²For example, the seer of the Sibyllines notes: "More than any men they
(Israelites) are mindful of the purity of marriage. Nor do they hold unholy intercourse with boys, as do the Phoenicians, Egyptians and Latins, and spacious
Hellas and many nations of other men, Persians and Galatians and all Asia
transgressing the holy law of the immortal God which he ordained" (*Sib. Or*
3:594–600, Charles); similarly Josephus: "what reason can there be why we
should desire to imitate the laws of other nations, while we see they are not
observed by their own legislators? And why do not the Lacedemonians think of
abolishing that form of their government which suffers them not to associate
with any others, as well as their contempt of matrimony? And why do not the
Eleans and Thebans abolish that unnatural and impudent lust, which makes
them lie with males?" (*Against Apion* 2.37.273, Whiston); or the Letter of Aristeas, constrasting Israel and "most other" ethnic groups: "For most other men
defile themselves by promiscuous intercourse, thereby working great iniquity,
and whole countries and cities pride themselves upon such vices. For they not
only have intercourse with men but they defile their own mothers and even
their daughters. But we have been kept separate from such sins" (*Ep. Aristeas*
152, Charles).

³Greek *Ioudaioi;* in historical perspective, the word "Jews" is properly used
only of persons in the Israelite tradition after the formation of the Jewish (Tal-
mudic) kinship religion in the fifth century C.E.; see Malina and Rohrbaugh
1992, 32–34.

⁴By the Hellenistic period Israelite-Gentile marriages were considered
"offering one's children to Molech" (Lev 18:21; 20:2), deserving the death
penalty since such unions are "contrary to nature," as we shall note below.
Paul's continued concern about Israel's purity laws can be seen in his assessment of offspring of a Jesus group member and an outsider, 1 Cor 7:14.

⁵"Degrading" of course points to a scale calibrated in terms of honor; see
Gilmore 1987; Giovannini 1987; Malina and Neyrey 1991; Malina 1993;
Neyrey 1998.

⁶The Israelite view is represented by Josephus: "for Scripture says: 'A
woman is inferior to her husband in all things' [Gen 3:16]. Let her, therefore, be
obedient to him; not so, that he should abuse her, but that she may acknowledge her duty to her husband; for God has given the authority to the husband"
(*Against Apion* 2.201, Whiston).

⁷While in the Israelite tradition guilty persons alone are to be killed, not
members of their family (Deut 24:16: "every man shall be put to death for his

own sin"), the death penalty attaches to all of the Ten Commandments apart from coveting (i.e., stealing):

Idolatry: those serving and worshiping other gods (Deut 17:7), as well as false prophets (Deut 13:5), are to be put to death.

Blasphemy: Blasphemers of the name of YHWH shall be put to death (Lev 24:16).

Temple Defilement: In Exod 19:12, going up Mount Sinai or touching the border of it while Moses was up there required the death penalty for the offender. The same rules were then applied to the Tent (and Temple: the altar and what is within the veil) where God dwelt in Israel (Num 1:51; 3:10; 18:7).

Sabbath Observance: Infractions of the Sabbath require the death penalty for the offender (Exod 31:14-15; 35:2; Num 15:35).

Parents: the death penalty is required for anyone who strikes father or mother, or who curses father or mother (Exod 21:15, 17; Lev 20:9); this is also the fate of a recalcitrant son disobedient to parents (Deut 21:21).

Adultery: the death penalty is commanded for adulterer and adulteress (Deut 22:22), consenting betrothed woman and another man (Deut 22:24), rapist of unconsenting betrothed woman (Deut 22:25), a wife without tokens of virginity (Deut 22:21).

Murder: "Whoever strikes a man so that he dies shall be put to death" (Exod 21: 12; also Num 35:16-21): murderers must be put to death; specifically, "the avenger of blood shall put the murderer to death, when he meets him"; for in Israel "you shall accept no ransom for the life of a murderer, who is guilty of death; but he shall be put to death" (Num 35:31; also Lev 24:17; 24:21). The owner of an ox known to kill must also be killed if the ox kills again (Exod 21:29); one disobedient to a priest-judge's judgment in a homicide case likewise gets the death penalty (Deut 17:12).

Kidnappers must be put to death (Exod 21:16; Deut 24:7).

False witnesses are to be put to death (Deut 19:19).

[8] But they could be written verbatim. Since these words were put in *tephilim* and *mezuzoth* by no command of God (unlike the *Shema* of Deut 6:4-9), it seems their presence there, "to the letter," was to serve as apotropaic, a prophylactic device to ward off hostile power, the evil eye, and the like.

[9] There are further truncated listings. For example, in the Sermon on the Mount the antitheses (Matt 5:21-36) cover five of the Ten Commandments. In the list of evils proceeding from the heart, while Mark 7:21-22 has three parallel categories: a. fornication, b. theft, c. murder; a'. adultery, b'. coveting, c'. wickedness; a". licentiousness, b". envy, c". slander and pride and foolishness (I would consider this only five of the ten: 3 x 3 plus pride and foolishness, that

is, other gods before God and idolatry), Matt 15:19 has a list of six (or seven or five), but these are the last five of a listing, just as in the antitheses in the Sermon on the Mount: evil thoughts: (1) murder, (2) adultery, fornication, (3) theft, (4) false witness, (5) slander.

9

Perfect Fear Casteth Out Love: Reading, Citing, and Rape[1]

Mary Rose D'Angelo

Only fragments remain, like fragments of shrapnel lodged in my subconsciousness. Once in a while they work themselves free. When they do, I see things more clearly: why I left the Church, why I have difficulties with relationships, and why I empathize with Matthew Shepard.

My two rapists, who were not gay, were rich, Catholic, white, and conservative. Knowing that the school had voted 99–1 Democrat in a poll at the time of the 1988 elections, they accused me of being "a faggot democrat who deserves to be raped."

They bragged about their conquests with women to me, claiming to have raped over twenty women on the campus alone.

They named the girl I had just broken up with as one of their "loyal subjects" who "needed to be taught a lesson when she was a Freshman."

My rape was about power, as all rape is. And in my case religion encouraged my rapists. I was choked with a rosary, and forced to

*recite the Apostle's Creed and Lord's prayer during the ordeal. In the
name of the Father I was nearly destroyed. How many other people
suffer in the same manner every day because of the church's disregard for their humanity and their dignity? It begins in the pulpit.*

*"My priest said fags are evil. I'm doing God's work," is the last thing
I remember before I began the task of editing out twenty minutes of
my life.*

John Andrew Murphy [2]

*A*n invitation to reflect on the "Biblical Renewal of Catholic Teaching on Homosexuality" cannot help but raise some speculation
as to its intent. The struggles of scholars of other Christian denominations with the biblical texts that have been read as prohibitions
of homoeroticism suggest that the Catholic tradition of ethics should
offer considerable advantages over "divine command" uses of Scripture
that are at times invoked as the basis of condemnations of same-sex love
among Protestant Christians.[3] "A tradition committed to a natural law
approach (that is, some form of ethical realism, however moderated)
should, more than any other tradition, take account of the empirical
findings, plausible psychological theories and human experience across
cultures."[4]

While recent years have seen this commitment transform many
areas of Catholic moral theology including thinking about sexuality, its
effect in leniating ecclesiastical pronouncements on homosexuality has
been limited. An attempt to renew Catholic ethical teaching by appealing to the very biblical texts that have caused so much anguish in other
Christian churches would seem unlikely to induce a fuller comprehension of contemporary moral realities in the ecclesiastical authorities
who insist that "Catholic teaching" is a province reserved to themselves.
But it may be that a careful examination of the biblical texts that are
used in the condemnation of same-sex love can provide an entreé into
the complex problem of the impact of biblical dicta on contemporary
moral responsibility.

The relation between contemporary ecclesiastical condemnations of
homosexual love and unions and the biblical texts to whose authority
they lay claim is by no means unexplored by scholars. Numerous biblical scholars (Catholic, Protestant, and Jewish alike) have already suggested that the biblical texts used by some Christian (including Roman

Catholic) authorities to condemn homosexuality and to promote homophobia offer a less than secure theological foundation. Two approaches to the very few texts that seem to refer to same-sex sexual contact have become virtually standard, and a third, more far-reaching and central analysis of the relation between ancient and contemporary sexual taboos has begun to emerge.

This essay will briefly summarize the first two approaches, designating them as relativizing the texts and recontextualizing them,[5] and then seek to make a contribution to the third, which I call interrogating the texts. Analyzing biblical texts that have contributed to contemporary constructions of sexuality does indeed inspire a call for renewal and revision of those constructions, but in ways that may be unexpected.

RELATIVIZING THE TEXTS

A first approach begins from the prohibitions and reflects on their relative weight in their literary and canonical contexts. This approach is important as a reminder that the real force behind the biblical prohibitions of homoeroticism is not the authority of the Bible but the homophobia that has characterized the interpretive communities. For instance, the Holiness Code in Leviticus includes two explicit prohibitions forbidding a man to "lie with a male as with a woman" (Lev 18:22 and 20:13);[6] the second version prescribes death as the penalty for this act. The "holiness code" (Leviticus 18–26) is an ancient collection of laws that includes the tables of forbidden relations among kin and applies the death penalty to men who have sex with their wives during their menses (20:18).[7] It also proscribes fabric blends, mules, and the planting of mixed crops (19:19). The laws of gleaning occur here too; they limit private profit from agricultural land by requiring harvesters not to strip a field but to leave some of the crop for the landless poor and sojourners (immigrants) to harvest (19:9-10).

The New Testament includes no explicit prohibitions of same-sex sexual contact. The undisputed letters of Paul make two very brief references to what at least appears to be same-sex sexual contact, both in vice lists. (The only other potential reference to same-sex sexual contact among the New Testament texts is a single word in another vice list in 1 Tim 1:10, a letter produced in Paul's name by a second-century interpreter of his person and mission.) Romans 1:26-27 gives the most attention to homoeroticism. Beginning by singling out an unspecified "unnatural use" by women, Paul proceeds to decry men who, "consumed with passion," gave up the 'natural use' (*physikē chrēsis,* "natural intercourse" NRSV) of the woman and worked shamelessness upon one another."

In another vice list in 1 Cor 6:9 two nouns (among a list of many) have been interpreted as indicating the active and passive partners in male homoerotic contact. As Choon-Leong Seow points out, 1 Cor 6:9 is a supporting element in a vehement argument against a practice Paul sees as deeply shameful—members of the Christian community suing each other in a civic court (1 Cor 6:1-11). "How do we decide, then, that Paul's central point in the passage is no longer relevant, but that a peripheral reference is?"[8] It is noteworthy that in the same letter Paul devotes far more energy to the demand that women cover their heads in the Christian assembly (1 Cor 11:2-16). Still more elaborate and lengthy is his carefully nuanced approach to the eating or refusal of temple sacrifices (1 Cor 8:1–11:1). And of course, 1 Corinthians 5 is devoted to Paul's demand that the community eject and curse a member who now "has" a woman who had once been his father's partner—a situation that might now be considered distasteful, but hardly incestuous.

RESTRICTING THE TEXTS' CONTEXT

The second approach is to reread the texts in their own social context, so as to demonstrate the very considerable distance between contemporary homoerotic partnerships and understandings of homosexuality and the practices and social meanings of the ancient text. This approach stresses the relative novelty of such concepts as "sexual orientation," drawing on scholarship that has described the ways that sexual experiences, including homoeroticism, have undergone historical transformations.[9]

Retrieving the historical context can, for instance, underline the inappropriateness of the term "sodomy." In common English sodomy refers to male homosexual intercourse and in legal terminology to anal or oral intercourse, whether homosexual or heterosexual. But the sin of Sodom is seen quite differently by interpreters within the biblical texts. In the story in Genesis 19, the assault the men of Sodom propose against the angels is only the culminating example of their lack of justice. It provides the final evidence that it is impossible to find ten just men there and so validates the "outcry against them" (Gen 18:20-21). And, as has often been remarked, the deed that illustrates their wickedness is not homosexuality, but the violent and gratuitous violation of guest-friendship, of the sacred and ultimate obligation to protect a guest that obtained throughout the ancient Mediterranean. In this they are contrasted both with Abraham, the perfect (and spectacularly rewarded) host (Gen 18:1-15) and with Lot (Gen 19:1-3, 8).

Texts from the Hebrew Bible other than Genesis mention the fate of Sodom (or Sodom and Gomorrah) as an example of the deity's wrath against sinners, as warnings to Israel or Judah or prophecies against their enemies. But they never identify the sins that cause the projected disasters as homosexuality, and rarely mention any sexual sin.[10] Violence, exploitation of strangers, and exploitation of the poor are the explicit concerns when Ezekiel uses Sodom as a cautionary example: "This was the guilt of your sister Sodom: she and her daughters had pride, excess of food and prosperous ease but did not aid the poor and needy" (Ezek 16:49 NRSV; see also Isa 1:10-18).[11] Even the Roman-era Greek work Wisdom of Solomon uses the men of Sodom to interpret the forced labor of the Israelites in Egypt as violating hospitality, or, in the terms of the Hebrew Bible, the protection of the *ger* (sojourner or immigrant):

> Others (i.e., the men of Sodom) had refused to receive strangers when they came to them
> But these (the Egyptians) made slaves of guests who were their benefactors . . .
> They (the Egyptians) were stricken also with loss of sight—
> Just as were those (the men of Sodom) at the door of the righteous man—
>
> (19:14, 17 NRSV; parentheses mine)

Through the rabbinic period this emphasis on the breach of hospitality and the rapaciousness of the Sodomites remains the "obvious" meaning of the text for Jewish interpreters in Hebrew and Aramaic. *Mekilta Shirata* 2:30-52 explains their hostility toward travelers as greed and cites Ezek 16:49 as the definition of their crime (neglect of the poor and needy). Other interpretations of Genesis 19 elaborate the greed and violence of the Sodomites. This is not to say that the rabbis had no objections to same-sex contact. In fact, *Shirata* itself interprets Pharaoh's boast, "I will bare my sword," as his intent to commit pederasty upon the Israelites (*Shirata* 7.35-45), but this interpretation is not connected with the Sodomites.

Yet another stream of interpretation sees the story as a narrative of lust, but links it with the "sons of God" who are said to have had sex with human women in Gen 6:1-5. This pairing seems to focus the outrage not on the "homosexual" character of the Sodomites' demand but on what might be termed its interspecies aspects: like the lustful "angels" of Gen 6:1-5, the guests threatened with rape are not human males but heavenly beings (*Jub* 20:5; Jude 6–7; cf. 2 Pet 2:6).[12]

RETHINKING THE PROBLEM

Both relativizing the texts within their literary settings and recontextualizing them within their historical and social locations are approaches that help to shift attention from the supposedly unalterable biblical texts to the investments of the interpreters who focus upon them. In addition, these approaches help to foreground biblical concerns with justice for the poor, issues that are much more central to the prophets and legal material of the Hebrew Bible but have been easily dismissed in the last two centuries.

But these approaches inspire my anxiety as a biblical scholar on two levels. First, either relativizing the texts or stressing their distance from the social world of contemporary Christianity runs the risk of trivializing the biblical texts, of rendering them unusable or even risible for the audience, and even in some cases for the interpreter. Some exegetes do indeed see the biblical texts as locked within the assumptions of their ancient culture, and view their own task as exposing their inapplicability to later lives.[13] On another level, the strategies of relativizing the texts and distancing them may spring from or result in an apologetic attempt to absolve the Bible from the condemnation of same-sex love, from homophobia.

The biblical texts, including these biblical texts, are in fact implicated in the production of twentieth-century homophobia and sexism in such a way that challenging them is essential to the safety of every woman, lesbian or straight, and of straight men (as John Andrew Murphy's narrative illustrates) as well as gays. Thus neither strategy can adequately deal with the problem of the Bible, the Christian communities, and homoeroticism. An ethically adequate approach to the biblical texts must investigate not only the ways that they evade the categories to which they have been assigned, and the distance between their worlds and the world in which they now act, but also their continuities with that world and the ways in which they have helped to construct current categories. This approach demands careful attention to the literary context and a searching examination of the historical and social context, but its aim is not (or not only) to disconnect these texts from the sources of their power in the present, but to recognize and interrogate their implication in the power struggles of the present.

INTERROGATING THE TEXTS

The biblical texts that have been read as condemnations of homosexuality originated in part as guardians of the kinds of sexual hierarchy that continue to produce the fear and hatred of sexual dissidents, the sexual hierarchy that is violated when a male is "reduced" to the status of a woman. Homophobia is a product of patriarchy: that is, it inheres in social systems in which a limited number of privileged males have power over women, children, and less-privileged males (clients, slaves, unemancipated sons). Within such systems homophobia is but one feature of a complex gender system that requires and enforces the subordination of women and of many, if not most, men. Homoeroticism is seen as wrong or unnatural because it interferes with, violates, the superior status of men and so endangers the homosocial bonding of privileged males.

THE TEXTS OF THE HEBREW BIBLE

Genesis 19 requires a rereading in light of this observation. In this text two heavenly beings are sent to Sodom to convince Abraham's relative Lot to flee the divine wrath coming upon Sodom (vv. 1-4). The men of Sodom demand that Lot put the visitors out of the house so they can rape them (v. 5). To avoid this violation of hospitality Lot offers his virgin daughters in their place (vv. 6-9). The angelic visitors intervene (v. 10), so that his offer is never acted upon. The father and his two daughters escape the destruction of the city under the tutelage of the angels, while the mother's regrets leave her frozen in place (vv. 12-26).

Genesis 19 has a shadow version in Judges 19, a "text of terror" whose central episode is nearly identical to Genesis 19, but whose details and issue are even grimmer, offering no *deus ex machina* salvation.[14] A Levite, his concubine, and his servant arrive in Gibeah and are offered hospitality by an old man (Judg 19:14-21). Once again the men of the town demand the opportunity to rape the male visitor (vv. 22-23). When the old man offers his own young daughter and the Levite's concubine as a substitute (v. 24), the Levite himself pushes the concubine out (v. 25). Raped all night (v. 25), she falls at the doorsill (v. 26). In the morning the Levite finds her there and dismembers her, using her body as the signal and bond to muster the Israelites to revenge the injury to him

(vv. 27-30). When his vengeance brings the tribe of Benjamin to near extinction (20:1–21:7) this wrong is righted by the rape of six hundred more women (21:8-24).

As I conceded above, these stories condemn the perpetrators not for "the homosexual act" but for the violation of hospitality. But the willingness of the hosts to offer their own daughters in place of the male guests casts light on the prohibition of "lying with a male as with a woman" (Lev 18:22; 20:13). They demonstrate the authors' cultural presupposition that while it is by no means "all right" to rape a woman, it is worse to rape a man, not because sex between men is "intrinsically evil" but because penetration of one man by another reduces one of the two supposedly superior males to the status of the "inferior" female.[15] This aspect is underlined by the invitation of the old man of Gibeah to the would-be rapists of the Levite: "here are my virgin daughter and his concubine; let me bring them out. Humble [NRSV ravish] them, but do not do this foul thing to this man" (Judg 19:24).

Thus, despite the vast historical, cultural, and social differences between the narratives of Genesis 19 and Judges 19 on the one hand and the narrative of John Andrew Murphy on the other, the motivations of the rapists appear strikingly similar. Even the proxy rape of the Levite through his concubine is echoed in the rapists' insinuation that they had also raped Murphy's former girlfriend.[16] Their purpose is to humiliate the lesser and vulnerable male guests: in the words of an anthropologist friend who studies abused children in war zones, "they do it because they can"—and beyond that, to make it clear that *they* can, and the lesser male cannot. Recognizing the content of these narratives in a sense vindicates readers who insist that the text is not about homosexuality "as we know it." As in the case of John Andrew Murphy, no one in these narratives is gay; the rapes that are at issue in his narrative and in the two biblical texts are not in any real sense "homosexual rapes," but rather acts by which men assert their own male power by violently denying that of another man.

It is possible that the prohibitions against lying with a male "as with a woman" in Lev 18:22 and 20:18 (NRSV) envisage precisely this sort of rape, though they do not refer explicitly to coercion. The Hebrew phrase translated "as with a woman" occurs only in these two verses; Robert Di Vito's discussion of it makes clear that interpreting the prohibition is a complex issue.[17] But the narratives of Genesis 19 and Judges 19 illuminate the context: they understand the penetration of a male by a male to involve hubris on the part of one and humiliation on the part of the other.

EARLY CHRISTIANITY AND IMPERIAL ROME

If the view that penetrating a male reduces him to female status is implicit in the Hebrew Bible, it is quite explicit in the Greek-speaking Roman imperial context of Paul and his interpreters. Scholarship on sexuality in Greek and Roman antiquity has increasingly recognized that, while since the late-nineteenth-century sexual experience has been constructed as an identity organized along an axis whose poles are heterosexual and homosexual desire, the ancients understood sexual experience in terms of activities organized along an axis that ran from active to passive.[18] John J. Winkler has argued convincingly that "natural" sex in Greek-speaking antiquity involved a penis, penetration, and an appropriate display of power relations: the penetrated passive partner is the inferior of the penetrating, active partner.[19]

The appropriate display of power differential is carefully observed within the "approved" form of Greek homosexuality, pederasty.[20] The age difference between the two partners assigned roles within the relationship. The adult, active partner was the lover, the passive boy the beloved, who might be or become the lover of a younger boy. These relationships were appropriated into the process of education and socialization in the Greek city. Both theory and social practice attempted to provide safeguards for the character and manliness of the young boy.[21] Pleasure was the prerogative of the pursuer; the youth was wooed with gifts, but expected not to enjoy the sexual act itself. In this he was and was expected to be distinguished from women, who were believed to experience more sexual pleasure and therefore less self-control than men.

Vase paintings depicting the pederastic pair show the courtship, or in a few cases what seems to be intercrural intercourse—the adult partner thrusting his penis between the youth's thighs.[22] Anal penetration appears not to have been a "licit" form of pederastic contact. Several vase paintings depict it being practiced by symposium participants on older, less attractive hetaerae; one displays a conquered Persian bending over for the advance of a victorious Greek soldier.[23] The viewer may have been intended to find these scenes amusing; they certainly suggest that anal penetration was a technique of humiliation and involved coercion akin to rape. The (much later) rabbinic interpretation of Pharaoh's pursuit of the Israelites as evidence of his intent to rape them likewise reveals the long-standing use of rape as a performance both aimed at and articulating the subjugation of the conquered.

Latin literature of the late Roman republic and imperial-period literature, whether in Greek or in Latin, tend to display wholesale disapproval of same-sex eroticism, whether between freeborn males or between women. This observation is not intended to approve Cicero's conclusion that pederasty (like other forms of pleasure and luxury) was a Greek import (*Tusculan Disputations* 4.70). While homoeroticism in both Athens and Sparta was not merely inculturated but deeply intertwined with political institutions, it is unlikely that Roman homoeroticism derived from foreign influence.[24] There are some real differences in Roman cultural perceptions and the practice of male homoeroticism, in particular the association of the passive role not with elite youth but with slaves, especially (though not exclusively) with young and pretty boy slaves. Cicero's claim reflects moralizing propaganda about true Roman manliness. Accusations of someone's having played the passive role in homoerotic contact, even as a boy, provided a valuable weapon in the repertoire of political and legal invective.[25] The condemnation of women for same-sex erotic contact was a particularly Roman-period concern.[26]

Moralizing invective, like recent complaints about a breakdown in religious, social, and sexual mores, had political uses in the struggles of the late Roman republic. Augustus exploited the accusations and plaints of his contemporaries in a sort of first-century "family values" campaign whose aim was to provide a moral pretext for the consolidation of his power. This interest inspired the marriage laws by which, according to his own boast, he restored the ancient customs (*Res Gestae* 2.8). These laws were promulgated in 18 B.C.E. and revised in 9 C.E.[27] They have often been dismissed as unenforceable, but enforcement is not the primary indication of their significance.[28] As a means of propaganda they were effective primarily as they both responded to and marshaled public opinion.[29] In the assessment of Catherine Edwards, "The *lex Iulia de adulteriis* was the last word in rhetorical invective."[30]

While it is difficult to gauge the precise degree to which the laws were effective as propaganda, there is every reason to see the atmosphere they reflected and generated as extremely important in the articulation of social mores among early Christians, and also among Jews. Both communities had to live within the empire, but were unable to affirm their loyalty by sharing its religious pieties. If they were unwilling to make offerings to Rome and Augustus, they could yet pray for the emperor and display for him the excellence of their marital chastity and their assiduousness in the raising and begetting of legitimate children.

One example is Philo of Alexandria, a Greek-speaking Jewish philosopher who was an older contemporary of Paul. His work appears to have aimed both at broadening the intellectual basis of Jewish communities and at explicating Judaism for the thinking imperial public. During the reign of Gaius (Caligula, 37–41) he undertook the even more public task of an embassy to the emperor on behalf of all Jews, entreating against the erection of a colossal statue of the emperor in the Temple in Jerusalem *(Embassy to Gaius)*.

A significant oddity appears in Philo's interpretation of Deut 24:4, which forbids a man to remarry a former wife who had in the interval been married to someone else. In *Special Laws* 3.31 Philo accuses the husband who does this of both adultery *(moicheia, adulterium)* and pandering *(prosagogeia, lenocinium)*. These crimes were the focus of Augustus's legislation.[31] The charge of pandering laid against a complaisant husband seems to have been a peculiarly Roman piece of invective.[32] These same crimes are also seen by Philo as indications of "unmanliness" *(anandria)* and "softness" *(malakia);* in other words, effeminacy. Adultery and effeminacy are a strange combination to modern ears, but the association is consistent with the Roman construction of sexuality.[33]

For Philo pederasty, castration, and the assumption of feminine dress and manner and of the passive role in intercourse all "debase the coin" of nature by changing the "character" stamped into a man to the inferior pattern of femaleness.[34] An evil even greater than this personal corruption, in Philo's view, is "the depopulation *(eremian)* of cities and the scarcity of the best sort" that they produce *(Contemplative Life* 62). This condemnation reflects Philo's conviction that the motive for sexual intercourse must be the production of legitimate heirs *(Special Laws* 3:32-39), but the Augustan laws' role in the campaign to increase the population of citizens and especially of the propertied classes should also be reckoned as indicative of the context in which he wrote.

At the end of the first century Josephus, the Jewish historian and client of the Flavian emperors, rephrased the prohibition of Lev 20:18 as a condemnation in his affirmation of the excellence of Jewish sexual mores against the accusations of Apion: "What then are the (Jewish) marriage laws? The law permits only union with a wife (woman) according to nature, and that only for the sake of children. It abhors the union of males with males, and death is the penalty if any should undertake it" *(Against Apion* 2.198). Likewise in retelling the Genesis narrative he remarks upon the beauty and youthful appearance of the angels, marking the rapists of Sodom as pederasts in the Greek manner (*Antiquities of the Jews* 1:200). In recounting that Herod refused to send the young prince Aristoboulos to Antony as a hostage (and potential rival to Herod for Antony's favor), Josephus recasts his refusal as a ploy to protect a handsome and royal youth from an arrogant and dissolute usurper of Roman power who, for all his sexual enthrallment to the threateningly oriental Cleopatra, was "ready to subject him to erotics . . . and the most powerful men among the Romans" (*Antiquities* 15:27-30). Thus he distances both Jews and their true Roman masters (as opposed to corrupt, dissolute, and orientalized Antony) from the "foreign" practice of pederasty.

These Jewish writers shared the disapprobation expressed by earlier and later Roman political theorists. In the early second century Dio Chrysostom played the role of a sort of philosophical chaplain to Trajan, to whom he appears to have addressed at least his four discourses *On Kingship*. Both the reading of penetration as humiliation and the continuity between "homosexual" and "heterosexual" lust appear in his work. In the conclusion to his idealized pastoral romance celebrating the love of Daphnis and Chloe he asserts that the desire for pederasty results from getting away with adulterous desire for other men's wives and daughters—if that is too easy, the perpetrators will "cross over into the men's quarters, lusting to humiliate those who will soon be rulers, judges and generals, so as to find there some difficult and recherché form of pleasure" (*Discourse* 7, *the Euboean* 151–52).

These writers illustrate the existence of both the assumed and the explicit construction of sexual relations in terms of power relations throughout the first century, a construction that is reflected in the two Greek words that are generally taken to refer to male homosexual contact in 1 Cor 6:9: *arsenokoites* (male-bedder? cf. 1 Tim 1:10) and *malakos* (softy). Dale Martin has rightly questioned the simple equation of these terms with the active *(arsenokoites)* and passive *(malakos)* partners in male homoerotic contact.[35] As he points out, *arsenokoites* occurs rarely, and the few contexts in which it appears might as easily suggest a crime of exploitation as a sexual sin.[36] While *malakos* is far more frequent and can refer to the pathic lover, it has a broader context, designating any form of luxury or "unmanliness."[37] But these caveats, if they preclude the certain identification of these two terms with the homosexual or pederastic pairs, ultimately testify to Paul's immersion in precisely the sexual ideology that constructs sexuality and gender as a display of social power and understands penetration as humiliation. Given Dio

Chrysostom's explanation of pederastic desire, it is no surprise to find *arsenokoites* among the perpetrators of fraud, theft, and exploitation, or to discover that the penetrated male and the adulterer are both *malakoi,* indulging in the same vice. These terms, like the texts in which they are found, function to maintain a sexual and social hierarchy, to distinguish the privileged males who can claim the title of father (or master or husband) not only from the women, children, and lesser males in their *potestas,* but also from those lesser males who might contest or usurp it.

Thus women who take an active role in sex, especially (but not exclusively) an active role in sex with another woman, are liable to the charge of unnameable and unnatural use (Rom 1:26-27).[38] They are imaginable to Paul's contemporaries only as competing "fuckers" *(futatores),* who manage by physical anomalies or primitive prosthetics to ape the accomplishments of male sexual omnivores.[39] Conversely, men who abdicate or exploit their status by sexual contact with another male are gender traitors who, as Philo charges, "debase the coin," traducing the status awarded them by "nature" (see Rom 1:27-28). The biblical texts that appear to condemn homosexuality function to maintain a social and sexual hierarchy, as do the deutero-Pauline household codes that demand submission from women and obedience from slaves (Col 3:18–4:1; Eph 5:22–6:9; 1 Pet 2:18–3:6). Whether *arsenokoites* refers to the "male-bedder" in the pederastic pair, to some other type of sexual or financial exploiter, or to some role that remains unknown to later interpreters, its referent is likely to be entirely harmonious with the "family values" of the codes. This is particularly manifest in its employment in 1 Tim 1:10. Here the vice list in which it occurs is part of the overture of a letter that is essentially a household code for "the household of God, which is the church" (1 Tim 3:15). From the community the letter requires prayers for the emperor and all in power (2:1-3), silence and submissiveness from women (2:9-15), reverent obedience from slaves (6:1-2), and the demonstrated ability to "rule" their own household from those men who are considered fit to oversee the community (3:4-5).

REMEDIAL READING

How then are these texts to be regarded in the search for a renewal of Catholic moral theology? I believe that they are in a strange way essential to that enterprise, although their significance can hardly be said to arise from their centrality to the biblical witness. Commentators who point to the relative insignificance of the texts in question within the larger scope of biblical narrative and imperative rightly ask why it is that Christians need to insist upon their clear and definitive bearing upon Christian mores. Those who argue that the ancient texts that are interpreted as applying to homosexuality do not speak of homosexuality "as we know it" also rightly turn the interpreters to the examination of their own contexts and investments. The construction of sexuality along an axis whose poles are activity and passivity cannot be equated with contemporary constructions of sexuality that polarize homoeroticism and heterosexual desire.

But the narrative of John Andrew Murphy demonstrates the degree to which that older axis perdures as a sort of *pentimento* behind and within contemporary sexual constructs. Another example of its survival occurred during the controversies over deregulating homosexuality in the U.S. military. One sailor told an interviewer that he didn't want gays in the Navy because he didn't want to be looked at "that way" in the shower. That is, if gays were allowed the same tolerance for expressing their desire that both society and the Navy have permitted him, he might be reduced to the status to which women are subject and are seen by men to be subject, that is, reduced to the status of sexual prey for the male gaze, available for consumption or rejection. His homophobia was a protection for male homosociality, and ultimately for patriarchal rule.

Some readers of Murphy's narrative might see his claim that "it begins in the pulpit" as overstatement. It seems improbable that anything said from a pulpit would have caused the rapists to choke him with a rosary or force him to recite the Apostles' Creed as they raped him. But the continuity between condemnations of homosexuality and violence against gays (and men who are inadequately "manly," and women, and children) should be a real concern. Writing about legislation that secures the basic civil rights of lesbians and gays, Margaret Farley observes:

> . . . the continuing massive societal resistance to this legislation is lodged, I believe, in the vehemence of the negative judgment that continues to be made regarding homosexual activity and relationships. This judgment, at least when it is put forward by church leaders and moral theologians, is frequently a carefully reasoned one. But its power as a social force is the power of an unreasoned taboo, lodged in and reinforcing a kind of unreflective repulsion that must be addressed if we are to move forward politically on these issues.[40]

The "unreasoned taboo" and "unreflective repulsion" arise because "the vehemence of the negative judgments" collaborates with the fear that any man who deviates from gender prescriptions can be reduced to, made into, a woman. This fear is strengthened by every reassertion and protection of gender hierarchy, and simultaneously it provides that hierarchy with a nearly perfect bulwark.

The damage done by the "vehemence of the negative judgments" thus cannot be undone by merely softening the tone of condemnation, or even by ceasing to make them. A first, indeed minimal, step is official ecclesiastical acknowledgment of and indeed advocacy on behalf of full civil rights, including domestic partnership rights, for gays and lesbians. But more than that is required, not only from Church officials but from theologians, biblical scholars, and ethicists who have recognized the need for serious revision of Church positions in this matter.

Choon-Leong Seow suggests "reorienting" the texts on the model of the interpretations of Scripture attributed to Jesus. He does this by drawing on that stream of the Wisdom tradition that resists claims to direct revelation and invites, in fact requires, the application of reason to nature, the endeavor of what contemporary people see as scientific thinking.[41] In theory this reorientation would place Protestant ethical approaches to the biblical texts precisely where Catholic moral theology has been strongest. Unfortunately, both popular understanding and official statements from the Roman Catholic hierarchy have found it quite easy to identify "natural law" with the conventional understanding of the biblical dicta. This identification short-circuits the work of reason in the method of natural law and, by confining thought to horizons established by ancient patriarchy, it enforces contemporary patriarchal power.

"Reorienting the text" in the light of Catholic experience thus requires something more than finding other texts with which to counter or realign these. It also requires reorienting the reader to be alert not only to what texts supposedly prescribe and proscribe, but also to how they have been inscribed in their afterlife. What is needed is a two-pronged campaign on the part of Christian thinkers: first to theorize and propagate "vehement negative judgment" upon homophobia and its sources in the tradition, and second to advocate a positive valuation of sexual love as a good in itself in ways that can integrate the experience of same-sex lovers.

Since both homophobia and the devaluation of sex are deeply rooted in gendered social hierarchy and the protection of patriarchal power, reorienting both the texts and the readers means a genuinely searching re-examination of the gender ideologies that have formed sexual meanings in the West. The aim of reading and writing must be the dismantling of sexual and gender hierarchies down to the point at which women and femaleness no longer occupy a scarecrow status. Such a dismantling is essential in removing from men the motivation to make abject both women and those men who can in some way be made lesser.

DISMANTLING SEXUAL AND GENDERED HIERARCHY

One point at which this reorienting might start is Rom 1:26-27: "Their women changed the *natural use* for the unnatural and likewise the men giving up the *natural use* of the female (NRSV "natural intercourse with women") burned with passion one for another, males performing the shameful deed on males, and receiving the recompense that was due their error in themselves." The use of "natural" and "unnatural" in these verses and in Paul generally has received considerable attention and will be discussed by others in this volume.[42] I want to focus on *chrēsis*. This term means both habit and custom (what is usual) on the one hand, and usefulness or utilization on the other. It is also a standard euphemism for sexual intercourse.[43] While *chrēsis* can be contrasted with *physis* ("nature"), here that contrast is collapsed in the expression "natural use." As in 1 Cor 11:13-14, Paul's use of *physis* conforms to other ancient uses that implicitly or explicitly see "nature" as produced by habit and convention.[44]

Paul's use of *chrēsis* makes sex parallel to food, drink, the world—something that can be used, and even something over which one may have an *exousia* (1 Cor 6:12-13, 9:1-6, 15), but something he chooses not to use or at least not to "use up." Perhaps a revision should be made here; it is not exactly sex that is "used" or over which one has an *exousia*. Romans 1:27 speaks of men turning from the natural *chrēsis* of the female; when Rom 1:26 castigates women who leave "the natural *chrēsis*" no object is expressed; it is not within nature for the male to be the object of use. While this may sound like an overly crass and partisan interpretation of *chrēsis*, it should be remembered that for Paul metaphors for sex and marriage routinely depict them in terms of bondage and slavery. For both partners, marriage involves exercising an *exousia* over each other's bodies and not over one's own; here Paul seems to have in mind the right to sexual intercourse acknowledged by Mishnaic and Roman law to apply to both partners, though not equally (1 Cor 7:3-4).[45]

For Paul both partners are "enslaved" (7:15) within a marriage, but this image comes to his mind most readily with regard to women (7:39-40, Rom 7:1-3). Paul himself refuses to be subjected to the *exousia* of anyone or anything else (1 Cor 6:12). All of this language indicates how deeply and determinatively Paul's understanding of sexuality (and that of the rest of early Christianity, like that of the rest of the ancient world) is imbued with a grammar of power, one that is not a grammar of empowerment, but a grammar of domination that can be escaped only by refusal of sexuality itself. In 1 Cor 6:13 Paul recognizes a distinction, even a contrast, between sexual experience and food. But the potential for recognition of sexuality as relationship rather than consumption is undercut by objectification of the hypothetical prostitute to whom the hypothetical believer might join his person (6:15-20). Here as elsewhere, sexuality remains in the realm of purity and danger rather than of relationship and justice.

In remarking these aspects of ancient understandings of sexuality I do not argue that they have disappeared from contemporary understandings and that Christian theology is "out of date" in retaining them. Rather I wish to point to their quite obvious endurance in contemporary mores and to argue that the Church's reluctance to reject them fosters thinking about sexuality as substance parallel to food and drink. The construction of sex as a commodity for which one has an appetite and whose true utility is the production of legitimate offspring continues to lurk in attempts to reconstruct sexuality as expression and conductor of relationship. For instance, the concern to defend homoeroticism against Paul's charge that it is "unnatural" has led too many well-meaning Christian readers and writers (including gays and lesbians) to argue that homosexual orientation is "not a choice," on the grounds that people are permanently and irretrievably oriented either toward the opposite sex or the same sex from at least early childhood. While an exclusive and early sexual preference describes the experience of some persons, this description accords ill with the experience of many lesbians.

More significantly, the plea that "they can't help it" is a poor basis for an ethical understanding of human sexual relations. At best such an argument can produce tolerance, often filled with distaste. At worst it leaves mature and loving lesbians and gays in the same category as compulsive pedophiles (who, as far as can be discerned, really cannot help it). My point is not to claim that all aspects of mature sexual experience are or should be subject to control, but that the moral character of sexual acts (as of all others) should be discerned in their locus in just and mutual relationships. Similarly, attempts to validate homoerotic experience by forcing it into the already troubled format of marriage too often do as much to propagate patriarchy as to alleviate it. At the same time, they stymie the potential of homoerotic and homosocial relationships to extend the range of human erotic and affectional experience.

PREFERENTIAL OPTION

Are there no points at which the biblical tradition offers a way of reorienting contemporary readers? There are some clues in the texts of antiquity. One can be sought in the complete disinterest in the production of legitimate offspring on the part of Paul and other early Christian writers, including the gospel writers. Another, I believe, lies in the early Christian rearrangements of household relations for the variety of pairings and other voluntary associations reflected especially in Romans 16, in the disciple lists of the synoptic gospels, and narratives like John's account of Martha, Mary, and Lazarus (John 11:1–12:19).[46] But these are not clues that will refute and convince by being cited. Rather they must be examined with a patient and discerning eye for their investments and horizons, as well as for those of later readers including ourselves. For this there is a need for more resources than the Bible provides. For this it is necessary to turn to the contemporary wisdom literature, the provisional but real wisdom that can be gained from the social sciences.[47] This must of course be read through all the wisdom that contemporary theology and ethics can bring to bear.

Margaret Farley has pointed to one "essential and even determinative source" in the "interpretation offered by individuals who experience same-sex relations," specifically those "whose whole lives evince integrity, and whose actions cohere with the general ethical norms of justice in human relationships."[48] This is a resource that becomes more available as social mores become more tolerant and accommodating of such lives. Increasing numbers of gays and lesbians provide not only witness to their own experience but also analysis of the social and theological contexts in which they must live out their call. Mary E. Hunt's essay in this volume is a salient example of lesbian experience talking back to and within theology. With her I suggest that what is needed is a "'preferential option' for lesbian voices that have been marginalized."[49] This option is essential not only as a matter of justice for lesbians, but also for the health of theological and ethical thought as a whole. Thinking about sexuality has evolved far too little from the period that, in Winkler's analysis, "assumes that what are significant in sexual activity are (i) men, (ii) penises that penetrate, and (iii) the articulation thereby of relative statuses through relations of dominance."[50]

A similar preferential option should be extended to the witness of all those who have suffered deeply, even devastatingly, from homophobia and other efforts to maintain the aging and leaky structures of patriarchy. In particular, voices that have been silenced require attentive hearing.[51] From these the Christian community should not ask or need the added testimony of an exemplary life or of Christian fidelity. Too often their inability to present such credentials is the first testimony to their tribulations. For many of the victims of patriarchy, their terrors form the "negative contrast experience" that clarifies many choices and the subjectivity from which they proceed: "Why I left the Church, why I have difficulties with relationships, and why I empathize with Matthew Shepard."[52]

CONCLUSION

Reading and citing the biblical texts is an activity with moral fallout, an activity that is deeply implicated in the social and ethical world and has a long and complex history of engagement. Relativizing the texts and returning them to their original contexts are essential steps in that they create distance, or rather honor the distance, between the worlds of the texts and the readers, and require readers to examine their own investments. But to stop with either or both of these approaches is inadequate. It is essential to interrogate the ways that the texts are implicated in the power struggles of both past and present, to be alert to the ways that readers collaborate with them in sustaining patterns of domination and submission. Making this effort for the texts that have been used to condemn homoerotic relations is only one step on the road; ending the condemnation of male homosexuality will not ensure the end of all forms of sexual and gender-based oppression, but sustaining homophobia is central to the maintenance of patriarchy. The story of John Andrew Murphy, like the saga of Abraham, the Sodomites, and the angelic visitors, like the horrifying tale of the Levite, the old man, and the concubine, makes clear that not only every woman, but also nearly any man, has overwhelming reason to contest this hierarchy.

NOTES: CHAPTER 9

[1] I am grateful to Margaret Farley of the Yale Divinity School, Kathleen Cannon of the University of Notre Dame, and Francine Cardman of Weston School of Theology for their reading and responses to this essay. It was completed with the help of a research leave supported by a Henry Luce III Fellowship in Theology and by the University of Notre Dame.

[2] "Hate and Homosexual Rape," *Common Sense* 13/2 (1998) 1, 5.

[3] See Choon-Leong Seow, "Textual Orientation," in Robert L. Brawley, ed., *Biblical Ethics and Homosexuality: Listening to Scripture* (Louisville: Westminster John Knox, 1996) n. 1; also Margaret Farley: "Roman Catholic moral thinking has . . . not been known for an allegiance to a 'divine command theory' but for a continuing affirmation of the ultimate intelligibility of reality and of the moral imperatives that emerge from reality." In "Moral Discourse in the Public Arena," in William W. May, ed., *Vatican Authority and American Catholic Dissent: The Curran Case and Its Consequences* (New York: Crossroad, 1987) 174.

[4] Margaret A. Farley, "Response to James Hannigan and Charles Curran," in Saul Olyan and Martha Nussbaum, eds., *Sexual Orientation and Human Rights in American Religious Discourse* (New York and Oxford: Oxford University Press, 1998) 106.

[5] See the similar description of these two approaches in Robert Di Vito, "Questions about the Construction of (Homo)sexuality: Same-Sex Relations in the Hebrew Bible," this volume.

[6] All translations are my own unless otherwise noted.

[7] Henry T. C. Sun, "Holiness Code," *ABD* 3:254–57.

[8] Seow, "Textual Orientation," 25.

[9] Michel Foucault, *The History of Sexuality Volume 1: An Introduction;* trans. Robert Hurley (New York: Random House, 1978) 105–6; David M. Halperin, *One Hundred Years of Homosexuality and Other Essays on Greek Love* (New York and London: Routledge, 1990); David M. Halperin, John J. Winkler, and Froma I. Zeitlin, *Before Sexuality: The Construction of Erotic Experience in the Greek World* (Princeton, N.J.: Princeton University Press, 1990) passim, but especially 1–7. John J. Winkler, *The Constraints of Desire: The Anthropology of Sex and Gender in Ancient Greece* (New York and London: Routledge, 1992) 17–23; Marilyn B. Skinner, "Introduction: *Quod multo fit aliter in Graecia*," in Judith Hallet and Marilyn B. Skinner, eds., *Roman Sexualities* (Princeton, N.J.: Princeton University Press, 1997) 1–3, as well as throughout the essays in the volume. See also Robert Di Vito in this volume. For a discussion of the question in terms of female homoeroticism see Bernadette J. Brooten, *Love Between Women: Early Christian Responses to Female Homoeroticism* (Chicago and London: University of Chicago Press, 1996) 17–26.

[10] Jeremiah 23:14 accuses the prophets of adultery, possibly metaphorically; the other accusations are that they "walk in lies; they strengthen the hands of evildoers" (NRSV). Thus it may mean that their prophecy has been corrupted.

[11] Most texts use Sodom (with or without the other cities of the plain) as a cautionary example, an example of destruction, but do not specify the crimes that brought the destruction about: Deut 29:22; 32:32; Is 3:9; 13:19; Jer 49:18; 50:40; Lam 4:6; Amos 4:11; Wis 10:6; Hos 11:8 refers to two of the other cities, Admah and Zeboiim, this way. Matthew 10:15; 11:23; Luke 10:12; 17:19; and Rev 11:8 use the same trope.

[12] See also Martti Nissinen, *Homoeroticism in the Biblical World,* trans. Kirsi Stjerna (Minneapolis: Fortress, 1998) 90–93.

[13] See, for instance, the cautions of Leland White and Bruce Malina in this volume.

[14] Phyllis Trible, *Texts of Terror: Literary-Feminist Readings of Biblical Narratives,* OTB 13 (Philadelphia: Fortress, 1984) 74–75 concludes that the women in the Genesis narrative are preserved not by divine action but by the hostility of the men of Sodom to Lot and his guests.

[15] See also Nissinen, *Homoeroticism,* 48–49.

[16] On the rape of the concubine as the proxy rape see ibid. 51.

[17] Di Vito, this volume.

[18] For the literature see Michael Satlow, "They Abused Him Like a Woman: Homoeroticism, Gender Blurring and the Rabbis in Late Antiquity," *Journal of the History of Sexuality* 5 (1994) 1–25, at 1, n. 1.

[19] Winkler, *Constraints of Desire,* 36–41.

[20] On Greek writers who call the practice into question see Nissinen, *Homoeroticism,* 79–88.

[21] Eva Keuls, *Reign of the Phallus: Sexual Politics in Ancient Athens* (New York: Harper and Row, 1985) 296–98, also Nissinen, *Homoeroticism,* 64–69.

[22] See the collection of illustrations in K. J. Dover, *Greek Homosexuality* (Cambridge, Mass.: Harvard University Press, 1989), also Keuls, *Reign of the Phallus,* figs. 245–60, 278–90.

[23] For illustrations of the former see fig. 261; of the latter, figs. 166–68 in Keuls, *Reign of the Phallus,* 292, 184–85.

[24] See Saara Lilja, *Homosexuality in Republican and Augustan Rome.* Commentationes Humanorum Literarum 74 (Helsinki: Societas Scientiarum Fennica, 1982) 123–29.

[25] Ibid. 88–97; also Catherine Edwards, *The Politics of Immorality in Ancient Rome* (Cambridge: Cambridge University Press, 1993) 63–97.

[26] Bernadette J. Brooten, "Paul's Views on the Nature of Women and Female Homoeroticism," in Clarissa W. Atkinson, Constance H. Buchanan, and

Margaret R. Miles, eds., *Immaculate and Powerful: The Female in Sacred Image and Social Reality.* Harvard Women's Studies in Religion Series (Boston: Beacon, 1985) 63–71; eadem, *Love Between Women,* 41–57.

[27] For a description and assessment see Susan Treggiari *Roman Marriage: Iusti Coniuges from the Time of Cicero to the Time of Ulpian* (Oxford: Clarendon, 1991) 277–98.

[28] Karl Galinsky claims that these laws ultimately "attracted more comment from the Roman jurists than did any other laws." *Augustan Culture: An Introduction* (Princeton, N.J.: Princeton University Press, 1996) 128.

[29] Catherine Edwards, *Politics of Immorality,* 34–62; even Galinsky, who generally rejects the term "propaganda" as applied to Augustus, concedes that these laws went well beyond the exercise of *auctoritas; Augustan Culture* 129.

[30] Ibid. 62.

[31] On *lenocinium* see Treggiari, *Roman Marriage,* 288–89.

[32] See Valerie Tracy, "The Leno-Maritus," *Classical Journal* 72 (1976) 62–64.

[33] See Catherine Edwards, "*Mollitia:* Reading the Body," in *Politics of Immorality,* 63– 97.

[34] *On the Special Laws* 3.38; cf. *On the Special Laws* 2.50; *On Abraham,* 135–36; *On the Contemplative Life,* 59–62.

[35] Dale Martin, "*Arsenokoites* and *Malakos:* Meanings and Consequences," in Robert L. Brawley, ed., *Biblical Ethics and Homosexuality,* 117–36.

[36] Ibid. 119–20.

[37] Edwards, "*Mollitia,*" in *Politics of Immorality,* 63–97, also the treatment of Philo above.

[38] Brooten, *Love between Women,* 44–49; eadem, "Paul's Views and Female Homoeroticism," 66–70.

[39] See especially Martial's description of Philaenis, *Epigrammata* 7, 67–70, described by Brooten in *Love between Women,* 46–47; eadem, "Paul's Views and Female Homoeroticism," 67.

[40] "Response" (see n. 4 above), 102.

[41] "Textual Orientation," also "A Heterotextual Perspective," in Choon-Leong Seow, ed., *Homosexuality and the Christian Community* (Louisville, Ky.: Westminster, 1996).

[42] Brooten, *Love Between Women,* 238–59, 267–301; Nissinen, *Homoeroticism,* 103–13; Leland White, "Romans 1:26-27: The Claim that Homosexuality Is Unnatural," in this volume.

[43] See discussion in Foucault, *History of Sexuality 2. The Use of Pleasure,* trans. Robert Hurley (New York: Random House, 1985) 53–62, and Brooten, *Love Between Women,* 245 and nn. 86–87.

[44] See especially Winkler's discussion of Aristotle, *Constraints of Desire,* 64–70.

[45] *M. Keth.* 5.7 prescribes financial penalties if the wife refuses the husband and also the reverse, but the penalties are less severe for the husband.

[46] Mary Rose D'Angelo, "Women Partners in the New Testament," *Journal of Feminist Studies in Religion* 6 (1990) 65–86; republished in Gary Comstock and Susan Henking, eds., *Que(e)rying Religion* (New York: Continuum, 1996) 441–55.

[47] See the summary provided by Isiaah Crawford and Brian Zamboni in ch. 11 of this volume.

[48] "Response," 106.

[49] See also Mary E. Hunt, *Fierce Tenderness: A Feminist Theology of Friendship* (New York: Crossroad, 1991); Carter Heyward, *Saving Jesus from Those Who Are Right* (Minneapolis: Fortress, 1999); eadem, *Staying Power: Reflections on Gender, Justice and Compassion* (Cleveland: Pilgrim Press, 1995); eadem, *Touching Our Strength: The Erotic as Power and the Love of God* (San Francisco: Harper & Row, 1989); Ellen, ed., *Speaking of Christ: A Lesbian Feminist Voice* (New York: Pilgrim Press, 1989); Janice Raymond, *A Passion for Friends: Toward a Philosophy of Female Affection* (Boston: Beacon, 1986); also the essays in Gary Comstock and Susan Henking, eds., *Que(e)rying Religion* (New York: Continuum, 1996).

[50] Winkler, *Constraints of Desire,* 39.

[51] Mary Rose D'Angelo, "Hardness of Hearing, Muted Voices: Listening for the Silenced in History," *Women and Theology.* Annual Publication of the College Theology Society 40 (1994), ed. Mary Ann Hinsdale and Phyllis Kaminski (Maryknoll, N.Y.: Orbis, 1995) 83–92.

[52] Murphy, "Hate and Homosexual Rape," 1.

Part Three:
Interpreting Secular Disciplines

10

Homosexuality, Moral Theology, and Scientific Evidence

Sidney Callahan

*T*oday Catholics are struggling to understand the moral and theological status of homosexuality in the Church. Of course the teaching on homosexuality does not stand alone, but is embedded in the larger body of Church teaching on human sexuality. It is also true that many of the current Church teachings on sexuality have been met with dissent from the faithful. I too find myself disagreeing with official Church positions. For dissenters, the current theology of human sexuality appears immobilized in a critical moment of transition and development.

Over the centuries our understanding of the Gospel has evolved. Christians of every age engage in the "endlessness of making sense" of the good news.[1] Pope John Paul II in his encyclical "Faith and Reason" proclaims the essential harmony of the two, yet adds "that reason must realize that human knowledge is a journey which allows no rest"; God as Truth has created rational human beings to be "explorers" and seekers of truth with the "mission to leave no stone unturned."[2] In seeking to understand the Christian truths of human sexuality, explorers will turn to Scripture, tradition, the teachings of the Church, scientific and humanistic knowledge, and their own lived Christian experience. In seeking to read "the signs of the times," Catholics follow the teaching of

Vatican II that instructs the faithful to pursue knowledge within all intellectual disciplines, including the human sciences. Indeed, Vatican II's teaching on human sexuality is an instance of the Church's development of new, personalist, psychosocial understandings of sexuality, in which human beings are viewed as a unity of mind, body, and spirit, and human sexual experience is accepted as good. Thus, declares Vatican II, the purpose of marital sexuality is twofold: to procreate offspring and to provide unity between the spouses.

Yet this movement toward a personalist vision of the goodness of sexuality has not progressed far enough. I judge the present teachings to be inadequate and in need of change and revision because I cannot in conscience agree with the current ban on the use of contraception, the refusal to ordain women, and the condemnation of all homosexual acts as intrinsically evil. Such teachings are discordant with (1) current Christian understandings of Gospel morality, (2) recent understandings of scientific and psychological findings about human nature and sexuality, and (3) the personal experiences of lay persons in their sexual and family lives. The interlocking assumptions and fundamental presuppositions that undergird current Roman Catholic teaching on sexuality are a tightly wrapped package, but they are not rationally convincing, morally helpful, or theologically adequate.

First, while the Church recognizes that human sexuality is ordered to marital unity as well as to procreation, the Church asserts that the link between these two ends can never be broken. Every act of sexual intercourse must be open to procreation. Openness to biological procreation can never be bypassed in order to serve some other human good. Although actual procreation is often impossible for natural reasons, as in an older or sterile heterosexual couple, the symbolic openness to procreation must be maintained by a ban on contraception. Second, when biological procreation is held to be a critical definitive purpose of sexuality, then the complementary reproductive roles of men and women become exaggeratedly important in defining gender differences. Gender differentiation becomes so central to human life that gender mandates different and complementary vocations in the family and in the Church. Aligned with these first two premises is the third: homosexuality, in both its gay and lesbian manifestations, is deemed a fundamental objective defect because it is not ordered to biological procreation. Same-sex unions cannot be allowed or considered to be marital commitments because marriage requires the union of a man and a woman in a heterosexual, gender-complementary relationship oriented to procreation.

Homosexual acts are intrinsically evil because they are not procreative and because they cannot take place within marriage.

Correspondingly, if you claim that gender differences are neither as fundamental to personhood nor as complementary as now asserted, you are likely to deny that gender can determine vocations and just as likely to affirm that the Church should ordain women. Reducing the essential centrality of gender complementarity will weaken arguments against same-sex unions as well. A concession that every sexual act need not be open to biological procreation as long as it is expressing love in a committed permanent union leads to the approval of contraception and non-procreative homosexual unions. If you agree that sexual unions can be fruitful and procreative in other than biological ways you support arguments for same-sex relationships. To accept homosexuality as a naturally occurring sexual variation, and not fundamentally as an objective defect, weakens the assertion that sexuality is, and must always be, ordered to biological procreation as well as unity. If loving, committed same-sex unions can be moral, what happens to the gender complementarity that sustains the ban on ordaining women? And so it goes, round and round, in a circle of interrelated arguments that resist change on any front.

The Church teaches that homosexuals must abide by the same sexual morality as heterosexuals. Well and good, a universal principle of moral responsibility applied equally to all validates the capacities of normal mature human beings to freely direct their sexual behavior in accord with their moral standards and personal commitments. Sexual promiscuity, exploitation, harassment, and abuse are immoral whether in homosexual or heterosexual lifestyles. Human beings are more than their sexual desires and have the free will to make sexual choices. No Christian has a religious duty that compels marriage, as in other religions. Nor is there some right to a sexual partner or progeny.

But ironies and contradictions exist as well. Single adult unimpaired heterosexuals have a reasonable hope of finding a partner, and when they do they can exercise their right to marry and express sexual love, whether procreation is possible or not. In contrast, homosexuals are encouraged to be sexually abstinent for life because the only sexual intimacy morally permitted is within marriage, and marriage is impossible for them. If they love, and desire to have a committed intimate sexual relationship, they cannot do so without engaging in intrinsically evil acts. Consequently, homosexual persons are required by the Church to endure the lifelong deprivation of sexual intimacy. Though some heterosexuals choose this path, as a group they are not required to do so. At least the present official teaching has progressed to the point of affirming that the homosexual orientation is not in itself sinful, nor is a homosexual orientation seen as the defining characteristic of the whole person. But it is painful and stigmatizing to be told that one's homosexual orientation is an objective disorder that predisposes the person to intrinsically evil acts.

In defending the Church's present teachings it is often admitted that these teachings impose suffering upon homosexuals. This suffering, however, is allegedly justified by the higher moral duty to follow God's will and preserve the goods of marriage and the family.[3] Certainly it is the case that the Christian life will often require one to endure morally necessary suffering rather than commit sin, harm another, or injure the common good. But the dispute over homosexuality turns on the question of whether it is actually God's will that homosexuals should suffer the burden imposed by the Church's teaching. Certain defenders of the faith minimize the weight of the burden by claiming that since gay single persons can pursue loving friendships, enjoy extended family bonds, pursue fulfilling work, and exercise a Christian life of charity, there should be little ground for complaint.[4] This argument, like the argument against married persons using contraception, seriously undervalues the goods to be found in the erotic union of a committed relationship. Yet in other developments in the theology of sexuality, such as in Pope John Paul II's writings, erotic love and sexual joy are exalted as good gifts from God, if, that is, they take place in heterosexual, noncontracepting marital unions.[5]

Unfortunately, current Church teachings erroneously overemphasize and overvalue the procreative purpose of human sexuality, wrongly overemphasize the importance of gender differences and the gender complementarity of men and women, wrongly condemn a homosexual orientation as a defect leading to intrinsically evil acts, and seriously undervalue the uniquely human gift from God of embodied sexual joy. These interdependent errors ensure that the Church's teaching on sexuality betrays the Christian call to exemplify love and justice within the human community. Unnecessary burdens are laid upon homosexuals, women, and married couples—all in Jesus' name. Yet the core of Christian morality consists of enacting God's merciful love in justice, and there can be no conflict between the two. As Pope Paul VI said, "Justice is love's absolute minimum." While my critique of the Church's moral teachings rests upon rational, normative judgments, these judgments are significantly informed by evidence emerging from the human sciences.

SCIENTIFIC EVIDENCE AND HUMAN SEXUALITY

I recognize that the natural and human sciences are, like moral and theological inquiries, always engaged in dynamic processes of acquiring more complete understandings of reality. It is also the case that no scientific theory or finding can decisively settle a question of moral and theological truth. In every pursuit of knowledge persons have to make evaluative reasoned judgments about how to read and synthesize the available evidence and arguments. All theories and observations in every discipline are to some degree value-laden and incomplete. There are no infallible formulas to guarantee absolute certainty. But those who believe in God as Truth will affirm the necessary unity of all truths in God. This faith begets a trust in the Creator's gift of human reason and sustains the search for valid objective knowledge in science, the humanities, morality, and theology.

When it comes to the study of human sexuality, it must be recognized that the inquiry has just begun. Still, it can be claimed with assurance from a scientific and psychological point of view that human sexuality should be analyzed from within the currently dominant evolutionary perspective on human life. Few doubt what is now called in science "the evolutionary synthesis."[6] Yet taking evolution seriously does not solve the complexities and questions of sexuality. Even the purpose of the evolution of sexual reproduction has been seen as a conundrum.[7] Why do species display sexual rather than the less costly means of asexual reproduction? Asexual reproduction is present in many forms of life, and some microorganisms move back and forth from asexual to sexual reproduction depending on the environmental conditions.

One conclusion to be drawn from taking an evolutionary perspective is the important role of the environment in the survival of the species as a whole. Evolutionary biology and psychology employ a species point of view and focus on the species' interactions with the conditions existing in the environment. When environmental resources become scarce, some species automatically suppress reproduction. The study of social insects such as bees shows that the good of a whole species is sometimes served by the suppression of reproduction on the part of certain individual organisms. In the human species also, the common good and survival of the group as a whole can be served by the altruistic self-sacrifices of life and reproduction that certain defenders of the group engage in. The analysis of altruism is a new frontier in evolutionary theory and evolutionary psychology.[8]

If we take a population and species point of view in analyzing human sexuality in different environments it becomes hard to claim that all sexual acts are naturally ordered to biological procreation. The nonprocreative outcomes of a minority of individuals will not necessarily harm the welfare of the group and may serve to increase its chances of survival. Homosexuality in higher social animals can be seen as a variation that exists and continues to exist in the human species because it does not threaten group survival.

Indeed, in human societies increasing population can put pressure upon the available resources in an environment. While non-human populations may decrease reproduction automatically, self-conscious human beings who foresee future consequences can make judgments and decide upon reproductive actions. Humans can judge that increasing the number of their offspring will harm their existing families as well as the common good of their communities. Humans must adapt to the ever-changing natural and social conditions of the environment. Today in modern industrialized societies there is an increased human life span and less mortality from diseases that once threatened human survival. Increased longevity means that human females can live for many decades beyond their reproductive years, yet remain sexually active while nurturing grandchildren or others. While most women are biologically sterile even during most of their reproductive years, increasing decades of postmenopausal life have enlarged even further the infertile portion of a female's life span. Female sterility is the more natural human norm from the statistical point of view since conception is possible for only a brief period during each reproductive cycle.

In technological and medically advanced countries many offspring do not have to be born in order to have a few survive to adulthood. At the same time rearing children for adult self-sufficiency in an advanced non-agrarian society requires long periods of expensive education and psychologically taxing care. The increasing psychosocial resources needed to provide adequate socialization for each child ensure that few families can successfully rear large numbers of children. Therefore Catholic parents in developed countries adapt to their environmental conditions and use contraception and sterilization to control their fertility. They act in good conscience to benefit the whole family. The technological medical revolution that brought the control of death and disease is used to control fertility. Such an adjustment of reproductive responses to a changing environment, called the demographic transition to small families, makes sense from an evolutionary point of view.

Studies of the evolution of sexuality reveal how unique human sexuality is. Sexual intercourse is no longer governed by the physiological controls that confine mating to the fertile period. As an evolutionary biologist puts it, humans "are extraordinary in that females can maintain continual receptivity, and ovulation is quite difficult to detect."[9] The result is that sexual intercourse becomes more frequent between two partners, and males and females form long-term mated pairs. Humans are also extraordinary in their cognitive and emotional capacities, which can transform and enlarge human physiological sexual drives into psychosocial bonds of emotional attachment. Sexual intercourse has been seen to create bonding because of the power of mutual pleasure to bind couples together.[10] The sexual bonding and intimate cooperative relationship of a mated pair work for the survival of the species because they increase the nurturing and emotional investment available to protect and socialize offspring. Affective bonds contribute to the creation of the family and kinship ties.[11] The expansion of sexual activity from the confines of the reproductive period was crucial to the cultural evolution of human groups.

A human couple can desire and choose to engage in sexual expressions of loving unity throughout their lives, while the fertile period enabling conception is not under voluntary control or consciously experienced. Physiological desire amplified by emotions and social attachments enables human sexual unions to include the different kinds of uniquely human emotions such as affection, friendship, charity, and erotic love. Of course, human freedom also means that humans can choose to engage in sexual domination, exploitation, and cruelty. Sexual abuse may be as longstanding a possibility as the freedom to sin. But love, including erotic love, focusing upon a specific preferred object of desire, also appears in all human cultures. Romantic love is not simply an artificial construct of medieval French troubadours, as the Song of Songs has long demonstrated.

With the evolution of human culture, the psychological and emotional expressive capacities of human beings have become more elaborate and highly valued. With civilization the erotic playful interpersonal potentials of sexual bonding become appreciated as an intrinsically joyful experience. Sexual love and pleasure, like beauty, music, and art, lift the heart and enhance human life. Sharing intense emotions and mutual sexual joy can expand the self, affirm the body, give mutual comfort, and mend psychic and social wounds. Loving sexual acts augment happiness and increase the energy to care for self, one's partner, and other dependent persons. Depression, loneliness, and sadness deplete energy for social living and threaten physical and mental health. Like all experiences of joy, which is a universal basic emotion, sexual joy helps persons remain healthy, bear the burdens of life, and believe in the goodness of the world.

To value and seek conscious experiences of sexual love and joy does not necessitate taking an instrumental or dualistic view of mind and body. To intend, seek, and express mutual love and pleasure cannot be equated with exploiting the body instrumentally since the brain/mind is embodied. Love and commitment enacted in erotic expression require uniquely human consciousness and intention. Conception, by contrast, occurs independently of consciousness and the human relationship. Surely it can be argued that the psychosocial unitive purpose of sexuality is the more uniquely human end. The evolution of human reproductive biology has made bonds possible by loosening the link between procreation and sexual expression. It seems unreasonable for the Church to insist that the end of biological reproduction must override all the other goods of human sexuality. It seems a mistaken understanding of evolution, human nature, and the common good to claim that each and every sexual act should be "reproductive in type" even when it is not possible to be "reproductive in effect."[12] In the present teaching, supposedly based on nature, one embodied capacity of human beings is being selected, valorized, and allowed to dominate other more uniquely embodied, conscious capacities for mutual lovemaking.

The evolution of human sexuality and the powerful positive psychosocial effects of pair bonding help explain why the urge to form pair bonds is so strongly present in human beings, whether homosexual or heterosexual. A human group may not need to increase its population, but it always needs to increase its emotional bonds of love, commitment, and mutual social support. With the continuing theological and moral development of a personalist perspective on sexuality, the concept of procreation can be expanded to include psychological and social fruitfulness as well as reproductive generativity. Fruitfulness implies attention and effort to altruistically care for the good of others, whether offspring, other family members, or the larger community. With such developments, moral judgments about sexual acts would be made with the guidance of Christian love and justice. Human acts and intentions would count for more than a human being's sexual characteristics. Yes, there remain intrinsically evil sexual acts—such as rape, abuse, pedophilia —but contraception and homosexual acts do not belong in that category. While monogamous marriage and faithful unity were blessed by Christ, it is not clear that such loving unity can only be achieved in heterosexual unions with reproductive-type acts. The goal of interpersonal unity must be achieved by conscious and embodied intentional acts that extend throughout the whole of the relationship.

EVOLUTIONARY PERSPECTIVES ON GENDER IDENTITY, GENDER DIFFERENCES, AND SEXUAL ORIENTATION

Taking an evolutionary perspective on gender differences, gender identity, and sexual orientation reveals that present Church teachings have oversimplified the complexities of human nature. Variation, change, contingency, and complexity rule human development and the development of sexual identities and preferences. Only by a selective narrowing of attention can one make the realities of human development fit into the ideology of current teachings. Since other chapters in this book deal with research on homosexuality and the theological exaggeration of gender differences, I will only offer a few brief comments on gender differences and sexual orientation.

Certainly evolutionary psychologists would affirm that innate, biologically programmed gender differences have evolved in the human species in order to facilitate courtship, mating, and reproduction. Those who would insist that gender differences are simply the result of social conditioning, cultural interpretation, and patriarchy's oppressiveness underrate the biological matrix of human life, an error that can be as misleading as overrating and exaggerating the importance of biological procreation in human sexuality. No psychologist denies that gender differences exist.[13] Clearly there exist innate programs for the development of gender identity and reproductive functions. But the interpretation of the importance of gender differences goes astray when it is not recognized that sex and gender development is only *one* of several critical innate developmental processes in human beings.

Always and everywhere humans are genetically programmed to produce language, logical reasoning, basic emotional responses, motor skills, temperamental patterns of personality, and cultural invention— along with gendered sexual and reproductive behavior.[14] Psychologists can speak of seven different kinds of intelligence, including logical, verbal, spatial, kinesthetic, musical, and intra- and interpersonal intelligence.[15] Emotional intelligence is also seen as important.[16] Human beings also develop free will and make choices that interact with all their other capacities to produce moral development and individual character. Therefore the question always arises as to how an individual's sexual development interacts with all the other innate developmental programs of an individual. Everyone grants that in a species there are many more similarities than differences between sexes because of the common species-specific genetic program. And in humans there exist many within-sex variations in each gender. For every trait that shows a sex difference there will be overlapping distributions. Since the development of culture is also innate within human groups, any cultural influences present in socialization will also affect the distributions of many gender differences. In a society like our own, the recent changes in education and opportunity for women have increased the convergence of many characteristics, as measured by test scores and performance measures.

Observers can either maximize the importance and role of existing gender differences or minimize them by focusing upon common characteristics, overlapping distributions, and the importance of individual differences. Maximizers argue that gender is a pervasive, powerful influence on the total organism and operates throughout the life span. They make a large leap from differences found in the sexual reproductive system in order to claim that essential gender differences exist in all other characteristics. These essential differences will mandate different complementary social roles for men and women. Minimizers of the importance of gender differences, who I think have the better arguments, claim that gender must be evaluated as but one variable in the whole multi-dimensioned system that makes up a person. Because of the interactions of sexuality and gender with the other central programs operating within an embodied person, gender differences cannot predict personal characteristics. Gender differences should not be exaggerated as essential categories because in nature there are too many basic similarities in the species program, too many interactions with other innate systems, too many within-sex differences, and too many influences from social, cultural forces interacting with free individual choices.

The minimalist approach also notes that gender differences vary over the life span: differences are most important during the mating period of adolescence and young adulthood and less important in maturity and old age. In old age men and women become more alike and the effect of individual difference increases. All in all, differences in intelligence, emotional temperament, cultural socialization, and the voluntary choices that produce moral character will affect individual character as much as or more than gender. Any two individual persons must work to achieve a complementary relationship and it follows that individuals of the same sex can be complementary.

Moreover, it is important for each human individual to be complementary to larger human groups, such as the community and Church. Human beings, as a highly social species, can only survive in cooperative communities. Human communities, including the body of the Church, include both men and women and individuals of different ages. Embodied human beings exist through time and range in development through the different stages of fetus, infant, toddler, child, adolescent, young adult, middle-aged, old, and old-old. In every human group there are the weak and the strong, the ill and the well, the handicapped and the fit. Focusing so much attention upon the reproductive mating period to define complementarity is too exclusive and narrow. When theologians speak of "the nuptial body" as the essential body, they simplify the complex reality of embodiment.

The development of gender identity and sexual orientation is also an incredibly complex and multi-dimensioned reality that should not be oversimplified. As more scientific inquiry into human sexual development has taken place, it can be seen that human sexuality is complex because it includes a genetic component, a hormonal component, a morphological bodily component, a psychological gender identity component, sexual orientation, sexual performance, sexual reproduction, and socially prescribed gender roles.[17] Sexual orientation is not the same thing as gender identity; orientation is defined as the preferred direction of sexual fantasy and desires, while gender identity is the sense of oneself as male or female. In the general population the different elements of the sexual system develop in a relay fashion, so that the majority of males and females arrive in adulthood with psychosocial identities that correlate with their genes, bodies, and psychosocial identities. The predominant orientation of sexual preference is for the other sex, although many persons are sexually attracted to both. But variations and contingencies in a human population ensure that differences will appear in each developmental history such that some individuals will be different from the majority of cases. The complexities of developmental processes and the possibility of different variations, for instance, make it difficult to understand and explain the causes of either heterosexual or homosexual preferences.

There may, however, be a critical period of development at a very young age at which the development of sexual orientation becomes imprinted and is irreversible. In language development the growing brain commits at an early age to certain paths that produce one set of linguistic responses rather than another. After a certain period a person cannot learn to speak a foreign language like a native speaker. All sexual orientations, including a homosexual orientation, may be the result of the same kind of commitment in a critical period. Here again, however, there may be many variations and differences in degree. Some persons and some psychologists make claims that same-sex sexual orientation can be reversed in so-called "reparative therapies." Other gay and lesbian persons also assert that they have freely chosen their orientation. Such reports of choices and change should not be discounted, but be seen as evidence, along with reports of bisexuality, of the wide variation in sexual orientations. Men and women, for instance, may follow different paths in developing same-sex orientations. Such variations have caused researchers to speak of "homosexualities" rather than homosexuality. As with gender differentiation, the presence of variation and individual differences works against claims for essential personal characteristics associated with gender identity and sexual preference. Stereotypes and prejudices also confuse issues of sexuality. One reason so many Catholics dissent from official Church teachings on sexuality is that their own experiences are discordant with Vatican pronouncements.

A BRIEF NOTE ON THE PERSONAL EXPERIENCES OF MANY CATHOLICS

Many married Catholics deny that the use of contraception in their committed marriages leads to a lessening of self-giving. The characteristic of their whole relationship is judged as more important than individual sexual acts. They affirm that mutual erotic joy is vital for marital bonding.

Those who have been long married and raised children of different genders can also question the rigid gender differentiations espoused in official Church teaching. They find that marital partners and children are shaped more by their individual differences, especially differences of character, than by gender differences. Gender roles can be experienced as fluid and flexible in family life.

Homosexual and lesbian Catholics testify to their experiences of love, fidelity, and commitment in their sexual relationships. They also report much pain and suffering arising from the Church's teachings. And while many families may reject their gay and lesbian children, others do not. These families who have homosexual children do not see that their sexual orientation determines their personalities or their character.[18] They often offer support to their homosexual children and hope that they too can find what they desire for their heterosexual children: faithful unions of love, sexual intimacy, and social support. Many Catholic parents of gay adult children welcome their children's lifelong partners as "in-laws" who become part of their extended families.

Finally, many of the married laity, along with others who fully accept their embodiment, do not find homosexuality to be a "disgusting" practice or condition.[19] Developing a loving sexual relationship, as well as childbearing, requires the full acceptance of all of the body's functions. Even though the bodily processes of childbirth and heterosexual intercourse were once stigmatized as ritually impure and polluting, they produce human goods that are now recognized by all. With the development of a new Christian sexual ethic that fully accepts erotic joy and embodiment, two moral truths of the Gospel will be made plain: Christ teaches that it is the human heart that determines what is pure or impure in human actions, and love fulfills the law.

REFERENCES

Buss, David M. "Evolutionary psychology: A new paradigm for psychological science," *Psychological Inquiry* 6/1 (1995) 1–30.

Cahill, Lisa Sowle. *Sex, Gender and Christian Ethics.* Cambridge: Cambridge University Press, 1996.

Gardner, Howard. *Multiple Intelligences: The Theory in Practice.* New York: Basic Books, 1993.

George, Robert P. "'Same-sex Marriage' and 'Moral Neutrality,'" in Christopher Wolfe, ed., *Homosexuality and American Public Life.* Dallas, Tex.: Spence Publishing Company, 1999, 142–53.

Goleman, Daniel. *Emotional Intelligence.* New York: Bantam Books, 1995.

Gudorf, Christine E. *Body, Sex and Pleasure: Reconstructing Christian Sexual Ethics.* Cleveland: Pilgrim Press, 1994.

Haas, Kurt, and Adelaide Haas. *Understanding Sexuality.* St. Louis: Mosby-Year Book, 1993.

Hefling, Charles, ed. *Our Selves, Our Souls & Bodies: Sexuality and the Household of God.* Cambridge, Mass.: Cowley Publications, 1996.

John Paul II. *Fides et ratio* ("Faith and Reason"). Encyclical text published in *Catholic New York,* October 29, 1998.

Kelly, Kevin T. *New Directions in Sexual Ethics: Moral Theology and the Challenge of AIDS*. London: Geoffrey Chapman, 1998.

Lash, Nicholas. *Believing Three Ways in One God*. Notre Dame, Ind.: University of Notre Dame Press, 1993.

Low, Bobbie S. *Why Sex Matters: A Darwinian Look at Human Behavior*. Princeton: Princeton University Press, 1999.

Maccoby, Eleanor E. *The Two Sexes: Growing Up Apart, Coming Together*. Cambridge, Mass.: Harvard University Press, 1999.

McCarthy, Donald G., ed. *Reproductive Technologies, Marriage and the Church*. Braintree, Mass.: The Pope John XXIII Medical-Moral Research and Education Center, 1988.

Neuhaus, Richard John. "Love, No Matter What," in Christopher Wolfe, ed., *Homosexuality and American Public Life*. Dallas, Tex.: Spence Publishing Company, 1999, 239–47.

Pinker, Steven. *How the Mind Works*. New York: W. W. Norton, 1997.

Pope, Stephen J. *The Evolution of Altruism & the Ordering of Love*. Washington, D.C.: Georgetown University Press, 1994.

Rychlak, Joseph F. *In Defense of Human Consciousness*. Washington, D.C.: American Psychological Association, 1997.

Shavanandan, Mary. *Crossing the Threshold of Love: A New Vision of Marriage in the Light of John Paul II's Anthropology*. Washington, D.C.: The Catholic University of America Press, 1999.

Sober, Elliott, and David Sloan Wilson. *Unto Others: The Evolution and Psychology of Unselfish Behavior*. Cambridge, Mass.: Harvard University Press, 1998.

Stenseth, Nils Christian. "The Evolutionary Synthesis," *Science* 19 (November 1999) 1490.

Tooby, John, and Lois Cosmides. "The past explains the present: Emotional adaptations and the structure of ancestral environments," *Ethology and Sociobiology* 11/4–5 (July–Sept., 1990) 375–424.

Wilson, Peter J. *Man the Promising Primate: The Conditions of Human Evolution*. New Haven: Yale University Press, 1980.

Wink, Walter, ed. *Homosexuality and Christian Faith: Questions of Conscience for the Churches*. Minneapolis: Fortress, 1999.

Wolfe, Christopher, ed. *Homosexuality and American Public Life*. Dallas: Spence Publishing, 1999.

Wright, Robert. *The Moral Animal: Evolutionary Psychology and Everyday Life*. New York: Vintage Books, 1994.

NOTES: CHAPTER 10

[1] Nicholas Lash, *Believing in One God Three Ways* (Notre Dame, Ind.: University of Notre Dame Press, 1993) 10.

[2] John Paul II, *Fides et ratio* ("Faith and Reason"). Vatican text published in *Catholic New York,* October 29, 1998, 18, 21.

[3] Michael Pakaluk, "Homosexuality and the Common Good," in Christopher Wolfe, ed., *Homosexuality and American Public Life* (Dallas: Spence Publishing, 1999) 179–91.

[4] Richard John Neuhaus, "Love, No Matter What," *Homosexuality and American Public Life,* 239–47.

[5] Mary Shavanandan, *Crossing the Threshold of Love: A New Vision of Marriage in the Light of John Paul II's Anthropology* (Washington, D.C.: The Catholic University of America Press, 1999).

[6] Nils Christian Stenseth, "The Evolutionary Synthesis," *Science* 19 (November 1999) 1490.

[7] Bobbie S. Low, *Why Sex Matters: A Darwinian Look at Human Behavior* (Princeton, N.J.: Princeton University Press, 1999) 35–37.

[8] Elliot Sober and David Sloan Wilson, *Unto Others: The Evolution and Psychology of Unselfish Behavior* (Cambridge, Mass.: Harvard University Press, 1998).

[9] Low, *Why Sex Matters,* 50.

[10] Christine E. Gudorf, "Sexual Pleasure as Grace and Gift," *Body, Sex and Pleasure* (Cleveland: Pilgrim Press, 1994) 81–138.

[11] Peter J. Wilson, *Man the Promising Primate: The Conditions of Human Evolution* (New Haven, Conn.: Yale University Press, 1980).

[12] Robert P. George, "'Same-sex Marriage' and 'Moral Neutrality,'" in Christopher Wolfe, ed., *Homosexuality and American Public Life,* 144.

[13] Eleanor E. Maccoby, *The Two Sexes: Growing Up Apart, Coming Together* (Cambridge, Mass.: Harvard University Press, 1999).

[14] Steven Pinker, *How the Mind Works* (New York: W. W. Norton, 1997).

[15] Howard Gardner, *Multiple Intelligences: The Theory in Practice* (New York: Basic Books, 1993).

[16] Daniel Goleman, *Emotional Intelligence* (New York: Bantam Books, 1995).

[17] Kurt Haas and Adelaide Haas, *Understanding Sexuality* (St. Louis: Mosby-Year Book, 1993) 117–48.

[18] Walter Wink, ed., *Homosexuality and Christian Faith, Questions of Conscience for the Churches* (Minneapolis: Fortress, 1999) 23–30.

[19] Richard John Neuhaus, "Love, No Matter What," 245.

11

Informing the Debate on Homosexuality: The Behavioral Sciences and the Church

Isiaah Crawford and Brian D. Zamboni

A s the Church moves into the next millennium it finds itself facing increased pressure both internally and externally to explicate and justify its moral position on homosexuality and homosexual behavior. Behavioral science has addressed many of the constructs moral theologians encounter when they confront these issues. In an attempt to facilitate and inform the discussion about the complex and impassioned questions homosexuality creates for the Church, this chapter will summarize and critically evaluate empirical behavioral research on the following aspects of homosexuality: (a) the etiology of sexual orientation, (b) the intimate relationships and the moral development of gay, lesbian, and bisexual people, (c) the impact of parental homosexuality on child development, and (d) the psychosocial factors associated with heterosexism.

THE ETIOLOGY OF SEXUAL ORIENTATION

The question of what causes a person to be homosexual has been a topic of considerable interest from both a scientific and a value-based perspective. Scientifically speaking, this question should be reformulated: how does sexual orientation develop? Researchers cannot study "the cause of homosexuality" without studying "the cause of heterosexuality." The scientific perspective is based on intellectual curiosity. By contrast, individuals operating with a value-based perspective may use the etiology of homosexuality as the basis of their social, political, or moral judgments of gay men and lesbians. The implicit idea behind this inquiry is: if homosexuality is genetic, then it is not a choice (i.e., "homosexuals cannot help the way they are and therefore are not blameworthy"). This notion can take a patronizing tone; it also assumes that any behavior that is genetically determined is not blameworthy. Because all behavior is assumed to have some genetic roots, it seems unwise to base one's attitude toward homosexuals solely on biological explanations for sexual behavior (see Bailey and Pillard, 1995). These issues will be revisited after a review of the approaches used to understand the development of sexual orientation has been completed.

Several theories have been proposed to explain how a person's sexual orientation develops. In the last ten years a number of studies with methodological strengths that improve upon prior research have been reported. These studies have attempted to explain the etiology of sexual orientation with as much scientific rigor as possible, but this research is not without flaws. Theories of sexual orientation can be grouped into genetic, hormonal, neuroanatomical, and environmental theories. Each of these explanations and the research associated with each theory will be summarized. Strengths and weaknesses of each body of research will be noted.

The Genetic Theory

Genes are the basic units of heredity that determine a person's traits. A trait such as eye color is genetic when people possess the trait because of different genes rather than different environments. Although genetics has been implicated in the development of sexual orientation of non-human species (e.g., fruit flies; see Burr, 1994), this review will focus on studies involving humans. Overall, the evidence that genetics is involved in the development of sexual orientation appears to be fairly strong. Genetic studies of sexual orientation use family, twin, and adoption studies. Studies involving molecular genetics will also be reviewed briefly.

Family Studies

In family studies a characteristic may be genetic if the trait runs in families (i.e., how many people in this family are gay or lesbian?) Because a trait may exist due to shared environmental conditions, the trait may not be genetic. Drawbacks to family studies include the difficulty of disentangling genetic and environmental factors and the lower reproduction rate of homosexuals (i.e., researchers must often examine the rate of homosexuality in siblings rather than between parents and their offspring, particularly across generations). A review of family studies (see Bailey and Pillard, 1995) shows that the rate of homosexuality among brothers is approximately 9 percent, which is higher than the rate for heterosexual controls (i.e., 3 percent). This suggests that male homosexuality may be familial (Bailey and Pillard, 1995; see also Dank, 1971). Although there is evidence for familial homosexuality among women, it is less consistent (Bailey and Pillard, 1995).

Twin Studies

Some of the best evidence for a genetic explanation of sexual orientation comes from maximizing genetic similarities between individuals (i.e., from working with identical or monozygotic twins) and minimizing similarities in environmental conditions (i.e., by studying monozygotic twins reared apart). Twin studies provide stronger evidence of a genetic explanation of sexual orientation because the two individuals have more in common genetically. Monozygotic twins are identical twins and share more similar genetic material than dizygotic twins, that is, than fraternal twins who are not identical. When twins are raised in the same family their shared environment creates a problem for the genetic theory of sexual orientation (i.e., the environment, rather than genes, could account for their sexual orientation). When twins are raised in different family environments (e.g., one was adopted away) yet still share the same trait, the genetic explanation for this trait is stronger.

Because homosexuality and monozygotic twins reared apart are both relatively uncommon phenomena, it is rare to be able to study homosexuality in monozygotic twins reared apart. Only one known study (Eckert, Bouchard, Bohlen, and Heston, 1986) has conducted such research. Eckert *et al.* (1986) described six pairs of separated monozygotic twins, two male pairs and four female pairs, in which one of the twins was gay or lesbian. (One of the female twins was bisexual.) One male pair was concordant for homosexuality (i.e., both males were gay) and the other male pair was not clearly concordant or discordant. All four female pairs were discordant for homosexuality. Eckert *et al.* (1986) suggested that male sexual orientation is influenced by interactive factors and that genes clearly play a role, but that female sexual orientation may be an acquired trait because environmental factors rather than genetic factors appear to influence it.

Based on the statistical likelihood of finding separated monozygotic twins concordant for homosexuality, Bailey and Pillard (1995) have argued that the study supports the role of genes in the development of male sexual orientation, but cannot deny the possible role of genetics in female sexual orientation. This study is clearly limited by its small and selective sample size. Regardless of these limitations, this study of such rare phenomena provides compelling evidence that genetics plays an etiological role in male sexual orientation, although genetics does not appear to be the only causal factor. Eckert *et al.* (1986) were not able to support the notion that genetics is involved in the etiology of female sexual orientation. Due to the rarity of separated and homosexual monozygotic twins, it is difficult to test the results of Eckert *et al.* (1986) by conducting similar studies. Examining the sexual orientation of monozygotic and dizygotic twins reared together provides the next best alternative to studying the genetics of sexual orientation.

If sexual orientation is genetic, monozygotic twins should show higher concordance rates for homosexuality compared to dizygotic twins because monozygotic twins share more similar genetic material. Early studies of twins conducted prior to 1970, flawed by small and biased samples, generally reported such findings (see Eckert *et al.*, 1986 for a brief overview). Fortunately, five larger studies of sexual orientation in twins were reported early in the 1990s (e.g., Bailey and Pillard, 1991; Buhrich, Bailey, and Martin, 1991; Whitam, Diamond, and Martin, 1993; see Bailey and Pillard, 1995). In general these more recent studies show higher rates of concordant homosexuality in monozygotic twins than in dizygotic twins (see Bailey and Pillard, 1995), a finding that is consistent with the theory that genetics plays a significant role in the development of sexual orientation. One study (King and McDonald, 1992) failed to find significantly higher rates in monozygotic twins, although it was in the hypothesized direction (see Bailey and Pillard, 1995).

Overall, these studies involve few, if any, female monozygotic twins, making the results largely applicable to the genetics of male sexual orientation. The exception to this rule is one study devoted to female twins conducted by Bailey, Pillard, Neal, and Agyei (1993). The results of this study mirror those of the other investigations: rates of concordant homosexuality or bisexuality in female monozygotic twins were higher than in dizygotic twins, supporting the etiological role of genetics in female sexual orientation (Bailey *et al.,* 1993). Because none of these recent twin studies report concordance rates of 100 percent for homosexuality among monozygotic twins, genetics can only be a partial etiological factor in sexual orientation. Other contributing causal factors may be biological (e.g., hormonal) or environmental (see Burr, 1994).

Criticisms of Twin Studies

Byne and Parsons (1993) have suggested that these studies of twins use potentially unrepresentative samples, do not control for environmental factors, assume equal environments between monozygotic and dizygotic twins, and fail to specify the intervening mechanisms between genes and sexual orientation (see also Muir, 1996). These are negligible criticisms because the former three points are issues for the majority of twin studies on any given topic. The latter point, however noteworthy, is beyond the scope of research, which must first determine the degree to which genetics plays a role in sexual orientation, if at all (see also Bailey and Pillard, 1995). Future studies must explore ways in which genes might become translated into sexual orientation. Other writers have stressed that the way sexual orientation is defined and measured remains inadequate (Looy, 1995; McGuire, 1995). These criticisms are theoretically interesting and have methodological implications, and in practice affect any study of sexual orientation. For the twin studies examining genetic explanations of sexual orientation where sexual orientation was adequately assessed, these criticisms do not appear to influence the results appreciably. Future studies of sexual orientation should still carefully assess sexual orientation using multiple methods (e.g., continuous scales, label preferences, sexual behavior reports).

One of the twin studies (i.e., Bailey and Pillard, 1991) was closely scrutinized because it was one of the first reported in the 1990s and received substantial publicity. In evaluating this study, Byne and Parsons (1993) pointed out that Bailey and Pillard (1991) did not use a systematically ascertained sample of twins and that one of their findings is at odds with the genetic theory of sexual orientation (i.e., the homosexuality concordance rate for non-twin biological brothers was similar to genetically unrelated adoptive brothers and lower than the dizygotic twins). The former criticism is an important point that can apply to other twin studies as well and has been acknowledged as a methodological challenge for future twin studies in the genetics of sexual orientation (Bailey and Pillard, 1995; McGuire, 1995). With regard to the latter criticism, the unusual finding may be due to sampling fluctuations (Bailey and Pillard, 1991), a concordance-dependent ascertainment bias in the dizygotic twins (Bailey and Pillard, 1995) or more similar environments among the dizygotic twins (Byne and Parsons, 1993). This odd result does not detract from the other findings in that study, which have been replicated by subsequent studies.

Studies in Molecular Genetics

Research into the molecular genetics of sexual orientation involves techniques that pinpoint the location and the specific genes that appear to be associated with sexual orientation. Hamer, Hu, Magnuson, Hu, and Pattatucci (1993) conducted the first such study using a linkage technique where family members with the same sexual orientation should have a high likelihood of sharing the gene in question. These authors found that a region called Xq28 was shared by most of the gay male brothers in their study, more than would be expected in general (Hamer *et al.*, 1993).

Concerns regarding this study's methodology have been raised, but none appears to be serious enough to cause us to disregard its results (see Bailey and Pillard, 1995). Nonetheless, subsequent research has not fully supported the Xq28 region as a genetic basis of sexual orientation. While one study found no excessively shared genetic material among families, another found modest support for the Xq28 as a genetic marker (see Bailey and Pillard, 1995). A recent study failed to identify Xq28 as a genetic marker for sexual orientation, but this does not preclude the possibility that this or another genetic marker might eventually be associated with sexual orientation (Rice, Anderson, Risch, and Ebers, 1999). The technology in molecular genetics is scientifically exciting. Because the current results are mixed, larger and numerous studies will be needed to ascertain whether the Xq28 area, or another location, contains a gene that is associated with sexual orientation.

Conclusions Regarding the Genetics of Sexual Orientation

The bulk of the evidence suggests that genes play a role in the development of sexual orientation. Several lines of research point toward this conclusion, with most of the evidence coming from twin studies. As noted, some of the criticisms directed toward twin studies are more important than others. The one odd finding reported in Bailey and Pillard's (1991) study is a small anomaly compared to the study's remaining results and findings of other twin studies.

Scientists should continue their efforts to conduct sound, rigorous research in this area and replication studies need to be done. In addition, more twin studies are needed with female monozygotic twins. The existing research on the genetic explanation of sexual orientation is impressive given the difficulty of conducting such investigations, and these studies offer the best available results to date. These results are consistent. Genes appear to be a significant contributing factor in the development of male sexual orientation, but these genes clearly must interact with other as yet unknown etiological factors in shaping a male's sexual orientation. The same conclusion can be offered tentatively with respect to female sexual orientation, but more studies are needed to support with greater confidence the idea that genes partially influence female sexual orientation.

Hormonal Theories

Another theory regarding the origins of sexual orientation concerns hormones. Hormones strongly influence the mating behavior of non-human species (Crews, 1994). According to this school of thought, certain hormone levels in men and women predispose them to behaving as a heterosexual, homosexual, or bisexual individual. Current research shows that hormone levels are not significantly different between homosexual and heterosexual individuals (Friedman and Downey, 1993; Gooren, Fliers, and Courtney, 1990; Meyer-Bahlburg, 1993). In addition, sexual orientation does not appear to be influenced by artificial or natural changes in hormone levels. Hormones appear to influence the degree to which a person is interested in sex, but not the type of individuals with whom one desires sex (Whalen, Geary, and Johnson, 1990).

As a result of these findings, the hormonal hypothesis of sexual orientation now focuses on the idea that prenatal and possibly early postnatal hormonal factors influence sexual orientation (see Ellis and Ames, 1987). Androgen is a hormone that typically shows high levels in young males and low levels in young females. Specifically, disruptions in androgen levels *via* a variety of mechanisms in males or females could lead to homosexuality (Ellis and Ames, 1987).

There have been relatively few studies conducted with humans to test the prenatal hormone theory of sexual orientation. Two recent studies with humans address the prenatal hormone notion directly, and both support the theory. One study compared the sexual orientation of normal control women and women who had prenatal exposure to synthetic estrogen (Meyer-Bahlburg, Ehrhardt, Rosen, and Gruen, 1995). Women who had exposure to the synthetic estrogen were more likely to have a homosexual or bisexual orientation than women without exposure to the synthetic hormone (Meyer-Bahlburg *et al.*, 1995).

Using a series of measures concerning sex- and gender-related behavior, Dessens *et al.* (1999) compared normal control men and women with men and women who had been exposed prenatally to anticonvulsant drugs (i.e., drugs that have led to altered sexual differentiation in animal studies). Although the two groups did not differ with respect to gender role behavior, more individuals in the prenatal drug exposure group reported past or current cross-gender behavior and gender dysphoria (Dessens *et al.*, 1999). Moreover, two prenatal drug-exposed males were homosexual and three prenatally drug-exposed individuals were transsexuals compared to no homosexuals or transsexuals in the control group (Dessens *et al.*, 1999).

Other scholars have described support for the prenatal hormone theory of sexual orientation by discussing theoretical issues and citing research that often involves non-humans (Ellis and Ames, 1987; Meyer-Bahlburg, 1991). Critics of the prenatal hormone theory question how well research with non-humans translates to humans where sexual behavior is concerned (Byne and Parsons, 1993). More research is clearly needed with humans to test the prenatal hormone theory of sexual orientation. Thus far, prenatal disturbances in androgen levels appear to influence sex- and gender-related behavior, but the role of prenatal hormones in shaping sexual orientation remains an open question. Future research should also consider that prenatal hormone levels might interact with a genetic predisposition toward a given sexual orientation.

The Neuroanatomical Theory

A final biological theory about the etiology of sexual orientation concerns neuroanatomy. The idea behind this theory is that sexual orientation is influenced by specific brain structures. To test this idea, researchers have looked for potential differences in brain structures between homosexual and heterosexual individuals. Unfortunately, aside from research with non-humans, only three known studies have examined postmortem differences in brain structures among humans. All three studies reported different brain structures varying by sexual orientation. One study reported that an area called the suprachiasmatic nucleus was larger in homosexual men than in heterosexual men (Swaab and Hoffman, 1990). Another study (LeVay, 1991) reported that a specific area of the hypothalamus (i.e., the third interstitial nucleus of the anterior hypothalamus) was comparably small in homosexual men and heterosexual women while larger in heterosexual men. A third study provided evidence that the anterior commissure is larger in homosexual men and heterosexual women when compared to heterosexual men (Allen and Gorski, 1992).

Unfortunately, there are several problems with the research in this area. These studies were generally unable to include homosexual women, preventing a complete examination of brain structures and sexual orientation. Some of these studies included individuals who had died from acquired immunodeficiency syndrome (AIDS), a medical condition that could have altered their brain structures. Moreover, the results focus on brain structures that are inconsistent across all studies. (For additional critical perspectives see Byne and Parsons, 1993; Harrison, Everall, and Catalan, 1994). Much more research is needed to examine the neuroanatomical theory of sexual orientation. The current evidence is inconclusive.

Environmental Theories

A variety of psychoanalytic, social-environmental, and experiential theories of sexual orientation have been suggested. Brief historical sketches of these theories have been described elsewhere (e.g., Ellis and Ames, 1987). A full exposition of these theories is not only beyond the scope of this chapter but also imprudent, given the lack of support for each school of thought.

The psychoanalytic perspective, originated by Freud, suggests that male homosexuality stems from a fixated psychosexual development due to a dominant mother and a submissive father (see Bieber and Bieber, 1979). Other theorists emphasized the influence of family environment (e.g., unhappy homes) on sexual orientation, rather than parent-child interactions specifically (e.g., Bene, 1965). Social-environmental theories suggested that homosexuality resulted from difficulty in learning proper social roles (e.g., Kagan, 1964), while others have argued that the reinforcement of same-sex sexual encounters leads to homosexuality (e.g., Acosta, 1975). The lack of consistent empirical support for these theories diminishes their value (Friedman, 1986).

The focus on biological explanations of sexual orientation seems to stem from advancing medical technology and dissatisfaction with research on environmental and psychosocial theories. Yet if sexual orientation is only partially shaped by genetics, as suggested by current research, then other factors must be involved. Other biological factors (e.g., prenatal hormones) might interact with genes, but environmental or psychosocial factors could play a role. Furthermore, genetics has not been implicated in all cases of homosexuality, suggesting that other factors, possibly environmental ones, may influence sexual orientation.

Retrospective studies of childhood cross-sex behavior show that, compared to heterosexuals, gay men recall effeminate childhood behavior and lesbians recall more masculine-type behavior (Bailey and Zucker, 1995). Nonetheless, some gay men and lesbians evidenced typical gender-type behavior and their childhood behavior varied considerably (Bailey and Zucker, 1995). Prospective studies show similar results for homosexual and heterosexual men (see Bailey and Pillard, 1995). Childhood gender-typed behaviors might differentiate some homosexuals from heterosexuals, but not all of the time. The meaning of these findings as they relate to sexual orientation remains unclear. Is childhood gender-typed behavior based on biological factors, or do biological factors predispose a person toward certain gender-typed play? Is there something early in a person's childhood that helps to shape sexual orientation? Bailey and Pillard (1995) state that environment is sometimes an important determinant of sexual orientation and suggest that research examining the experiences or developmental antecedents of homosexual and heterosexual co-twins might be critical.

There can be no question that environment plays some type of role in the development of sexual orientation. The important questions at this point seem to be what these environmental factors are, and how much they contribute to the development of sexual orientation. If these factors occur early in infancy they may be difficult to pinpoint. Moreover, there may be considerable variability in terms of the environmental factors that influence sexual orientation. These factors may be so inconsistent that research may not be able to identify the most salient ones. Research on the environmental factors associated with the etiology of sexual orientation appears to be the most daunting in this area.

Implications of Research on the Etiology of Sexual Orientation

Studies regarding the origins of sexual orientation can have an impact on society in many ways. For example, recent studies may have shaped professionals' attitudes toward the etiology of homosexuality. In a recent survey psychiatrists endorsed a theory of genetic inheritance as the primary causal agent in male homosexuality, including psychiatrists with a psychoanalytic orientation (Vreeland, Gallagher, and McFalls, 1995).

Some scholars suggest that research on the etiology of sexual orientation should not be conducted because of the potential misuses and abuses of the findings. Such authors apparently fear that homosexuality will be viewed as normal or natural, that homosexuality will be assumed good if a genetic or biological basis for sexual orientation were found (see Schuklenk, Stein, Kerin, and Byne, 1997). Similarly, other writers dispute genetic or other biological evidence (Byne and Parsons, 1993; Muir, 1996; Schuklenk *et al.*, 1997), possibly fearing that gay men and lesbians will be positively valued when genetic explanations appear robust. Still other writers suggest that it is unethical to conduct research into the origins of sexual orientation due to the researchers' possible biases (Schuklenk *et al.*, 1997). Researchers are never completely objective and should certainly strive to conduct research that is as free as possible from their own biases. Yet a close reading of these critics' evaluation of genetics and sexual orientation (e.g., Byne and Parsons, 1993; Muir, 1996; Schuklenk *et al.*, 1997) suggests that they may be working out of their own biased "anti-homosexual" framework.

Writers who do not seem to work from an anti-homosexual framework also have concerns regarding this research. Political groups may want to see research that supports a genetic or biological basis for homosexuality because such findings would buttress legal arguments to afford the same civil protections to homosexuals that other minorities have in the United States (Gabard, 1999). Yet individuals concerned about the welfare of non-heterosexuals are troubled that such research may not add to the public's understanding of homosexuality and in fact detracts from studies that refute misconceptions regarding gay men and lesbians (Gabard, 1999). People concerned with the welfare of homosexuals do not want homosexuality to be seen as a defect or a dysfunction, possibly increasing the chances that research findings will be used to develop treatments for preventing homosexuality or "reorienting" homosexuals (Gabard, 1999).

All individuals, regardless of their backgrounds or sociopolitical views toward homosexuality, must recognize the difference between scientific facts and personal values. Genetics may partially influence sexual orientation, but this does not imply a complete lack of free will or choice regarding sexual behavior (see Bailey and Pillard, 1995). Furthermore, genetic or other etiological differences in sexual orientation between individuals do not imply that any one etiological path is dysfunctional (e.g., left-handed people are not dysfunctional). As noted earlier, all behavior shows genetic or biological underpinnings. Indeed, basing one's attitudes toward homosexuality on its apparent etiology seems unwise.

INTIMATE RELATIONSHIPS AMONG GAY MEN AND LESBIANS

The socially sanctioned desire to partake in and maintain a romantic relationship is a goal that gay men, lesbians, and heterosexuals alike share (Meyer, 1990). Yet lesbians and gay males have been stereotyped as: (a) lacking the desire and the ability to achieve enduring relationships and (b) experiencing unhappy, dysfunctional, and aberrant relationships (Peplau, 1993). Another common misconception revolves around the idea that masculine and feminine roles in relationships are universal and that lesbians and gay men must somehow adhere to these role expectations (Peplau, 1993). As this forthcoming review shows, research consistently contradicts these stereotypes of gay male and lesbian relationships. Research on gay male and lesbian couples can be divided into studies that describe such relationships, research that compares gay male couples and lesbian couples, and research that compares same-sex couples with opposite-sex couples.

Descriptive Studies: Gay Men and Lesbians

Several studies indicate that gay men and lesbians are quite interested in maintaining lasting, loving relationships and that most are currently in such relationships (see Bell and Weinberg, 1978; Harry, 1983; Peplau and Cochran, 1981). These studies generally show that 40 to 60 percent of gay men and 45 to 80 percent of lesbians are currently in ongoing relationships (see Peplau, 1993). These are probably underestimates because early studies of gay male and lesbian relationships tended to use convenience samples (e.g., surveys in bars), where individuals who are in a relationship are less likely to be found (Peplau, 1993).

Eldridge and Gilbert (1990) conducted a survey of over 270 lesbian couples from across the United States. The average duration of the lesbians' current relationship was 5.4 years, with one relationship lasting as long as twenty-two years (Eldridge and Gilbert, 1990). Many participants (65 percent) had not disclosed their sexual orientation to their employers, to coworkers (37 percent), to their fathers (over 50 percent), or to their mothers (over 33 percent; Eldridge and Gilbert, 1990). The lesbians in this sample reported satisfaction with their relationships, satisfaction with life in general, experience with intimacy in their relationships, and commitment to their careers (Eldridge and Gilbert, 1990). The high levels of self-esteem and life satisfaction among the lesbians in this sample have been previously documented (Bell and Weinberg, 1978) and run counter to the stereotype of lesbians as unhappy persons with a low self-esteem (Eldridge and Gilbert, 1990). Contrary to the stereotype of lesbian relationships as transient and primarily sexual, the study indicated that the lesbians surveyed remained in stable, lasting, and committed relationships (Eldridge and Gilbert, 1990).

A smaller study followed the relationships of lesbian couples over a two-year period (Green, Bettinger, and Zacks, 1996). Forty-eight of the original fifty-two couples were tested at follow-up and 71 percent of these couples were still together (Green *et al.*, 1996). Couples that had separated reported lower relationship cohesion and flexibility during the initial testing (Green *et al.*, 1996). For the couples who were still together, higher levels of relationship cohesion and flexibility during the initial testing were associated with higher relationship satisfaction two years later (Green *et al.*, 1996). An earlier, larger longitudinal study of lesbian, gay male, and heterosexual couples found similar results (Blumstein and Schwartz, 1983). After eighteen months the vast majority of gay male and lesbian couples were still together (Blumstein and Schwartz, 1983). These findings, again, contradict the stereotype that same-sex couples cannot maintain enduring relationships.

Generally, studies do not report differences between gay male and lesbian relationships. Still, differences have been reported. Gay males seem to be more likely than lesbians to allow sexual activity outside the couple, but the levels of relationship satisfaction do not differ by sexual exclusivity status in the gay male relationships (see Kurdek, 1991). Lesbian relationships may also be more cohesive (i.e., the degree of closeness *via* emotional bonding) and enjoy greater role flexibility than gay male relationships (Green *et al.*, 1996; see also Blumstein and Schwartz, 1983). These differences may reflect differences in gender roles. Males may have stronger sex drives and more permissive sexual attitudes, but are not encouraged to express emotions and are not allowed a great deal of gender role flexibility (e.g., see Blumstein and Schwartz, 1983).

Kurdek (1988) found that the predictors of relationship quality for lesbian and gay male couples were the same: high motivation to be in the relationship, high trust, high satisfaction with social support, high shared decision-making, and low autonomy. In addition, both gay and lesbian partners in a couple are similar to each other (Kurdek, 1988). Over time, the relationships of both gay men and lesbians become more satisfying (Kurdek, 1988).

One study found that lesbians report higher relationship satisfaction than gay men (Kurdek, 1988) while another study found that lesbians report more rewards from their relationship than gay men (Kurdek, 1991). Yet these two studies, as well as several other investigations, fail to find differences between gay males and lesbians in their relationships on a variety of other measures. In contrast to Kurdek (1988), Duffy and Rusbult (1986) as well as Kurdek (1991) found no differences in reported relationship satisfaction between gay men and lesbians. Kurdek (1991) also found no differences between gay men and lesbians on measures of emotional expressiveness, relationship beliefs, self-consciousness, relationship conflict, relationship autonomy, and problem-solving techniques. Other studies have reported few differences between the relationships of gay men and lesbians, supporting the notion that these relationships are more similar than they are different (Blumstein and Schwartz, 1983; Duffy and Rusbult, 1986; Falbo and Peplau, 1980; Kurdek, 1988; Kurdek and Schmitt, 1986; Peplau and Cochran, 1990).

Comparing Homosexual and Heterosexual Relationships

Research suggests that heterosexual and homosexual relationships are more similar than different. Some of the similarities might be simple (e.g., jewelry, clothing) to show commitment to one another (Meyer, 1990). Other similarities might be as profound as feelings of love and relationship satisfaction (see Peplau, 1993). These studies do not suggest that same-sex couples are free of problems or that they are better than other-sex couples, but instead suggest that gay male and lesbian relationships are not more prone to difficulties than heterosexual relationships.

Relationship Values and Satisfaction

Lesbians and heterosexual women do not appear to differ with respect to measures of self-esteem, capacity for intimacy, or values in romantic relationships (Rosenbluth, 1997). Rosenbluth (1997) has reported that over half of the lesbians and over half of the heterosexual women in her sample endorsed "mutual trust" and "mutual respect" as important aspects of intimate relationships. Lesbians, gay men, and heterosexuals appear to have the same likes and dislikes with regard to these aspects of their relationships (see Peplau, 1993). Moreover, Peplau (1993) has indicated that lesbians, gay men, and heterosexuals alike appear to share two independent personal values with respect to relationship needs: dyadic attachment (i.e., knowing one is loved and needed by a partner) and personal autonomy (i.e., being able to maintain one's independence). Other research supports the notion that heterosexual and homosexual individuals share the same values with respect to romantic relationships (Laner, 1988; Ramsey, Lathem, and Lindquist, 1978; Peplau and Cochran, 1990). One exception to these findings suggests that sexual exclusivity is more important to heterosexuals than to gay men or lesbians (Peplau and Cochran, 1990). This issue will be addressed in greater depth later in this chapter.

Lesbians have reported higher levels of trust in their partners compared to heterosexual women (Zak and McDonald, 1997). The authors of this study suggested that lesbians may report higher levels of trust due to the partners' increased similarity of goals, which may be partly motivated by the limited number of available partners (Zak and McDonald, 1997). These findings may also reflect the lack of trust that may exist in heterosexual relationships due to the differences in economic and social power between men and women and the justified perceptions that men are more likely to be sexually unfaithful than women (Michael *et al.,* 1994). Research has suggested that both lesbian and gay male relationships are more cohesive (i.e., having a sense of interconnectedness) than heterosexual relationships (Green *et al.,* 1996). This finding runs counter to the stereotype that gay male couples are disengaged compared to heterosexual couples (Green *et al.,* 1996). Another study reported that 72 percent of its sample of lesbians endorsed "emotional fulfillment and intimacy" as a reason for being in their relationship compared to 20 percent of the heterosexual women endorsing the same reason, a significant difference between the groups (Rosenbluth, 1997). This finding may reflect a difference between lesbians and heterosexual women in their primary motivations for intimate relationships. Indeed, although intimacy was valued by all respondents in this study, more lesbians and fewer heterosexual women perceived lesbian relationships as offering a greater opportunity to achieve such intimacy (Rosenbluth, 1997).

One group of researchers reported that lesbians had higher relationship satisfaction than heterosexual couples and that gay men had slightly lower relationship satisfaction than heterosexual couples (Green *et al.*, 1996). Unfortunately, these findings resulted from two different measures of relationship satisfaction, making the results somewhat tenuous. A recent study compared heterosexual women and lesbian women in their ratings of relationship satisfaction, but no significant differences were found between the groups (Zak and McDonald, 1997). These findings are consistent with prior studies showing that lesbians and heterosexual women report comparable levels of satisfaction in their love relationships (Cardell, Finn, and Marecek, 1981; Eldridge, 1987; Fogarty, 1980; Peters and Cantrell, 1993). Furthermore, no differences in relationship satisfaction were found in a study that included lesbians, gay men, and heterosexuals (see Peplau, 1993). Kurdek and Schmitt (1986) also found no differences among lesbian, gay male, and heterosexual couples in terms of their relationship satisfaction and feelings of love. Levels of sexual satisfaction also appear to be similar across gay male, lesbian, and heterosexual couples (Peplau, 1993).

Sexual Exclusivity

Sexual exclusivity appears to be an issue in all relationships (see Peplau, 1993). There is limited evidence that some gay men engage in sexual activity outside their relationships, more than lesbians (as previously noted), and more than heterosexual men. According to one study, 79 percent of gay men in a relationship reported sex with another partner in the previous year compared to 11 percent of heterosexual men (Blumstein and Schwartz, 1990). Due to the considerable interest that this topic can generate, the issue of sexual exclusivity warrants close examination.

Some authors have argued that this in part reflects a gender difference, showing that men have stronger sex drives and are more sexual (Mannino, in press). For gay men, love and sex may be viewed separately (Mannino). More specifically, it is possible that more gay men have successfully adopted a norm for extracurricular sex than have heterosexual men. Some gay couples may come to an understanding that outside sex is permitted, but only under mutually defined circumstances (e.g., sex without an emotional bond). A recent study supports this idea. Wagner, Remien, and Carballo-Diéguez (in press) studied sixty-three gay male couples and found that in the past year 30 percent were monogamous, 29 percent were sexually open, 21 percent had been secretly unfaithful, and 21 percent were unfaithful without complete secrecy. Monogamous and open couples had lower scores of psychological distress and higher levels of relationship quality compared to "secretive" and "partial knowledge" couples, but these differences were not statistically significant (Wagner *et al.,* in press). Monogamous and open couples had significantly higher levels of relationship consensus, affectional expression, relationship satisfaction, and sexual satisfaction compared to the partial knowledge and secretive couples (Wagner *et al.,* in press). The notion that gay male couples can successfully integrate outside sexual activity into their lives is supported by earlier research that demonstrates that equality and lack of possessiveness (particularly in sexual relations) are important factors in maintaining gay male relationships beyond ten years' duration (McWhirter and Mattison, 1984; see also Blumstein and Schwartz, 1983; Kurdek, 1988).

It should be noted that another study of gay male couples has shown that 73 percent are monogamous (Mohr and Fassinger, personal communication), a figure that is higher than other reports. There is considerable variation in terms of the sexual exclusivity and other relationship characteristics among gay male, lesbian—and heterosexual—couples (Blumstein and Schwartz, 1983; Peplau, 1993; Mannino, in press). It should also be noted that substantial percentages of heterosexual men and women have been shown to engage in a variety of unfaithful behaviors while in a dating relationship and up to 25 percent of married men *report* marital infidelity (Laumann, Gagnon, Michael, and Michaels, 1994; Yarab, Sensibaugh, Allgeier, 1998; see also Blumstein and Schwartz, 1983). The existing studies are somewhat contradictory on this issue. Because some gay male relationships involve outside sexual activity and some do not allow any extracurricular sexual activity, sexual exclusivity may be influenced by several factors. The degree to which any relationship is sexually open may depend upon the partners' personalities, goals in the relationship, the status of the relationship (e.g., dating versus cohabiting), the duration of the relationship and/or the degree to which the couple idealize the concept of monogamy. More research is needed to compare gay men and heterosexual couples in terms of sexual exclusivity, and such studies should examine the factors that lead to a decision of sexual openness versus sexual exclusivity.

Social Support, Life Roles, and Relationship Roles

There is generally little support from nuclear families and the community at large for gay men and lesbians who are seeking to create a loving dyadic relationship (Meyer, 1990). Although this can be a burdensome stressor, gay men and lesbians have been able to overcome such difficulties and create their own systems of support (Peplau, 1993). Gay men and lesbians may be more likely to rely on friends for support in contrast to heterosexuals who are more likely to rely on family for support (Peplau, 1993). Nonetheless, family can be a source of support for many gay male and lesbian couples, and same-sex couples have reported comparable levels of and satisfaction with overall support (see Peplau, 1993).

Life roles refer to the notion that each person maintains multiple capacities in everyday life (e.g., a career role, a parenting role). For example, an intimate partner role refers to the expectations a person plays out as part of a committed romantic relationship (i.e., like the script for being a spouse). There is evidence that lesbians experience more conflict regarding their various roles in life when compared to heterosexual women, particularly with respect to intimate partner roles. Compared to heterosexual women, lesbians have reported more conflict regarding their intimate partner role and their role as a daughter (Peters and Cantrell, 1993). Similarly, lesbians have reported more conflict regarding their roles as intimate partners and employees (Peters and Cantrell, 1993). These conflicts appear to stem from the inability to communicate with parents and coworkers about their intimate relationships, as well as disapproval from parents and coworkers (Peters and Cantrell, 1993). Such role conflicts reflect the lack of familial and social support for lesbian relationships.

In contrast to various life roles, an individual can experience various roles within an intimate relationship (e.g., dominant versus submissive; masculine versus feminine). Role flexibility has been defined as the ability of a couple to change the rules and power structure in the relationship in response to stress (see Green *et al.*, 1996). Past research shows that gay male and lesbian relationships show greater equality and gender-role flexibility when compared to heterosexual couples (Bell and Weinberg, 1978; Blumstein and Schwartz, 1983; Peplau, 1991; Kurdek,

1995; see also Rosenbluth, 1997). These findings run counter to the stereotype of same-sex couples as assuming fixed gender roles (e.g., lesbians do not assume "butch/femme" roles to match masculine/feminine roles). More recent research continues to support the notion that both lesbian and gay male relationships are characterized by substantially greater role flexibility compared to heterosexual relationships (see Green *et al.*, 1996).

A Note on Morality: A Study of Deception

Lesbians and gay men have been stereotyped as individuals who are immoral in both specific and vague ways. One specific charge of immorality holds that homosexual individuals are pedophiles and attempt to convert or recruit others (especially youths) into their lifestyle. Research debunks this myth and shows that the vast majority of pedophiles are heterosexual, some of whom molest same-sex children (see Freund and Watson, 1992; Blanchard *et al.*, 1999). As noted previously, lesbians, gay men, and heterosexual individuals share similar values with respect to intimate relationships. Few studies have examined morality among homosexual and heterosexual individuals, but one investigation (Burdon, 1996) has examined deception among same-sex and other-sex couples.

Burdon's (1996) sample included forty-one heterosexual males, fifty-two heterosexual females, thirty-two gay and bisexual men, and thirty-four lesbian and bisexual women. The participants read three scenarios that could occur while one is in an intimate relationship. The vignettes involved the target person joining a former lover for a drink, failing to attend a current lover's dinner party, and receiving flirtation from a former sex partner at a party (see Burdon, 1996). Participants were asked how they would handle the situation (e.g., what would the current lover be told?), and responses were coded according to an established definition of deception and guidelines to maintain coding consistency (Burdon, 1996). The coder was blind to the sexual orientation of the participant.

The results indicated that heterosexuals engaged in more deception than homosexual or bisexual participants and that homosexual/bisexual men and women were truthful in their responses to the same degree (Burdon, 1996). Heterosexual women were more truthful in their responses than heterosexual men (Burdon, 1996). These results are consistent with a similar pilot study conducted by the author, but the pilot study showed no differences in deception between homosexuals and heterosexuals when non-intimate situations were involved (see Burdon, 1996). The author suggested that the intimate situations used in the current study may not have been threatening or important to gay, lesbian, or bisexual individuals compared to heterosexuals, possibly because the role expectations for homosexual/bisexual couples are not as demanding or constraining (Burdon, 1996).

This study is not without flaws. It did not include non-intimate situations and apparently only one coder was employed. Nonetheless, the results are intriguing and more research on deception and moral issues among gay, lesbian, and heterosexual individuals is needed. Burdon's (1996) findings run counter to the stereotype that gay men and lesbians are immoral in general and in their intimate relationships.

Conclusions on Gay and Lesbian Relationships

Simply stating that there are far more similarities among gay male, lesbian, and heterosexual relationships than there are differences can summarize the literature on gay and lesbian relationships. Without question, these studies debunk the stereotypes that gay males and lesbians do not seek intimate relationships, are unhappy in their relationships, cannot have stable and loving relationships, follow gender-typed roles in a couple, and are immoral in their relationships.

Research indicates that the majority of gay men and lesbians are interested and currently involved in committed relationships. Gay male and lesbian relationships are stable, long-lasting, intimate and loving. Gay men and lesbians are happy and satisfied with their lives and relationships. When gay male couples are compared to lesbian couples, few differences (e.g., sexual exclusivity; life roles) have been consistently identified and these may be due to differences in the gender roles into which they were socialized. Gay male and lesbian couples appear to be equally satisfied in their relationships and report comparable beliefs about relationships, conflicts within relationships, autonomy in relationship, and problem-solving techniques. When same-sex couples are compared to heterosexual couples, few differences are apparent: gay males may be less sexually exclusive than other types of couples, same-sex couples may employ different sources of social support and experience greater cohesion and role flexibility, and heterosexuals may engage in more deception, possibly due to more inflexible gender roles. Despite these differences, gay male, lesbian, and heterosexual couples report similar relationship values, motivations for being in a relationship, levels of relationship satisfaction, levels of sexual satisfaction, and levels of overall social support.

When and if differences are found between same-sex and heterosexual couples, these differences do not result in consequences for the relationships themselves that are self-evidently good or bad. For example, gay male couples may be more likely to adopt sexually open relationships, but this does not appear to create a problem for the average gay male couple: Some couples appear to have successfully adopted this type of relationship and in fact levels of relationship satisfaction are similar for sexually open and non-open gay male couples. In addition, the greater role flexibility among same-sex couples may be a strength of such relationships. Of course, gay male and lesbian couples experience many of the same difficulties heterosexual couples encounter (e.g., career/job stress, financial strain, family pressures and dynamics, domestic chores etc.).

Undoubtedly, more research in this area is needed, particularly to clarify discrepant findings in the literature. A meta-analysis, a statistical way of analyzing several studies on a given topic, should be conducted in the near future. Future research should continue to test the ability of relationship theories to describe all couples regardless of sexual orientation and examine the impact of gender on relationship dynamics by comparing same-sex and other-sex couples (Peplau, 1993). Understanding the similarities and unique differences among gay male, lesbian, and heterosexual couples can dispel misconceptions toward diverse couples. Consequently, professionals (e.g., clergy, therapists) and laypersons can become more sensitive to gay male and lesbian couples, and ways of supporting them can be identified.

THE IMPACT OF PARENTAL HOMOSEXUALITY ON CHILD DEVELOPMENT

Over the last decade gay men and lesbians have increasingly expressed and realized their hopes of having, nurturing, and parenting children. A popular writer (Kantrowitz, 1996) referred to the growing number of children within non-heterosexual families as the "gayby boom." It is estimated that up to eight million children in the United States have lesbian mothers and gay fathers (Harry, 1990; Rothblum and Cole, 1989). Most of these parents had their children in other-sex relationships prior to identifying themselves as gay or lesbian; however, many of these parents utilized options such as adoption, artificial insemination, surrogacy, and foster parenting to realize their dream of becoming parents. Controversy has accompanied this postmodern expansion of the notion of family, and it has centered primarily on the following: (a) whether gay men and lesbians are fit to be parents, and (b) the effect parental homosexuality may have on child development. A summary of the behavioral science research that has addressed these concerns will now be presented.

Empirical research indicates that children of gay and lesbian parents do not differ from children of heterosexual parents in psychosocial adjustment (Gottman, 1990; Kirkpatrick, Smith, and Roy, 1981; Miller, 1979; Patterson, 1992, 1997; Patterson and Chan, 1996; Patterson and Redding, 1996). With regard to the issue of "stigmatization," researchers found no differences in the manner in which lesbian and heterosexual mothers assessed the social skills and popularity of their children among their peers (Green, Mandel, Hotvedt, Gray, and Smith, 1986). In addition, the children in this study also did not demonstrate differences in their own ratings of their popularity among same-sex and opposite-sex peers.

The idea that gay or lesbian parents might influence their children's psychosexual development (i.e., make them non-heterosexual) has not been supported by empirical research (Bigner and Bozett, 1990; Cramer, 1986; Gottman, 1990; Patterson, 1992). A longitudinal study conducted in Great Britain by Golombok and Tasker (1996) found no significant differences in sexual attraction or self-declared sexual orientation between adult children of lesbian and heterosexual mothers. Examining data regarding sexual orientation in their sample of eighty-two adult sons of gay fathers, Bailey *et al.* (1995) found that 91 percent of them were heterosexual. Evidence indicates that children of gay parents do not differ from children of heterosexual parents with regard to gender identity, gender role behavior, or psychosocial adjustment (Gottman, 1990; Green *et al.*, 1986; Kirkpatrick, Smith, and Roy, 1981; Patterson, 1992, 1997).

Research also disputes the notion that gay men and lesbians are unfit to be parents (Bigner and Bozett, 1990; Bigner and Jacobsen, 1992; Gottman, 1990; Harris and Turner, 1986; Patterson, 1992, 1997; Ricketts and Achtenberg, 1990). Results from studies have consistently indicated that the parenting abilities and child-rearing practices of gay men and lesbians are similar to those of heterosexual parents (see Patterson, 1992, 1997 for a comprehensive review). Harris and Turner (1986) report that the gay parents in their study indicated that their sexual orientation had been a strengthening experience for their children. Gay parents in another study offered that the honesty and openness related to their sexual orientation created greater interpersonal intimacy between them and their children (Bigner and Bozett, 1990). Patterson (1992) suggests that children reared by gay parents may be better prepared to approach their own sexuality with greater acceptance and be more empathic and tolerant of different viewpoints and human diversity.

Flaks, Ficher, Masterpasqua, and Joseph (1995) compared lesbian mothers who conceived through artificial insemination to married heterosexual parents. Results from their study revealed that both groups exhibit similarly satisfying relationships with their partners. The quality of the "spousal" relationships of lesbian mothers was comparable to the established norms of married couples. Findings from the study also indicated that lesbian mothers were as knowledgeable of effective parenting skills as their heterosexual counterparts, could identify critical factors in child-care situations, and could develop suitable responses to the problems they encountered. In summary, the study suggested that lesbian mothers can create stable environments for their children and that they are knowledgeable about and are capable of executing effective parenting skills.

Comparable studies have been conducted examining these variables among gay and heterosexual fathers. Results from this research suggest that gay fathers' parenting styles and attitudes toward fathering are more similar than different from those of heterosexual fathers (Bigner and Jacobsen, 1992). No differences between gay fathers and heterosexual fathers were found with regard to degree of involvement with children's activities, intimacy with children, problem solving, provision of recreational activities, encouragement of child autonomy, and the manner in which problems of child-rearing are handled (Bigner and Bozett, 1990; Bigner and Jacobsen, 1992; Harris and Turner, 1986; Miller, 1979).

In a comprehensive analysis of the research examining the role of fathers on child development, Silverstein and Auerbach report:

> In contrast to the neoconservative perspective, our data on gay fathering couples have convinced us that neither a mother nor a father is essential. Similarly, our research with divorced, never-married, and remarried fathers has taught us that a wide variety of family structures can support positive child outcomes. We have concluded that children need at least one responsible, caretaking adult who has a positive emotional connection to them and with whom they have a consistent relationship (1999, p. 9).

Moreover, Silverstein and Auerbach's (1999) critical review of the literature suggests that the stability of the emotional connection and the predictability of the caretaking relationship (regardless of the sexual orientation of the caretaker) are the significant variables that predict positive child adjustment.

PSYCHOSOCIAL FACTORS ASSOCIATED WITH HETEROSEXISM

Heterosexism has been defined as an individual's intolerance of gays and lesbians as well as the institutionalization of these attitudes that is maintained by a heterosexual-dominated power structure (Neisen, 1990). Jung and Smith (1993) assert that heterosexism indicates prejudice in favor of heterosexual people and prejudice against non-heterosexuals. The term heterosexism, in comparison to the now outdated term "homophobia," which obscures the notion of a prejudicial attitude with its misleading suffix -phobia (Neisen, 1990), captures the multi-dimensional composition of anti-gay attitudes as well as their complete range of expression *via* cognition, affect, and behavior. The construct of heterosexism redefines the ethical issues by moving the problem away from homosexuality and relocating it with the individuals and/or institutions that hold attitudes condemning of homosexuality, or conversely, attitudes exalting heterosexuality (McLeod, 1999, p. 3). Over the last twenty years a substantial amount of behavioral science research has identified proximal and distal factors associated with heterosexism. A report of these findings is presented below.

What causes people to be heterosexist? Empirical research suggests the following: men tend to be more homonegative than women; hostility toward gays is also associated with the extent to which one perceives that one's friends are in agreement with one's own negative attitudes toward homosexuality; interpersonal contact with non-heterosexuals is associated with more positive attitudes toward homosexuality; disapproval of homosexuality is mediated by higher levels of religiosity and traditional ideologies of family and gender; and the belief that homosexuality is a matter of choice is associated with less favorable attitudes toward non-heterosexuals (Herek, 1984b 1988; Herek and Glunt, 1993; Gentry, 1987; Kite, 1984; Whitley, 1990). Other studies have indicated that individuals who maintain negative attitudes toward gays and lesbians have an authoritarian personality structure (Altemeyer, 1998; Haddock, Zanna, and Esses, 1993; Karr, 1978; Larsen, Reed, and Hoffman, 1980;

MacDonald and Games, 1974; Smith, 1971). The authoritarian personality is characterized by submission to authorities, adherence to social
conventions, and generalized aggression directed toward others (Adorno,
Frenkel-Brunswik, Levinson, and Sanford, 1950; Altemeyer, 1981, 1988).

Personality variables such as cognitive rigidity, ambiguity intolerance, and dogmatism have also been found to be related to heterosexist
attitudes (Morin and Garfinkle, 1978). Although several studies have
suggested that heterosexism is part of an overarching prejudicial attitude
(Bierly, 1985; Henley and Pincus, 1978), Ficarrotto (1990) found that
sexual conservatism was a more significant predictor of heterosexism
than general social prejudice, implying that heterosexist attitudes may
be distinctive in origin and serve specific psychological needs. The most
comprehensive analysis of these needs has been provided by the work of
Herek (1986a, 1986b, 1987a). Utilizing Katz's (1960) functions of attitudes, Herek investigated the various functions served by an individual's attitudes toward gay men and lesbians. Herek advanced that these
attitudes may serve two different functions: one experiential and the
other expressive. The experiential function helps one organize reality.
According to Herek (1986b), if one anticipates having unpleasant or
negative experiences with a particular object (i.e., gay men or lesbians)
he/she will have more negative attitudes toward that object. Conversely,
if an individual perceives an object as a source of reward or pleasure
he/she is more likely to have positive attitudes toward the object. Empirical research seems to support Herek's theory (Gentry, 1987; Herek,
1986a, 1987a, 1988; Herek and Capitanio, 1995; Herek and Glunt, 1993;
Lance, 1987; Pagtolun-An and Clair, 1986; Whitley, 1990). This body of
research suggests that across levels of education, age, political ideology,
and gender the more interpersonal contact an individual has with gay
men and lesbians, the more likely that individual is to relinquish his/her
preconceived notions of homosexuality and to ultimately hold significantly more favorable attitudes toward gays and lesbians.

Herek's expressive attitudes are divided into three subcategories:
social expressive, value expressive, and ego defensive, and are related to
one's need for identity and self-esteem (Herek, 1986a). Herek's research
(1987a) revealed that individuals who endorsed social expressive
attitudes evidenced a stronger need for acceptance and/or approval
from others and were more likely to hold attitudes they believed would
be favorably viewed by others. Utilizing a questionnaire designed to
evaluate attitudes, Herek found that individuals who reported social
expressive attitudes toward gay men and lesbians tended to engage in

more self-monitoring, to be more self-conscious, and to belong to very cohesive social groups. Research also indicates that those who hold negative attitudes toward non-heterosexuals are more likely to believe that their peers hold similar attitudes (Herek, 1988; Larsen, Reed, and Hoffman, 1980). Collectively, these findings suggest that for some, heterosexist beliefs are intricately tied to their sense of identity, personal value, and emotional connection with a social group. As a consequence they are more likely to hold negative attitudes toward gay men and lesbians because they believe they will gather social approval for holding and expressing these beliefs.

The value expressive attitude suggests that attitudes are stimulated by one's need to be consistent with and committed to the values associated with a more abstract reference group (Herek, 1987a). Herek found that individuals with value expressive attitudes toward gays and lesbians were very committed to a particular doctrine and were likely to verbalize negative attitudes toward individuals who were perceived to violate that doctrine. It is Herek's contention (1986a, 1987a) that condemning that which violates an exalted value system is a way to reaffirm one's identification with that value system. A significant portion of the literature on heterosexism involves these various value systems and their impact on attitudes toward gay men and lesbians. Fidelity to politically conservative ideologies (Herek and Capitanio, 1995; Seltzer, 1992), sexism (Ficarrotto, 1990; Stark, 1991), sexual conservatism (Dunbar, Brown, and Amoroso, 1973), and traditional family and gender ideologies (Herek, 1984a; Herek, 1988; Kerns and Fine, 1994; Krulewitz and Nash, 1980; Marsiglio, 1993; Whitley, 1987) have all been found to predict heterosexist attitudes. Numerous studies have demonstrated that religiosity is correlated with negative attitudes toward homosexuality (Hansen, 1982b; Herek, 1987b, 1988; Herek and Capitanio, 1995; Herek and Glunt, 1993; Seltzer, 1992). Collectively, the findings from the aforementioned studies indicate that homosexuality is believed by some to violate cherished doctrines of Western culture. A recent study by Wells and Daly (1992) seemed to support Herek's theory that the rejection of homosexuality helps to reaffirm one's connection with these doctrines. In brief, these researchers found that individuals who held more positive attitudes toward non-heterosexuals tended to report more pronounced feelings of social alienation.

Herek's theory about the defensive function of attitudes toward homosexuals is based upon the belief that negative attitudes toward gays and lesbians originate from insecurities related to one's own gender or sexuality (Herek, 1986a, 1986b). Grounded in psychodynamic theory, this approach contends that individuals who experience intrapersonal conflicts associated with the attitudinal object are more likely to encounter emotional discomfort (i.e., anger, hostility, revulsion, dread, *etc.*) in relation to the object (Lock and Kleis, 1998). For example, a heterosexually identified man who is conflicted about his sexual orientation or meeting the standard of masculinity associated with Western culture may project his own feelings of anxiety, anger, and/or self-loathing outward (McLeod, 1999). A possible outlet for these feelings may be a non-heterosexual who represents the homosexuality or femininity that a heterosexual man may feel pressured to deny (Lock and Kleis, 1998). These feelings may be manifested by verbally or physically assaulting the non-heterosexual. Steering his feelings toward the object rather than himself preserves his sense of self as a heterosexual masculine male. A recent study seems to provide a modest amount of support for this psychodynamic theory of homonegativity. Adams, Wright, and Lohr (1996) found a relationship between high levels of heterosexism in men and an increase in penile erections in response to male homoerotic stimuli. It is not clear from the study if the erections were caused by sexual stimulation or anxiety; however, the findings do suggest that homosexuality may be threatening to heterosexist men, providing credibility to the defensive function of heterosexism.

CONCLUSION

An abundance of sound, empirical behavioral science research has been conducted on various aspects of homosexuality over the last twenty-five years. This research disputes conclusions drawn from the poorly-designed and biased research of Paul Cameron and his research group (e.g., Cameron and Cameron, 1996; Cameron, Cameron, and Proctor, 1989; Cameron, Proctor, Coburn, and Forde, 1985; Cameron, Proctor, Coburn, Forde, Larson, and Cameron, 1986), and clearly indicates that there is nothing inherently pathological or disordered about homosexuality or individuals who possess a homosexual orientation. The Church should utilize this scientific information to guide its pastoral responses to the needs of its gay and lesbian parishioners and their families. Contrary to the perspective of Jones and Workman (1994), we exhort the Church to allow this scholarship to inform in a meaningful way the Church's debate on the morality of homosexuality. To do otherwise would be both anti-intellectual and immoral.

REFERENCES

Acosta, F. (1975) *"Etiological and Treatment Literature on Homosexuality:* A Review," *Archives of Sexual Behavior,* 4, 9–29.

Adams, H. E., W. W. Lester, and B. A. Lohr. (1996) "Is Homophobia Associated with Homosexual Arousal?" *Journal of Abnormal Psychology,* 105, 440–45.

Adorno, Theodor W., E. Frenkel-Brunswik, D. J. Levinson, and R. N. Sanford. (1950) *The Authoritarian Personality.* New York: Harper.

Allen, L. S., and R. A. Gorski. (1992) "Sexual Orientation and the Size of the Anterior Commissure in the Human Brain," *Proceedings of the National Academy of Sciences,* 89, 7199–202.

Altemeyer, Bob. (1981) *Right-wing Authoritarianism.* Winnipeg: University of Manitoba Press.

_____. (1988) *Enemies of Freedom: Understanding Right-wing Authoritarianism.* San Francisco: Jossey-Bass Publishers.

Bailey, J. M., D. Bobrow, M. Wolfe, and S. Mikach. (1995) "Sexual Orientation of Adult Sons of Gay Fathers," *Developmental Psychology,* 31, 124–29.

Bailey, J. M., and R. C. Pillard. (1991) "A Genetic Study of Male Sexual Orientation," *Archives of General Psychiatry,* 48, 1089–96.

_____. (1995) "Genetics of Human Sexual Orientation," *Annual Review of Sex Research,* 6, 126–50.

Bailey, J. M., R. C. Pillard, M. C. Neale, and Y. Agyei. (1993) "Heritable Factors Influence Female Sexual Orientation," *Archives of General Psychiatry,* 50, 217–23.

Bailey, J. M., and K. J. Zucker. (1995) "Childhood Sex-typed Behavior and Sexual Orientation: A Conceptual Analysis and Quantitative Review," *Developmental Psychology,* 31, 43–55.

Bell, Alan P., and Martin S. Weinberg. (1978) *Homosexualities: A Study of Diversity among Men and Women.* New York: Simon & Schuster.

Bene, E. (1965) "On the Genesis of Male Homosexuality: An Attempt in Clarifying the Role of the Parents," *British Journal of Psychiatry,* 3, 803–13.

Bieber, I., and T. B. Bieber. (1979) "Male Homosexuality," *Canadian Journal of Psychiatry,* 24, 409–21.

Bierly, M. M. (1985) "Prejudice toward Contemporary Outgroups as a Generalized Attitude," *Journal of Applied Social Psychology,* 15, 189–99.

Bigner, J. J., and Frederick W. Bozett. (1990) "Parenting by Gay Fathers," in Frederick W. Bozett and Marvin B. Sussman, eds., *Homosexuality and Family Relations,* 155–76. New York: Harrington Park.

Bigner, J. J., and R. B. Jacobsen. (1992) "Adult Responses to Child Behavior and Attitudes toward Fathering: Gay and Non-gay Fathers," *Journal of Homosexuality,* 23, 99–112.

Blanchard, R., M. S. Watson, A. Choy, R. Dickey, P. Klassen, M. Kuban, and D. J. Ferren. (1999) "Pedophiles: Mental Retardation, Maternal Age and Sexual Orientation," *Archives of Sexual Behavior,* 28, 111–27.

Blumstein, Philip, and P. Schwartz. (1983) *American Couples: Money, Work, Sex.* New York: William Morrow.

Buhrich, N. J., J. M. Bailey, and N. G. Martin. (1991) "Sexual Orientation, Sexual Identity and Sex-dimorphic Behaviors in Male Twins," *Behavior Genetics,* 21, 75–96.

Burdon, W. M. (1996) "Deception in Intimate Relationships: A Comparison of Heterosexuals and Homosexuals/bisexuals," *Journal of Homosexuality,* 32, 77–93.

Burr, C. (1994) "Homosexuality and Biology," in Jeffrey S. Siker, ed., *Homosexuality in the Church: Both Sides of the Debate,* 116–34. Louisville, Ky.: Westminster John Knox.

Byne, W., and B. Parsons. (1993) "Human Sexual Orientation: The Biologic Theories Reappraised," *Archives of General Psychiatry,* 50, 228–39.

Cameron, P., and K. Cameron. (1996) "Homosexual parents," *Adolescence,* 31, 757–76.

Cameron, P., K. Cameron, and K. Proctor. (1989) "Effect of Homosexuality upon Public Health and Social Order," *Psychological Reports,* 64, 1167–79.

Cameron, P., K. Proctor, W. Coburn, and N. Forde. (1985) "Sexual Orientation and Sexually Transmitted Diseases," *Nebraska Medical Journal,* 70, 292–99.

Cameron, P., K. Proctor, W. Coburn, N. Forde, H. Larson, and K. Cameron. (1986) "Child Molestation and Homosexuality," *Psychological Reports,* 58, 327–37.

Cardell, M., S. Finn, and J. Marecek. (1981) "Sex-role Identity, Sex-role Behavior and Satisfaction in Heterosexual, Lesbian and Gay Male Couples," *Psychology of Women Quarterly,* 5, 488–94.

Cramer, D. (1986) "Gay Parents and Their Children: A Review of Research and Practical Implications," *Journal of Counseling Development,* 64, 504–7.

Crews, D. (1994) "Animal Sexuality," *Scientific American,* 270, 108–14.

Dank, B. M. (1971) "Six Homosexual Siblings," *Archives of General Psychiatry,* 1, 193–204.

Davies, P. T., and E. M. Cummings. (1994) "Marital Conflict and Child Adjustment," *Psychological Bulletin,* 116, 387–411.

Dessens, A. B., P. T. Cohen-Kettenis, G. J. Mellenbergh, N. Poll, J. G. Koppe, K. Boer. (1999) "Prenatal Exposure to Anticonvulsants and Psychosexual Development," *Archives of Sexual Behavior,* 28, 31–44.

Duffy, S., and C. E. Rusbult. (1986) "Satisfaction and Commitment in Homosexual and Heterosexual Relationships," *Journal of Homosexuality,* 12, 1–23.

Dunbar, J., M. Brown, and D. M. Amoroso. (1973) "Some Correlates of Attitudes toward Homosexuality," *Journal of Social Psychology,* 89, 271–79.

Eckert, E. D., T. J. Bouchard, J. Bohlen, and L. L. Heston. (1986) "Homosexuality in Monozygotic Twins Reared Apart," *British Journal of Psychiatry,* 148, 421–25.

Eldridge, N. S. (1987) "Gender Issues in Counseling Same-sex Couples," *Professional Psychology: Research and Practice,* 18, 567–72.

Eldridge, N. S., and L. A. Gilbert. (1990) "Correlates of Relationship Satisfaction in Lesbian Couples," *Psychology of Women Quarterly,* 14, 43–62.

Ellis, L., and M. A. Ames. (1987) "Neurohormonal Functioning and Sexual Orientation: A Theory of Homosexuality-heterosexuality," *Psychological Bulletin,* 101, 233–58.

Falbo, T., and L. A. Peplau. (1980) "Power Strategies in Intimate Relationships," *Journal of Personality and Social Psychology,* 38, 618–28.

Ficarrotto, T. J. (1990) "Racism, Sexism and Erotophobia: Attitudes of Heterosexuals toward Homosexuals," *Journal of Homosexuality,* 19, 111–16.

Flaks, D. K., I. Ficher, F. Masterpasqua, and G. Joseph. (1995) "Lesbians Choosing Motherhood: A Comparative Study of Lesbian and Heterosexual Parents and Their Children," *Developmental Psychology,* 31, 105–14.

Fogarty, E. L. (1980) "'Passing as Straight': A Phenomenological Analysis of the Experience of the Lesbian Who Is Professionally Employed," *Dissertation Abstracts International,* 41 (6-B) 2384–85.

Freund, K., and R. J. Watson. (1992) "The Proportions of Heterosexual and Homosexual Pedophiles among Sex Offenders against Children: An Exploratory Study," *Journal of Sex and Marital Therapy,* 18, 34–43.

Friedman, R. C. (1986) "Male Homosexuality: On the Need for a Multiaxial Developmental Model," *Israel Journal of Psychiatry and Related Sciences,* 23, 63–76.

Friedman, R. C., and J. Downey. (1993) "Neurobiology and Sexual Orientation: Current Relationships," *Journal of Neuropsychiatry and Clinical Neurosciences,* 5, 131–53.

Gabard, D. L. (1999) "Homosexuality and the Human Genome Project: Private and Public Choices," *Journal of Homosexuality,* 37, 25–47.

Gentry, C. S. (1987) "Social Distance Regarding Male and Female Homosexuality," *Journal of Social Psychology,* 127, 199–208.

Golombok, S., and F. Tasker. (1996) "Do Parents Influence the Sexual Orientation of Their Children? Findings from a Longitudinal Study of Lesbian Families," *Developmental Psychology* 23, 3–11.

Gooren, L., E. Fliers, and K. Courtney. (1990) "Biological Determinants of Sexual Orientation," *Annual Review of Sex Research,* 1, 175–96.

Gottman, J. S. (1990) "Children of Gay and Lesbian Parents," in Frederick W. Bozett and Marvin B. Sussman, eds., *Homosexuality and Family Relations,* 177–96. New York: Harrington Park.

Green, R. J., M. Bettinger, and E. Zacks. (1996) "Are Lesbian Couples Fused and Gay Male Couples Disengaged? Questioning Gender Straight Jackets," in Joan Laird and Robert-Jay Green, eds., *Lesbians and Gays in Couples and Families*, 185–230. San Francisco: Jossey-Bass.

Green, R., J. B. Mandel, M. E. Hotvedt, J. Gray, and L. Smith. (1986) "Lesbian Mothers and Their Children: A Comparison with Solo Parent Heterosexual Mothers and Their Children," *Archives of Sexual Behavior*, 15, 167–84.

Haddock, G., M. P. Zanna, and V. M. Esses. (1993) "Assessing the Structure of Prejudicial Attitudes: The Case of Attitudes Toward Homosexuals," *Journal of Personality and Social Psychology*, 65, 1105–18.

Hamer, D. H., S. Hu, V. L. Magnuson, N. Hu, and A.M.L. Pattatucci. (1993) "A Linkage between DNA Markers on the X Chromosome and Male Sexual Orientation," *Science*, 261, 321–27.

Hansen, G. L. (1982) "Androgyny, Sex-role Orientation and Homosexism," *Journal of Psychology*, 112, 39–45.

Harris, M. B., and P. H. Turner. (1986) "Gay and Lesbian Parents," *Journal of Homosexuality*, 12, 101–13.

Harrison, P. J., I. P. Everall, and J. Catalan. (1994) "Is Homosexual Behavior Hard-wired? Sexual Orientation and Brain Structure," *Psychological Medicine*, 24, 811–16.

Harry, J. (1983) "Gay Male and Lesbian Relationships," in Eleanor D. Macklin and Roger H. Rubin, eds., *Contemporary Families and Alternative Lifestyles: Handbook on Research and Theory*, 216–34. Beverly Hills, Calif.: Sage.

_____. (1990) "A Probability Sample of Gay Males," *Journal of Homosexuality*, 19, 89–104.

Henley, N. M., and F. Pincus. (1978) "Interrelationship of Sexist, Racist and Anti-homosexual Attitudes," *Psychological Reports*, 42, 83–90.

Herek, Gregory M. (1984a) "Beyond 'Homophobia': A Social Psychological Perspective on Attitudes toward Lesbians and Gay Men," *Journal of Homosexuality*, 10, 1–21.

_____. (1984b) "Attitudes Toward Lesbians and Gay Men: A Factor Analytic Study," *Journal of Homosexuality*, 10, 39–51.

_____. (1986a) "The Social Psychology of Homophobia: Toward a Practical Theory," *Review of Law & Social Change*, 14, 923–34.

_____. (1986b) "The Instrumentality of Attitudes: Toward a Neofunctional Theory," *Journal of Social Issues*, 42, 99–114.

_____. (1987a) "Can Functions Be Measured? A New Perspective on the Functional Approach to Attitudes," *Social Psychology Quarterly*, 50, 285–303.

_____. (1987b) "Religious Orientation and Prejudice: A Comparison of Racial and Sexual Attitudes," *Personality and Social Psychology Bulletin*, 13, 34–44.

_____. (1988) "Heterosexuals' Attitudes Toward Lesbians and Gay Men: Correlates and Gender Differences," *The Journal of Sex Research*, 25, 451–77.

Herek, Gregory M., and John P. Capitanio. (1995) "Black Heterosexuals' Attitudes Toward Lesbians and Gay Men in the United States," *The Journal of Sex Research*, 32, 95–105.

Herek, Gregory M., and John P. Capitanio. (in press) *Some of My Best Friends: Intergroup Contact, Concealable Stigma and Heterosexuals' Attitudes Toward Gay Men and Lesbians*.

Herek, Gregory M., and E. K. Glunt. (1993) "Interpersonal Contact and Heterosexuals' Attitudes Toward Gay Men: Results from a National Survey," *Journal of Sex Research*, 30, 239–44.

Jones, S. L., and D. E. Workman. (1994) "Homosexuality: The Behavioral Sciences and the Church," in Jeffrey S. Siker, ed., *Homosexuality in the Church*, 93–115. Louisville, Ky.: Westminster John Knox.

Jung, Patricia Beattie, and Ralph F. Smith. (1993) *Heterosexism: An Ethical Challenge*. New York: SUNY Press.

Kagan, J. (1964) "Acquisition and Significance of Sex Typing and Sex Role Identity," in Martin L. Hoffman and L. W. Hoffman, eds., *Review of Child Development Research*, 137–67. New York: Russell Sage Foundation.

Kantrowitz, B. (November 4, 1996) "Gay Families Come Out," *Newsweek*, 51–57.

Karr, R. G. (1978) "Homosexual Labeling and the Male Role," *Journal of Social Issues*, 34, 73–83.

Katz, D. (1960) "The Functional Approach to the Study of Attitudes," *Public Opinion Quarterly*, 24, 163–204.

Kerns, J. G., and M. A. Fine. (1994) "The Relation between Gender and Negative Attitudes Toward Gay Men and Lesbians: Do Gender Role Attitudes Mediate This Relationship?" *Sex Roles* 31, 297–307.

King, M., and E. McDonald. (1992) "Homosexuals Who Are Twins: A Study of Forty-six Probands," *British Journal of Psychiatry*, 160, 407–9.

Kirkpatrick, M., C. Smith, and R. Roy. (1981) "Lesbian Mothers and Their Children: A Comparative Survey," *American Journal of Orthopsychiatry*, 51, 545–51.

Kite, M. E. (1984) "Sex Differences in Attitudes Toward Homosexuals: A Meta-analytic Review," *Journal of Homosexuality*, 10, 69–81.

Krulewitz, J. E., and J. E. Nash. (1980) "Effects of Sex Role Attitudes and Similarity on Men's Rejection of Male Homosexuals," *Journal of Personality and Social Psychology*, 38, 67–74.

Kurdek, Lawrence A. (1988) "Relationship Quality of Gay and Lesbian Cohabiting Couples," *Journal of Homosexuality*, 15, 93–118.

_____. (1991) "Correlates of Relationship Satisfaction in Cohabitating Gay and Lesbian Couples: Integration of Contextual, Investment and

Problem-solving Models," *Journal of Personality and Social Psychology,* 61, 910–22.

———. (1995) "Lesbian and Gay Couples," in Anthony R. D'Augelli and Charlotte J. Patterson, eds., *Lesbian, Gay and Bisexual Identities Over the Lifespan: Psychological Perspectives,* 243–61. New York: Oxford University Press.

Kurdek, Lawrence A., and J. P. Schmitt. (1986) "Relationship Quality of Partners in Heterosexual Married, Heterosexual Cohabitating and Gay and Lesbian Relationships," *Journal of Personality and Social Psychology,* 51, 711–20.

Lance, L. M. (1987) "The Effects of Interaction with Gay Persons on Attitudes Toward Homosexuality," *Human Relations,* 40, 329–36.

Laner, M. R. (1988) "Permanent Partner Priorities: Gay and Straight," in John P. De Cecco, ed., *Gay Relationships,* 133–55. New York: Haworth Press.

Larsen, K. S., M. Reed, and S. Hoffman. (1980) "Attitudes of Heterosexuals Toward Homosexuality: A Likert-type Scale and Construct Validity," *Journal of Sex Research,* 16, 245–57.

Laumann, Edward O., J. Gagnon, R. Michael, and S. Michaels. (1994) *The Social Organization of Sexuality: Sexual Practices in the United States.* Chicago: University of Chicago Press.

LeVay, S. (1991) "A Difference in Hypothalamic Structure between Heterosexual and Homosexual Men," *Science,* 253, 1034–37.

Lock, J., and B. Kleis. (1998) "Origins of Homophobia in Males: Psychosexual Vulnerabilities and Defense Development," *American Journal of Psychotherapy,* 52, 425–36.

Looy, H. (1995) "Born Gay? A Critical Review of Biological Research on Homosexuality," *Journal of Psychology and Christianity,* 14, 197–214.

MacDonald, A. P., and R. G. Games. (1974) "Some Characteristics of Those Who Hold Positive and Negative Attitudes Toward Homosexuals," *Journal of Homosexuality,* 1, 9–27.

Mannino, J. Davis. (in press) *Sexual Themes and Variations: The New Millennium.* McGraw-Hill.

Marsiglio, W. (1993) "Attitudes Toward Homosexual Activity and Gays as Friends: A National Survey of Heterosexual Fifteen to Nineteen Year Old Males," *The Journal of Sex Research,* 30, 12–17.

McGuire, T. R. (1995) "Is Homosexuality Genetic? A Critical Review and Some Suggestions," *Journal of Homosexuality,* 14, 115–45.

McLeod, A. (1999) *Understanding Heterosexism: The Personal Need for Structure and the Gender Role Conflict Models.* Unpublished doctoral dissertation, Loyola University of Chicago.

McWhirter, David P., and Andrew M. Mattison. (1984) *The Male Couple: How Relationships Develop.* Englewood Cliffs, N.J.: Prentice-Hall.

Michael, Robert T., J. Gagnon, E. Laumann, and G. Kolata. (1994) *Sex in America: A Definitive Survey.* Boston: Little, Brown.

Meyer, J. (1989) "Guess Who's Coming to Dinner This Time? A Study of Gay Intimate Relationships and the Support for Those Relationships," *Marriage and Family Review,* 14, 59–82.

Meyer-Bahlburg, H.F.L. (1991) "Will Prenatal Hormone Treatment Prevent Homosexuality?" *Journal of Child and Adolescent Psychopharmacology,* 1, 279–83.

———. (1993) "Psychobiologic Research on Homosexuality," *Child and Adolescent Psychiatric Clinics of North America,* 2, 489–500.

Meyer-Bahlburg, H.F.L., A. A. Ehrhardt, L. R. Rosen, and R. S. Gruen. (1995) "Prenatal Estrogens and the Development of Homosexual Orientation," *Developmental Psychology* 31, 12–21.

Miller, B. (1979) "Gay Fathers and Their Children," *Family Coordinator,* 28, 544–52.

Morin, S. F., and E. M. Garfinkle. (1978) "Male Homophobia," *Journal of Social Issues,* 34, 29–47.

Muir, J. G. (1996) "Sexual Orientation—Born or Bred?" *Journal of Psychology and Christianity,* 15, 313–21.

Neisen, J. H. (1990) "Heterosexism: Redefining Homophobia for the 1990s," *Journal of Gay and Lesbian Psychotherapy,* 1, 21–35.

Pagtolun-An, I. G., and J. M. Clair. (1986) "An Experimental Study of Attitudes Toward Homosexuals," *Deviant Behavior,* 7, 121–35.

Patterson, C. J. (1992) "Children of Lesbian and Gay Parents," *Child Development,* 63, 1025–42.

———. (1997) "Children of Lesbian and Gay Parents," *Advances in Clinical Child Psychology,* 19, 235–82.

Patterson, C. J., and R. W. Chan. (1996) "Gay Fathers and Their Children," in Robert P. Cabaj and Terry S. Stein, eds., *Textbook of Homosexuality and Mental Health,* 371–93. Washington, D.C.: American Psychiatric Press.

Patterson, C. J., and R. Redding. (1996) "Lesbian and Gay Families with Children: Implications of Social Science Research for Policy," *Journal of Social Issues,* 52(3), 29–50.

Peplau, L. A. (1993) "Lesbian and Gay Relationships," in Linda D. Garnets and Douglas C. Kimmel, eds., *Psychological Perspectives on Lesbian and Gay Male Experiences,* 395–419. New York: Columbia University Press.

Peplau, L. A., and S. D. Cochran. (1981) "Value Orientations in the Intimate Relationships of Gay Men," *Journal of Homosexuality,* 6, 1–19.

———. (1990) "A Relational Perspective on Homosexuality," in David P. McWhirter, Stephanie A. Sanders, and June M. Reinisch, eds., *Homosexuality/Heterosexuality: Concepts of Sexual Orientation,* 321–49. New York: Oxford University Press.

Peters, D. K., and P. J. Cantrell. (1993) "Gender Roles and Role Conflict in Feminist Lesbian and Heterosexual Women," *Sex Roles,* 28, 379–92.

Rice, G., C. Anderson, N. Risch, and G. Ebers. (1999) "Male Homosexuality: Absence of Linkage to Microsatellite Markers at Xq28," *Science,* 284, 665–67.

Ramsey, J., J. Lathem, and C. Lindquist. (1978) "Long-term Same-sex Relationships: Correlates of Adjustment." Paper presented at the annual meeting of the American Psychological Association, Toronto, Canada.

Ricketts, W., and R. Achtenberg. (1990) "Adoption and Foster Parenting for Lesbian and Gay Men: Creating New Traditions in Family," in Frederick W. Bozett and Marvin B. Sussman, eds., *Homosexuality and Family Relations,* 83–118. New York: Harrington Park.

Rosenbluth, S. (1997) "Is Sexual Orientation a Matter of Choice?" *Psychology of Women Quarterly,* 21, 595–610.

Rothblum, Esther D., and Ellen Cole, eds. (1989) *Loving Boldly: Issues Facing Lesbians.* New York: Harrington Park.

Schuklenk, U., E. Stein, J. Kerin, and W. Byne. (1997) "The Ethics of Genetic Research on Sexual Orientation," *Hastings Center Report,* 27, 6–13.

Seltzer, R. (1992) "The Social Location of Those Holding Antihomosexual Attitudes," *Sex Roles,* 26, 391–98.

Silverstein, L. B., and C. F. Auerbach. (1999) "Deconstructing the Essential Father." *American Psychologist,* 54(6), 397–407.

Smith, K. T. (1971) "Homophobia: A Tentative Personality Profile," *Psychological Reports* 29, 1091–94.

Swaab, D. F., and M. A. Hoffman. (1990) "An Enlarged Suprachiasmatic Nucleus in Homosexual Men," *Brain Research,* 537, 141–48.

Vreeland, C. N., B. J. Gallagher, and J. A. McFalls, Jr. (1995) "The Beliefs of Members of the American Psychiatric Association on the Etiology of Male Homosexuality: A National Survey," *The Journal of Psychology,* 129, 507–17.

Wagner, G., R. H. Remien, and A. Carballo-Diéguez. (in press) "Prevalence of Extradyadic Sex in Male Couples of Mixed HIV Status and Its Relationship to Psychological Distress and Relationship Quality," *Journal of Homosexuality.*

Wells, J. W., and A. Daly. (1992) "University Students' Felt Alienation and Their Attitudes Toward African Americans, Women, and Homosexuals," *Psychological Reports,* 70, 623–26.

Whalen, R. E., D. C. Geary, and F. Johnson. (1990) "Models of Sexuality," in David P. McWhirter, Stephanie A. Sanders, and June M. Reinisch, eds., *Homosexuality/Heterosexuality: Concepts of Sexual Orientation,* 61–70. New York: Oxford University Press.

Whitam, F. L., M. Diamond, and J. Martin. (1993) "Homosexual Orientation in Twins: A Report on Sixty-one Pairs and Three Triplet Sets," *Archives of Sexual Behavior,* 22, 187–206.

Whitley, B. E. (1990) "The Relationship of Heterosexuals' Attributions for the Causes of Homosexuality to Attitudes Toward Lesbians and Gay Men," *Personality and Social Psychology Bulletin,* 16, 369–77.

Yarab, P. E., C. C. Sensibaugh, and E. R. Allgeier. (1998) "More than Just Sex: Gender Differences in the Incidence of Self-defined Unfaithful Behavior in Heterosexual Dating Relationships," *Journal of Psychology and Human Sexuality,* 10, 45–57.

Zak, A., and C. McDonald. (1997) "Satisfaction and Trust in Intimate Relationships: Do Lesbian and Heterosexual Women Differ?" *Psychological Reports,* 80, 904–6.

12

Harming by Exclusion: On the Standard Concepts of Sexual Orientation, Sex, and Gender

David T. Ozar

"Filled with compassion, Jesus reached out his hand and touched the leper" (Mark 1:41).

INTRODUCTION AND A STORY

I want to change how we speak and how we think. I want to change the sets of concepts and the corresponding language that are standard in contemporary American culture for describing and categorizing people in terms of sexual orientation, biological classification by sex (male, female, etc.), and gender. This essay cannot do this task thoroughly, of course, but I hope these reflections will be sufficient to make the continued use of the standard concepts and terms uncomfortable for my readers and therefore a subject for caution and careful reflection.

For the sets of concepts and words that we commonly use to refer to sexual orientation, biological classification by sex, and gender exclude large numbers of our fellow human beings altogether. By excluding these persons conceptually they also exclude their concerns and interests, the good or harm done to them, their rights, and the respect due to them as persons from counting at all in our reflections about how people ought to act toward one another. Indeed, our standard concepts about these matters exclude large numbers of people from being counted in the human family at all, even by people who care very much about being inclusive. This is the most radical form of exclusion, that the persons excluded do not so much as exist in the minds of others.

To explain this claim I must first tell a story. Six years ago I learned that someone who is a very close friend of mine is transgendered. He is someone I knew as happily married, the father of six children grown to adulthood, an active, successful businessman, a good and valued neighbor, a leader in the life of his Catholic parish. In a moment of special candor he shared with me the reality that he is transgendered, not by being a transsexual, which is the form of transgendered experience with which the public are probably most familiar, but as a heterosexual male cross-dresser; or more accurately, as bi-gendered. I will explain this way of describing him more fully in a moment.

The conversation in which I learned my friend is transgendered was a very moving one for both of us. Good friendships do not exist solely for powerful moments of revelation, but they do facilitate them and can grow greatly as a result. Because he is my friend I wanted to learn more, and he is a good teacher. In fact, over the last three years my friend has spoken to several classes of mine and of other professors at my university and at other schools in his feminine *persona*. Both faculty and students who have met my friend in this way concur in what I already knew, that the person whose femme name is Amanda is a very impressive person.

My friend and I have talked a lot. I have also studied a lot; and we have talked more. I also asked if I could meet other members of my friend's support group, which is called Tri-Ess, for "Society for the Second Self." This is a support group specifically for heterosexual male cross-dressers and their spouses and significant others. One of its principal missions, besides providing a strong base of mutual support for each member and a monthly opportunity for the members to cross-dress in safety, is to help marriages and other relationships between the members and their significant others survive and grow. Obviously the ways in which male cross-dressing is conceptualized in contemporary American culture, together with the powerful stigma against it, mean that the male partner's need to cross-dress makes for powerful challenges to the stability of a heterosexual relationship. In fact, so powerful is this stigma and so deeply internalized in most men of our culture that many men are afraid to reveal this aspect of themselves, even to their wives in otherwise exemplary marriages. From what I have observed in now knowing a number of members of the support group, such groups do a great deal of good.

Before long I also saw a connection between what I was learning about gender—and especially about gender-identity, as I shall explain—and the underlying theme of most of my scholarly work for the last thirty years. What I have chiefly studied as a moral philosopher are the ethical standards that operate within complex social systems. I have studied and written about property relations, law, professions, and other important social roles, business and health-care organizations and other social systems. I have explored how the set of concepts that defines such a system and its component roles and relations is typically used in turn to justify the whole system and its activities within the larger society. I have observed how the concepts that define most social systems are ordinarily learned and employed by persons within these systems without careful examination of their presuppositions or implications. The view of the world that these concepts shape and limit is typically accepted as simply how-the-world-is by those living and interacting within that system.

It is certainly not an original insight to say that gender roles constitute such a system. But personal contact with transgendered people has taught me something that I have not heard proposed before. It is now clear to me that those of us who have not experienced a mismatch between our gender—that is, between the gender role with which we identify, what I will call our gender-identity—and other aspects of ourselves—for example, how others assign or conceive of our gender—may have to listen to those who have experienced this mismatch in order to understand not only the experience of mismatch, but even what is involved in identifying with a gender role, in "having a gender identity," in the first place.

So I have both personal and professional motivation to learn more about and especially more from my transgendered friends and to support my friend and others in the support group as they deal with their difficult situation. One aspect of my effort to assist them has been to apply the skills that come from my years as a philosopher in the development of a draft educational document that critiques the standard concepts and terms and articulates a more inclusive set of concepts and terms to describe people in terms of their biology as male, female, etc., their sexual orientation, and their gender-identity. The material offered below on these concepts could not have been written without my involvement in this drafting project.

I should mention that the membership in the Tri-Ess support group cuts across social class, economic categories, educational achievement, race, religion, and ethnic background. I also need to mention that the first rule of the support group is privacy. Members of the group are known to one another by their feminine names, and any question about what a member does for a living or where a member lives, etc., may always be comfortably and appropriately answered with "I'd rather not say." I certainly can appreciate this. Transgendered people not only live under the deep stigma our society imposes on them, but suffer as well that which comes from their inevitably internalizing that stigma as they are growing up. They are also without any legal protection in most places in the United States if anyone would refuse to serve them or would fire them from their jobs or discriminate against them in some other way because of their cross-dressing. If they are attacked, or even killed because they cross-dress, that act is not even considered a hate crime.

Why is this? The answer to this question restates the central thesis of this essay and is, from a philosophical perspective, very simple. Conceptually speaking, transgendered people and another group of people of whom I will speak in a moment, the intersexed, simply do not exist. That is, they have no standing within the sets of concepts about sexual orientation, biological sex, and gender that are commonly used in our society. It is not just that they are unusual, outliers from the curve. Instead, they have no conceptual standing at all. In terms of the standard concepts we use to understand these aspects of the world these people are excluded from existing altogether.

By far the most efficient way to exclude a class of persons from the realm of ethics and obligations is for our operative system of concepts to have no place for them whatsoever. When that is so, there is no need to ask ethical questions about how to deal with them. There are no ethical questions to ask because the ethical questions about properly addressing their situation cannot, strictly speaking, even be formulated. Their situation is not beneath deserving our attention. Rather it does not exist at all in the system of concepts taken for granted by those judging.

CORRECTING OUR CONCEPTS

The Distinctness of the Three Categories

There are three important themes that need to be addressed before we have any hope of reconstructing our concepts, so they are inclusive of all the relevant human experience. The first theme concerns the distinctness of three ways of describing or categorizing human beings. These three ways of categorizing people are: (1) as biologically male, female, etc., (2) according to a person's preferred partner for intimacy or sexual orientation, (3) according to a person's gender identity.

The point to be stressed here is that the characteristics of persons that these three categories pick out are distinct from one another in people's experience. We all know, for example, that persons from both of the two largest biological categories, typical males and typical females, are to be found in all the subcategories of sexual orientation, however that category is subdivided. The same is true of every other subcategory of the three ways of categorizing just mentioned. Every possible combination is to be found in the human family. Consequently, if a society's system of concepts does not allow for this range of experiences, for example by excluding the possibility of a biological female with a masculine gender-identity, not only is that system of concepts inadequate to describe human experience accurately, but those members of the human family who experience life in the excluded ways have no conceptual standing in that society. And since they do not exist, the question of how we ought or ought not to interact with them cannot even be formulated, much less thoughtfully addressed.

Setting Aside Either/Or
Preferred Partner for Intimacy (Sexual Orientation)

The second theme is that the notion of "two and only two" does not apply to any of these three ways of categorizing. Consider preferred partner for intimacy or sexual orientation. Most people now know that, in addition to persons who are sexually attracted exclusively to persons with typical female anatomies and persons who are sexually attracted to persons with typical male anatomies, there are people who are sexually attracted to members of both groups. Such people are referred to as bisexual.

It is important to remember in this, however, that many persons who experience sexual attraction to both males and females are not equally attracted to members of both groups. They are not all fifty-fifty, so to speak. In the experience of such persons there is a broad range of attraction in the two directions. To use mathematical imagery again, some people are 60/40, others 40/60, some 20/80, others 10/90 and so on. Indeed, it is likely that many people who would describe themselves either as straight or as gay or lesbian are in fact 90/10 or 80/20 in their orientation, but view the admixture of the other element of attraction as a kind of breadth of perspective. In other words, the subcategories of sexual orientation cover a whole spectrum from 100/0 to 0/100 and every combination in between. This is what it means to say about sexual orientation that either/or ways of thinking do not apply.

Biological Classification as Male, Female, etc.

It is common knowledge that the description of someone as biologically male or female actually involves a number of distinct aspects of human biology, and that people vary considerably in all of them. Among these are genetic and chromosomal characteristics, hormonal characteristics, reproductive physiology, internal anatomy, external anatomy, and possibly the structure of the brain. These matters vary considerably and the notion of a spectrum of subcategories might seem quite appropriate. Yet our culture's concept system persists in categorizing people into two and only two rigid biological categories, male and female. It might be argued that this is appropriate because there are two and only two body types, or perhaps two and only two ways in which human gonads occur. But in fact there are many persons who have biological characteristics of both typical males and typical females. In fact, approximately one in every two thousand infants is born intersexed; that is, with a combination of external anatomical features associated with both typical females and typical males, or with a combination of external and internal (including gonadal) features associated with both typical males and typical females.

Such persons were once called "hermaphrodites" and "pseudo-hermaphrodites" (these words come from the name of a character in Greek mythology) because nineteenth-century medicine taught that there were only two important subcategories to which all such persons belonged. The more common term today is "intersex." This single summary term is used in part to recognize that there are more than just two combinations of biological characteristics in this group, more in fact than have been carefully counted or distinguished to date, and that there are many different, and often not well understood, medical conditions that cause such combinations of biological characteristics. Using this single summary term also recognizes the many similar challenges that almost all such persons face in American society, where their condition is widely thought either not to exist at all or to be extremely rare, or to be so different from what is typical as to be defective or objectively disordered. It underscores the fact that persons who have biological characteristics of this sort are certainly full human beings, deserving of respect, affirmation, and support.

For a number of years medical treatment of intersexed infants and children has typically focused on reconstructing their external genitals so they match as closely as possible either typical male or typical female age-appropriate anatomy. Such treatment has been based on two un-proved assumptions that are sharply debated today: first, that gender identity is completely formed through early social influences, and sec-ond that the intersexed child's gender identity, formed by the child's parents and others, will match whatever gender-role is assigned to the child when the child's external genital anatomy is surgically recon-structed (first as an infant, and then ordinarily through a number of other surgical procedures, hormone treatments, etc.). Many adults who received such surgeries as infants and children are now actively chal-lenging this approach on the basis of their experience. Note that this pattern of medical practice, which is now being challenged from within the medical community as well, depends for its rationale on an either/ or system of biological (and gender) concepts that excludes the experi-ence of many members of the human family.

Gender and Gender-Identity

The third way of categorizing people mentioned above is in relation to gender. This way of categorizing people appears simple to many people, but it is much more complicated than it seems. One thing about it that makes it seem simple is the fact that in contemporary American culture there are two and only two genders or gender-roles.

In this essay the terms "feminine" and "masculine" are used to refer to these two gender-roles when an adjective is needed, and the terms women and men (and girls and boys) to refer to them when a noun is needed. These six words will be used here only to refer to gender-roles, never to biological categories (which will be referred to, as above, by the words male, female, and intersex).

It is important to keep in mind, when thinking about gender, that there are other cultures in the world where the gender-roles are not the same as they are in American culture. It is not only the case that other cultures have masculine and feminine categories that are different from the masculine and feminine roles in contemporary American culture (even though they are similar enough to our masculine and feminine categories that the same words can be meaningfully used to name them). It is also the case that there are cultures that have more than two genders or gender-roles. That is, there are cultures that have more than two divisions in a categorization of people that functions in those cultures in about the same way that categorization of people by gender-role does in ours.

As mentioned, the topic of gender is much more complicated than it might seem. The same word, gender, is used with at least four different meanings in ordinary speech today. The first of these relates to roles in terms of which people in a society are categorized: gender-roles. The other three relate to three different contexts for categorizing people in terms of these gender-roles: gender assignment, gender expression, and gender identity.

Gender-Roles

First, there are the gender-roles, which are complex sets of human characteristics, behaviors, and expectations that are constructed (gradually, and gradually changed) by a culture so its people can more easily describe one another, assign tasks and statuses within the society, and have fairly stable expectations of one another. As was mentioned above, American culture presently has two and only two gender-roles, the feminine gender-role and the masculine gender-role: women and men.

Some elements of these two gender-roles have undergone significant change in American society in recent decades. For example, some behaviors and tasks that were narrowly associated with only one of these gender-roles fifty years ago—e.g., competitiveness for the masculine role and nurturing for the feminine role—can today be properly undertaken by individuals in the other role, at least under certain circumstances. But these adjustments in the behaviors considered appropriate in the two roles have not changed the reality that there are still two and only two gender-roles in contemporary American culture. The fact that there are people who are viewed as transgendered is itself evidence that there are gender-role boundaries that such people are considered to be crossing. There are many other forms of evidence of the reality and significance of our culture's two gender-roles.

Gender Assignment

A second use of the word gender refers to the assignment of a particular gender-role to an individual person by others who interact with that person. This is one of the contexts in which categorization of people in terms of gender takes place: people in a culture perceive and describe one another as belonging to one or other of the culture's gender-roles, an activity that will here be called gender-assignment.

Assignment here does not refer only to official forms of assignment, as when a newborn is declared to be a boy or a girl. In fact, we all do this assigning all the time, routinely identifying the individuals we encounter in our lives as participants in one gender-role or the other. Using various kinds of evidence (which function as evidence because of their connection to the characteristics, behaviors, tasks, etc. of the culture's two gender-roles), we identify each other as a participating in the masculine gender-role or as participating in the feminine gender-role, as being either a man or a woman, and then we typically act accordingly in our interactions with and our expectations of the person.

In this connection it is worth saying that the expectation that an infant categorized as a boy will grow up to be a man and an infant categorized as girl will grow up to be a woman is not only or even primarily a biological prediction. It is rather a statement of expectations associated with gender-assignment. Note that in common speech all the words reserved here for gender-roles are also often used to refer to biological categories, and they often are used to refer to biological and gender categories simultaneously, as if these two sets of categories were always paired together in human experience. Thus when an infant is declared to be a boy or a girl, the infant is typically being categorized into a gender-role, as masculine or feminine, and a biological category, as male or female, at one and the same time, lending credence to the mistaken idea that biological categories and gender identity are always nicely matched.

Gender Expression

The third meaning of the word gender concerns how we humans express ourselves in action, speech, carriage, dress, ornament, etc. Associated with each of the gender-roles is a complex set of forms of gender expression. Phrases like "looked very feminine," "sounded like a man," "didn't act like a woman," and "wasn't very masculine" are common in ordinary speech and always presuppose a set of gender-role-typical forms of speech, appearance, bearing, movement, etc., which the speaker takes for granted as being well understood within the speaker's culture. Most such statements also imply a value judgment regarding the person's manner of expressing or presenting himself/herself because, in addition to there being a set of gender-role-typical forms of self-expression, there are also gender-role-based limitations on people's ways of expressing themselves within a culture. Expressing oneself in ways that are outside those limits usually evokes a negative judgment against the person who does so.

The reason for distinguishing gender expression from both gender assignment and gender identity is that a person's expression may not be consistent with his/her gender identity or with how she/he is gender-assigned. In some settings, for example, gender expression inconsistent with gender assignment is ordinarily considered acceptable, as when a woman (a person gender-assigned in the feminine gender-role) wears the costume of a man (clothing etc. typically associated with the masculine gender-role), or vice-versa, at a costume party. But in other settings expression inconsistent with assignment may be severely stigmatized, as has long been the case in the United States for males wearing feminine clothing and makeup, unless there are special excusing circumstances like a costume party. On the other hand, if a person's gender identity was at odds with her/his gender assignment, but he/she engaged in gender expression consistent with assignment, the person could experience conflict and psychological pain by reason of the mismatch between identity and expression. So there is real descriptive value in distinguishing gender expression as a separate concept.

Gender Identity

Fourth, the word "gender" is also used to refer to a person's own identification with the society's gender-roles. This aspect of human experience will be referred to here as "gender identity." In this activity the context of categorization is self-categorization. Although there is some disagreement and the matter has not been fully studied, most psychologists who study gender identity agree, and most persons who have experienced a conflict between their gender identity and other aspects of their lives support the view, that people's experience regarding their gender identity should be thought of as an orientation, in the sense of this word used in connection with preferred partner for intimacy. That is, gender identity is a deeply embedded characteristic of a human being that is present in people from their earliest years of awareness of distinct gender-roles and of themselves in relation to them; and it is a characteristic that does not ordinarily change across a person's lifetime.

Gender identity is frequently what is being expressed when a person says "I am a woman" or "I am a man," and then draws a conclusion from this about how to act or react, or about how other persons should act on the basis of this identification. But in ordinary speech, as was mentioned, statements using these words could easily be intended to describe the person's biological characteristics because the words man and woman are also used in that way in ordinary speech. Or they could be about how the person perceives the gender assignments that others are making about him/her. But such statements are often intended to articulate something about the person's identity, about how the person perceives or understands herself/himself. They are about the kind of self the person has been, about the kind of self that he/she is trying to become, and about the kinds of actions and reactions that are consistent with or called for by this identity.

Many people now understand that there are persons who identify with one of the gender-roles within the culture, but it is not the gender-role to which they have previously been assigned by others in the society and in which they have lived and which has typically been assigned to them on the basis of their biological categorization at birth. Some persons who experience life in this way choose to live with the conflicts and psychological pain that such a mismatch between identity and assignment (and its consequences in the actions and expectations of others) produces. Others choose to change the way they live in order to live in the gender-role with which they identify. In order to do this they set aside the other gender-role to which they had previously been assigned and in which they have previously lived and take up the gender-role with which they identify. In doing this, because gender-roles pervade so many aspects of human life, these persons may have to set aside many other elements of their previous lives, including possibly very important relationships with other persons if these persons cannot incorporate the person's change of gender-role into their own lives. Persons who make such a thorough going change, and fully and permanently take up the other gender-role, are now generally called "transsexuals" (even though this term used to refer more narrowly to persons making this change who also seek changes their external genital anatomy).

What is not widely known in American culture is that there are also many people who identify deeply with both gender-roles of our culture, who experience themselves as being both deeply masculine persons and deeply feminine persons. People of this sort will be referred to here as "bi-gendered."

Those who experience their sense of who they are in this way sometimes describe themselves by saying they "have two genders." But properly speaking it is cultures that have genders, namely gender-roles. A more precise way of describing the experience of bi-gendered persons is to say that, as stated above, they identify with both gender-roles that our culture provides. That is, with regard to gender identity it is not a matter of either/or for bi-gendered people. For them it is a matter of both/and. Just as our standard system of concepts is mistaken in holding that, in terms of biological categorization, every person is either simply female or simply male, so also is our culture's system of concepts about gender mistaken in holding that every person's gender identity is either simply masculine or simply feminine. Some people are deeply both.

It is important to note how dependent these discussions about identity are on the use of the words he/she, her/him, his/her, etc. It has not been easy to avoid these words in the paragraphs just written. But in English these words only come in gender-assigned forms: he/him/ himself/his and she/her/herself/hers. For speakers of English, whenever a word of this sort is needed one cannot avoid assigning a single gender (either/or) to the person referred to. (In some languages there are pronouns that mean simply the person, without gender assignment in the very saying of the words.) In addition, these same gendered words are used, in ordinary speech, to assign persons to biological categories. There would be no problem here, of course, if these aspects of life—biological categorization regarding a person, gender assignment regarding the person, and the person's gender identity—always matched up perfectly. But they do not always match up perfectly. So the English language has significant potential for describing people incorrectly and supporting a set of concepts that systematically excludes large numbers of persons.

This fact about the English language is not only a matter of inconvenience for speakers who want to speak accurately. It also shapes people's thinking in English-speaking cultures, leading them without noticing it to believe that everyone's gender identity is either masculine or feminine and that, in regard to biological characteristics, everyone is either simply male or simply female. No matter how much these patterns are taken for granted and seem supported by our use of English pronouns, however, neither of these either/or patterns is accurate.

Among bi-gendered persons, some strongly identify with the gender-role different from the gender-role in which they ordinarily live and to which they have been assigned by others throughout their life (which gender-role has typically been assigned on the basis of their biological categorization at birth). Other bi-gendered persons genuinely identify with the other gender-role, but not as strongly. That is, not all bi-gendered persons are 50/50, so to speak. In a manner that parallels what was said earlier about bisexuals, some bi-gendered persons are 60/40, others 40/60, others 20/80, others 90/10, and so on.

Among the bi-gendered who strongly identify with the other gender-role, some choose to live with the conflicts and psychological pain produced by the mismatch between this aspect of their identity and their actual life. Others choose to change the way they live in order to participate in the other gender-role as well as continuing to participate in their assigned gender-role. But it is not possible to participate to any full degree in both gender-roles simultaneously in a society with two and only two definitely distinct gender-roles. So typically such a person lives the majority of his or her life in one gender-role and spends briefer amounts of time and engages in a more limited range of activities and relationships in the other.

Obviously, change of gender-role includes changes in gender expression. When a bi-gendered person changes gender-role, this involves expressing the other gender-role with which the person identifies. For being in a gender-role includes being assigned that gender-role by other persons, and it certainly includes self-assignment of that gender-role. Gender assignment is significantly dependent upon gender expression; our culture's system of concepts is not open to assigning a person to both gender-roles simultaneously. Therefore when a bi-gendered person chooses to express the other gender-role with which he/she identifies, the bi-gendered person will aim through details of gender expression to be assigned by others in that other gender-role, both in order to experience a proper "match" in his/her identification with that other gender-role and also to avoid the negative judgment of others for transgressing gender-role boundaries.

Given the extent to which body-shape and other visible characteristics are used as evidence in gender assignment in our culture, a person changing gender-roles will typically work hard to express the body-shape and other visible characteristics typically associated with the gender-role she/he is adopting. This activity is often called "cross-dressing." But it would be a serious mistake to think that a bi-gendered person's expression of his or her other gender-role is simply a matter of clothing, even though many bi-gendered people are comfortable with this term. What is happening here is something far more personally significant than putting clothes on one's body. It is an expressing of the person's identity to himself/herself and an expressing of himself/herself to other

members of the human family in a manner in accord with her/his genuine gender identity. Note also that the bi-gendered person, because
he/she identifies with both gender-roles, is in a certain sense always
cross-dressed, always presenting himself or herself to the world in a
gender-role that does not express all of his or her identity.

There is another term that deserves a comment, the term "transves-
tite," which is simply the Latin word for the same idea. But this term is
one that the transgendered community does not care to use because it
was invented by and long used by psychiatry as the name of a pathology
or mental illness. While the conflicts and psychological pain experienced by many bi-gendered people are very real, neither they nor most
mental health professionals who assist them consider their identification with both gender-roles to be a pathology. They experience this aspect of their identity simply as one way of being a human being who
deserves respect, affirmation, and support.

One of the hardest aspects of being bi-gendered in our society is
that, at least for males, for cultural reasons (some of which are explored
in this volume), there is a profound stigma in American society attached to males if they engage in gender expression appropriate to the
feminine gender-role, except under special excusing conditions such as
a costume party (and many people in American culture do not consider
that an exception). This stigma, especially when it has been powerfully
learned in youth and has been deeply internalized in the bi-gendered
person, as is often the case, creates a profound fear of expressing the
other gender-role, as well as profound guilt for even wanting to do so.
Bi-gendered persons who feel a deep need to express the gender-identity
that does not match their typical gender assignment ordinarily need to
muster a lot of courage, and often need the help of counselors or a support group to deal with the power of this internalized stigma.

NO LONGER HARMING BY CONCEPTUAL EXCLUSION

I began by saying that I want to change how we speak and how we
think because the system of concepts that we commonly use in American culture to refer to people in terms of biology, sexual orientation,
and gender excludes important groups within the human family. In
fact, the most common academic way of referring to sexual orientation,
categorizing (most) people as heterosexual and homosexual, pre-
supposes the either/or conceptualization of both biology and gender.
Sexual orientation is thus ordinarily conceptualized in terms of likeness

and unlikeness, but likeness and unlikeness to what? To typical male and typical female gender anatomy, and to typical masculine and feminine gender characteristics, with the assumption that everyone fits either one category or the other. There is, as in so much of our culture, no conceptual room for both/and, and those who are intersexed or bi-gendered are simply excluded from notice.

What is it like to be without conceptual standing? Consider this analogy. You cannot make your case in court before a judge if you do not have standing in that jurisdiction. If you are a citizen of Illinois or of Texas, even if they would let you into a courtroom in Ohio, your statement of the words of a claim you have about a matter in your home state would have no consequence whatsoever to the Ohio judge. It is not only that your words would not be judged legally sound in that court. Your words would be empty, meaningless, would not count for anything but noise because you lack standing in that courtroom. And in fact, because of this, they would not let you in!

Persons who are excluded by our commonly used concepts are similar, but their lack of standing is more radical. They are not even lepers, who exist but must be shunned and certainly never touched. These persons do not exist. How can their lives, well-being, interests, or rights be weighed when our concepts have no room for them at all? Without standing in the world of meaning, their words and their concerns are empty noise, the words and the concerns of persons who do not exist.

To extend our hand to these, as Jesus did to the leper, we must reject the systems of concepts we are familiar with and construct concepts that include them and their ways of experiencing life in the human family. And to do that well, as Jesus did, we may actually have to touch them.

Part Four:
Interpreting Human Experience

13

Papal Ideals, Marital Realities: One View from the Ground [1]

Cristina L. H. Traina

This work is open to every echo of experience, from whatever quarter it comes, and it is at the same time a standing appeal to all to let experience, their own experience, make itself heard, to its full extent: in all its breadth, and all its depth. When we speak here of depth we have in mind all those things which do not always show themselves directly as part of the content of experience, but are nonetheless a component, a hidden dimension of it, so much so that it is impossible to omit them, if we want to identify fully the contents of experience. If we do omit them, we shall be detracting from and impoverishing experience, and so robbing it of validity, though it is the sole source of information and the basis of all reliable knowledge on whatever subject. *Love and Responsibility*, with this sort of methodological basis, fears nothing from experience. Experience does not have to be afraid of experience. Truth can only gain from such a confrontation. [2]

So begins Pope John Paul II's 1960 treatise on sexuality, the book that lays the theological and philosophical groundwork for all his papal writings on gender and sexual ethics. He seems to have meant this explicit nod to experience as a reassurance of his theories' objectivity and coherence with everyday life. That experience had a "hidden dimension" whose discernment required special theological and philosophical expertise (if not charismatic authority, here) was for him an obvious and unproblematic caveat. If implicit and explicit experience were in contradiction, he assumed, then there must have been some error in interpreting the latter.

Forty years later, experience is perhaps both the most-cited factor and wildest variable in debates over methods and questions in ethics.[3] Far from comforting the reader or foreclosing debates over the natures and ends of things, appeals to experience raise questions about perspective and authority and are widely thought to reveal as much about speakers as about the phenomena they address.[4]

Concern for the credentials of experience certainly dominates Roman Catholic discussions of sexuality. One important critical task has been identifying and ranking the experiential tributaries that flow into an author's moral judgments. In this volume, for example, James Hanigan and Susan Ross illustrate in different ways how Pope John Paul II grounds his vision of procreative complementarity in the authority of charismatic insight and in an experience formed by Scripture, traditional norms and practices, mariology, and his own deeply held, particular ideals of masculinity and femininity, perhaps unconsciously universalized from the events of his childhood.

But all experience is not equal. A second essential task is criticism of these sources and the relative weight they are given in moral argument. Hanigan sees John Paul II's central source as Scripture interpreted in light of traditional mores. But Ross joins critics like Peter Hebblethwaite in arguing that this narrow interpretation of experience leaves important personal and cultural assumptions unexamined and dismisses concrete, practical experiences as morally irrelevant. According to Hebblethwaite, John Paul II's sources are limited and primarily textual, theoretical, or reflective rather than broad and practical or concrete; in his search for "the unchanging essence of things" John Paul II seems to have "a preference for introspection over evidence—or rather the introspection provides the evidence."[5] Nowhere is this clearer than in his discussions of sex and sexuality. John Paul II insists that accounts of concrete experience may enter moral argument only *after* universal norms are established, and then solely to confirm them. For example, "sexology"—scientific knowledge of human sexuality and sexual function—"does not have to furnish arguments from which we can deduce these rules—it is enough if it incidentally confirms rules already known from elsewhere and established by other means"(*Love,* 276).

In the case of homosexuality this reasoning implies that pessimistic sociological and psychological data on "the gay lifestyle" may provide legitimate outrigger support for established arguments in favor of essential gender complementarity. Thus many Roman Catholic authors cite disease, despair, breakdown of essential gender characteristics, and the decline of the two-parent family as observable, measurable consequences of homosexual (primarily gay) promiscuity.[6] These arguments typically treat homosexual relationships as mere long-term affairs, despite the fact—as Isiaah Crawford and Brian Zamboni demonstrate in this volume—that the "homosexual lifestyle" of the gay and lesbian bar circuit is no more similar to the stable homosexual household than the straight "swinging singles" scene is to a mutual, cooperative marriage.[7] Evidence of stability, fidelity, or emotional health is seen as irrelevant to the argument because this sort of success is assumed to occur in spite of the essential gender conflict that compromises the relationship.

When the topic is heterosexual marriage the criteria for admissible data reverse. Measurable benefits experienced by heterosexual married couples provide outrigger support for the assumption in favor of the essential morality of heterosexual marriage. Statistics to the contrary are simply the fruit of poor approximation of the ideal; they are read as evidence of individual weakness rather than as indicators of flaws inherent in the institution, which is assumed to be unproblematic. There is, in other words, a double standard for the use of concrete evidence: it may support but not question ruling assumptions about gender and marriage.

Yet if "experience does not have to be afraid of experience" this double standard is both unnecessary and insidious. Indeed, the particular version of natural law method that underlies moral theology actually demands that, if the Roman Catholic community is responsibly to confirm, revise, or replace current official teachings on any subject, then knowledge must be sought from all quarters.[8] The net must be cast as widely as possible, and the information it gathers must be interpreted within a number of competing or overlapping frameworks, including some that challenge established assumptions. For instance, as Jon Nilson and Mary Hunt imply in this volume, other readings of the same experiential sources that underlie John Paul II's theology can produce visions of sexuality, procreativity, and gender quite different from his; and as Bishop Thomas Gumbleton argues, intimate gay and lesbian relationships can reveal and embody divine love just as marriages do. Dialogue that includes these voices is crucial to the evaluation of the version of ontological, procreative gender complementarity that undergirds all contemporary Roman Catholic ecclesiastical teachings on homosexuality.

What significance can a straight, married woman's experiential reflections have for this volume's critical reexamination of the sources and norms of Roman Catholic teaching on homosexuality? To extrapolate from straight experience seems presumptuous and irrelevant: gay, lesbian, bisexual, and transsexual (GLBT) theologians speak quite eloquently for themselves, here and elsewhere. But while straight, married voices should not dominate the conversation, to exclude them risks impoverishing it in two important ways. First, it perpetuates the assumption that GLBT sexual experiences necessarily differ radically and essentially from married heterosexual experiences. Second, presuming to know the "hidden dimension" of the ideal of married sexuality already, it misses an opportunity to criticize this ideal in light of the concrete experiences of the married couples whom it in theory governs. Thus one key to authentic dialogue about homosexuality is candid talk about married sexuality's joys and frustrations, as well as its approximation to or distance from traditional Roman Catholic moral norms as interpreted by John Paul II. Where does the reigning ecclesiastical account of married sexuality—marvelously articulated by Ross and Hanigan— ring true with the concrete experience of particular married people and where is it false? How might questions like these help us to approach discussions of sexuality more constructively? Such conversations do not—because they cannot—arise among members of the ecclesiastical hierarchy, but they must be carried out.

In what follows I draw inspiration from Mary Pellauer's more rigorous moral reflections on women's sexual pleasure, seen through the lens of her own marriage, and on Christine Gudorf's sexual ethics of mutual pleasure.[9] I concentrate on procreativity and complementarity, the most prominent Vatican concerns; I remain largely within the paradigm of sexual self-gift; and I work from a sample size of one: my own experience as a married person hewing fairly close to Vatican ideals of sexuality and family structure.[10] The account is therefore neither comprehensive, representative, nor conclusive. But I hope that it inspires a conversation that is both.

UNION ON ALL LEVELS

> [Persons have] an inborn need . . . to give [themselves] to another. . . .
> The need to give oneself to another person has profounder origins than
> the sexual instinct and is connected above all with the spiritual nature of
> the human person. . . . It is the need to give oneself, latent in every

human person, which finds its outlet in physical and sexual union, in matrimony (*Love,* 253).

The rough outlines of my sexuality and procreativity are unremarkably orthodox. I saved sexual intercourse for marriage, and I married a man for whom equality and mutuality are indisputable goals in sexuality as in all other dimensions of our lives. This has meant learning to understand and accommodate each other's different and changing sexual personalities. The effort has been worth it. Sexual affection is part of the "glue" that holds us together, providing refreshment in smooth times and expressing love and reassurance when words fail (or, worse, harm). In periods when we have felt precariously close to coming unglued, we have later realized, more intimate physical connection would have helped us to bridge or accept our emotional distance. We have three children, all of whom were conceived intentionally and easily and whose arrival caused no severe hardship to health or family security. And, while we are avoiding another birth, we are committed to mustering the resources to love and raise another child should we conceive again. By no means has either of us habitually ranked either procreation or our own pleasure above the other goods of intercourse. If we had, we would not still be married.

Not surprisingly, there is resonance between this experience and John Paul II's descriptions of spousal procreative love. His assertion of the latent need to give oneself physically, in sex, rings true for me (*Love,* 253). So does his insistence that "[sexual] intercourse is necessary to [married] love" (*Love,* 233): intercourse not in a reductive sense, but a physical, ecstatic intimacy that is so necessary to a relationship that (for example) a husband has a moral obligation to learn and respond to his wife's erotic rhythms (*Love,* 272–74). Likewise familiar is the "general disposition toward parenthood" that, according to John Paul II, characterizes "a true union of persons" even when they are not seeking pregnancy (*Love,* 229, 233).

This resonance is not merely theoretical or abstract, however. For example, for me intentionally procreative intercourse is an experience unto itself. Other than childbirth, I can think of nothing that compares with the physical, psychological, and spiritual exhilaration of intentionally procreative lovemaking. With pregnancy a hope rather than a worry, there is a giddy, thrilling sense of abandon; I have the psychological freedom to commit all of my energy to sensing, caressing, and responding, to (as Pellauer says) "being here-and-now."[11] Here too the papal model matches my experience; for me, as long as conception seems both likely and wise, intentionally procreative intercourse eliminates anxieties over unwanted pregnancy that have stood in the way of attentive, loving intercourse on other occasions.[12] In this sense procreative sex sometimes achieves the relational or "unitive" goods of love-making better than intercourse that is not aimed at procreation.

This difference is not merely freedom from inhibition. There is a new focus, a shared delight in a common project that really is a "total self-gift" to each other and our hoped-for future child. Our joy in each other and our mutual excitement about the project of conceiving can be nearly overwhelming. The Spirit's presence is palpable. Physical climax, in the end, plays a minor role. For me, as for many women, procreative intercourse typically does not lead to thrilling orgasmic release; at ovulation, although I feel aroused, my body is so sensitive to touch that intercourse is actually uncomfortable.[13] Yet the experience as a whole brings a different array of pleasures and goods: "warmth, comfort, intimacy, the experience of belonging in an embrace"—and the prospect of a new child.[14] In spite of all of this, as long as we anticipate no difficulty in conceiving, neither do I replace a focus on mutual erotic pleasure with an instrumental desire to conceive. The intention to conceive is rather a second layer of meaning, an extra dimension: *through* loving, we may create a child (see *Love*, 18, 234). Here again my experience echoes John Paul II's description: our physical connection is only one dimension of our love, which "must possess a fertility of its own in the spiritual, moral, and personal sphere" in order to sustain the productive work of parenthood (*Love*, 55).

But here the resemblance to papal descriptions of appropriate marital sexuality breaks down. It fails precisely along the two axes upon which the papal argument for traditional sexual norms is constructed: procreativity and complementarity. The ecstatic joys and profound peace of procreativity have characterized our sexual encounters on perhaps ten occasions. Otherwise our sexual relationship, while not antiprocreative in any ideological sense, has been intentionally—often anxiously—non-procreative. And the moments when we have experienced our sexual complementarity as in any way essential to the business of our marriage have been limited to these same ten occasions. Otherwise the fact that I am a woman and my husband is a man fades back into the many other circumstances, personal and social, that more strongly mold the intimate dimensions of our lives together. If these insights—arising out of a faithful, prayerful, procreative marriage—make moral sense, then the two strongest current Roman Catholic objections to homosexual unions ring hollow.

Interpreting these departures from the presumptive norm demands an inductive process that begins with listening to details and circumstances: literally, *circum stantia,* the facts that stand around an event. Because in Roman Catholic moral theology the circumstances are in every case relevant to the evaluation of the act (in direction and degree), we ignore these at our peril. Circumstances reveal morally significant textures, contingencies, and interdependencies that introspective abstraction can easily elide in its quest for universal insight. Most importantly for us, they forbid a reductionist simplification that erroneously treats sexuality as an issue unto itself, isolated from all other moral commitments.[15] Circumstances on all scales—personal, political, environmental—are relevant here. But because John Paul II's arguments on sexual affection are personalist rather than social justice arguments, I argue primarily on this intimate level.

NON-PROCREATIVITY

To put it simply, in my experience there is no necessary, exclusive connection between physical openness to procreation and genuine attentiveness to my husband in a particular sexual encounter. Even in loving procreative sex, I may not focus on him; in intentionally non-procreative sex, I generally do; and in sex that even minutely risks pregnancy when it is unwise, unsafe, or both, I welcome neither partner nor child.

Whether this departure from the papal ideal is a result of sin I leave others to judge. But I am sure of three things. First, I do not have the energy to erect a buffer wide enough to protect a focus on mutual self-gift in intercourse open-to-but-not-desiring conception from the many other real and good emotional, economic, and social demands on me. Second, although these other demands can be harmful distractions from selfless sexual intimacy, they are also integral to the selves my husband and I bring to lovemaking in our best moments. A truly personal, mutual, intimate sexual relationship is a connection between our whole persons; a joining of only a few elements of our lives would be exploitative and dishonest. Finally (assuming that "intercourse is necessary to love"), generous, unprotected intercourse does not seem to me to be an absolute good, able to trump all my other obligations. Each of these realizations severely qualifies John Paul's psychology and his view of the connections between intimacy and procreativity.

1. The desire to have a child is naturally awakened by marriage and marital intercourse, whereas resistance to this desire in the mind and the will is unnatural (*Love*, 280).

> The factors which disturb the regularity of the biological cycle in women are above all of psychological origin. . . . Of the psychological causes, fear of conception, of becoming pregnant, is the commonest. . . . Clinical experience also confirms the thesis that fear of pregnancy also deprives a woman of that "joy in the spontaneous experience of love" which acting in accordance with nature brings (*Love*, 281).

Although I have desired pregnancy, I have also been terrified of it. After our third child was born, I continued to teach full-time while my husband, who earned less, worked part-time and cared for our children. Our remaining in the town where we had put down roots depended entirely on my working hard enough to retain my position. I was exhausted by sleeplessness, nursing, and the combined responsibilities of work, parenthood, and citizenship in church and community. For the first time I knew that another pregnancy would spell physical and professional disaster for me and economic hardship for my family, not to mention a move down the professional ladder to a strange city and an uncertain, even more difficult future. This was a rational judgment. It stemmed from concern for my family's needs; it was consistent with my "natural" ends of responsible parenthood and citizenship; and it was based on data on tenure and on my own realistic evaluation of my husband's and my physical and emotional stamina.

John Paul II is not wrong about the consequences of fear, either: this fear of pregnancy became a visceral fear of sex itself. It knotted my whole body so tightly that I could not even consent to intercourse, far less enjoy it, no matter how many protections were built into it. This too was a rational judgment. My fertility symptoms were in uninterpretable chaos for well over a year, making intercourse an unconscionable risk. Although I was certainly under stress and psychologically "resistant" to further children (plainly not to motherhood!), this entirely normal "disturbance" had biological roots as well: fatigue and the hormonal suppression caused by nursing. These factors prayer, confidence in God, and willingness to accept another pregnancy were unlikely to alter.

If these biological factors are both almost ubiquitous and impossible to overcome even for the comparatively wealthy, we cannot forget the circumstances of women who are not healthy middle-class college professors. Pregnancy is physically dangerous for many otherwise healthy women and for all who are ill or malnourished. Stress caused by insufficient wages, uncertain work, poor nutrition, violence, or displacement actually tends to decouple ovulation from classic fertility symptoms, so that non-contraceptive pregnancy prevention—even with a husband's cooperation—becomes very difficult.[16] Similarly, if I could be rationally certain that a "total self-gift" resulting in pregnancy would overdraw my family's emotional and economic reserves, what of women who earn far less, who are far more precariously and less flexibly employed, whose husbands are far less committed to the home? These stresses do not, *pace* John Paul II, originate in the individual psyche. Their alleviation is not the emotional responsibility of individual women or couples but the economic and political responsibility of society on a national—and sometimes international—scale. And they are unlikely to disappear.

When we add the biological, economic, and political factors together we see that only women who typically have regular menstrual periods, who are not currently post-partum, lactating, or pre-menopausal, and who are not subjected to social, physical, and emotional stresses can rely on periodic abstinence to prevent the births that John Paul II himself argues they can and should prevent (*Love*, 243). Nevertheless, John Paul II's prototypical married woman has two options: abstaining from intercourse for long periods or overcoming her "unnatural" resistance to motherhood (*Love*, 237–39). In John Paul's mind the ideal is to choose both; they work together for the good of the woman and her family. Yet abstinence, though a woman might desire it, is rarely within her control; John Paul himself, despite his ideal of mutuality, admits that "in the majority of cases it is [the man] who makes the decision" when to conceive (*Love*, 279). Even if a husband is willing to accept abstinence, alternative paths to sexual delight are forbidden, reducing by one the number of precious resources that enable a couple to maintain their connection in demanding, fragmenting surroundings. And overcoming resistance means accepting as many children as may come, a decision normally antithetical to women's and children's health and family welfare, not to mention profession, community, and global flourishing—all goods that the Pope, and modern Vatican documents generally, subordinate to the absolute good of "natural" intercourse. Consequently, if, as John Paul II insists, mutual delight in intercourse is proper only when conception is not impeded and when the possibility of its occurrence is met with relaxed, joyful expectation; and if, as he also insists, intercourse is the only proper structure of marital sexuality; then for the typical couple enmeshed in ordinary responsibilities, opportunities for generous, appropriate marital sexual expression are few in a lifetime. This is not, in my experience, a path to happy marriage and responsible parenthood.

2.When a man and a woman who have marital intercourse decisively preclude the possibility of paternity and maternity, their intentions are thereby diverted from the person and directed to mere enjoyment: "the person as co-creator of love" disappears and there remains only the "partner in erotic experience" (*Love*, 234).[17]

John Paul II never claims that lovemaking must be carried out with procreative intent (*Love*, 233–36). He argues only that it must involve intercourse and that there can be no interruption of the physical processes of ovulation, ejaculation of sperm, meeting of sperm and ovum, or implantation. Only the act of unprotected intercourse, for him, symbolizes the total self-gift of spouses, who must always pursue mutual ecstasy accepting the possibility that it may result in a new child.

On the contrary, I am able to give myself most fully to my husband in two circumstances: on those rare occasions when pregnancy is a hope, as above, or when it is not a worry. Not surprisingly, I first discovered the latter while pregnant. While I was open to the idea of children —after all, we were expecting one—there was no chance of conceiving another. Once I overcame my first-timer's fear of "hurting the baby," I could focus on our mutual pleasure, undistracted by the nagging anxiety that we might have a child at the wrong time. The obligation to be open to conception seemed beside the point.

These new pleasures of worry-free intercourse inspired another realization: during pregnancy especially the Roman Catholic objection to non-coital ejaculation becomes ludicrous.[18] Since conception is impossible, there is no longer any biological reason why sexual pleasure should include intercourse. The same doubt arises whenever surgery, age, or circumstances of birth make a couple infertile.[19] Arousal and orgasm in all of these circumstances—both in and outside intercourse— can express and symbolize self-gift in mutual pleasure without any explicit reference to procreation. These realizations are, to most of the Western world, old news; my point here is that they can arise precisely out of marital, procreative experience, not merely in protest against it.

As the reader may have guessed by now, my significant departures from the Roman Catholic script on marital sexuality have been first actively preventing, and then foreclosing, pregnancy. I am hardly alone in this.[20] All sorts of arguments have been launched for it since 1968, from personalist revisions of moral theology (judge by the procreativity of the marriage as a whole, not the act in isolation) to statistical arguments (God can as easily—perhaps more easily—cause sperm to pass around a diaphragm as cause a child to be conceived other than during ovulation).[21] But experience provides other arguments as well. For me contraception does not impede self-gift but, like pregnancy, allows it the freedom to proceed unworried by consequences. This does not mean that our lovemaking disregards children, even now. First, they are almost always in the house, and therefore at the fringes of our awareness, potentially waking for breakfast or for comfort from a dream or illness. Second, as our marriage matures I become increasingly aware that lovemaking involves our whole selves, including and especially our parental selves. Our children have in a certain respect made us, have shaped our minds, spirits, and even bodies. This awareness is always implicit and sometimes explicit in our lovemaking, especially when we remember and celebrate our children's conceptions.

In addition, a significant share of my role as spouse and parent has been the financial support of my family. The parental identity I bring to lovemaking has in recent years been much more that of "wage-earner" than "potential mother." My work may be a path to self-fulfillment and a contribution to the common good, but it is has also been a gift to my family, often an indispensable one. The enormity of this economic demand—to say nothing of the emotional resources that work and parenting always require—requires that true sexual self-gift, except in rare circumstances, exclude procreation.[22] My sexual self-gift remains fully spousal and parental precisely through contraception rather than in spite of it.

3. The lust of the flesh directs these desires [for personal union] to satisfy the body, often at the cost of a real and full communion of persons (*Blessed*, 68).

John Paul II implies that our greatest obstacles to ethical sexual relations are lust—viewing partners not as persons but as mere bodies capable of awakening and satisfying our purely physical longings—and lack of self-control; he is convinced that eliminating the possibility of conception merely exacerbates these failings.[23] This may be true for single people, or for cruel or inattentive spouses, but they do not, in my experience, apply to loving marital sexuality. The challenge my husband and I face is not controlling our desire but finding time and energy to make love. Our sexual lives are already disciplined, not only by external factors like schedules but also by internal curbs. We face trade-offs among sex, sleep, recreation, and conversation; often, in need of all four, we settle for one, and quite frequently it isn't sex. In these cases we make conscious decisions to shunt or avoid awakening desire in order to pursue some other good. Some couples find that natural family planning helps them to develop this sort of discipline, but it clearly is not the only path to this end.[24]

In addition, John Paul II's writings seem too easily to equate intense physical desire with the exploitive objectification of lust, which sees the spouse as a convenient and acceptable opportunity for the satisfaction of physical longings that might be met just as well by anyone else. In my experience an input of desire does not necessarily produce an output of mere physical release. Even when my desire for sex with my husband is overpoweringly physical, the connection I gain from making love is still emotional and even spiritual; in fact at this stage in my marriage greater sexual desire for my husband yields, paradoxically, greater generosity toward him: fuller self-gift. From my point of view this fact manifests God's brilliance: we get more than we ask for.

COMPLEMENTARITY

Of all John Paul II's arguments for limiting sexual expression to potentially procreative marital sexuality, perhaps the most deep-seated is his doctrine of sexual complementarity. According to this doctrine, sexual difference extends to our very psychological and spiritual cores. Marriage completes men's and women's inherent and natural deficiencies, creating out of two partial persons a healthy, dynamic, mutually supportive whole. The procreative physical union of (active) male with (passive) female enacts and symbolizes the overcoming of these ontological differences. This foundational belief permeates John Paul II's writings:

> Knowledge of man passes through masculinity and femininity, which are . . . two ways, as it were, of "being a body" and at the same time a man, which complete each other—two complementary dimensions, as it were, of self-consciousness and self-determination.[25]

> In the mystery of creation . . . man was endowed with a deep unity between what is, humanly and through the body, male in him and what is, equally humanly and through the body, female in him. On all this, right from the beginning, the blessing of fertility descended, linked with human procreation (cf. Gen 1:28).[26]

> Genesis 2:24 . . . proves that in every conjugal union of man and woman, the same original consciousness of the unifying significance of the body in its masculinity and femininity is discovered again. At the same time, the biblical text indicates that each of these unions renews, in a way, the mystery of creation in all its original depth and vital power (*Unity*, 50).[27]

> The man must reckon with the fact that the woman is in a sense in another world, unlike himself not only in the physiological but also psychological sense (*Love*, 275).

The symbolic power of this wholeness-in-union is undeniable. Yet of all John Paul II's claims about marital sexuality, the one that has least resonance for me, even in my heterosexual, married experience, is his insistence that the complementarity out of which marriages are made is primarily and essentially the ontological complementarity of the sexes. This is not to say that reproductive complementarity cannot be a great blessing. As a fertile heterosexual couple, we are able to conceive children through the physical, sacramental, ecstatic union of our bodies. This marvelous privilege should be neither denied nor downplayed.

It is also not to say that complementarity does not have an essential role in my marriage; it simply does not fall along the stereotypical gender lines that John Paul II suggests are engraved in our sexual natures. My husband may be carpenter and mechanic, but he is also uncannily perceptive, better at the intimate "girl talk" that typically connects women, and much more gifted at arranging colors and objects to create a comfortable living space. I may be cook, but I am also more comfortable debating and making utilitarian conversation, not so good at showing affection, and skilled at dispassionately analyzing and organizing ideas. Our relative skill as nurturers depends upon which of us is currently getting more practice at it. And passivity? We are two headstrong, oldest children; deference never had a chance. The fit and misfit of our personalities have everything to do with the successes and strains in our marriage, but they bear almost no relationship to our biological sexes.

Likewise, our physical complementarity—our anatomical maleness and femaleness—is increasingly insignificant in our love-making. My sense of us as "man" and "woman" in magnetic attraction, strongly and exotically present when we met in our teens, has given way to my sense simply of two people in erotic partnership. Our lovemaking is inspired much more by our knowledge of each other as particular persons—the fit of our whole bodies, our common histories, what pleases us—than by our awareness of each other as male and female. I make love with a particular person, not with a generic man, or even with a specific man. For me, sex and marriage with a different man would likely have been just as like and unlike ours as a long-term union with a woman would have been. Thus what is essential to my marriage is a complementarity grounded not in ontology or anatomy but in personality. This "good fit"—combined with love, friendship, and a desire to please, excite, and comfort—sustains our marriage, in physical love as in the give and take of daily life.

This does not mean that the world agrees. Assumptions about sexual complementarity are built into the core and trivia of our culture. Somehow my husband's name rises to the top of all deeds and other official documents, no matter where it starts out; teachers and school nurses always call me first—at home and at work—before they try to reach my husband; people try to talk to my husband about football and to me about fashion. But because we are culturally and economically privileged—and married and heterosexual—these assumptions are minor and often amusing irritations rather than threats to our equality and mutuality. For other couples, both heterosexual and homosexual, these cultural assumptions reinforce power differentials that in turn yield real relational and economic imbalances; these cannot be so easily shut out of the relationship, not to mention the bedroom.

TOWARD A REALISTIC ETHIC OF SEXUALITY

In my experience John Paul II is correct: loving, intentionally procreative intercourse has goods—textures, emotions, intentions—particular to it that non-procreative sex lacks. But his critics have been correct as well: sex can be genuinely mutual, loving, just, fun, good, and even holy without having any procreative intent or being referred even remotely to procreation.[28] Its goods and pleasures, in turn, may be absent from procreative sex. Neither form of lovemaking—nonprocreative or procreative—is normative. Rather, each is a genuine dimension of sexual expression, each has its own goods and its own times, and each can sustain partners in relationship.

Is this self-deception, a lustful captivation with evil? Sin can and does blind us to our hypocrisies, but according to Roman Catholic moral theology we also possess the tools to examine pleasure of any sort critically: how does it reverberate in the rest of our lives? John Paul II himself holds that true happiness comes from conforming willingly to our ontological "finality": harmony with God's intentions for humanity adds to any pleasure (or pain) of the moment growth in virtue and promotion of justice and mercy. Conversely, disharmony with this end brings profound unhappiness that, in its blind pursuit of pleasures for their own sakes, destroys self and others. By this measure, at least, the dual character of sexuality that I have described seems to pass the test of virtue. My husband and I are grateful for both of our "sexual identities": the procreative, complementary union in which we conceived our children, and the more fungible, fluid, nonprocreative partnership in which we have lived the rest of our lives. And we are as sure that the first is inessential to the second as we are that the second is essential to the first.[29] Contraception and fluid gender roles have been indispensable to our individual growth, to the success of our relationship in all its dimensions, to our parenthood, and to our lives in the broader world. Sex has harmed these same goods only when we have communicated badly and so felt rejected or coerced, or when we have risked pregnancy at the wrong time.

With the exception of easy procreativity, how different, really, is this rather orthodox marital connection from the everyday sexual intimacy of gay and lesbian couples? There are, I would wager, more overlaps than differences.[30] In both cases energy arises from committed, nonprocreative sexual union, sustaining and deepening the relationship, providing refreshment and stamina for what needs to be done both inside and outside the home. Heterosexual couples could learn much, in fact, from lesbian authors' explicit focus on the necessity and fruitfulness of struggling simultaneously on two fronts: for just and mutual sexual relationship and for social justice.[31] Like heterosexual couples, gay and lesbian couples often find that their non-procreative energy eventually becomes generative, inspiring them to share their love with children; some lesbian couples even practice procreative sexuality, incorporating lovemaking into their efforts to conceive.[32]

The concrete similarities in the ways we link commitment, sex, and parenting certainly have much to do with culture, class, educational level, and expectations of a monogamous relationship. But I believe that they also have something to do with the fact that, formally married or simply steadfastly committed, we are people, pure and simple. Our partnered covenants are formed within patterns of social, economic, and political commitments and exigencies; within these boundaries, our unions must be nurtured regularly by both divine grace and the ecstatic and comforting union of mind, spirit—and body. Any ethic of sexuality that truly "confronts experience" must begin here.

I do not mean to argue by this that experience and moral norms should be arrayed as natural adversaries. Rather, I want to suggest that norms limiting sex to marriage may be informed by a doctrine of pro-creative complementarity that reflects incomplete, immature experience. Partly because of the dominant language of heterosexual romance in our culture, complementary sexual anatomy can indeed play a large, even overpowering role in sparking a relationship, especially when we are young. At fifteen, when I met my husband, I found his masculine charm electrifying. Celibate moral theologians likely have similar vivid memories of their own youthful longings. But, lacking the experience of a sustained, faithful sexual relationship, they may not be able to imagine or discover what I—now at the brink of my forties—could not have imagined at fifteen myself: no matter how important it may have been at the beginning, anatomy's importance can fade until gender is the least relevant factor in the sustenance of a relationship. If so, the ultimate fruitfulness and durability of any union—heterosexual or homosexual—have nothing to do with gender complementarity or lack thereof. But they have everything to do with faith, friendship, generosity, communal support, the serendipity of personalities, sexual and verbal affection, and the hard work that goes into mutual formation of a working partnership.

NOTES: CHAPTER 13

[1] Special thanks to all who have helped shape this article: Isiaah Crawford, Robert DiVito, Mary Hunt, Patricia Beattie Jung, and Susan Ross; Gloria Albrecht, who generously provided references; and my husband, Bill Hutchison, who is its reason for being.

[2] Karol Wojtyla, *Love and Responsibility*, trans. H. T. Willetts (New York: Farrar, Straus, and Giroux, 1981; 1st Polish edition 1960) 10. Hereafter *Love*.

[3] In Christian writings, Scripture is equally contentious; see essays in this volume by Mary Rose D'Angelo, Robert DiVito, Patricia Beattie Jung, Bruce Malina, and Leland White.

⁴ See, for example, Sandra G. Harding, *Whose Science? Whose Knowledge? Thinking From Women's Lives* (Ithaca, N.Y.: Cornell University Press, 1991); a good ecclesiastical example of the latter is John Paul II, *Veritatis splendor, Origins* 23, no. 18 (October 14, 1993) 299–334.

⁵ Peter Hebblethwaite, "The Mind of John Paul II," *Grail* 1 (March 1985) 23.

⁶ See Congregation for the Doctrine of the Faith, "Letter to the Bishops of the Catholic Church on the Pastoral Care of Homosexual Persons," in Jeannine Gramick and Pat Furey, eds., *The Vatican and Homosexuality: Reactions to the "Letter to the Bishops of the Catholic Church on the Pastoral Care of Homosexual Persons"* (New York: Crossroad, 1988) 5; for a critical assessment of these arguments see Patricia Beattie Jung and Ralph F. Smith, *Heterosexism: An Ethical Challenge* (Albany: SUNY Press, 1993) 90–103.

⁷ See also Dan Perreten's 1996–1997 columns in *Windy City Times;* e.g., Dan Perreten, "Where I'm Coming From," *Windy City Times* (February 6, 1997); and Mary Hunt, "Catholic Lesbian Feminist Theology," in this volume.

⁸ Cristina L.H. Traina, *Feminist Ethics and Natural Law: The End of the Anathemas* (Washington, D.C.: Georgetown University Press, 1999).

⁹ Mary D. Pellauer, "The Moral Significance of Female Orgasm: Toward Sexual Ethics That Celebrates Women's Sexuality," *Journal of Feminist Studies in Religion* (1993) 161–82; Christine E. Gudorf, *Body, Sex and Pleasure: Reconstructing Christian Sexual Ethics* (Cleveland: Pilgrim Press, 1994). See also Sidney Callahan's essay in this volume.

¹⁰ I am leaving other dimensions of sex, good and bad, nearly unexplored: comfort, spirituality, relief, excitement, apology, forgiveness, but also anger, boredom, etc. Thanks to Susan A. Ross for this list.

¹¹ Pellauer, "Moral Significance," 170.

¹² Couples with severe fertility problems tend to find intercourse a chore, or at least a highly ambiguous experience, rather than pure pleasure. See Sheila Kitzinger, *Woman's Experience of Sex: The Facts and Feelings of Female Sexuality at Every Stage of Life* (New York: Penguin, 1983) 197.

¹³ Ibid. 61.

¹⁴ Pellauer, "Moral Significance," 175.

¹⁵ On the ways in which obligations qualify each other see Margaret A. Farley, *Personal Commitments: Beginning, Keeping, Changing* (San Francisco: Harper and Row, 1986).

¹⁶ For this reason failure to abstain when a woman is under stress raises the annual failure rate of the ovulation method of periodic abstinence to nearly 100 percent (James Trussell and Laurence Grummer-Strawn, "Contraceptive Failure of the Ovulation Method of Periodic Abstinence," *Family Planning Perspectives* 22 [March/April 1990] 70).

[17] See also John Paul II, *Blessed Are the Pure of Heart: Catechesis on the Sermon on the Mount,* in John Paul II, *The Theology of the Body: Human Love in the Divine Plan,* foreword by John S. Grabowski (Boston: Pauline Books and Media, 1997) 150–2. Hereafter *Blessed.*

[18] Female orgasm tends either to be ignored or to occupy murky territory; John Paul II clearly values it, but only as part of non-contraceptive marital intercourse. On the invisibility and ambiguity of female orgasm in Christian writings see Pellauer, "Moral Significance," 178; also Susan A. Ross, "The Bride of Christ and the Body Politic: Body and Gender in Pre-Vatican II Marriage Theology," *Journal of Religion* 71 (July 1991) 345–61.

[19] Non-fertile intercourse is redeemed by its unitive quality, which in turn depends upon openness to conception. John Paul II's rejection of the "bio-logic" of non-coital sex in nonfertile circumstances follows Paul VI, although the former stresses the need for psychological and intentional openness to conception more than the latter. See Pope Paul VI, *Humanae Vitae* (Boston: The Daughters of St. Paul, 1968) pars. 12–16; and John Paul II, *Love,* 235–36, 240–41.

[20] In 1988, 75 percent of all married, white, non-Hispanic American women between the ages of fifteen and forty-four practiced some form of birth control; of these, only 4 percent used periodic abstinence methods, but 43 percent relied on male or female sterilization. See Calvin Goldscheider and William D. Mosher, "Patterns of Contraceptive Use in the United States: The Importance of Religious Factors," *Studies in Family Planning* 22 (March/April 1991) 104.

[21] E.g., Richard A. McCormick, *The Critical Calling: Reflections on Moral Dilemmas Since Vatican Council II* (Washington, D.C.: Georgetown University Press, 1989) 19.

[22] A parent who works only in the home may expend as much or more energy in support of the family as a wage-earning parent; this identity and responsibility can just as easily make further births ill-advised, population considerations notwithstanding.

[23] John Paul II, *Life According to the Spirit: St. Paul's Teaching on the Human Body,* in John Paul II, *The Theology of the Body: Human Love in the Divine Plan,* foreword by John S. Grabowski (Boston: Pauline Books and Media, 1997) 216. Hereafter *Life.*

[24] For some accounts and arguments in favor of agreed abstinence see John F. Kippley, *Birth Control and Christian Discipleship,* 2nd edition (Cincinnati: The Couple to Couple League International Inc., 1994); John and Sheila Kippley, *The Art of Natural Family Planning,* 3rd edition (Cincinnati: The Couple to Couple League, 1994); and, from a feminist perspective, Sondra Zeidenstein, "The Naked Truth," *Ms.* vol. 9, no. 5 (August/September 1999) 55–59. In a Christian Family movement survey conducted to inform Pat and Patty Crowley's work on the Papal Birth Control commission, 64 percent of couples who used

periodic continence found it helpful in some way to their marriages, but 78 percent said that it had (in many cases also) wounded their relationships. Failure rates were high (Robert McClory, *Turning Point: The Inside Story of the Papal Birth Control Commission, and How* Humanae Vitae *Changed the Life of Patty Crowley and the Future of the Church* [New York: Crossroad, 1995] 86–95).

[25] This is a considerably stronger claim than even that of *Humanae vitae,* which he approvingly quotes: "a man who grows accustomed to the use of contraceptive methods *may* forget the reverence due to a woman, and, disregarding her physical and emotional equilibrium, reduce her to being a mere instrument for the satisfaction of his own desires, no longer regarding her as his partner whom he should surround with care and affection" (*Humanae vitae,* 17, italics added; quoted in John Paul II, *Life,* 216).

[26] John Paul II, *Original Unity of Man and Woman: Catechesis on the Book of Genesis,* in John Paul II, *The Theology of the Body: Human Love in the Divine Plan,* foreword by John S. Grabowski (Boston: Pauline Books and Media, 1997) 47. Hereafter *Unity.*

[27] For the connection between John Paul II's theological anthropology and his trinitarian theology see especially *Unity,* 46–7.

[28] See, e.g., Carter Heyward, *Touching Our Strength: The Erotic as Power and the Love of God* (San Francisco: HarperSanFrancisco, 1989); eadem, *Staying Power: Reflections on Gender, Justice, and Compassion* (Cleveland: Pilgrim Press, 1995) 112–20; Margaret Farley, "An Ethic for Same-Sex Relations," in Robert Nugent, ed., *A Challenge to Love: Gay and Lesbian Catholics in the Church* (New York: Crossroad, 1983) 93–106; Mary Hunt, "Lovingly Lesbian: Toward a Feminist Theology of Friendship," in ibid., 135–55; eadem, *Fierce Tenderness: A Feminist Theology of Friendship* (New York: Crossroad, 1991); Beverly Wildung Harrison, *Our Right to Choose: Toward a New Ethic of Abortion* (Boston: Beacon, 1983) 39; see also Jung and Smith, *Heterosexism,* 167–86.

[29] This is not to deny that during rough periods children are a powerful incentive for working out differences; we and they stand to lose much more from marital failure than a childless couple might.

[30] The same seems to be true for parenting. See Sandra Pollock and Jeanne Vaughan, eds., *Politics of the Heart: A Lesbian Parenting Anthology* (Ithaca, N.Y.: Firebrand Books, 1987), and April Martin, *The Lesbian and Gay Parenting Handbook: Creating and Raising Our Families* (New York: HarperCollins, 1993). These texts focus more attention than heterosexual parenting literature on the struggles of bringing a child into the family (with the exception of heterosexual infertility literature), but their handling of the joys and frustrations of parenting is similar—if frequently less breezy and more honest. For an unromantic look at the division and performance of pedestrian domestic labor by gay and lesbian couples see Christopher Carrington, *No Place Like Home:*

Relationships and Family Life among Lesbians and Gay Men (Chicago: University of Chicago Press, 1999).

Plainly there are still important differences between us and gay or lesbian couples: we are married, according to civil and ecclesiastical law; we are male and female; we have conceived our children by ourselves through sexual intercourse. No one must discount the barriers that nonconformity to these cultural standards still creates for homosexual couples in adoption and conception, childrearing, medical benefits, and legal rights.

[31] See especially the works of Hunt and Heyward, above; also Carter Heyward, *Our Passion for Justice: Images of Power, Sexuality, and Liberation* (New York: Pilgrim Press, 1984).

[32] See Martin, *Lesbian and Gay Parenting*, 64–65; also Mary Hunt, personal communication. For a humorous twist see Sophie Cabot Black, "The Boys," in Jill Bialosky and Helen Schulman, eds., *Wanting a Child: Twenty-two Writers on Their Difficult But Mostly Successful Quests for Parenthood in a High-Tech Age* (New York: Farrar, Straus, and Giroux, 1998) 33–34.

14

Catholic Lesbian Feminist Theology

Mary E. Hunt

atholic lesbian feminist theology is no longer an oxymoron. Like
the gay Catholic work of John McNeill and the queer Catholic
work of Robert Goss, it simply reflects another perspective within
a wide tradition that is always getting wider.[1] Catholic feminist theology
is well established.[2] But the lesbian dimension is only now surfacing as
part of a larger debate.

One reason for this lacuna is the mistaken but widespread notion in
a patriarchal culture that homosexuality is really a male experience. Or,
if women are involved, we are involved in a way that is derivative of
men. Androcentric readings of scriptures and the erasure of lesbian experiences as such have allowed theologians and ethicists (both male and
female) to ignore the specificity of lesbian women. For example, it is not
clear that Catholic moral theology on homosexuality is based on any
knowledge of lesbians' lives. We are understood, if at all, as some dim
reflection of gay men, or some odd permutation of heterosexuality.
Happily, this is not the case in real life. Our experience needs to be reflected in theology. And, just as important, we need to "do theology" out
of our particularity if the Christian community is to be whole and its
reflections on questions of ultimate meaning and value are to be valid.

The Vatican intensified the contradiction by silencing Sr. Jeannine
Gramick, S.S.N.D., and Fr. Robert Nugent, S.D.S., in 1999 because of
their pioneering work to build bridges between lesbian/gay and other

Catholics. At that time Joseph Cardinal Ratzinger reiterated the kyriarchal position that homosexual orientation is "disordered" and that
homosexual acts are "intrinsically evil."[3] But many Catholics who love a
lesbian daughter or a gay son, who live next door to a lesbian couple, or
who work with a gay man have come to realize that this is simply
wrong. They add their common sense to the range of psychological,
philosophical, sociological, and theological arguments marshaled in
opposition to the institutional Catholic Church's view.

In this climate I offer with caution a Catholic lesbian feminist starting point for theological reflection. First, the dangers of essentialist
thinking lurk. Just as there is a wide spectrum encompassing what we
call "Catholic," so too is "lesbian" disputed territory in the sexual arena.
Is one born a lesbian? Does one become a lesbian? If so, how and why?
Likewise, "feminist" has grown from its gender-based origins to encom-
pass analyses and strategies aimed at overcoming many inequalities, including racism, economic deprivation, and other forms of structured/
interstructured injustice. Nonetheless, I believe that a well-defined
Catholic lesbian feminist perspective can contribute clarity and, with
luck, insight to the discussion.

I begin this sketch for a portrait, as surely more extensive treatment
is required in the future, in three steps. First, I note that the kyriarchal
view of homosexuality is based on male experience in a patriarchal
church and that it ignores women's experiences. I do so not to claim the
moral superiority of lesbians, but to suggest that our rejection of the
male-defined policy goes well beyond feeling excluded. It is sympto-
matic of structures of exclusion and of sex-specific kyriarchal policies
promulgated without women's input, such as the non-ordination of
women, that affect the whole church. Second, I outline five theological/
theoretical sources offered by feminist/womanist/*mujerista* theologians
and writers that help to shape a Catholic lesbian feminist theological
starting point in an increasingly pluralistic religious context. Third, I
suggest what a Catholic lesbian feminist theology might look like in
such a setting as we expand the horizons of contemporary spirituality.

My approach is speculative, relying on analysis and imagination as
well as on data and history. It is fundamentally theo-ethical, aimed at
taking seriously the experiences of women that have yet to inform kyriarchal Catholicism. From a feminist liberation theological perspective, I
am concerned with how theology emerges from human experiences
and how theological teachings influence the faith lives of adherents.
Such a theology is rooted in Catholic social justice teachings and culture,

coheres with the reality on which it is based, and fosters the faith of those for whom it is intended. In this case I have a "preferential option" for lesbian voices that have been silenced. I join the other authors in this anthology in renewing Catholic moral theology through tradition-conscious and community-respecting work.

KYRIARCHAL CATHOLICISM, THE BAN ON MALE HOMOEROTIC ACTIVITY, AND THE TELLING ABSENCE OF WOMEN

Feminist critiques of kyriarchal Catholicism began with language and imagery, as Mary Daly so nimbly pointed out more than thirty years ago.[4] Among the well-known sticky wickets of contemporary Catholicism are male names for the Divine, symbols and images such as Father, Lord, Ruler, King; the right to test a vocation to the priesthood reserved to males only, coupled with most significant decision-making left in the hands of ordained men; and male-centered sexual ethics, especially the ban on women's reproductive choice.

There is substantive disagreement between the teachings of the kyriarchal Church and the theological practices and teachings of many Catholic feminists. For example, female language for the Divine, including pronouns and images like the name Sophia, is used commonly in feminist liturgical base communities, those places where so many Catholic feminists worship. Priesthood is redefined in feminist theological terms, and its duties, including celebrating the Eucharist, are shared in feminist Catholic groups. These are serious disagreements that admit of no easy resolution, but Catholic life goes on despite them. Of course there are penalties. A case in point is the Massachusetts Women-Church group being banned from church property by Bernard Cardinal Law. Likewise, privileges are conferred on those who conform, as in the extension of a mandatum to teach in Catholic higher education according to the specifications of *Ex Corde Ecclesiae* only to those whose theology matches that of the kyriarchal Church.

While the substance of such theological disagreements is not trivial, and the price is often high, even more problematic is the fact that structures of power have not evolved to foster new ideas based on the diversity of human experience. Despite decades of feminist work, the androcentric bias remains firmly in place because there is literally no opening for women at the highest levels of church life where policy is decided. Nor is there any move toward renewed institutional structures that would include more and varied people in the process. I believe that this failure to bring about structural changes is, in the long run, far more serious than any of the gender-specific matters at hand. A more participatory process would allow other information to surface because respected members of a mature community would bring those experiences to the table.

The non-ordination of women is a case in point.[5] Whether women are eventually ordained is for many feminist theologians less important than whether decision-making structures are changed to reflect a more inclusive, participatory model. In fact, we are skeptical whether the ordination of women to the priesthood as presently conceived will ever achieve that goal. Even if a few conforming women are ordained and placed in positions of decision-making, the fundamental model will not be altered. This exclusive dynamic is clear in the institutional Church's position on homosexuality, formulated by clerics in the absence of a range of lesbian/gay/bisexual and transgendered peoples' experiences. Anecdotal and some survey research on the high percentage of male priests who are gay adds the pathetic dimension of self-hatred to this scene.

Pre-Vatican II Catholic theology relied relatively little on Scripture. But in this case, texts that condemn male homosexual behavior were part of the weight of evidence: Gen 19:1-29, the misinterpreted story of inhospitality from which the dreaded word "sodomy" was born; Gen 38:1-11, the spilling of seed which is seen as a violation of procreative laws; Lev 18:22, men who lie with men commit an abomination; Lev 20:13, men who commit this sin are to be killed.[6] Nary a mention of lesbian women, who certainly were not spilling seeds, much less treating strangers inhospitably! I think rather of Ruth and Naomi who, if anything, were a suggestive prototype of committed women's friendship, whether lovers or not. But they are oddly missing from the discussion.

Nonetheless, when it comes to policy, lesbian women are equally enjoined from same-sex sexual practices. Why? Because the general Catholic theological approach before feminist correctives, and still today in those unreconstructed Catholic approaches, was to assume, however falsely, that women's experiences were included in male experiences. It is only with Rom 1:26 that women merit a mention on their own terms: "Their women exchanged natural intercourse for unnatural . . ." But even this portion of the text is left aside in most interpretative arguments, which end with sweeping condemnations based on male experience.

Bernadette Brooten, in her impressive study on female homoeroticism in the early Christian period, claims that Paul "used the word 'exchanged' to indicate that people knew the natural sexual order of the universe and left it behind."[7] In her view, the Pauline idea of female sexuality was based on presumed gender differences and a hierarchically dualistic way of thinking about sex, with men in charge and women in a receiving mode. This model was foisted onto same-sex couples such that one homosexual partner was thought to act as a male and the other as a female.[8] She observes that in the Pauline world gay men gave up status by allegedly adopting a passive role in homosexual conduct, while lesbian women theoretically gained status by giving up a passive role.[9] Some critics argue that Dr. Brooten's reading gives far more credit for nuance to Paul than he deserved. In any case, the differences between women and men in same-sex relations seem to have gotten lost when it comes to the use of Scripture to inform policy.

Far more weight in Catholic theology was placed on philosophical teachings, especially natural law, where the hetero-bias is strong. Still, no one seems to have probed the obvious, namely, what women thought was natural, how women experienced their love for one another, what women felt about making love with each other without fear of pregnancy or the need for an abortion. But now we know better, and it is time to formulate Catholic lesbian feminist theology accordingly.

It is hard to imagine a contemporary discussion, one that might have been part of the Gramick/Nugent case, for example, in which Church officials would make a blanket argument against homosexuality in the face of the abundant data on lesbian lives. First they would have to discuss the matter *with* lesbian women, not talk *about* people who are fully capable of representing their own position. This would be a breakthrough, signaling the willingness of kyriarchal Catholic theological policy makers to engage in dialogue, not rule by fiat.

Then they would have to reject, or at least counter, the abundant psychological evidence that finds most lesbian women healthy and well adjusted despite social pressures, as Isiaah Crawford and Brian D. Zamboni have shown in their chapter in this volume.[10] They would need to bypass the thousands of lesbian-led families in which children are being raised to be productive citizens. They would be forced to ignore the testimony of Catholic lesbian women who find that root values of love and justice from our religious tradition inform our lives and relationships.[11] Such a conversation would be evidence of an historic methodological shift, as well as, presumably, one that reflects new content.

Church officials would have to deal with the fact that lesbian women, like gay men, are more than the sum of our genitalia. As such, we expect

to be treated like all other persons who make up the Catholic community, not pigeonholed and denounced with terms that have no bearing
on our being. We expect to be agents in the formation of, and not passive recipients of, the theo-ethical teachings of our tradition. This requires changes in structures that are finally far more profound than
changes in teachings on homosexuality, however revolutionary such
positive teachings would be. These changes require a democratic, participatory approach to being Church that has thus far been roundly
rejected by those who make decisions, and vigorously endorsed by those
who engage in Church reform.

Up to now I have passed over the matter of lesbian sexuality as such.
I do so not because it is irrelevant. To the contrary, it is important as
part of the data of revelation that go into theological reflections. But
part of the patriarchal trap in Catholic theology is the presumption that
what is at stake is primarily sex and not also, and perhaps in fact more
foundationally, power. I see the structural power issues as critical to renewed theo-ethical work. While it might make life slightly easier to
accomplish a repeal of the "disordered," "intrinsically evil" language,
I consider it even more important that we challenge the way in which
such policy is made and the notion that there is one Catholic position
on the question. Learning to live with and value a diversity of opinions
among Catholics will, in my judgment, stand us in better stead in an
increasingly pluralistic context.

Further, the "sex" in question as the parameters of debate are set
within Catholicism is normatively heterosexual and open to procreation.
Any other kind of sex is automatically defined as "objectively immoral."
On those terms there can be no fruitful discussion that does not put lesbian women in a defensive position with regard to our own lives and in
an oppositional posture with regard to gay men. I refuse to start there.

Rather, I insist that what is in play is precisely who decides, and how
we decide, what is important in the moral arena, what will be priori-
tized for discussion and how issues will be couched. From a lesbian
feminist perspective, the most important issue is not sex as such, however defined, but how we learn to live respectfully as a Christian community of people who share a diversity of lifestyles. Privileging one, in
this case heterosexuality, is patriarchy's trick to which feminists are now
wise. Its widespread implications in employment, inheritance, and
family law are too devastating to be ignored.

Part of the patriarchal furor over homosexuality is caused by undue
emphasis on the genital sexual component to the detriment of any

careful analysis of the "homo," or social, dimension of same-sex love, much less any analysis of the love component. Let's start there. Two women or two men who fall in love, just like their hetero counterparts, experience feelings that not even the most competent poet can capture on a page. They are attracted to each other, an attraction they live out physically as well as emotionally. They enjoy life together—meals, sex, movies, sports—and do not want that time to end, ever. So they commit to each other, work out the parameters of their relationship, figure out finances, children, aging parents, and all the other aspects of daily life that shared love involves. With luck, Catholics might say with grace, they enjoy a long life together in the company of friends and family. Same-sex love is, after all, first and foremost love.

I am not naïve about the fact that many people—heterosexual and homosexual, bisexual and transgendered (though those terms are now problematic and contested)—have no such storybook experiences. Nor am I unaware that the lack of support systems for same-sex love propels some people, especially some gay men, toward anonymous sex and a bar/bath scene that leave much to be desired. But those realities have as little to do with homosexuality as such as brothels and wife abuse have to do with heterosexuality as such. They need to be looked at critically, of course, but not on the basis only of sexuality. They need to be evaluated as potential health risks, just as sexual abuse is evaluated not primarily in terms of sex but of violence. To do otherwise is to miss the obvious, and/or to actualize an anti-homosexual agenda.

Moreover, lesbian women and gay men have less in common than is sometimes thought. I say this not to disconnect us in the struggle for justice, and not to imply any moral superiority of women, whose opportunities for casual sex are generally fewer. To the contrary, I want to clarify our respective starting points to highlight the "lesbian" on its own terms, something rarely done in discussions where the gendered aspects of homosexual experience are conflated.

For example, economic resources are different when two men form a bond versus when two women come together. Two white male incomes usually outweigh two female incomes, with all of the accompanying privilege, access, and entitlement of white men in a patriarchal society. Racial and class differences affect this dynamic, but the general trend toward male hegemony is clear and not trivial in Catholic circles where such privilege is codified. Differences in the power to ensure their own safety accrue variously to men and women. Two men can be mutual protection, much needed as hate crimes mount. But as Adrienne Rich wrote, "Two women sleeping together have more than their sleep to defend."[12] These differences point to deep issues that require ethical problematizing so as to approximate justice for all.

Add sex-role socialization, access to work and legal protections, and we find extremely varied experiences for lesbian women and gay men.[13] This is not to mention the complexities for bisexual and transgendered people, whose situations are beyond the scope of this essay. All of this raises ethical work to do and still not a mention of lesbian genital sex. In short, there is much more at stake than who sleeps with whom. Yet kyriarchal Catholic theologians persist in offering a blanket condemnation of that about which they know so little. They seem to have no regard for the many complexities of same-sex love in a heterosexist context. There must be a better way that does not play lesbian women and gay men off against one another and us against our heterosexual, bisexual and transgendered friends, a way that serves to make the world safer for people of all lifestyle choices.

FEMINIST THEOLOGICAL/THEORETICAL SOURCES AND STRATEGIES THAT PAVE THE WAY FOR LESBIAN CLAIMS

Feminist theologians/theorists have been in the vanguard of those promoting social justice through careful consideration of the interlocking structures of kyriarchy. What began as a gender analysis is now, thanks to womanist, *mujerista,* and other women's challenges, a full-scale social change project encompassing racial and economic issues, attention to nationality and ability, age and gender, and including attention to the earth and all of its inhabitants. It is from this rich resource that I cite five insights that help to situate a Catholic lesbian feminist theological starting point.

Women's Moral Agency and Bodily Integrity

Feminist Christian ethicist Beverly Wildung Harrison, in her landmark book on abortion *Our Right to Choose,* makes the case for women's moral agency.[14] She cites the history of philosophy as full of impediments to women's decision making, from women barred from giving testimony to pregnant women kept from deciding whether to continue or terminate their pregnancies. Human history is proof that women can and do make good decisions on reproductive health as in other matters.

Coupled with this ability to be a moral agent is what she calls "women's bodily integrity," the extent to which women have responsibility for our bodies. Pregnancy makes this obvious, but so, too, I believe, does lesbian life wherein the female body is also central. Against the tide of patriarchal logic, women who love women are moral agents fully capable of making good decisions to love others whose bodies are similar. This does not mean that all lesbian relationships are good. Indeed, just like some heterosexual relationships, some lesbian relationships are morally dubious, as when they contain violence or otherwise inhibit the growth of the partners. But in principle lesbian relationships are rooted in the bodily integrity of women who choose women for their intimate companions, respecting their bodies as bodies.

Community Focus

A second insight comes from *mujerista* Catholic theologian Ada Maria Isasi-Diaz, whose insistence on community helps to mitigate what might be the privatizing aspects of an individual focus.[15] She argues for this in light of the Hispanic women with whom she lives and works, contending that it is not her view as a theologian but the community's considered judgment that counts. In so doing she reverses the Anglo tendency to tout the rugged individual.

The tendency toward privatized analysis that might emerge from a lesbian starting point needs to be countered by understanding how wider communities of women, including heterosexual and bisexual women, understand issues. It is often the case, for example in the ordination of Catholic women, that what excludes one excludes all, albeit for lesbian women on more virulent terms. Such solidarity is key to avoiding co-optation, and such communal thinking is a check against privatization.

Erotic Power

A third useful idea comes from the brilliant work of poet and essayist Audre Lorde, who wrote about "the erotic as power."[16] Here the insight comes specifically from a lesbian woman's experience of just how powerful erotic attractions and attachments can be. She saw this as a force for social change, "a well of replenishing and provocative force."[17]

For Catholic lesbian feminist theological work it is this positive possibility that sets the stage for discussion of lesbian sexuality. Far from

298 Mary E. Hunt

denying or degrading women's sexual pleasure, far from minimizing or magnifying its importance, Audre Lorde names all women's sexuality, using that of lesbian women as a prototype, as "creative energy empowered."[18] She explains why those who would contain it so often relegate it to the bedroom, when in fact erotic energy "becomes a lens through which we scrutinize all aspects of our existence . . . {causing us} not to settle for the convenient, the shoddy, the conventionally expected, nor the merely safe."[19] It is on these terms that I would begin a conversation with Vatican officials on the "ordered" nature of same-sex love and the "intrinsically good" nature of same-sex acts.

Justice Connections

Episcopal priest Carter Heyward contributes "our passion for justice" to the theological mix.[20] She insists that issues of sexuality are intimately connected to other justice struggles, beginning with racism and economic inequalities. Likewise, she implies that working on one issue propels one to see these connections because they are embodied in real people who suffer. From the experience of oppression comes a perhaps-heightened sense of the need for solidarity. This lesbian feminist analysis is a major strategic offering. It is what allows those of us who are white lesbian women to relativize our struggle alongside that of people who are discriminated against on account of their race or ethnicity. It compels those of us who are economically affluent lesbians to put our energies into social change for economic justice. It helps to redirect our focus from sex to power so that we avoid the traps of arguing the wrong question.

Feminist Friendships

A fifth feminist insight comes from my own work on friendship as the normative adult relationship.[21] I believe that friendship, unlike marriage, is available to everyone, and that it has the potential to level the ethical playing field when it comes to evaluating relationships in communities. Far from being a privatized, romantic notion, friendships have political, practical implications. Building social structures on the basis of friends and not family allows everyone to benefit; everyone can be a friend, while not everyone can be married. Major legal and social changes would follow. For example, the case for universal health coverage would be made on the basis of our being/having bodies rather than on the current thinking that links coverage to having a job that provides coverage or being married to someone who does. Wholesale new ways of thinking come from a friend-based model rather than a family-based model.

The priority on friendship comes from a lesbian feminist perspective, but it does not stay there. Widely applied, it heads off the potentially atomizing aspects of postmodern life. It helps to counter the temptation to repeat the heterosexual model of marriage in an effort to be inclusive. Instead, it offers to heterosexual, bisexual, transgendered, and homosexual people alike (however helpful/unhelpful those categories may turn out to be) the chance to think and act anew. A number of scholars have taken up this theme as a normative model of adult relating, both in theology and biblical studies, from a range of perspectives.[22]

Taken together, these five insights—women's moral agency and bodily integrity, a community focus, erotic power, the justice connections, and friendship as the normative adult relationship—form a solid feminist basis on which to critique patriarchal ways of thinking about homosexuality. It is the larger dimension of women's well-being and justice, not simply the lesbian dimension, that is crucial. These form a starting point from which to construct a Catholic lesbian feminist theology.

A CATHOLIC LESBIAN FEMINIST THEOLOGY

It is relatively easy to deconstruct patriarchal theology, especially when it is so clearly rooted in assumptions and practices that postmodern life has replaced, such as the assumed connection between sex and reproduction. It is more difficult to propose a constructive Catholic approach, since there is so little practice at offering new models that take women's experiences seriously. But before talking about the divine it is important to clarify some of the more accessible human dimensions. I begin the theological and ethical conversation from this Catholic lesbian feminist starting point in the interest of moving the discussion forward on a fresh footing. I choose three issues central to contemporary lesbian life as the foci in the hope that they reveal contours of a larger whole.

Lesbian Sexual Expression

Lesbian sexual expression is, I daresay, as far from the experience of kyriarchal churchmen as possible. I shudder to think what they imagine lesbian women do in bed, in the shower or on the beach, at the grocery store or on vacation, at the movies or in a car, at work, or wherever else human beings express affection, care, and love for one another in genital and non-genital ways. What is it about how we play tennis or feed our children, volunteer in the community or take naps that makes us "disordered"? What is the difference between these ordinary things done by homosexual women (making them, strictly speaking, homosexual acts) and homosexual *sexual* acts? Are they all "intrinsically evil"? The real issue this question raises, of course, is how sexual expression is part of a larger relational constellation, and how that relationship is conducive of community. The rest, as the rabbis say, is commentary.

Lesbian women, like all human beings, seek to get and give love, enjoy expressing that love in physical ways including genital contact when appropriate, and integrate our affective lives into complex and differentiated wholes. What we do in bed need not be objectified and labeled any more than any other sexual expression as long as it is safe and consensual. Survey evidence and my several dozen years of practice make me confident in saying that pleasure is pleasure, all the more so when one's partner is beloved and trusted.

What does call for moral scrutiny is the extent to which we act safely, responsibly, mutually, and with care in our sexual dealings, the same criteria I would apply to all sexual behavior, no more, no less to lesbian women. With the HIV/AIDS pandemic full blown, the moral compass points toward prevention, even for lesbian women, who are among those at lowest risk. Then the intimate link between spirituality and sexuality can be nurtured in a Catholic lesbian feminist way and its fruits shared abundantly.

Shared Motherhood

One of the delights of the contemporary lesbian/gay life is the so-called "baby boom," with thousands of lesbian and gay people having and/or adopting children. What could be more pleasing music to Catholic ears? From the Virgin Mary on, motherhood has always been valued. Now, in some happy cases, it is doubled! "Be fruitful and multiply" seems newly to apply to us! At least it is easier than it used to be for lesbians to have children, a substantive change in the thirty years since the Stonewall riots launched a wholesale lesbian/gay movement.

Reliable statistics do not exist because of the Catch-22 of custody and the continued stigma in some circles about same-sex parenting. But anecdotal evidence abounds for the fact that new families are springing up where couples used to dwell. In the case of lesbians, there are now families with two mothers, whether both adopt a child or one bears and the other adopts.

Such a boom has its pluses and minuses. Like the move toward same-sex marriage, it can lead to a certain pressure to have children, subtly reinforcing the heterosexist notion that to live responsibly without children of one's own is somehow a lesser life choice. I reject that, knowing many people who nurture and care in ways other than child rearing. But the delights (not to mention the challenges) of forming a family and bringing up children are now experienced by a growing number of lesbian women and gay men.

I see this as evidence of the goodness of same-sex relationships, requiring the same degree of commitment, stability, and intention, and perhaps a little more, than for heterosexual couples. In fact, I see parenting as a more productive starting point than same-sex marriage for leveling the ethical playing field when it comes to some social benefits.

Some stable lesbian families have much to teach some unstable heterosexual couples about providing for the needs of children, balancing the demands of work and home life, keeping a relationship fresh in the midst of diapers and homework. But it is precisely in such an everyday situation that religious faith is helpful for orienting decision-making, setting priorities, and coping with the inevitable problems. More so, faith communities, especially active parishes or small base communities like women-church groups, are the logical places for Catholic lesbian-led families to worship and expect support.

A Lesbian Call to Holiness

All theological projects are finally larger than any theo-political goals, any structural changes or dogmatic differences. They are aimed at fostering the spiritual well-being of faithful people, nurturing the divine-human love in its myriad forms. That is why, at base, the Vatican's claims about "disordered" and "intrinsically evil" dimensions of homosexuality are so destructive. People who hear such rhetoric rightly question the wisdom of everything else that comes from the same dubious source.

Catholic lesbian feminist spirituality is set in an increasingly pluralistic religious context. With more Muslims than Presbyterians, and spiritual options growing by leaps and bounds, the U.S. religious landscape

is changing, dotted with opportunities for those who leave their traditions of origin in search of a closer fit with their current beliefs. I respect
this and realize why it is the preferred mode of so many Catholic lesbians. But for those who wish to remain part of the tradition into which
they were born or which they chose at an earlier time in life, it seems
unjust to have a Vatican-promulgated anti-lesbian/gay policy act as a
barrier. Hence my effort to develop a theology that is fully consistent
with the best of Catholic social teaching and sacramental life: the call to
holiness for all Catholics emphasized by Vatican II and the invitation to
break bread and do justice.

CONCLUSION

The development of a systematic Catholic lesbian feminist theology
is a larger project than one essay and a task for more than one person. But
I hope that the groundwork laid here will serve as a foundation for others
who seek to move beyond the parameters of a heretofore-unproductive
debate. At least a Catholic lesbian feminist starting point signals another community at the table, another group bringing abundant resources to share, and an eagerness to do so. At most, such a theological
perspective signals that the Catholic tradition is worthy of its name,
universal, when those who have been marginalized join the community.
Then the hard work of learning to live fruitfully with difference will
start in earnest.

NOTES: CHAPTER 14

[1] John McNeill's trilogy is foundational to Catholic gay theology: *The
Church and the Homosexual* (Boston: Beacon, 1976); *Taking a Chance on God*
(Boston: Beacon, 1988); *Freedom, Glorious Freedom* (Boston: Beacon, 1995).
Robert Goss's *Jesus Acted Up: A Gay and Lesbian Manifesto* (San Francisco:
Harper San Francisco, 1993) is the basic text in queer Catholic work. There is
simply no Catholic lesbian equivalent yet.

[2] Catholic feminist theology in the U.S. is grounded in the foundational
work of Mary Daly, Rosemary Radford Ruether, and Elisabeth Schüssler
Fiorenza, among others. It includes such scholars as Sandra Schneiders, Shawn
Copeland, Elizabeth Johnson, and Margaret Farley, to name just a few of the
dozens whose work is changing the face of the field.

[3] "Kyriarchal" is a word coined by biblical scholar Elisabeth Schüssler
Fiorenza to describe the interlocking forms of oppression such as racism,

gender discrimination, economic injustice, and the like that combine in patriarchy to oppress people. See her *But She Said: Feminist Practices of Biblical Interpretation* (Boston: Beacon, 1992) 117, 123.

[4] Mary Daly included a savvy treatment of lesbian issues in *Beyond God the Father* ([Boston: Beacon, 1973] 124–27), arguing that being a lesbian does not make one a feminist any more than being heterosexual excludes one from being involved in social change.

[5] The issue is framed helpfully in *The Non-Ordination of Women and the Politics of Power. Concilium* 1999/3, eds. Elisabeth Schüssler Fiorenza and Hermann Häring (Maryknoll, N.Y.: Orbis, 1999).

[6] Walter Wink distinguishes between these "unequivocal condemnations" and several other more ambiguous ones, for example, 1 Cor 6:9 and 1 Tim 1:10. See his "Homosexuality and the Bible" in idem, ed., *Homosexuality and the Christian Faith: Question of Conscience for the Churches* (Minneapolis: Fortress, 1999) 33–49.

[7] Bernadette J. Brooten, *Love Between Women: Early Christian Responses to Female Homoeroticism* (Chicago: The University of Chicago Press, 1996) 244.

[8] Ibid. 303.

[9] Ibid. 266.

[10] See chapter 11 of this volume.

[11] An early Catholic collection is Barbara Zanotti, ed., *A Faith of One's Own: Explorations by Catholic Lesbians* (Trumansburg, N.Y.: Crossing Press, 1986).

[12] Adrienne Rich, "The Images," *A Wild Patience Has Taken Me This Far* (New York: Norton, 1981) 3.

[13] Bisexual people's religious experiences are only now being taken seriously on their own terms. See Debra R. Kolodny, ed., *Blessed Bi Spirit: Bisexual People of Faith* (New York: Continuum, 2000). Transgendered peoples' faith perspectives remain to be published.

[14] Beverly Wildung Harrison, *Our Right to Choose* (Boston: Beacon, 1983).

[15] Ada Maria Isasi-Diaz, *En La Lucha/In the Struggle: A Hispanic Women's Liberation Theology* (Minneapolis: Augsburg Fortress, 1993).

[16] Audre Lorde, "Uses of the Erotic: The Erotic as Power," in *Sister Outsider* (Trumansburg, N.Y.: Crossing Press, 1984) 53–59.

[17] Ibid. 54.

[18] Ibid. 57.

[19] Ibid.

[20] Carter Heyward, *Our Passion for Justice: Images of Power, Sexuality and Liberation* (New York: Pilgrim Press, 1984).

[21] Mary E. Hunt, *Fierce Tenderness: A Feminist Theology of Friendship* (New York: Continuum, 1991).

[22] See, for example, Janice Raymond, *A Passion for Friends* (Boston: Beacon, 1986); Sharon H. Ringe, *Wisdom's Friends: Community and Christology in the Fourth Gospel* (Louisville: Westminster John Knox, 1999).

Contributors

Sidney Callahan is a psychologist and author of many books and articles. She writes on interdisciplinary questions concerning ethics, religion, and psychology. She has been a tenured college professor of psychology, served on many national boards, and lectures widely.

Joseph Andrew Coray is a doctoral student and adjunct instructor in New Testament and Early Christianity at Loyola University Chicago. His interests include gay and lesbian liberation theology and hermeneutics, as well as pastoral care, education, and outreach activities in regard to the HIV and AIDS pandemic.

Isiaah Crawford is Professor and Chairperson of the Department of Psychology at Loyola University of Chicago. He maintains an active psychotherapy practice, specializing in the treatment of individuals living with HIV disease, depression, and addictive behaviors. He has published in the areas of HIV/AIDS prevention and treatment, human sexuality, and attitudes toward individuals marginalized in society.

Mary Rose D'Angelo is Associate Professor in the Department of Theology and a former director of the Gender Studies Program at the University of Notre Dame. She teaches New Testament and Christian Origins, specializing in women and gender. With Ross Kraemer she edited *Women and Christian Origins* (New York: Oxford University Press, 1999); she has published numerous articles on women, gender, imperial politics, theological language, and sexual practice in the beginnings of Christianity.

Robert A. Di Vito is an associate professor in the Department of Theology at Loyola University of Chicago, where he is director of the graduate program and teaches courses related to the study of the Old Testament and its cognate disciplines. Author of a book on ancient Near Eastern religion and articles on subjects ranging from palaeography to the anthropology of the Old Testament, he is currently one of the editors-in-chief of the forthcoming revision of the New American Bible sponsored by the Catholic Biblical Association of America and the National Conference of Catholic Bishops. He resides in Chicago with his wife and two children.

Thomas J. Gumbleton, a Roman Catholic priest for forty years, is an Auxiliary Bishop in the Archdiocese of Detroit, Michigan, since 1968, and a pastor of St. Leo Parish, an inner-city Catholic community. He has spoken extensively on Catholic pastoral practice with regard to gay and lesbian Christians as well as on the moral and theological issue of homosexuality and Catholic tradition. Bishop Gumbleton is extensively involved in international justice and peace initiatives, especially in Iraq, Colombia, Chiapas, and Haiti.

James P. Hanigan is Professor of Moral Theology and Chairperson of the Theology Department at Duquesne University, Pittsburgh, Pennsylvania. In addition to several essays, he is the author of four previous books in the area of Catholic moral theology.

Mary E. Hunt is a Catholic feminist theologian. She is the co-founder and co-director of the Women's Alliance for Theology, Ethics and Ritual (WATER) in Silver Spring, Maryland and author of *Fierce Tenderness: A Feminist Theology of Friendship.*

Patricia Beattie Jung is Associate Professor of Moral Theology at Loyola University Chicago. She and her husband, Shannon, have enjoyed each other's company for over 25 years and have been blessed with three sons: Michael, Robert, and Nathan. She co-authored with the late Ralph F. Smith *Heterosexism: An Ethical Challenge* (New York: SUNY Press, 1993).

Bruce J. Malina is Professor of Biblical Studies at Creighton University. His best-known book is *The New Testament World: Insights from Cultural Anthropology* (Louisville: Westminster John Knox 1993). He is co-author of three volumes in the Fortress Press series of

Social Science Commentaries on the New Testament. His latest book with The Liturgical Press is *The New Jerusalem in the Revelation of John: The City as Symbol of Life with God.*

Jon Nilson is Associate Professor of Theology at Loyola University Chicago. He has taught at Illinois Benedictine College and the University of Dallas, in addition to visiting professorships at the Catholic Theological Union and the General Theological Seminary. Among other affiliations, he is a member of the Anglican-Roman Catholic Consultation in the United States and the editorial board of *Theological Studies.*

David T. Ozar is Professor of Philosophy and Director of the Center for Ethics at Loyola University of Chicago. He is the author of two books and more than seventy professional articles and book chapters. His principal area of scholarly research and reflection is the content and implications of and the foundations for the ethical standards that operate in human social systems. This is his first essay on the ethical implications of gender roles in American society.

Susan A. Ross teaches Theology at Loyola University of Chicago, where she also served as Director of the Women's Studies Program. She is the author of *Extravagant Affections: A Feminist Sacramental Theology* (Continuum, 1998), co-editor of *Broken and Whole: Essays on Religion and the Body* (University Press of America, 1994, with Maureen A. Tilley), and the author of numerous articles and book chapters on issues related to women, sacraments, and the body.

Cristina L. H. Traina is Associate Professor of Religion at Northwestern University. Author of a book on method in feminist ethics and in the moral theological tradition, she has also written articles on family, children, sexuality, and environmental ethics. She resides in Evanston, Illinois, with her husband and three children.

Leland J. White is Editor of *Biblical Theology Bulletin.* This lifelong South Carolinian is a member of the South Carolina Bar, a priest of the Diocese of Charleston, and active in the Charleston County and South Carolina Democratic Party. He is also Professor of Religion and Culture at St. John's University (New York), Adjunct Professor of Philosophy at the College of Charleston, and Associate Counsel to the New Jersey Law Revision Commission.

Brian Zamboni is an advanced graduate student in the Ph.D. Clinical Psychology Program at Loyola University of Chicago. His research interests focus upon aspects of sexual health, attitudes toward and psychosocial support of individuals who are marginalized in society, sexual dysfunction, and body image. His clinical work includes a specialty in couples and sex therapy.

Subject Index

Love
  homosexual, 295
  marital, 282
  sexual expression of, 208, 213
Lust, 279

Magisterium, xvi, xxii, 65, 71
Marriage, 22–23, 31
  nuptial metaphor, 40ff
Mary, Blessed Virgin, 42
Moral argument (*see* sexual ethics)
  place and use of scientific data,
    205ff
Moral wisdom, xiv–xvii, 84
Motherhood, 300

Natural law, 24, 189, 293
Nature, Natural, 135ff, 151–54, 190

Pederasty, 165, 183
Pontifical Biblical Commission, 80,
  85
Procreativity (*see* reproduction), xiii,
  22–23, 61
  and marriage, 31
Protestant ethics, xvi, 77

Rape, 175, 182, 188
Relationships, gay and lesbian, 227

Scripture (*see also* Bible)
  applicability of, 108–9
  dialogue with tradition, 90
  inspiration of, 85
  interpretation of, xx
  place and use in moral arguments,
    xiv, xv

Texts:
  Genesis 1:27-28, 126
  Genesis 19:1-29, 81, 109, 178ff,
    181ff, 292
  Genesis 38:1-11, 292
  Leviticus 18:22, 109ff, 159, 177,
    182, 292
  Leviticus 20:18, 109ff, 159, 177,
    182, 292
  Judges 19:16-29, 81, 109–10
  Matthew 5:48, 3
  Mark 10:2-12, 25
  Romans 1:18-32, 152ff, 165ff
  Romans 1:26-27, 134ff, 144ff,
    177, 187, 189, 292
  Romans 7:25, x
  1 Corinthians 6:9-11, 166, 177
  1 Timothy 1:8-11, 166
  1 John 4:16, 17
Sexism (biblical witness regarding),
  180
Sexual abstinence, 277
Sexual complementarity, 280ff
Sexual ethics (role of experience in),
  269–70
Sexual identity, 144
Sexual orientation, 150, 211
  etiology of 216–27
  genetics and, 217
  theories for origin of, 222ff
Shame, and submission, 141
Sin, 3
Slavery, 86ff
Social roles (and luxury), 141, 233ff
Social science criticism, 137

Transgendered, 253

Womanist, *mujerista* theology, 296ff

Index of Ecclesial Documents